9th EAI International Conference on Simulation Tools and Techniques (SIMUTools 2016)

Prague, Czech Republic
22 - 23 August 2016

ISBN: 978-1-5108-8173-0

Printed from e-media with permission by:

Curran Associates, Inc.
57 Morehouse Lane
Red Hook, NY 12571

Some format issues inherent in the e-media version may also appear in this print version.

Printed by Curran Associates, Inc. (2019)

For permission requests, please contact European Alliance for Innovation (EAI)
at the address below.

European Alliance for Innovation (EAI)
c/o Volha Shaparava , Dr
Publications
Via alla Cascata 56/D - 38123 Povo,
Trento - Italy

publications@eai.eu

Additional copies of this publication are available from:

Curran Associates, Inc.
57 Morehouse Lane
Red Hook, NY 12571 USA
Phone: 845-758-0400
Fax: 845-758-2633
Email: curran@proceedings.com
Web: www.proceedings.com

Proceedings of the 9th EAI International Conference on Simulation Tools and Techniques

22–23 August 2016, Prague, Czech Republic

SIMUTools 2016

General Chairs

Gary Tan, National University of Singapore, SINGAPORE

Technical Programme Chair

Yong Meng Teo, National University of Singapore, SINGAPORE

Wentong Cai, Nanyang Technological University, SINGAPORE

Contents

SHORT PAPERS

Fairness-aware Update Schedules for Improving Consistency in Multi-server Distributed Virtual Environments

Li Yusen*†
s080007@e.ntu.edu.sg

Yunhua Deng†
yhdeng@ntu.edu.sg

Wentong Cai†
aswtcai@ntu.edu.sg

Xueyan Tang†
asxytang@ntu.edu.sg

*Department of Computer Science and Information Security
Nankai University
Tianjin, China

†School of Computer Science and Engineering
Nanyang Technological University
Singapore

ABSTRACT

In Distributed Virtual Environments (DVEs), how to guarantee consistency and fairness is a primary concern for improving user experience. As the scale of DVE systems grows fast, multi-server architecture has been widely used in large scale DVEs such as Massively Multiplayer Online Games (MMOGs). In multi-server DVEs (MSDVEs), servers may get saturated with resources such as network bandwidth due to huge resource demand and workload variability. With resource limitations, state updates cannot be disseminated timely and inconsistency and unfairness will be greatly increased if the resources are not allocated properly. In this paper, we propose a fairness-aware state update scheduling algorithm which can minimize total inconsistency while guarantee fairness in MSDVEs under servers' network bandwidth constraints. Experimental results show that the proposed algorithm significantly improves the consistency and fairness compared to other existing update algorithms.

CCS Concepts

•Computing methodologies → Distributed simulation; *Distributed algorithms;* **•Computer systems organization →** Client-server architectures;

1. INTRODUCTION

Distributed Virtual Environment (DVE), a virtual world deployed on a group of computers connected via network, allows multiple geographically distributed participants, also known as clients, to communicate and interact with each other through the shared virtual world. In the virtual world, each client is often represented by an entity, called an avatar.

SIMUTOOLS 2016, August 22-23, Prague, Czech Republic

tual world and communicate and interact with other clients. DVEs have been widely used in many different applications such as military training, e-learning and online games [1, 4, 17, 21].

The client-server architecture is the most popular one to support DVEs. In client-server DVEs, the virtual world is maintained by a server and each client maintains a copy of the (relevant) virtual world state on his computer. When one client performs an action that affects the virtual world (e.g., the client controlled avatar moves to a new position), the state of the virtual world maintained by other clients must be updated in a timely manner. However, due to transmission delay and clock asynchrony, different clients may receive the same state update at different times, which will result in inconsistency and unfairness. Inconsistency refers to the differences between the virtual worlds seen by clients and the virtual world maintained by the server. Unfairness refers to the differences among the virtual worlds seen by different clients. It has been shown that both inconsistency and unfairness are crucial for user experience in DVEs [2]. Inconsistency may deteriorate the game responsiveness and playability while unfairness may provide unfair advantages or disadvantages to different players. Therefore, how to reduce inconsistency and unfairness is very important for DVEs.

As the development of the DVE applications, the scale of DVE systems becomes larger and larger. Like the most popular online game WoW [21], the peak number of simultaneous active users has exceeded 5 million [22]. Multi-server architecture, especially the zone based multi-server architecture, has become a popular platform to support large scale DVEs. In zone based multi-server DVEs (MSDVE), the virtual world is usually spatially partitioned into several disjoint zones, with each zone managed by only one server. A client interacts only with other clients in the same zone, and may move to other zones. As a server only needs to handle one or more zones instead of the entire virtual world, the system is more scalable. The zone based architecture has been used in many large-scale virtual environments such as RING [7], CittaTron [8] and many existing Massively Multiplayer Online Games (MMOGs) [6, 14].

At present, a large scale MSDVE like MMOGs can include millions of concurrent users spread across the world, which demands huge amount of resources such as computing power and network bandwidth on various servers [22]. Adding clients to a MSDVE will increase the resource requirement of servers. As the number of clients increases, the total resource demand may become huge. Moreover, a DVE system is highly dynamic. A client can join or leave a DVE at any given time. Therefore, the number of participating clients is dynamically changing over time, which results in dynamic workload requirement at servers. In addition, the workload like network bandwidth in a DVE is also highly dependent on avatars' interactions [18]. When avatars are crowded in the virtual world, more network bandwidth for each client is required. For instance, the peak value of the network bandwidth requirement from server to a client in WoW can exceed 64kbps, which is much larger than the median value 6.9kbps [18]. Facing huge resource demand and workload variability, servers may get saturated with resources like network bandwidth. If resources are not allocated properly, inconsistency and unfairness will be greatly increased.

In our previous work [9, 11], we have studied how to schedule state updates for minimizing inconsistency in MSDVEs with network bandwidth constraints of servers. However, unfairness is not considered in the proposed update algorithm. In this paper, we take unfairness into account and reconsider the state update scheduling problem in MSDVEs. The aim is to minimize inconsistency while guarantee fairness in MSDVEs when the network bandwidth is constrained for servers. The contributions of this paper are three-fold. First, we propose a new metric using time-space inconsistency to measure unfairness in a DVE. The new metric takes both spatial and temporal differences into account in the measurement, which is more effective in reflecting the impact of unfairness on users' experiences. Second, we propose a fairness-aware update scheme which ensures the same update can be issued at the same time by different clients so that the unfairness among clients is eliminated. Third, we propose a heuristic update algorithm that can minimize inconsistency with fairness guarantees in a MSDVE with network bandwidth constraints of servers. The proposed update algorithm has been shown to outperform other algorithms by experimental results.

The rest of the paper is structured as follows. The system model and problem definition are introduced in Section 2. In Section 3, the proposed update schedules are presented. The experimental evaluations are presented in Section 4. The related work is summarized in Section 5. In the last section, a conclusion is given and the future work is discussed.

2. SYSTEM MODEL

In this paper, we focus on zone based MSDVEs. However, the proposed approach can be easily applied to other types of MSDVEs. In zone based MSDVEs[1], as shown in Figure 1, the virtual world is assumed to be partitioned into zones and each zone is maintained by one server. For instance, in Figure 1, the virtual world is partitioned into three zones z_1, z_2 and z_3 which are maintained by servers s_1, s_2 and s_3 respectively. Avatars located in a zone are maintained by the server that is in charge of this zone. Generally, an avatar is only allowed to interact with the avatars in the same zone

[1]In the rest of the paper, MSDVE refers to the zone-based MSDVE

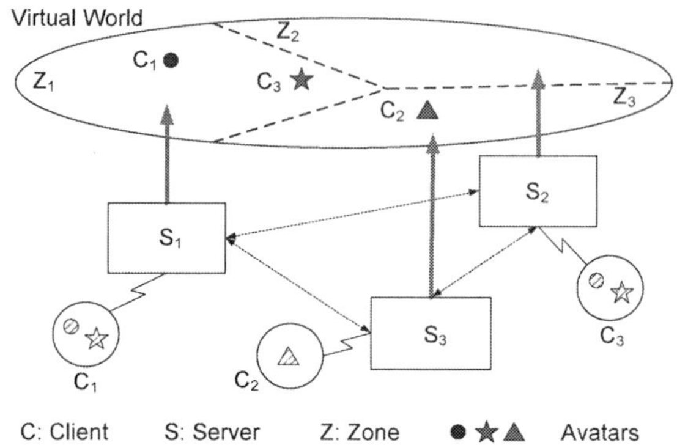

Figure 1: System Model of a MSDVE

where the avatar is residing.

Traditionally, clients can be assigned to servers in two different ways: based on virtual position or based on physical position. In the virtual position manner, each client is connected to the server that maintains the zone where his avatar is. The server-to-server communication is avoided in this case. However, the network delay between a client and the server may be large. In the physical position manner, each client is connected to the closest server that incurs minimum network delay. In this case, the network delay between a client and its connected server is small. However, if the connected server is not the server that maintains his avatar, the state updates need to be forwarded by the connected servers, thus the communications between servers are required. Therefore, client assignment will affect the transmission delays from servers to clients, and cause inconsistency. In our previous work [10, 12], the client assignment problem has been studied and a new client assignment approach was proposed. In that approach, a client is allowed to connect to any server, which is not necessarily the server that maintains his avatar or the closest server. The clients are assigned to servers with the purpose of minimizing inconsistency. In our system model, the client assignment will be determined by the approach proposed in [12].

In this paper, we focus on the position update of avatars, which are the most common type of avatar states requiring constant updates. Based on the above system model, the position update in a MSDVE is accomplished as follows. The server maintaining the avatar updates the position of the avatar according to user's input commands and periodically (generally by frame) disseminates the position updates to the clients in the same zone. To improve accessibility and responsiveness, each client in the same zone will maintain a replicated copy of the avatar. When a new position update is received by a client, the replica of the avatar will be updated and reflected to the user.

Note that when a server disseminates position update to a client, the client may not be connected to the server. In this case, the position update should be forwarded by the server that is connected to the client. Consider an avatar and a replica of the avatar, we define *target server* of the replica as the server maintaining the avatar and *contact server* of the replica as the server that is connected by the client where the replica is. To send position update to the replica, if the contact server and the target server of the replica are the same (e.g., the replicas maintained by client c_1 in Figure 1), the target server will directly disseminate position update to the replica. Otherwise, if the target server and the contact server are different (e.g., the replicas maintained by client c_3 in Figure 1), the target server will first send position update to the contact server in the manner of forwarding request, and then the contact server will forward position update to the replica.

In our system model, network bandwidth consumption on position update at each server can be divided into three parts. The first part is used to disseminate position updates to the replicas whose target server and contact server both are this server. The second part is used to send position updates in the manner of forwarding request for the replicas whose target server is this server and contact server is different. The third part is used to forward position update for the replicas whose contact server is this server and target server is another one. Suppose the network capacity for the position updates (the sum of three parts) is constrained for some servers, that is, each saturated server is allowed to send or forward position updates to only a given number of replicas. The aim of this paper is to investigate position update scheduling strategies for those saturated servers to reduce inconsistency while guarantee fairness in the whole DVE.

Based on the system model, we formally define inconsistency and unfairness using the metric of time-space inconsistency in a MSDVE. Time-space inconsistency is defined based on the following observation: participants make their judgements of a specific situation in a DVE based not only on the positions of entities, but also on the duration of this situation [25]. It has been shown that time-space inconsistency can effectively reflect the impact of inconsistency on a participant's perception and decision making. Therefore, it would be more reasonable to use time-space inconsistency to evaluate inconsistency and unfairness.

Consider a replica r of an avatar a. Let $\Delta(r, a, t)$ denote the spatial difference between the position of replica r at client side and the position of avatar a at server side at time t, the time-space inconsistency between r and a in a time session $[t_s, t_e]$ (denoted by s) is defined by

$$\Omega(r, a, s) = \int_{t_s}^{t_e} \Delta(r, a, t)dt \tag{1}$$

The total inconsistency associated with an avatar a in session s is defined as the total time-space inconsistency of all replicas of a in session s, which is given by

$$\Theta(a, s) = \sum_{r \in \mathcal{R}(a)} \Omega(r, a, s) \tag{2}$$

where $\mathcal{R}(a)$ denotes the set of all replicas of a. The total inconsistency of the DVE in session s is defined as the total inconsistency of all avatars in session s in the DVE, which is given by

$$\Theta(s) = \sum_{a} \Theta(a, s) \tag{3}$$

Consider an avatar a. Let $p(a, t)$ denote the position of a at server side at time t. For a replica r of a, let $p(r, t)$ represent the position of r at client side at time t. The divergence associated with a at time t is defined by

$$D(a, t) = \sqrt{\frac{1}{NR(a)} \cdot \sum_{r \in \mathcal{R}(a)} (p(r, t) - \overline{p}(a, t))^2} \tag{4}$$

where

$$\overline{p}(a, t) = \frac{1}{NR(a)} \cdot \sum_{r \in \mathcal{R}(a)} p(r, t) \tag{5}$$

and $NR(a)$ denotes the size of $\mathcal{R}(a)$. The unfairness associated with avatar a in session s is defined by

$$\Gamma(a, s) = \int_{t_s}^{t_e} D(a, t)dt \tag{6}$$

The unfairness of the MSDVE in session s is then defined by

$$\Gamma(s) = \sum_{a} \Gamma(a, s) \tag{7}$$

Based on the above definitions, this paper aims at two objectives:

1. The first objective is to minimize unfairness of the system in all sessions, i.e.,

$$minimize \sum_{s} \Gamma(s) \tag{8}$$

2. The second objective is to minimize total inconsistency of the system in all sessions, i.e.,

$$minimize \sum_{s} \Theta(s) \tag{9}$$

3. UPDATE SCHEDULES

In this section, we investigate position update schedules to minimize inconsistency while guarantee fairness in MSDVEs with network bandwidth constraints of servers. We first propose a fairness-aware update scheme which can guarantee fairness in a MSDVE. Based on the fairness-aware update scheme, we then propose an update scheduling algorithm which can minimize total inconsistency in a MSDVE. The basic idea of the scheduling algorithm is to update avatars according to their update priorities which are defined according to their potential impacts on inconsistency. When the network bandwidth is limited, the avatars with higher update priorities are updated first.

3.1 Fairness-aware Update Scheme

According to the definition, fairness can be achieved if each update of avatars is applied on the relevant replicas at the same time. Local lag is the most commonly used technique to achieve such goal [13]. For our problem, the basic idea is to add additional "lag" to the updates with smaller transmission delays so that the updates with larger transmission delays can be applied simultaneously. The "lag" can be performed either at server side (i.e., delaying disseminate update after it is generated) or at client side (i.e., delaying application of update after it is received) or both at server and client sides.

Consider a replica r. Let d_r denote the transmission delay of a position update from r's target server to r. Consider an avatar a. Let d_a^{max} denote the maximum transmission delay of a position update from the server maintaining avatar a

to all the replicas of a, i.e., d_a^{max} is the maximum d_r for all $r \in \mathcal{R}(a)$. Suppose a position update of avatar a is generated at time t. In the fairness-aware update scheme, the position update will be applied on all replicas of avatar a at time $t + d_a^{max}$. The time $t + d_a^{max}$ is defined as the *due time* of the position update of avatar a generated at time t. The additional lag to be added for replica r ($r \in \mathcal{R}(a)$) is $d_a^{max} - d_r$. In practical system, where the additional lag is performed will be flexibly determined by the update schedules according to the system context.

3.2 Derivations of Update Priority

The overview of the derivations of update priorities is as follows: firstly, we formulate the problem of finding optimal update schedule to minimize total inconsistency as an inequality constrained problem (ICP) for a static MSDVE. Secondly, Lagrange Multipliers are used to help derive the update priorities that can be estimated in practical systems.

Consider an avatar a. Due to transmission delay (including the lag that may be added by the fairness-aware update scheme), position update will not take effect on each replica until d_a^{max} later after it is generated. The growth of time-space inconsistency between each replica of avatar a and avatar a is given by

$$\Omega = \int_{t_{last}+d_a^{max}}^{t} \Delta(r, a, s)ds \tag{10}$$

where r is a replica of a and t_{last} is the time of the update last generated by the server maintaining a before $t - d_a^{max}$ [12]. To simplify the problem definition, we assume after each update of a is applied on the replicas, the difference between each replica's position and avatar a's position grows in the same manner following an increasing function $\delta(\cdot)$. Therefore, for a replica r of avatar a, we have $\Delta(r, a, t) = \delta(t - (t_{last} + d_a^{max}))$ and $\frac{d\delta(t)}{dt} > 0$. It is plausible to assume $\delta(\cdot)$ to be increasing, otherwise, the difference between the replica and the avatar is unchanged or getting smaller between two successive updates, position update is no longer needed in that case. With this assumption, Equation (10) can be rewritten as

$$\Omega = \int_{0}^{t-(t_{last}+d_a^{max})} \delta(s)ds \tag{11}$$

Note that $\delta(t)$ is the same for all the replicas of avatar a since update is applied with all the replicas at the same time. Similarly to Theorem 1 in [11], it can be proved that under fairness-aware update scheme, given a fixed number of updates allowed in a period for an avatar in a MSDVE, the updates should be generated periodically at server side over this period for minimizing total inconsistency over all replicas of this avatar. Therefore, to minimize total inconsistency, it just needs to determine the optimal update period for each avatar.

Suppose there are NA avatars in the DVE, which are denoted by $a_1, a_2, ..., a_{NA}$. Consider an avatar a_i ($1 \leq i \leq NA$). Suppose the update period of a_i is p_i, then the inconsistency between a_i and the replicas between two successive updates applied on the replicas is given by

$$NR(a_i) \cdot \int_0^{p_i} \delta_i(t)dt \tag{12}$$

The total inconsistency of the virtual world over period T is given by

$$\sum_{i=1}^{NA} \left(\frac{T}{p_i} \cdot NR(a_i) \cdot \int_0^{p_i} \delta_i(t)dt \right) \tag{13}$$

Then, we analyze the constraint of network bandwidth for each server. Suppose there are NS servers in the DVE, which are denoted by $s_1, s_2, ..., s_{NS}$. Consider a server s_j ($1 \leq j \leq NS$). s_j needs to send position updates directly to the replicas whose target server and contact server are both s_j. Moreover, s_j needs to send forwarding requests for the replicas whose target server is s_j but contact server is different. Let α denote the bandwidth consumption for disseminating one position update directly or in the manner of forwarding request. The total network bandwidth requirements for these two parts over T are

$$\alpha \cdot \left(\sum_{a_i \in \mathcal{R}(s_j)} NR(a_i) \cdot \frac{T}{p_i} \right) \tag{14}$$

where $\mathcal{R}(s_j)$ denotes the set of avatars maintained by s_j. In addition, s_j needs to forward position updates to the replicas whose contact server is s_j but target server is different. The bandwidth consumption on this part over T is given by

$$\alpha \cdot \left(\sum_{a_k \notin \mathcal{R}(s_j)} NR(a_k, s_j) \cdot \frac{T}{p_k} \right) \tag{15}$$

where $NR(a_k, s_j)$ denotes the number of replicas of avatar a_k whose contact server is s_j. Suppose the network capacity of s_j for position update at each update frame is constrained by c_j. Let f denote the update frame length of each server. The total network capacity over T will be constrained by $c_j \cdot \frac{T}{f}$. Therefore, we have

$$\alpha \cdot \left(\sum NR(a_i) \cdot \frac{T}{p_i} + \sum NR(a_k, s_j) \cdot \frac{T}{p_k} \right) \leq c_j \cdot \frac{T}{f} \tag{16}$$

Thus, the problem can be defined as the following inequality constrained problem (ICP), the objective is to minimize

$$f(p) = \sum_{i=1}^{NA} \left(\frac{T}{p_i} \cdot NR(a_i) \cdot \int_0^{p_i} \delta_i(t)dt \right) \tag{17}$$

subject to

$$g_j(p) \leq 0, \quad 1 \leq j \leq NS \tag{18}$$

, where $p = [p_1, ..., p_{NA}]$ and $g_j(p)$ is defined as

$$g_j(p) = \alpha \cdot \left(\sum NR(a_i) \cdot \frac{T}{p_i} + \sum NR(a_k, s_j) \cdot \frac{T}{p_k} \right) - c_j \cdot \frac{T}{f}$$

Based on the ICP formulated above, using Lagrange Multipliers, the update priority of avatar a_i at time t can be defined by

$$\frac{1}{\varphi_i(t)} \cdot \left((t - t_{last}) \cdot \Delta(r, a_i, t + d_{a_i}^{max}) - \int_{t_{last}+d_{a_i}^{max}}^{t+d_{a_i}^{max}} \Delta(r, a_i, s)ds \right) \tag{19}$$

φ_i is defined as

$$\frac{\alpha \cdot NR(a_i) \cdot \mu_k + \alpha \cdot \sum_{j=1, j \neq k}^{NS} (NR(a_i, s_j) \cdot \mu_j)}{NR(a_i)} \qquad (20)$$

where μ_i ($1 \leq i \leq NS$) are Lagrange Multipliers. The derivations are similar to that in [11]. The only difference is the update priority was derived in terms of each replica in [11], while the update priority is derived in terms of each avatar whereas in this paper.

To calculate the update priority, the values of $\Delta(r, a_i, t + d_{a_i}^{max})$, $\int_{t_{last}+d_{a_i}^{max}}^{t+d_{a_i}^{max}} \Delta(r, a_i, s)ds$ and μ_i ($1 \leq i \leq NS$) should be estimated by the server at time t. The estimations of these values in practical systems have been discussed in [11].

3.3 Update Scheduling Algorithm

Based on the above analysis, we investigate a fairness-ware update scheduling algorithm for minimizing total inconsistency. The update scheduling algorithm is designed towards achieving the following two targets:

- To maintain fairness, each position update of an avatar should be applied on all replicas of the avatar at same time.
- To minimize inconsistency, the avatar with highest update priority among all avatars in the virtual world should be updated.

The update scheduling algorithm is denoted as Fair-LMH. There are two data structures maintained by each server for running Fair-LMH.

- **AvatarList**: the avatar list maintained by each server. At each update frame, the avatars maintained by each server are sorted according to update priorities and put into the AvatarList.
- **RequestList**[]: an array of lists for storing updates (position update or forwarding request). If an update is stored in the list **RequestList[i]**, it means that the update can be delayed at most i frames at this server.

As has been mentioned earlier, each server will generate position updates (for the replicas whose target server is this server) and receive forwarding requests (for the replicas whose contact server is this server but target server is different). All the generated position updates and received forwarding requests will be first placed in **RequestList** before sent out.

Consider a position update generated by server s_i. Suppose the update is for replica r (s_i is the target server of r). The update will be put into the list **RequestList[j]** at server s_i, where j is equal to

$$\lfloor \frac{d_{a(r)}^{max} - d_r}{f} \rfloor \qquad (21)$$

Consider a forwarding request received by server s_i. Suppose the request is received at time t and the update is for replica r (r's contact server is s_i but target server is not s_i). Let t' denote the time when the update is generated at r's target server. The forwarding request will be put into the list **RequestList[j]** at server s_i, where j is equal to

$$\lfloor \frac{d_{a(r)}^{max} - (t' - t)}{f} \rfloor \qquad (22)$$

Algorithm 1 Fair-LMH (Server Side)

1: Put all avatars into **AvatarList** and sort them according to update priority
2: Move the items in list **RequestList[i]** to list **RequestList[i-1]** for all $i > 0$
3: Put each received forwarding request since last update frame into **RequestList**
4: Disseminate the updates in **RequestList[0]** as many as possible
5: **while** (**AvatarList** is not empty and bandwidth is not used up) **do**
6:     Select the avatar with highest priority in **AvatarList**
7:     Generate position updates for the selected avatar and put each of them into **RequestList**
8:     Disseminate the updates in **RequestList[0]** as many as possible
9:     Remove the selected avatar from **AvatarList**
10: **end while**
11: **while** (There are some unempty lists in **RequestList** and bandwidth is not used up) **do**
12:     Disseminate the updates in the unempty list with smallest index
13: **end while**

Algorithm 2 Fair-LMH (Client Side)

1: Assume the client receives an update at time t. Suppose the due time to apply the update (according to the fairness-aware update scheme) is t_d. If $t_d > t$, the update will be applied $t_d - t$ time later, otherwise, the update is applied immediately.

The Fair-LMH algorithm has two parts, which run at server side and client side respectively. The part for server side, shown in Algorithm 1, runs at each update frame. At each update frame, all the avatars maintained by the server are first put into **AvatarList** and sorted according to update priority which can be calculated by (19) (line 1). Then, items in list **RequestList[i]** are moved to list **RequestList[i-1]** for all $i > 0$ (line 2) since one update frame has elapsed. After that, each received forwarding request since last update frame is placed in **RequestList**, where the index of the list is calculated according to (22) (line 3). Then, the most urgent updates which are in list **RequestList[0]** are sent out first (line 4). Next, avatars are handled in decreasing order of their update priorities as long as there is network bandwidth available (lines 5 to 10). To handle an avatar, the position updates are generated first and placed in **RequestList**. Then, the most urgent updates which were placed in list **RequestList[0]** are sent out. If the network bandwidth is still available after all the avatars in **AvatarList** are handled, we continue processing each unempty list in **RequestList** (lines 11 to 13). Each time, the list with smallest index is processed and all updates in the list will be disseminated if there is sufficient bandwidth.

The part for client side is shown in Algorithm 2. When a client receives an update, if the receiving time is earlier than the due time of the update, the update will be issued at the due time. Otherwise, the update is applied on the replica immediately.

4. EXPERIMENTAL EVALUATION

4.1 Simulation Setup

We implemented an event-driven simulator to simulate a MSDVE. The virtual world is of scale 10000 x 10000, which was divided into 25 equal sized squares, each of them represents a zone. A total of 10 servers and 20000 clients were simulated. Each avatar is associated with a client, which was randomly distributed in the virtual world initially. The client assignment and zone mapping were determined by the approaches proposed in [12]. The length of a frame was set at 0.025 seconds, i.e., there are 40 frames per second.

The avatars move around the virtual world with random way point (RWP) mobility model. Specifically, as the simulation starts, each avatar selects one location in the virtual world as the destination. It then travels towards this destination with constant velocity chosen uniformly and randomly from [0.1, 1] distance units per frame. Upon reaching the destination, the avatar again chooses another random destination in the virtual world and move towards it.

In our simulation, the transmission delay from a server to a client was generated according to a shifted exponential distribution with probability density function $f(x) = \lambda e^{-\lambda(x-\tau)} (x \geq \tau)$ [5]. To generate a mean transmission delay d with a variance of v $(0 < v < 1)$, τ and λ should be set to $v * d$ and $\frac{1}{(1-v)*d}$ respectively.

Without loss of generality, the bandwidth consumption of position update and forwarding request, i.e., α was set at 1. The bandwidth capacity at each server was set to allow the server to send a given number of c_i updates at each frame, where c_i was varied in the experiments.

4.2 Update Algorithms to Compare

We also implemented the LMH algorithm for comparison, which is the optimal update algorithm proposed in our previous work for minimizing total inconsistency in MSDVEs [11]. However, the fairness is not considered in LMH. Moreover, we implemented some intuitive fairness-aware update algorithms including Fair-FF and Fair-SPACE. The Fair-FF and Fair-SPACE also follow the updating algorithm described in Algorithm 1 and Algorithm 2. The only difference between Fair-FF, Fair-SAPCE and Fair-LMH is on how the update priority of each avatar is calculated.

- Fair-RR: the update priority of each avatar is defined as the time since last update was generated.
- Fair-Space: the update priority of each avatar is defined as the spatial difference between the avatar and the replicas of the avatar.

4.3 Experimental Results

In the simulations, each experiment runs for a period of 30 minutes where the first 10 minutes was considered the warup period. Statistics were collected for the remaining 20 minutes of simulated time. In the results, the inconsistency and unfairness are presented as a ratio between 0 and 1 after normalization. For each group of result, let v_{min} and v_{max} denote the maximum value and the minimum value of the data respectively. The normalized ratio of a value v is calculated by $(v - v_{min})/(v_{max} - v_{min})$.

4.4 Impact of Bandwidth Capacity

We first evaluated the impact of bandwidth capacity on the performance of the algorithms. For each experiment, the bandwidth capacity was set in a range from 100 to 6000 updates per frame at each server. The average network delay was set at 0.1s with a variance of 0.95.

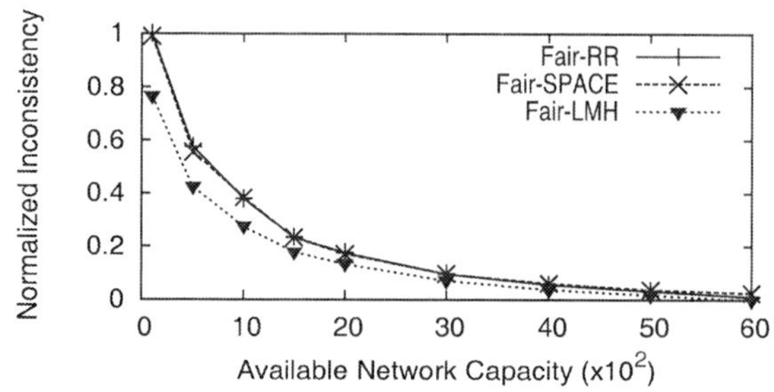

Figure 2: Impact of Bandwidth Capacity on Inconsistency

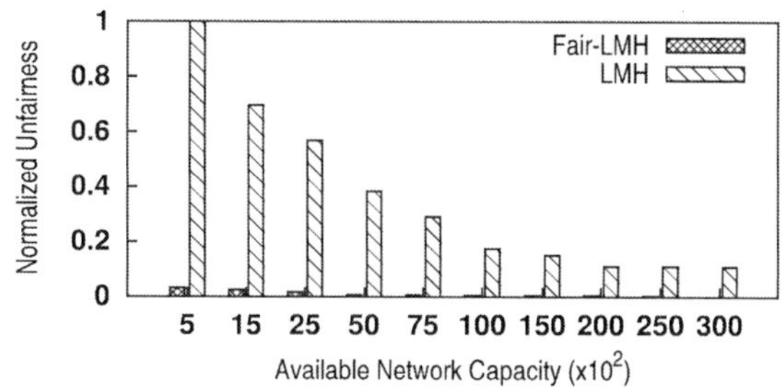

Figure 3: Impact of Bandwidth Capacity on Unfairness

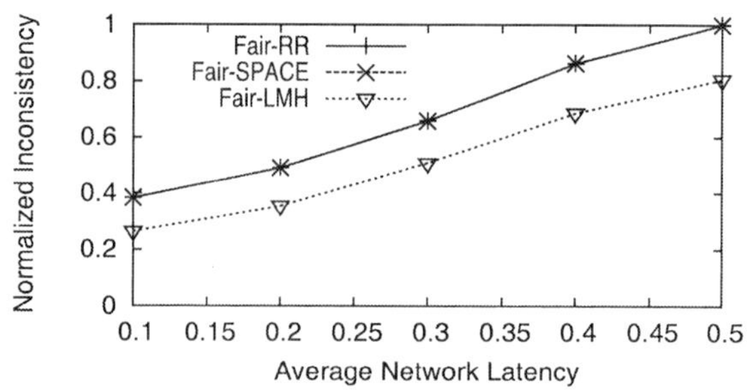

Figure 4: Impact of Network Delay on Inconsistency

Figure 2 shows the normalized inconsistency achieved by different algorithms. As can be seen, lower bandwidth makes larger inconsistency for all algorithms. For small bandwidth capacity, which implies more serious bandwidth constraints, Fair-LMH performs much better than other algorithms. For large bandwidth capacity, all algorithms get similar performance. This is because all the replicas can be updated frequently so the inconsistency is small.

Figure 3 shows the normalized unfairness achieved by LMH and Fair-LMH. As can be seen, Fair-LMH can greatly decrease the unfairness compared to LMH for all bandwidth capacities.

4.5 Impact of Network Delay

Next, we evaluated the impact of network delay on the performance of the algorithms. For each experiment, the

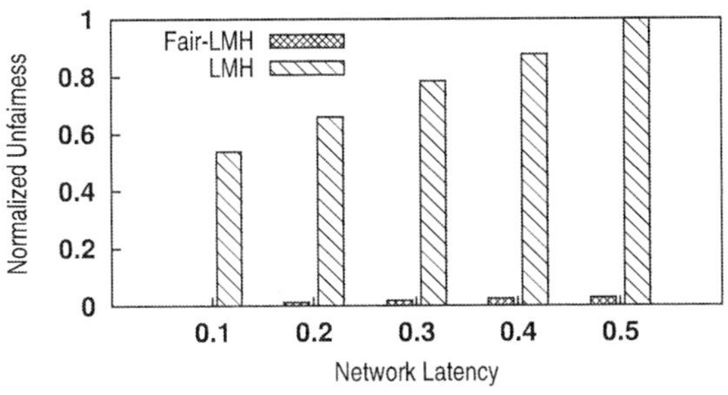

Figure 5: Impact of Network Delay on Unfairness

mean network delay was set in a range of 0.1s to 0.5s. The variance of network delay was set at 0.95. The bandwidth capacity was set at 1000 updates per frame at each server.

Figure 4 shows the normalized inconsistency achieved by different algorithms. As can be seen, the total inconsistency gets larger as the average network delay increases. This is because time-space inconsistency is affected by transmission delays and generally increases with the delays. The Fair-LMH algorithm alway outperforms other algorithms for various network delays.

Figure 5 shows the normalized unfairness incurred by Fair-LMH and LMH with different network delays. As can be seen, as the network delay increases, the unfairness incurred by the two algorithms both increases. For various network delays, the unfairness incurred by Fair-LMH is much smaller than the unfairness incurred by LMH.

4.6 Impact of Network Delay Variance

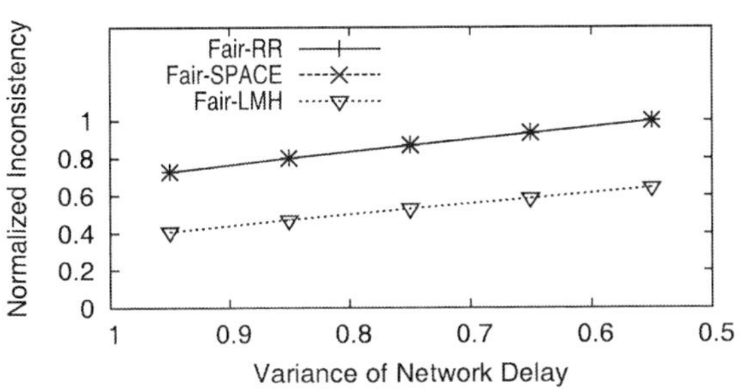

Figure 6: Impact of Network Delay Variance on Inconsistency

At last, we evaluated the impact of the variance of network delays on the performance of the algorithms. For each experiment, the mean network delay was set at 0.1s. The variance of network delay was set in a range of 0.55 to 0.95. The bandwidth capacity was set at 1000 updates per frame at each server.

Figure 6 shows the normalized inconsistency incurred by different algorithms. As can be seen, the total inconsistency gets larger as the variance of network delay increases. However, the growth is not quite obvious. The Fair-LMH algorithm always performs better than other algorithms for all variance settings.

Figure 7 shows the normalized unfairness incurred by Fair-LMH and LMH. As can be seen, similar to the inconsistency, the impact of network variance on the unfairness is also not

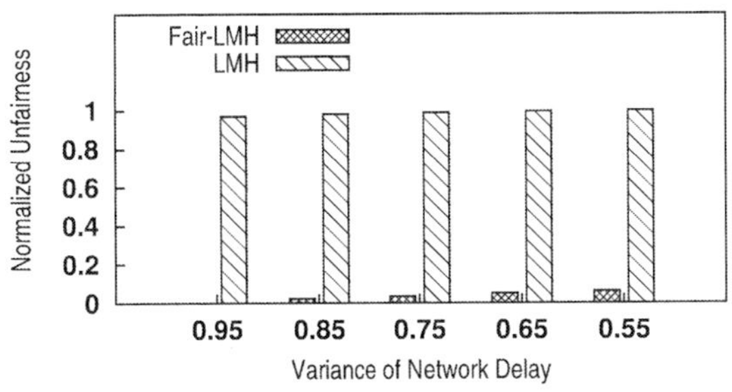

Figure 7: Impact of Network Delay Variance on Unfairness

obvious. The Fair-LMH algorithm always performs better than LMH for all variance settings.

5. RELATED WORK

The update scheduling problem for improving consistency in DVEs has been studied a lot in the literature. A state update scheduling algorithm to minimize total inconsistency in single server DVEs with constraint of network bandwidth was proposed in [19]. The proposed algorithm can be easily extended for multi-server DVEs where a client is allowed to directly connect to multiple servers. In our previous work [9, 11], we considered MSDVEs and proposed a heuristic update algorithm to prioritize state updates from a global perspective for improving consistency in MSDVEs where each server has a limit network bandwidth. However, the unfairness is not considered in any of the work mentioned above.

Research has also been carried out to address unfairness in DVEs. The causal relationship between propagation time, inconsistencies, playability and fairness in online multiplayer games was explored in [3]. Two strategies were proposed for managing playability and fairness in online games. Zander et.al [23] studied the impact of delay differences among players on the fairness in multiplayer network gaming. An approach that can be used with the existing network games to equalize the delay differences was designed and implemented. However, in all the work mentioned above, only network delay is considered while the spatial difference is not considered in the measurement.

Many research activities have been carried out to address the bandwidth reduction issues in DVEs. For example, dead reckoning [3, 16, 24] and relevance filtering [15, 20] are widely used in DVEs to compensate the network latency and reduce the network traffic. By maintaining a DR prediction model, remote node can predict the state of the replicated entity between two consecutive update packets thus update frequency can be reduced. Relevance filtering can eliminate the irrelevant information by using the concept of Area of Interest (AOI). For a single avatar, if some entities are not in the avatar's AOI (that implies the avatar is not interested in these entities), state updates of these entities can be saved. Although the total network traffic can be greatly reduced by using these techniques, the total bandwidth requirement may still be very high as the population of the DVE grows. If servers are not able to disseminate all state updates due to the constraints of network capacity, our algorithm is to determine the updating priority for each state update according to their potential impact on inconsistency and unfairness. Therefore, our algorithm can be easily used on top of those techniques.

6. CONCLUSIONS

In this paper, we investigated update schedules for improving fairness and consistency in MSDVEs with network bandwidth constraints for servers. A fairness-aware update scheme was proposed to guarantee fairness among clients in a MSDVE. Based on the fairness-aware update scheme, a distributed state update scheduling algorithm was proposed to minimize total inconsistency. A variety of experiments were performed to evaluate the proposed algorithm. From the results we can see that the proposed algorithm outperforms other algorithms. However, the proposed algorithm is only evaluated by simulations. In the future, we would like to evaluate the proposed algorithm in some real large scale DVE systems.

7. ACKNOWLEDGMENTS

This research is supported by the National Research Foundation, Prime Minister's Office, Singapore under its IDM Futures Funding Initiative, and Singapore Ministry of Education Academic Research Fund Tier 2 under Grant MOE2013-T2-2-067.

8. REFERENCES

[1] C. Bouras, G. Hornig, V. Triantafillou, and T. Tsiatsos. Architectures supporting e-learning through collaborative virtual environments: the case of INVITE. In *IEEE International Conference on Advanced Learning Technologies*, pages 13–16, 2001.

[2] J. Brun, F. Safaei, and P. Boustead. Fairness and playability in online multiplayer games. *Faculty of Informatics-Papers*, page 232, 2006.

[3] J. Brun, F. Safaei, and P. Boustead. Managing latency and fairness in networked games. *Communications of the ACM*, 49(11):46–51, 2006.

[4] J. Chim, R. W. H. Lau, H. V. Leong, and A. Si. Cyberwalk: A web-based distributed virtual walkthrough environment. *IEEE Transactions on Multimedia*, 5:503–515, 2003.

[5] A. Corlett, D. Pullin, and S. Sargood. Statistics of one-way internet packet delays. *53 rd IETF*, 2002.

[6] Everquest. http://everquest.station.sony.com.

[7] T. Funkhouser. Ring: a client-server system for multi-user virtual environments. In *Proceedings of Symposium on Interactive 3D graphics*. ACM, 1995.

[8] M. Hori, T. Iseri, K. Fujikawa, S. Shimojo, and H. Miyahara. Scalability issues of dynamic space management for multiple-server networked virtual environments. In *IEEE Pacific Rim Conference on Communications, Computers and Signal Processing*, volume 1, pages 200–203. IEEE, 2001.

[9] Y. Li and W. Cai. Determining optimal update period for minimizing inconsistency in multi-server distributed virtual environments. In *2011 IEEE/ACM 15th International Symposium on Distributed Simulation and Real Time Applications (DS-RT)*, pages 126–133. IEEE, 2011.

[10] Y. Li and W. Cai. Consistency-aware partitioning algorithm in multi-server distributed virtual environments. In *2012 IEEE 26th International Parallel & Distributed Processing Symposium (IPDPS)*, pages 798–807. IEEE, 2012.

[11] Y. Li and W. Cai. Update schedules for improving consistency in multi-server distributed virtual environments. *Journal of Network and Computer Applications*, 41:263–273, 2014.

[12] Y. Li and W. Cai. Consistency-aware zone mapping and client assignment in multi-server distributed virtual environments. *IEEE Transactions on Parallel and Distributed Systems*, 26(6):1570–1579, 2015.

[13] Z. Li, X. Tang, W. Cai, and S. J. Turner. Fair and efficient dead reckoning-based update dissemination for distributed virtual environments. In *Principles of Advanced and Distributed Simulation (PADS), 2012 ACM/IEEE/SCS 26th Workshop on*, pages 13–22. IEEE, 2012.

[14] B. Ng, A. Si, R. Lau, and F. Li. A multi-server architecture for distributed virtual walkthrough. In *Proceedings of the ACM Symposium on Virtual Reality Software and Technology*, 2002.

[15] K. Pan, W. Cai, X. Tang, S. Zhou, and S. Turner. A hybrid interest management mechanism for peer-to-peer networked virtual environments. In *IEEE International Symposium on Parallel and Distributed Processing (IPDPS)*, 2010.

[16] L. Pantel and L. Wolf. On the suitability of dead reckoning schemes for games. In *Proceedings of the 1st Workshop on Network and System Support for Games (NetGames)*, 2002.

[17] SecondLife. http://secondlife.com.

[18] P. Svoboda, W. Karner, and M. Rupp. Traffic analysis and modeling for world of warcraft. In *IEEE International Conference on Communications (ICC)*, pages 1612–1617, 2007.

[19] X. Tang and S. Zhou. Update scheduling for improving consistency in distributed virtual environments. *IEEE Transactions on Parallel and Distributed Systems (TPDS)*, 21:765–777, 2010.

[20] D. Van Hook, S. Rak, and J. Calvin. Approaches to relevance filtering. In *Proc. of 11th DIS Workshop*, 1994.

[21] WoW. http://www.worldofwarcraft.com/index.xml.

[22] WoWCencus. http://www.warcraftrealms.com/censusplus.php.

[23] S. Zander, I. Leeder, and G. Armitage. Achieving fairness in multiplayer network games through automated latency balancing. In *Proceedings of the 2005 ACM SIGCHI International Conference on Advances in Computer Entertainment Technology*, pages 117–124. ACM, 2005.

[24] Y. Zhang, L. Chen, and G. Chen. Globally synchronized dead-reckoning with local lag for continuous distributed multiplayer games. In *Proceedings of 5th ACM SIGCOMM Workshop on Network and System Support for Games (NetGames)*, 2006.

[25] S. Zhou, W. Cai, B.-S. Lee, and S. J. Turner. Time-space consistency in large-scale distributed virtual environments. *ACM Transactions on Modeling and Computer Simulation (TOMACS)*, 14(1):31–47, 2004.

Design, Use and Evaluation of P-FSEFI: A Parallel Soft Error Fault Injection Framework for Emulating Soft Errors in Parallel Applications

Qiang Guan[1], Nathan BeBardeleben[1], Panruo Wu[3], Stephan Eidenbenz[2],
Sean Blanchard[1], Laura Monroe[1], Elisabeth Baseman[1], and Li Tan[1]

[1]Ultrascale Systems Research Center, Los Alamos National Laboratory, Los Alamos, USA,
{qguan,ndebard,seanb,lmonroe,lissa}@lanl.gov,darkwhite29@gmail.com
[2]Information Science and Technology Institute, Los Alamos National Laboratory, Los Alamos, USA, eidenben@lanl.gov
[3]Department of Computer Science and Engineering, University of California Riverside, Riverside, USA, pwu011@cs.ucr.edu

ABSTRACT

Future exascale application programmers and users have a need to quantity an application's resilience and vulnerability to soft errors before running their codes on production supercomputers due to the cost of failures and hazards from silent data corruption. Barring a deep understanding of the resiliency of a particular application, vulnerability evaluation is commonly done through fault injection tools at either the software or hardware level. Hardware fault injection, while most realistic, is relegated to customized vendor chips and usually applications cannot be evaluated at scale. Software fault injection can be done more practically and efficiently and is the approach that many researchers use as a reasonable approximation. With a sufficiently sophisticated software fault injection framework, an application can be studied to see how it would handle many of the errors that manifest at the application level. Using such a tool, a developer can progressively improve the resilience at targeted locations they believe are important for their target hardware.

In this work, we present the Parallel Fine-grained Soft Error Fault Injector (P-FSEFI), an extended fault injection tool designed to inject faults in parallel applications. P-FSEFI inherits all the features from F-SEFI but adds support for parallel applications as well as an expanded fault model. Like, F-SEFI, P-FSEFI uses the QEMU processor emulation virtual machine and injects faults at the virtual hardware layer. We discuss the design of P-FSEFI and a case study on the NAS Parallel Benchmark which includes a breakdown between silent data corruption, hangs, and benign faults. We find portions of the benchmark that are more and less resilient to corruption and discuss why we believe that to be the case.

[1]This work was performed at the Ultrascale Systems Research Center (USRC) at Los Alamos National Laboratory, supported by the U.S. Department of Energy contract AC52-06NA25396. The publication has been assigned the LANL identifier LA-UR-16-

SIMUTOOLS 2016, August 22-23, Prague, Czech Republic

Keywords

soft error; MPI; fault injection; resilience; vulnerability; High Performance Computing

1. INTRODUCTION

Resilience will play a key role in next-generation supercomputer systems [39, 9]. Although the high performance computing (HPC) community tends to consider all aspects of reliability under the umbrella term of "resilience," failures can affect supercomputers and their running applications in a wide variety of complicated ways. Soft errors on hardware can be transient, intermittent, or permanent. They can cause silent data corruption (SDC), outright crash the application itself, or cause hardware components to fail. Faults can come from any range of events, including aging [8, 35], material impurities/packaging [34], neutron ("cosmic") radiation [11], electromagnetic interference [17], electromigration [25], and temperature [5, 24] or voltage extremes/fluctuations [10]. Furthermore, faults are not only driven by hardware influences. Software plays a non-trivial part in the rate of faults on computing systems today [38]. The lack of tools for characterizing and studying these kinds of faults is regarded as one of the current challenges of resilient exascale computing[18]. Without sufficient characterization and analysis tools it seems unlikely that key advancements in HPC resilience will occur in a timely fashion.

To date,the primary focus of HPC reliability has been on defensive I/O techniques , particularly checkpoint/restart (C/R). C/R enables a model of tenacious computing, playing a vital role in making it possible to perform reliably while using unreliable parts . However, expected increases in failure rates on future machines will reduce the amount of useful work performed between C/R cycles. The HPC community is already seeing significant effort from industry, academia, and national laboratories to advance this technique. In contrast, the subject of silent data corruption remains relatively unaddressed.

Silent Data Corruption (SDC) is characterized as any event that causes application data to be corrupted in a way that is not discernable to the system. SDC would be a common occurrence if not for techniques that protect memory systems and logic circuits. Main memory, registers, and caches have succeeded with resilient techniques such as SECDED (single error correct, double error detect), chipkill [15], and parity. Logic circuitry has protections built in as well , but at the expense of die space, performance, and power levels. To date, SDC mitigation techniques have led to computers being widely viewed as reliable digital machines. However, due to the large scale of deployed machines, the HPC community must account for what would otherwise be rare fault scenarios such as SDC.

Meanwhile, in order to cope with the high number of fault injection experiments and slowing-down due to the injection, especially for the large scale HPC application which usually use a large dataset as the input. Parallel fault injection tool can make a better utilization to the computation power of hardware [43], while multiple processes can be running at the same time to reduce the fault injection cycle.

While some current efforts attempt to address soft error resilience from the programming model perspective , such as using containment domains [12], this and other popular approaches are predicated on an underlying understanding of an application's vulnerability. This vulnerability can take the form of entire functions, regions of an application, or specific variables. While techniques such as compiler directed redundancy, automatic triple modular redundancy (voting), and rollback can protect such vulnerable structures, the programmer is left to identify the vulnerable regions of his/her application.

We believe there is a missing piece to addressing soft error resilience. That piece is a tool providing a gprof-like [19] profile of an application. However, we propose to profile an application for its resilience and vulnerability to a range of different faults rather than profiling the application's performance. Such a tool would enable new scientific discovery, expose new resilient programming techniques, and enable evaluation and validation of resilient middleware. With this sort of tool, programmers and application architects could focus their attention on "problem spots" in an application and apply resilient techniques where appropriate. We believe that this would enable a targeted resilience approach providing reliability at a much lower cost than is often incurred by other approaches.

In order to facilitate this targeted resilience approach for HPC supercomputer applications, we have developed a Parallel Fine-grained Soft Error Fault Injection tool (P-FSEFI). P-FSEFI inherits the functionality of F-SEFI[21], its sequential predecessor, and builds upon the previous work by adding the following features:

- Tools to configure, launch, and manage multiple sequential instances of F-SEFI, including virtual network interfaces, MPI environments, and Copy On Write (COW) virtual machine images. This allows P-FSEFI to emulate a cluster of hosts that can communicate in parallel.
- An extended, pluggable, and flexible interface for inserting fault models so that a user can develop their own fault injection techniques.
- Using the above interface, the addition of permanent, high-locality persistence, and low locality persistence faults.
- The ability to inject faults into parallel programs running on multiple virtual machines on the same, or different physical hosts. These faults can affect as many or as few VMs as desired and, for instance, could be used to watch fault propagation as parallel messages are exchanged.

In this paper, we demonstrate P-FSEFI's capability of injecting faults into the parallel applications. We use the NAS benchmark as a fault injection showcase. We also show direct injection comparisons between P-FSEFI and FSEFI.

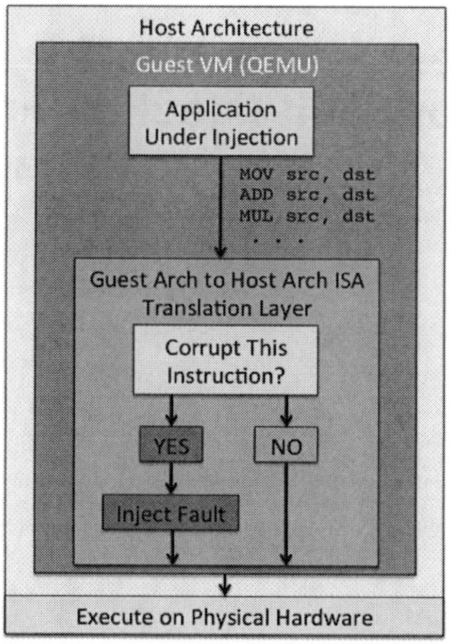

Figure 1: F-SEFI monitors applications running in a guest VM and precisely inserts faults to corrupt a given application in a specific location, with a user-specified fault model. This corruption is passed to the physical hardware without triggering application or operating system. For further details on F-SEFI, please refer to [14, 21].

The rest of the paper is organized as follows. In Section 2 we discuss the design of P-FSEFI and how it improves upon F-SEFI. The new fault models supported by P-FSEFI are discussed in Section 3. A case study of using P-FSEFI on the NAS Parallel Benchmarks is presented in Section 4. Performance overhead of using P-FSEFI is shown in section 5. In section 6 we discuss related work. We conclude in Section 7 and discuss some future work.

2. P-FSEFI DESIGN

P-FSEFI builds upon F-SEFI [21, 14], a sequential fault injection tool previously used to study a number of applications[23, 20, 22, 3]. Our extension adds support for injecting faults into parallel applications, a vitally important feature for advancing the original tool to be useful in the high performance computing and supercomputing fields. As a reminder of how fault injection in F-SEFI works, Figure 1 shows how F-SEFI inserts faults without alerting the application.

Building upon the F-SEFI sequential model, P-FSEFI allows multiple F-SEFI instances to be connected. Each F-SEFI instance can be deployed on the same physical host, or multiple, different physical hosts. A parallel program, such as an MPI program, is then run within this collection of F-SEFI instances. The parallel program communicates outside of the VM and into other F-SEFI VM instances as it passes data to perform a parallel calculation. This capability makes P-FSEFI unique and extensible to emulate a parallel process running on a virtual cluster. Figure 2 depicts P-FSEFI's parallel architecture and illustrates how its fault injection controller monitors and controls fault injection into each F-SEFI controller.

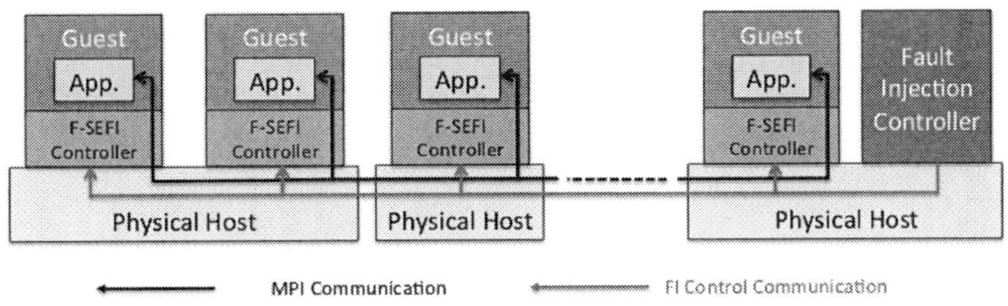

Figure 2: Parallel processes run in different guest VMs on possibly different physical hosts, each controller by an F-SEFI controller. P-SEFI manages the fault injection externally.

One of the interesting features of using QEMU as our virtual machine processor emulation framework, is that QEMU allows for virtual architectures to be emulated on different physical hardware. For instance, it is possible to have ARM as a guest architecture while running on an x86 physical host. This enables interesting possibilities which are impossible through classical software fault injection techniques.

To enable parallel fault injection we need multiple QEMU VM instances that can communicate and support MPI applications. Each VM instance needs a properly configured VM image, network interfaces, and MPI environment to support MPI applications and their deployments. For the network interfaces, each VM instance is configured with two interfaces — one for communicating with other VM instances, and one for management from the host. To communicate with other VM instances, each VM instance is configured with a virtual NIC with an unique IP. These VM instances then are connected by a multicast port on the hosts therefore avoiding the need of root privilege on hosts to configure networks. To manage the VM from the hosts another network interface is configured using port forwarding on the host. From this port on the host scripts can be written to fully automate VM images and instance provision, MPI application deployment, fault injection configuration, result collection and analysis, and cleanup.

Every VM instance needs a disk image and to save disk space and speed up VM instance provision we use Copy On Write (COW) images. Each VM image derives from a base image and configures its network interfaces and MPI environments upon boot based on its assigned MAC address. P-FSEFI uses MAC address, an easily specified command line argument in QEMU, to uniquely identify VM instances. The derived VM images are stateless and disposable, further simplifying automatic management.

As was noted above, and as was a key feature of F-SEFI, all of P-FSEFI exists entirely in user space. That is, no privileged (root) access is required. Neither F-SEFI nor P-FSEFI require any kernel modifications, special drivers, or changes to the operating system. In particular, this means that P-FSEFI can be used on production supercomputing resources that often have strict security restrictions. P-FSEFI is practical and functional for users in HPC environments.

P-FSEFI inherits "batch" fault injection capabilities which allow the user to perform, for instance, parameter sweeps and as many trials as desired. In this way, a user can modify and configure fault models to his interest and perform many experiments. Results from these trials, such as those presented in Section 4, are assembled together and ingested into R scripts for analysis.

Dynamic fault injection and binary fault injection are two key features of P-FSEFI. Many important DOE applications are large, and complex, performing radically different operations given different inputs. As such, static analysis of this class of applications is largely uninformative. P-FSEFI adapts to the dynamicity of data objects, covering all static and dynamic data, a feature especially valuable for applications that operate on random processes. Furthermore, the batch capabilities of P-FSEFI allow for statistical analysis given potentially differing inputs.

3. FAULT MODEL

It is very important for a fault injection tool to support multiple fault models to satisfy the requirements of reliability evaluation, verification, and validation. Different fault models could provide various emulated environments and manage the occurrences of faults temporally as well as spatially. The P-FSEFI fault model is pluggable and extensible. The fault models that P-FSEFI currently provides and a brief description of how these faults might manifest at the application level are as following:

- Single Bit Upset (**SBU**): A transient or permanent single bit flip to CPU logic units, registers, caches, and memory.
- Multiple Bits Upset (**MBU**): Transient or permanent multiple bit flips to CPU logic units, registers, caches, and memory.
- High Locality Persistence (**HLP**): A short term "stickiness" of flipped bit(s) to the higher level cache.
- Low Locality Persistence (**LLP**): A long term "stickiness" of flipped bit(s) to the lower level cache and memory.
- Permanent (**P**): A permanent malfunction of a memory location.

In addition to injecting a fault at a precise line number of a source program, P-FSEFI can also inject faults into a set of instructions with a user-defined probability. For instance, using P-FSEFI, one can specify that a floating point multiply should produce a multi-bit error over a bit range with 0.001% probability. That is, every single multiply of a target application (or region of an application if desired) would be subject to this probability of seeing a fault. As an example of why this is useful, in [16] the error rate percentage is shown with respect to supply voltage of an FPGA array multiplier block. Using P-FSEFI, one can "dial in" error rates of interest and study how an application targeting that platform would tolerate the errors.

As shown in Figure 3, P-FSEFI supports both permanent and semi-permanent faults in the memory hierarchy. Figure 4 demonstrates the logic for simulating memory system faults with different locality persistence. As load/store are the only instructions that access memory, P-FSEFI intercepts load/store in the intermediate code, or the TCG code. If P-FSEFI decides to inject a memory fault to a memory address, it marks the memory address as corrupted and keeps the correct value as a shadow copy. Afterwards, another load accessing the corrupted memory address will read the

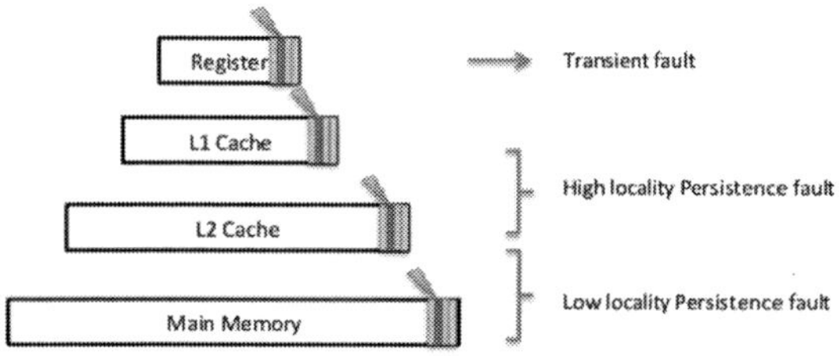

Figure 3: P-FSEFI supports a variety of fault models that emulate faults at different levels of the memory hierarchy. The user can easily add additional custom fault models.

corrupted value if the corruption persists, or the correct value if the corruption clears due to either expired locality persistence or the memory address overwrites. The store instruction will clear the corruption on the memory address.

The P-FSEFI user configures how long the fault will be persistent, that is, how long accessing that location will produce the fault. After this persistence period, the memory location returns to normal and subsequent accesses return the uncorrupted result. Any store operation to this faulty memory address will turn off the fault injection mechanism.

4. CASE STUDY

We demonstrate P-FSEFI injecting faults into seven parallel benchmark applications from NAS Parallel Benchmark (NPB) [1]. The test computing system comprises 4 Intel Haswell servers connected by gigabit Ethernet. The servers are equipped with 20 Intel Xeon cores and 128 GB of RAM. We installed P-FSEFI hypervisors on the servers , each of which hosts up to twenty VMs. A VM is assigned up to two VCPUs and the amount of memory allocatable by a VM is capped at 1 GB. Recall that the setup is as shown previously in Figure 2.

Motivated by the fault pattern described in [40], we focus our experiments on single bit faults. Again, P-FSEFI is a tool that can be configured in many ways and this is just how we have chosen to configure this experiment. This might be useful to look at single bit faults on a system that did not have error protection, for instance. We injected $10,000$ faults into $10,000$ runs of all seven kernel programs in the NPB suite.

At run-time in each injection run, we randomly inject either a single bit HLP or LLP fault into a randomly chosen load instruction. This load instruction is chosen from *all possible* loads for the entire NPB kernel program under evaluation. The HLP and LLP "stickiness" for these experiments, θ, was set to 2. That is, loads accessing a chosen fault location will return the same fault twice after which the fault will go away. A store before the second load would overwrite and clear the fault. The choice of 2 in our experiments is configurable. For instance, if a user had detailed hardware fault models (such as RTL cache simulations) then they would set this value accordingly.

We combine the results from HLP and LLP injection for brevity.

After a fault is injected, the program runs to completion, after which we determine the impact of the injection. In the case of the NPB, there is a "checker" that determines if the result passes after the completion of a benchmark run. In the experiment presented here for both the HLP and LLP fault models, one of three things can occur:

- **Benign**: There are no differences in results of the benchmark between the faulty run and fault-free "golden" run.
- **Hang**: The execution of the benchmark hangs at some point after the fault is injected. We use a software-defined timeout watchdog to detect the hang.
- **SDC**: The NPB "checker" reports that the result is corrupted.

Note that there is no **Crash** case in the case study presented here. This is because we target data regions for our fault injections and do not corrupt memory addresses or jumps that might cause access to protected memory space (usually resulting in a segmentation fault).

The benchmarks that make up the NPB are listed in Table 1 lists the benchmarks making up the NPB and used in these experiments.

Figure 5 shows the results of the fault injection campaign using both FSEFI and P-FSEFI. In NPB benchmark suite, the first four benchmarks are compute kernels and the last three benchmarks are mini-apps that solve nonlinear partial differential equations. Different applications exhibit nonhomogeneous characteristics under faults. All seven benchmarks are floating point applications and thus are not supposed to generate a bit-wise correct result — rather the result is considered correct if it falls within a small threshold [6]. As mentioned above, for this we use the "checkers" that come with the NPB.

The fault injection results suggest that certain kernels and numerical algorithms are more resilient to transient memory faults than others, thus adding one more dimension to the tradeoffs in choosing numerical algorithms. For example, MG, CG, and FT can all be used to solve certain PDEs. From the perspective of resilience one would consider choosing MG in addition to other considerations, as the MG kernel is 6x less likely to be affected by a memory fault. The same goes for the last three mini apps. They are all designed to solve a CFD problem but with different performance characteristics. The results suggest that the newer LU (lower upper Gauss-Seidel) method is significantly better in terms of resilience, with about 75% of faults masked by the LU application. It seems that the more tightly coupled the parallel application is, the more vulnerable it is to faults. For example, EP is the least tightly coupled thus least vulnerable. CG, characterized by its irregular communication pattern, is the most vulnerable.

Comparing the results of FSEFI injection into the serial version of benchmarks (denoted by S-FSEFI) with parallel injection (P-FSEFI), it is clear that parallel injection makes a significant difference in the outcome. In general, the simple compute kernels exhibit a larger fraction of SDCs in their parallel versions while parallel injection into mini-apps exhibits fewer relative SDCs compared to their serial version. We will explore this phenomenon in greater detail in future work.

Fault injection campaigns such as this one can help in understanding, choosing, designing, and optimizing numerical applications to achieve better resilience. On the contrary, numerical applications like CG and FT are good candidates for testing the resilience of large-scaled systems, because they are very "sensitive" to transient faults.

5. PERFORMANCE OVERHEAD

P-FSEFI and F-SEFI are intended to be used when a developer is studying their application for its resiliency and vulnerability. In this way it is similar to a debugger or profiler. As such, performance is not our main concern but much like these tools it is important to understand the performance impacts to make sure that the tool is fundamentally usable.

Compared to the application running on the host hardware, the application running under P-SEFI runs slower due to the emulation overhead in QEMU, the instrumentation of P-FSEFI, and further

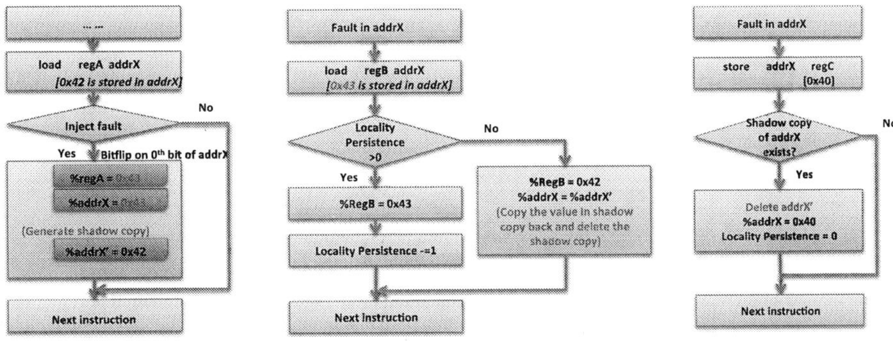

(a) When a single bit fault is injected into the memory address of a load instruction, P-FSEFI will also keep a shadow copy of the original value in the register or memory location and mark the specific memory address as contaminated. After then, any attempts to load the value from this contaminated address will automatically load the corrupted value.

(b) If a persistence values has been specified, any attampts to load the value from the contaminated address will automatically load the corrupted value *until the local persistence expires.*

(c) If an attempt is made to store a value from the register back to the memory location, P-FSEFI will automatically release the locality persistence and the contamination to the specific memory address.

Figure 4: Flowcharts for the simulation of memory system faults with varying persistence.

Table 1: The NAS Parallel Benchmarks

	Benchamrk	Description
Kernels	MG	Multi-Grid method; structured grids.
	CG	Conjugate gradient; unstructured grids.
	FT	3D Fast Fourier Transform; spectral method
	EP	Embarrasingly Parallel; Intensive in floating point computation but almost no communication.
Mini Apps	BT	Block Tri-diagonal solver
	SP	Scalar Penta-diagonal solver
	LU	Lower-Upper Gauss-Seidel solver

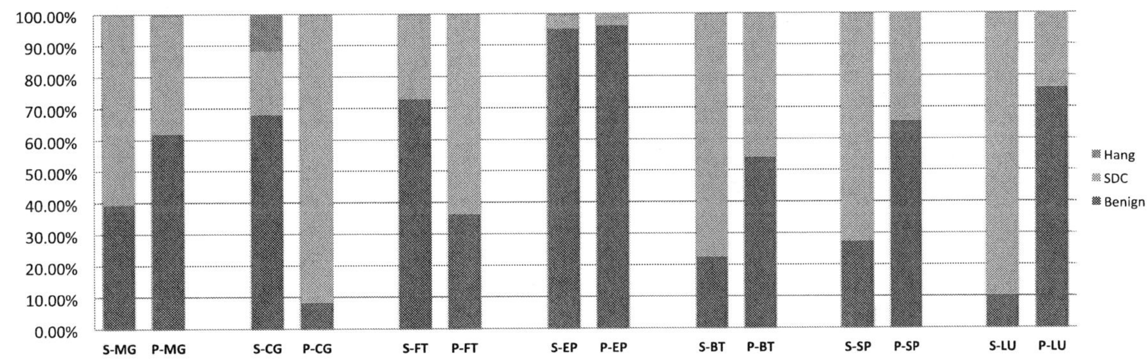

Figure 5: Fault injection campaign study on NAS Parallel Benchmark. all "*S-*" results mean the faults are injected into the serial version of NPB benchmark and all "*P-*" results mean the faults are injected into the parallel version of NPB benchmark. $10,000$ faults are injected into $10,000$ runs of the MG, CG, FT, EP, BT, SP and LU for both serial and parallel injection. In parallel fault injection, only a small number of "Hang" outcomes are collected from the fault injection campaign. MG and CG have only 0.5% of the total results as "Hang". FT and BT have only 1 "Hang" among all $10,000$ injections and EP, SP and LU have none of the "Hang" results. EP shows the highest percentages of fault tolerance which tolerates over 96% of the injected faults and produces benign results while EP is embarrassly parallel and generates little communication. On the contrary, CG shows the lowest capability in fault tolerance with only about 8% of injected faults are masked. In serial fault injection, EP shows similar result as parallel fault injection while CG, BT, SP and LU produce more SDCs with serial injection. On the other hand, CG and FT shows more benign errors in serial compared to parallel injection. Moreover, CG has a significant number of Hangs while injecting faults into its serial version.

Table 2: The performance overhead of using P-FSEFI comparing to the physical environment

Benchmark	MG	CG	FT	EP	BT	SP	LU	Geometric Average
Emulation slowdown - QEMU (x)	6.36	6.09	9.02	13.59	10.61	7.25	9.31	8.57
P-FSEFI slowdown (x)	39.53	44.46	33.25	16.72	30.08	44.12	30.96	32.72
Distributing VM slowdown (x)	1.01	1.00	1.29	1.01	1.08	1.01	1.04	1.06
Aggregate slowdown (x)	252.86	269.78	388.12	230.31	345.57	322.67	300.37	297.08

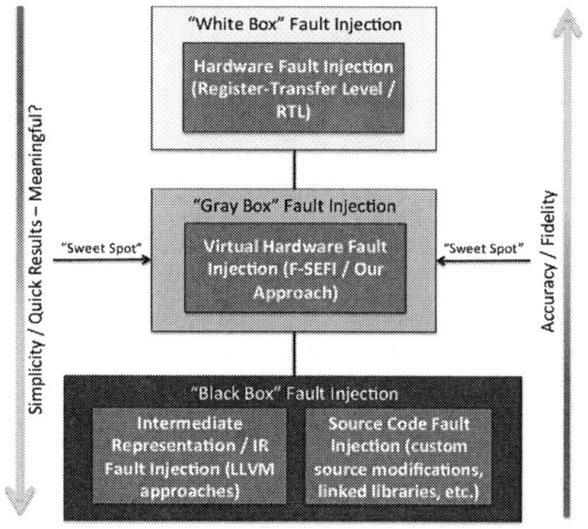

Figure 6: Fault injection techniques can be roughly categorized as "white box", "black box" and "gray box". White box fault injectors are those with detailed hardware knowledge, high accuracy, but slow and complex and usually requiring specialized vendor hardware. Black box injectors are fast and rely on source code or intermediate representation modification but genearlly lack accuracy. Gray box fault injectors, like P-FSEFI, exist somewhere in the middle.

overhead incurred due to distributing VMs across multiple nodes. Table 2 demonstrates the contribution of these three factors. In summary, the QEMU emulation slows down the application about 10x, P-SEFI instrumentation slows an additional 30x, and the VM distributing across multiple nodes adds some 1.06x slowdown on top. Overall, P-SEFI runs about 300x slower than under no emulation on the host hardware.

P-FSEFI uses a somewhat older version of QEMU that has higher overheads than newer versions. We are actively improving the performance of P-FSEFI and are currently testing a prototype which incurs considerably less overhead. At this time, it is not yet fully functional so is not discussed here.

6. RELATED WORK

Currently there exists a large uncertainty about the frequency of soft errors. Evaluation of the system's ability to withstand hardware soft errors in real systems is challenging because capturing a soft error at runtime is difficult and reproducing a transient soft error is practically impossible. Therefore, fault injection techniques are used to analyze the impact of soft errors.

In general, fault injection at the hardware level can be thought of as white box fault injection. That is, extremely high-fidelity results are produced with extremely detailed information about the hardware makeup of a particular device. This requires information that is usually vendor proprietary and also suffers from being extremely slow. So while the results are meaningful, it is impossible to simulate large-scale parallel applications in this manner and otherwise in-feasible given inaccessibility to vendor-protected device designs. It is important to note that with hardware fault injection it is generally impossible to connect application behavior under fault with specific lines of a source program. This makes it useful for studying hardware but difficult to use to iteratively create more resilient applications. The other extreme can be considered black box fault injection. Here, little is known about the architecture and applications are modified at the source, library, or an intermediate representation (IR) level. This is simple and produces fast results but it is unclear how meaningful the results are for resiliency-based hardware-software co-design. P-FSEFI, the software fault injector we described, fills a role in the middle of these two approaches and provides a very practical alternative which we refer to as gray box fault injection. This approach uses partial information of hardware design, and enough information about the application to facilitate actionable experiments. P-FSEFI together with its predecessor, FSEFI [21], takes advantage of major advances in virtualization and processor emulation to achieve as close to real hardware fault injection.

6.1 Black Box : Intermediate Representation Fault Injection and Source Code Fault Injection

Much recent research focuses on injecting soft errors in the binary level by modifying the the intermediate representation codes to inject faults dynamically on real systems. Lu et al. [30] proposes LLFI, a programming level fault injection tool using the LLVM [27] Just-In-Time Compiler (JITC) to allow injections to the compiler's intermediate code according to the different data categories (pointer data and control data). But performance of LLVM is restricted by the limitations of the compiler specification (only GCC is supported), the heuristic study of the source codes and the intrusion of instrumented Intermediate Representation (IR) in machine codes. Ashraf et al. [2] proposed LLFI++, an extended version of LLFI. The biggest limitation for LLFI++ is that it requires a modification the MPI layer for sharing the contaminated memory location in MPI through the message protocol. Instead, P-FSEFI relies on the hypervisor to exchange the contamination information between VMs and ranks.

BIFIT proposed by Li et al [29]] investigates the application's vulnerability to soft errors, which is designed closely upon PIN [31], a binary instrumentation tool for IA-32 and x86-64. BIFIT can inject faults at an arbitrarily chosen execution point and any data structures, but it depends on the application knowledge through profiling the application to generate a memory reference table of all data objects. This approach becomes less practical when the application uses a random seed to dynamically initialize the input data set. While the architecture restriction of PIN is not terribly limiting, it does restrict evaluations of different architectures (such as probabilistic and approximate computing, ARM, PowerPC, etc.). Moreover, to the best of our knowledge it is unable to support parallel programs.

Feng et al [26] introduced Fast Fault Injection and Sensitivity

Analysis Tool (FastFIT) to conduct fast fault injection and characterize the application sensitivity to faulty collectives. For each fault injection test, the injected fault is manifested by one bit flip in one of the input parameters. The source code and variable mutation based fault injection only provide limited set of injection instants at variables, the very high abstraction level only and it cannot inject faults into the locations that are invisible to the program. Modifying the source code means that the program under test is not the same as code that will be running in the real system.

FIMD-MPI [7] is designed to inject faults into MPI-based applications. It functions by providing a set of fault-injection versions of MPI message passing calls by replacing the regular MPI calls with the fault-injection versions at runtime. FIMD-MPI can only inject faults into the MPI calls to contaminate the message and requires re-compilation to the source code. While P-FSEFI is not specially designed for MPI message fault injection, it is capable of targeting the functions/calls of MPI. Meanwhile P-FSEFI does not require instrumentation to the source code as it works at a virtual architecture layer.

6.2 White Box : Hardware Fault Injection

Hardware-based fault injection involves augmenting the system under test with specially designed test hardware to allow for the injection of faults into the hardware. It either requires a pre-production hardware with enabled features to support the fault injector, which is designed for vendor testing only or it uses additional hardware to introduce faults into the target system's hardware.

HEARTLESS (Hierarchical Register-Transfer-Level Fault Simulator for Permanent & Transient Faults) [36] was developed to simulate the flow of signals between registers and the operations performed on those signals to represent the operation of the design. Madeira et al [32] proposed RIFLE, a general purpose Pin-level fault injector. Faults were mainly injected into the processor pins. External bi-/uni-direction fault injection elements were attached to the pins of CPU. Bacha et al [4] leveraged the reduction of voltage to force the hardware to work under unstable condition thus to generate numerous transient faults. The experiment was applied on a pre-production Intel Itanium II processor.

In general, hardware-based fault injection techniques have constraints that either the fault injection relies on the external device, circuit or hardware, or only vendor approved pre-production hardware has the capability to inject the faults through the hardware specific interface. These interfaces are usually disabled on the production hardware. Therefore, it is impossible to inject faults without specific hardware or the help of the vendors.

Tambara et al. [41] proposed to introduce the neutron beam to accelerate the fault occurrence and generate more samples of radiation-induced errors on the GPU hardware. Rech et al. [33] utilize similar neutron induced single event generation mechanisms to assess neutron sensitivity of GPU caches and register files. There are several limitations of this technology. Firstly, the neutron beam test requires special equipment and environment and it is usually very expensive to do the experiment. Secondly, we cannot control the locations of the faults because the radiation effect will be very random. The single event upset could happen to any components and make the outcome hard to study and summarize.

6.3 Gray Box : Virtualization-based Fault Injection

Virtualization provides an infrastructure-independent environment for injecting hardware errors with minimal modification and intrusion to the system. In addition, processor emulation virtualization is an enabling technology that allows one to evaluate and explore new architectures. However, there exists a semantic gap between the VMM and guest OSs for virtualization-based fault injection technologies. VMMs only see the instruction stream if no further heuristic knowledge or application knowledge is provided. Consequently, application semantics and fine-grained fault injection are difficult to attain.

Levy et al. [28] propose a virtualization-based framework that injects memory scrubber errors to guest physical address and evaluates the fault tolerance technologies for HPC system (e.g. Palacios). But their Virtual Hardware Fault Injector is only able to inject crash failures into an application and IDE disk failures, which can be easily captured by the system state monitor. CriticalFault [44] and Relyzer [37] are based on Simics, a commercial infrastructure simulator. With static pruning technology and dynamic profiling analysis of the application, instructions are categorized into several classes, i.e., control, data store and address. This process reduces the number of potential fault injection sites by pruning the injection space. Depending on the test scenario, soft errors are injected into different categories. This produces different faulty outputs; for example crash and SDC. However, CriticalFault and Relyzer cannot establish the correlations between instruction level fault injection and the faulty behaviors because tracing back from instructions to high-level languages is difficult. Therefore, only coarse-gained injection is available in these frameworks.

Wanner et al. [42] design VarEMU, an emulation testbed for studying fault characteristics built on top of QEMU. The injection is controlled by the guest system call rather than the hypervisor. In order to inject faults, users have to import the library to get the support from system calls and insert fault injection source code into applications that run in the guest OSs. VarEMU accomplishes this through a custom kernel / kernel modification in the guest OS. However, the user space control for injections cannot convincingly guarantee that the injections to the specific instructions belong to the user space application. If another user space application is running the same type of instructions and sharing the CPU cycles with the injector targeted application, the consequence of fault injection is unpredictable and uncontrollable. QEFI is another QEMU-based fault injection framework. It is quite similar to our work, but QEFI is designed to inject faults into the USB OHCI (Open Host Controller Interface) emulated device. It is used to test the kernel reaction to faults. For example, QEFI studies how the linux kernel will detect and attempt to reset the device. Faults are injected into the payload of USB tokens and QEFI aims to permentantly inject inrecoverable faults into the PC registers and introduce the crash scenarios. This fault model is different from the one used in P-FSEFI and is unrelated to what we are studying. Geissler et al. [13] also designed a QEMU-based fault injector for accessing the reliability of the run-time operating system. However, it only supports only one fault model which inject faults into the eight general purpose registers.

7. CONCLUSIONS

In this paper we have presented P-FSEFI, the Parallel Fine-grained Soft Error Fault Injector. We have discussed the need for parallel fault injectors, how P-FSEFI is designed and what it improves upon over its predecessor, F-SEFI. We have discussed the new fault models added in P-FSEFI and demonstrated their use by studying the popular NAS Parallel Benchmark suite. Using P-FSEFI one can reason about the resiliency and vulnerability of an application and the application's functions. This can then become part of a design-code-test cycle where the results of P-FSEFI inform the programmer where to add more resiliency into their code so as to protect from faults that they are concerned about. The extensible and already robust fault model helps to provide the basis for these experiments. P-FSEFI is currently under evaluation to be open sourced and it is our hope to have it available to the community for others to contribute to in the very near future.

8. REFERENCES

[1] NAS parallel benchmarks, nasa. Available at: http://www.nas.nasa.gov/Software/NPB.

[2] ASHRAF, R. A., GIOIOSA, R., KESTOR, G., DEMARA, R. F., CHER, C.-Y., AND BOSE, P. Understanding the propagation of transient errors in hpc applications. In *Proceedings of the International Conference for High Performance Computing, Networking, Storage and Analysis* (New York, NY, USA, 2015), SC '15, ACM, pp. 72:1–72:12.

[3] ATKINSON, B., DEBARDELEBEN, N., GUAN, Q., ROBEY, R., AND JONES, W. Fault injection experiments with the clamr hydrodynamics mini-app. In *Software Reliability Engineering Workshops (ISSREW), 2014 IEEE International Symposium on* (Nov 2014), pp. 6–9.

[4] BACHA, A., AND TEODORESCU, R. Dynamic reduction of voltage margins by leveraging on-chip ecc in itanium ii processors. *SIGARCH Comput. Archit. News 41*, 3 (June 2013), 297–307.

[5] BAGATIN, M., GERARDIN, S., PACCAGNELLA, A., ANDREANI, C., GORINI, G., AND FROST, C. Temperature dependence of neutron-induced soft errors in {SRAMs}. *Microelectronics Reliability 52*, 1 (2012), 289 – 293. 2011 Reliability of Compound Semiconductors (ROCS) Workshop.

[6] BAILEY, D., BARSZCZ, E., AND BARTON, J. The nas parallel benchmark rnr technical report rnr-94-007, 1994.

[7] BLOUGH, D., AND LIU, P. Fimd-mpi: a tool for injecting faults into mpi application. In *Parallel and Distributed Processing Symposium, 2000. IPDPS 2000. Proceedings. 14th International* (2000), pp. 241–247.

[8] CANNON, E., KLEINOSOWSKI, A., KANJ, R., REINHARDT, D., AND JOSHI, R. The impact of aging effects and manufacturing variation on sram soft-error rate. *Device and Materials Reliability, IEEE Transactions on 8*, 1 (March 2008), 145–152.

[9] CAPPELLO, F., GEIST, A., GROPP, W., KALE, S., KRAMER, B., AND SNIR, M. Toward exascale resilience: 2014 update. *Supercomputing frontiers and innovations 1*, 1 (2014).

[10] CHANDRA, V., AND AITKEN, R. Impact of technology and voltage scaling on the soft error susceptibility in nanoscale cmos. In *Defect and Fault Tolerance of VLSI Systems, 2008. DFTVS '08. IEEE International Symposium on* (Oct 2008), pp. 114–122.

[11] CHUGG, A., BURNELL, A., DUNCAN, P., PARKER, S., AND WARD, J. The random telegraph signal behavior of intermittently stuck bits in sdrams. *Nuclear Science, IEEE Transactions on 56*, 6 (Dec 2009), 3057–3064.

[12] CHUNG, J., LEE, I., SULLIVAN, M., RYOO, J. H., KIM, D. W., YOON, D. H., KAPLAN, L., AND EREZ, M. Containment domains: A scalable, efficient, and flexible resilience scheme for exascale systems. In *High Performance Computing, Networking, Storage and Analysis (SC), 2012 International Conference for* (Nov 2012), pp. 1–11.

[13] DE AGUIAR GEISSLER, F., LIMA KASTENSMIDT, F., AND PEREIRA SOUZA, J. Soft error injection methodology based on qemu software platform. In *Test Workshop - LATW, 2014 15th Latin American* (March 2014), pp. 1–5.

[14] DEBARDELEBEN, N., BLANCHARD, S., GUAN, Q., ZHANG, Z., AND FU, S. Experimental framework for injecting logic errors in a virtual machine to profile applications for soft error resilience. In *Euro-Par Workshops 2011* (2011).

[15] DELL, T. J. A white paper on the benefits of chipkill-correct ecc for pc server main memor. *White paper* (1997).

[16] ERNST, D., DAS, S., LEE, S., BLAAUW, D., AUSTIN, T., MUDGE, T., KIM, N. S., AND FLAUTNER, K. Razor: circuit-level correction of timing errors for low-power operation. *Micro, IEEE 24*, 6 (Nov 2004), 10–20.

[17] GAILLARD, R. Single event effects: Mechanisms and classification. In *Soft Errors in Modern Electronic Systems*, M. Nicolaidis, Ed., vol. 41 of *Frontiers in Electronic Testing*. Springer US, 2011, pp. 27–54.

[18] GEIST, A., SNIR, M., ROMAN, E., STILL, B., CLAY, R., ENGELMANN, C., ROSS, R., SCHULZ, M., KRISHNAMOORTHY, S., VISHNU, A., LUCAS, B., BORKAR, S., ELNOZAHY, M., CHIEN, A., WU, J., DEBARDELEBEN, N., KAPLAN, L., HEROUX, M., NOWELL, L., AND TALLEY, L.-A. US Department of Energy Fault Management Workshop Report. BWI Airport Marriott, Maryland, June 6, 2012.

[19] GRAHAM, S. L., KESSLER, P. B., AND MCKUSICK, M. K. Gprof: A call graph execution profiler. In *Proceedings of Symposium on Compiler Construction* (1982).

[20] GUAN, Q., DEBARDELEBEN, N., ARTKINSON, B., ROBEY, R., AND JONES, W. Towards building resilient scientific applications: Resilience analysis on the impact of soft error and transient error tolerance with the clamr hydrodynamics mini-app. In *Cluster Computing (CLUSTER), 2015 IEEE International Conference on* (Sept 2015), pp. 176–179.

[21] GUAN, Q., DEBARDELEBEN, N., BLANCHARD, S., AND FU, S. F-sefi: A fine-grained soft error fault injection tool for profiling application vulnerability. In *Parallel and Distributed Processing Symposium, 2014 IEEE 28th International* (May 2014), pp. 1245–1254.

[22] GUAN, Q., DEBARDELEBEN, N., BLANCHARD, S., AND FU, S. Addressing statistical significance of fault injection: Empirical studies of the soft error susceptibility. In *The 21st IEEE Pacific Rim International Symposium on Dependable Computing (PRDC 2015)* (Nov 2015).

[23] GUAN, Q., DEBARDELEBEN, N., BLANCHARD, S., AND FU, S. Empirical studies of the soft error susceptibility of sorting algorithms to statistical fault injection. In *Proceedings of the 5th Workshop on Fault Tolerance for HPC at eXtreme Scale* (New York, NY, USA, 2015), FTXS '15, ACM, pp. 35–40.

[24] JAGANNATHAN, S., DIGGINS, Z., MAHATME, N., LOVELESS, T., BHUVA, B., WEN, S.-J., WONG, R., AND MASSENGILL, L. Temperature dependence of soft error rate in flip-flop designs. In *Reliability Physics Symposium (IRPS), 2012 IEEE International* (April 2012), pp. SE.2.1–SE.2.6.

[25] KAHNG, A., NATH, S., AND ROSING, T. On potential design impacts of electromigration awareness. In *Design Automation Conference (ASP-DAC), 2013 18th Asia and South Pacific* (Jan 2013), pp. 527–532.

[26] KUN FENG, MANJUNATH GORENTLA VENKATA, D. L., AND SUN, X.-H. Fast fault injection and sensitivity analysis

for collective communications. In *Proceedings of the International Conference on Cluster Computing* (2015).

[27] LATTNER, C., AND ADVE, V. Llvm: a compilation framework for lifelong program analysis transformation. In *International Symposium on Generation and Optimization (CGO)* (2004).

[28] LEVY, S., DOSANJH, M. G. F., BRIDGES, P. G., AND FERREIRA, K. B. Using unreliable virtual hardware to inject errors in extreme-scale systems. In *The 3rd Workshop on Fault-Tolerance for HPC at Extreme Scale (FTXS)* (2013).

[29] LI, D., VETTER, J., AND YU, W. Classifying soft error vulnerabilities in extreme-scale scientific applications using a binary instrumentation tool. In *IEEE/ACM International Conference on High Performance Computing, Networking, Storage and Analysis (SC)* (2012).

[30] LU, Q., FARAHANI, M., WEI, J., THOMAS, A., AND PATTABIRAMAN, K. Llfi: An intermediate code-level fault injection tool for hardware faults. In *Software Quality, Reliability and Security (QRS), 2015 IEEE International Conference on* (Aug 2015), pp. 11–16.

[31] LUK, C.-K., COHN, R., MUTH, R., PATIL, H., KLAUSER, A., LOWNEY, G., WALLACE, S., REDDI, V. J., AND HAZELWOOD, K. Pin: building customized program analysis tools with dynamic instrumentation. In *Proceedings of ACM conference on Programming Language Design and Implementation (PLDI)* (2005).

[32] MADEIRA, H., RELA, M. Z., MOREIRA, F., AND SILVA, J. A. G. Rifle: A general purpose pin-level fault injector. In *Proceedings of the First European Dependable Computing Conference on Dependable Computing* (London, UK, UK, 1994), EDCC-1, Springer-Verlag, pp. 199–216.

[33] RECH, P., CARRO, L., WANG, N., TSAI, T., HARI, S. K. S., AND KECKLER, S. W. Measuring the radiation reliability of sram structures in gpus designed for hpc. *IEEE 10th Workshop on Silicon Errors in Logic-System Effects (SELSE)* (2010).

[34] ROBERSON, M. Soft error rates in solder bumped packaging. In *Advanced Packaging Materials, 1998. Proceedings. 1998 4th International Symposium on* (Mar 1998), pp. 111–116.

[35] ROSSI, D., OMA, M., METRA, C., AND PACCAGNELLA, A. Impact of aging phenomena on soft error susceptibility. In *Defect and Fault Tolerance in VLSI and Nanotechnology Systems (DFT), 2011 IEEE International Symposium on* (Oct 2011), pp. 18–24.

[36] ROUSSELLE, C., PFLANZ, M., BEHLING, A., MOHAUPT, T., AND VIERHAUS, H. A register-transfer-level fault simulator for permanent and transient faults in embedded processors. In *Design, Automation and Test in Europe, 2001. Conference and Exhibition 2001. Proceedings* (2001), pp. 811–.

[37] SASTRY HARI, S., ADVE, S., NAEIMI, H., AND RAMACHANDRAN, P. Relyzer: Application resiliency analyzer for transient faults. *Micro* (2013).

[38] SCHROEDER, B., AND GIBSON, G. A. A large-scale study of failures in high-performance computing systems. *IEEE Trans. on Dependable and Secure Computing 7* (2010), 337–351.

[39] SNIR, M., WISNIEWSKI, R. W., ABRAHAM, J. A., ADVE, S. V., BAGCHI, S., BALAJI, P., CARLSON, B., CHIEN, A. A., DINIZ, P., ENGELMANN, C., GUPTA, R., JOHNSON, F., BELAK, J., BOSE, P., CAPPELLO, F., COTEUS, P., DEBARDELEBEN, N. A., EREZ, M., FAZZARI, S., GEIST, A., KRISHNAMOORTHY, S., LEYFFER, S., LIBERTY, D., MITRA, S., MUNSON, T., SCHREIBER, R., STEARLEY, J., AND HENSBERGEN, E. V. Addressing failures in exascale computing. ICiC workshop, 2013.

[40] SRIDHARAN, V., DEBARDELEBEN, N., BLANCHARD, S., FERREIRA, K. B., STEARLEY, J., SHALF, J., AND GURUMURTHI, S. Memory errors in modern systems: The good, the bad, and the ugly. In *Proceedings of the Twentieth International Conference on Architectural Support for Programming Languages and Operating Systems* (New York, NY, USA, 2015), ASPLOS '15, ACM, pp. 297–310.

[41] TAMBARA, L., KASTENSMIDT, F., RECH, P., BALEN, T., AND LUBASZEWSKI, M. Neutron-induced single event effects analysis in a sar-adc architecture embedded in a mixed-signal soc. In *VLSI (ISVLSI), 2013 IEEE Computer Society Annual Symposium on* (Aug 2013), pp. 188–193.

[42] WANNER, L., ELMALAKI, S., LAI, L., GUPTA, P., AND SRIVASTAVA, M. Varemu: An emulation testbed for variability-aware software. In *Proceedings of the International Conference on Hardware/Software Co-design and System Synthesis* (2013).

[43] WINTER, S., SCHWAHN, O., NATELLA, R., SURI, N., AND COTRONEO, D. No pain, no gain? the utility of parallel fault injections. In *Software Engineering (ICSE), 2015 IEEE/ACM 37th IEEE International Conference on* (May 2015), vol. 1, pp. 494–505.

[44] XU, X., AND LI, M.-L. Understanding soft error propagation using efficient vulnerability-driven fault injection. In *Proceeding of IEEE/IFIP International Conference on Dependable Systems and Networks (DSN)* (2012).

Bayesian Optimization in High Dimensional Input Space

Jaemin Son
School of Computing
National University of Singapore

Samarth Gupta
School of Computing
National University of Singapore

Gary Tan
School of Computing
National University of Singapore

{jaemin,samarth,gtan}@comp.nus.edu.sg

ABSTRACT

Many simulations include design parameters that influence the terminal outcome. Often, our aim is to optimize these design parameters through recursive simulation in order to gain the outcome in favor of our interests. However, unlike usual objective functions, simulation cannot be directly expressed in analytic forms. Thus, conventional optimization methods such as gradient descent and convex optimization do not apply straightforwardly. Also, simulation usually incurs high computational costs. Therefore, less number of function evaluations is preferred during the optimization process. We present Bayesian Optimization (BO) to deal with such challenges in simulation-based optimization. BO constructs surrogates of the true function and evaluates the most promising points based on the surrogates. Also, we consider issues in applying BO to problems with high dimensional input space. Dealing with high dimensional input space is especially critical in simulation-based optimization if there exist multiple design parameters. In this paper, we discuss related theory and demonstrate experiments of BO on analytic functions.

CCS Concepts

•**Computing methodologies → Gaussian processes; Model development and analysis; Simulation evaluation;** *Machine learning approaches;*

Keywords

Experiment Design, Simulation-based Optimization, Bayesian Optimization, Optimization in High Dimensional Input Space

1. INTRODUCTION

In many cases, the fundamental purpose of simulation has to do with optimizing interesting features of the modeled phenomena. Given a set of design parameters that would affect the trajectory of the simulation, we aim to find an of interest. In traffic simulation, for instance, we may wish to find configuration of road network or road pricing policy that can improve traffic flow by reducing congestion rate and preventing potential traffic accidents. In the case of design simulation where a product is being verified on computational models before actual production, we are essentially interested in finding designs that ensure functionality as well as manufacturability.

However, analytic expressions are unknown for the objective function in simulation-based optimization. Thus, one cannot simply rely on gradient-based optimization methods since exact forms of gradients are unknown and the existence is also not guaranteed. Additionally, functions that cannot be described in analytic forms are likely non-linear and non-convex. For this reason, standard optimization methods such as linear programming and convex optimization methods would not fit to simulation-based optimization.

To make things worse, simulation is usually computation-intensive. In large scale simulation, running time of several hours or days can be a norm even with cutting edge hardware. This means that function evaluations act as significant bottleneck in the loop of optimization. Therefore, suitable optimization algorithm should be able to reduce the number of function evaluations as well.

In order to tackle these challenges, researchers have introduced the notion of surrogate functions or response surfaces [8]. The surrogate function is a computationally inexpensive function that is designed to replace the true function. The basic idea of application in simulation-based optimization is to estimate outputs from the surrogate function and choose the most promising inputs for actual simulation.

Bayesian Optimization [14] is one approach that exploits surrogate functions assuming that the objective function follows a certain process [1]. The most frequently used process is Gaussian Process [15]. Several literature has reported successful application of Bayesian Optimization with Gaussian Process prior [5, 18, 11, 20, 23, 12].

The surrogate function derived from Gaussian Process prior provides two advantages in optimization compared to other surrogate functions. First, it is a non-parametric model. In other words, we need not introduce more parameters to achieve higher complexity as we evaluate more points. Second, it quantifies uncertainty in the output value with posterior Gaussian distribution.

Additionally, Bayesian Optimization can balance two key factors in solving global optimization problems, namely, exploration and exploitation [1, 19]. A global optimization algorithm should explore the input domain enough to guar-

SIMUTOOLS 2016, August 22-23, Prague, Czech Republic

antee global optimality. At the same time, it requires to exploit the previous observations to avoid unnecessary function evaluations. In Bayesian Optimization, the potential optimality for each input can be quantified by considering the two factors at the same time.

The treatment of high dimensional input space is also critical in real applications. The number of input points grows exponentially as dimension increases. Then, evaluation of all potential candidates quickly becomes infeasible with high dimensional input space. In order to tackle such a challenge, several methods are proposed in machine learning community [24, 4, 10].

In this paper, we discuss Bayesian Optimization and various issues in applying Bayesian Optimization to simulation-based optimization problems. First we present the notion of Bayesian Optimization and related concepts. Then, we discuss several methods that are suggested to deal with high dimensional input space. Finally, we compare experimental results of the suggested methods on benchmark functions concluding with practical insight and future research direction.

For the clarity, we deal with maximization problems. Also we confine our subject to objective functions that are smooth and single output ($f : \mathbb{R}^D \rightarrow \mathbb{R}$). Still, f can be expensive to evaluate and have no analytic forms such as simulation.

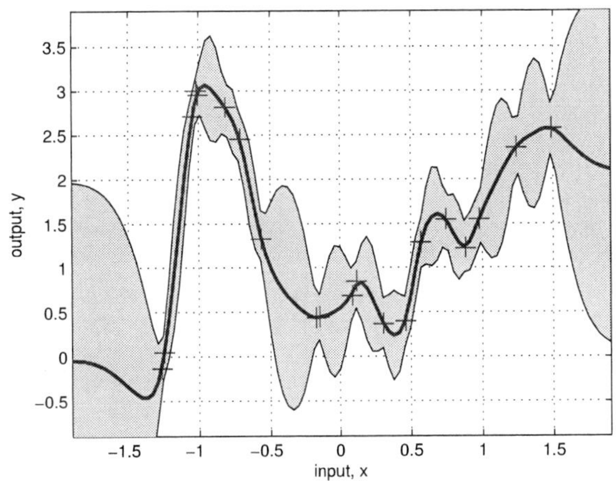

Figure 1: An example of Gaussian Process Regression in noisy function evaluation. Cross points are previously evaluated points (data) and solid blue line is posterior mean and shaded region represents standard deviation. Note that uncertainty (variance) is low near the data and high away from the data.

2. BAYESIAN OPTIMIZATION

Bayesian Optimization with Gaussian Process prior mainly consists of two parts, modeling a surrogate function from previous evaluations and selecting the next evaluation point based on the current surrogate function. A surrogate function is frequently modeled by posterior Gaussian distribution from Gaussian Process prior on the objective function. The choice of the next evaluation point, on the other hand, has a few variations since multiple criteria are viable for quantifying potential optimality. The function that encodes a criterion of potential optimality is referred to as *acquisition function* and each acquisition function has its own characteristics.

The complete algorithm of Bayesian Optimization is given in algorithm 1. The number of iteration T is chosen by the user typically based on computational budgets. Note that GP model is used as a surrogate function in evaluating acquisition function $\alpha(\mathbf{x}|\mathcal{D}_{1:t-1})$.

Algorithm 1 Bayesian Optimization

for $t = 1, 2, ..., T$ **do**
  $\mathbf{x}_t = \arg\max_{\mathbf{x}\in\mathcal{X}} \alpha(\mathbf{x}|\mathcal{D}_{1:t-1})$
  Evaluate $y_t = f(\mathbf{x}_t) + \epsilon_t$
  Augment the data $\mathcal{D}_{1:t} = \mathcal{D}_{1:t-1} \cup \{(\mathbf{x}_t, y_t)\}$
  Update the GP model with $\mathcal{D}_{1:t}$
end for

2.1 Gaussian Processes

Gaussian Process is a process in which a finite number of outputs follow Gaussian distribution. Gaussian Process is fully specified by mean function $\mu(\mathbf{x})$ and covariance function $k(\mathbf{x}, \mathbf{x})$. Formally, it is written as

$$f \sim \mathcal{GP}(\mu(\mathbf{x}), k(\mathbf{x}, \mathbf{x})). \quad (1)$$

Suppose N input points $\mathbf{X} = \{\mathbf{x}_1, \mathbf{x}_2, \cdots, \mathbf{x}_N\}$ and corresponding outputs $\mathbf{Y} = \{y_1, y_2, \cdots, y_N\}$ with $y_i \triangleq f(\mathbf{x}_i) + \epsilon_n$ in noisy evaluation. Noise is usually modeled with Gaussian distribution as $\epsilon_n \sim \mathcal{N}(0, \sigma_n^2)$. For noise-free evaluation, suppose that $\epsilon_n = 0$ with $\sigma_n^2 \rightarrow 0$.

Then, the joint distribution of $f(\mathbf{x}_*)$ and $\mathbf{Y}$ follows Gaussian distribution,

$$\begin{bmatrix} f(\mathbf{x}_*) \\ \mathbf{Y} \end{bmatrix} \sim \mathcal{N}\left(\begin{bmatrix} \mu(\mathbf{x}_*) \\ \mu(\mathbf{X}) \end{bmatrix}, \begin{bmatrix} k(\mathbf{x}_*, \mathbf{x}_*) & \mathbf{k}(\mathbf{X}, \mathbf{x}_*) \\ \mathbf{k}(\mathbf{x}_*, \mathbf{X}) & \mathbf{K}(\mathbf{X}, \mathbf{X}) + \epsilon_n^2 \mathbf{I} \end{bmatrix} \right) \quad (2)$$

where $\mathbf{I}$ is identity matrix and $\mathbf{K}(X, X)$ is a data kernel matrix where $\mathbf{K}(\mathbf{X}, \mathbf{X})_{ij} = k(\mathbf{x}_i, \mathbf{x}_j)$ and $\mathbf{k}(\mathbf{X}, \mathbf{x}_*)$ is a cross kernel matrix between data and the evaluation point where $\mathbf{k}(\mathbf{X}, \mathbf{x}_*)_i = k(\mathbf{x}_i, \mathbf{x}_*)$.

The posterior distribution of $f(\mathbf{x}_*)$ given $(\mathbf{X}, \mathbf{Y})$ can be derived through Bayesian statistics which results in posterior Gaussian distribution

$$f(\mathbf{x}_*)|\mathbf{x}_*, \mathbf{X}, \mathbf{Y} \sim \mathcal{N}\left(\mu_{\mathbf{x}_*|\mathbf{X},\mathbf{Y}}, \Sigma_{\mathbf{x}_*\mathbf{x}_*|\mathbf{X}}\right). \quad (3)$$

where posterior mean and posterior variance are defined as

$$\mu_{\mathbf{x}_*|\mathbf{X},\mathbf{Y}} \triangleq \mu(\mathbf{x}_*) + \mathbf{k}(\mathbf{x}_*, \mathbf{X}) \left(\mathbf{K}(\mathbf{X}, \mathbf{X}) + \epsilon_n^2 \mathbf{I}\right)^{-1} \mathbf{Y} \quad (4)$$

$$\Sigma_{\mathbf{x}_*\mathbf{x}_*|\mathbf{X}} \triangleq k(\mathbf{x}_*, \mathbf{x}_*) - \mathbf{k}(\mathbf{x}_*, \mathbf{X}) \left(\mathbf{K}(\mathbf{X}, \mathbf{X}) + \epsilon_n^2 \mathbf{I}\right)^{-1} \mathbf{k}(\mathbf{X}, \mathbf{x}_*). \quad (5)$$

Deriving posterior mean and posterior variance given the evaluated points can be thought as function regression. Unlike other regression methods, Gaussian Process Regression provides uncertainty measurement represented by posterior variance. An example is illustrated in Fig. 1.

Practically, mean function is set to 0 if there is no strong prior knowledge while covariance function is given with analytic forms [17].

2.1.1 Covariance Function

Two popular covariance functions are Squared Exponential and Matérn. Squared Exponential covariance function is given by

$$k_{SE}(\mathbf{x}, \mathbf{x}') \triangleq \sigma^2 \exp\left(-\frac{1}{2}\sum_{i=1}^{D}\frac{([\mathbf{x}]_i - [\mathbf{x}']_i)^2}{l_i^2}\right) \quad (6)$$

where $[\mathbf{x}]_i$ denotes ith dimensional value of $\mathbf{x}$. In the expression, l_i determines the distance of statistical independence in ith dimension and σ amplifies overall covariance value. For these reasons, l_i, σ are referred to as lengthscale and signal. Matérn covariance function is given by

$$k_{Matern}(\mathbf{x}, \mathbf{x}') \triangleq \sigma^2 \frac{2^{1-\nu}}{\Gamma(\nu)}\left(\frac{\sqrt{2\nu}d}{l}\right)^{\nu} B_{\nu}\left(\frac{\sqrt{2\nu}d}{l}\right) \quad (7)$$

where $d = \|\mathbf{x} - \mathbf{x}'\|$ and Γ, B_ν are Gamma function and Bessel function of the second kind. ν quantifies smoothness and l, σ are the lengthscale and signal. When $\nu \to \infty$, Matérn converges to the Squared Exponential.

2.1.2 *Hyperparameter Tuning*

As shown in SE and Matérn, covariance functions involve hyperparameters that regulate the form of covariance. For accurate estimation, the hyperparameters should be chosen in a way that previous evaluations are well understood as realization of the specified Gaussian Process. There are several ways of treating hyperparameters including point estimate, MCMC sampling and Variational Inference [17]. Maximum Likelihood (ML) and Maximum A Posteriori (MAP) are commonly used point estimate whose forms are given by

$$\boldsymbol{\theta}_{ML} \triangleq \arg\max_{\boldsymbol{\theta}} \Pr(\mathbf{Y}|\mathbf{X}, \boldsymbol{\theta}) \quad (8)$$

$$\boldsymbol{\theta}_{MAP} \triangleq \arg\max_{\boldsymbol{\theta}} \Pr(\boldsymbol{\theta}|\mathbf{X}, \mathbf{Y}) \quad (9)$$

where $\boldsymbol{\theta}$ is a set of hyperparameters.

2.2 Reproducing Kernel Hilbert Space

Reproducing Kernel Hilbert Space (RKHS) is a Hilbert Space where inner product is specified by the given kernel. Since RKHS is a function space induced by a specific kernel, we can analyze any machine learning algorithms that rely on kernel methods in RKHS. In Bayesian Optimization, theoretical analysis of convergence is established upon RKHS for several acquisition functions such as Expected Improvement [22, 2] and Upper Confidence Bound [21].

Formally, given a symmetric and positive definite kernel function $K : \mathcal{X} \times \mathcal{X} \mapsto \mathbb{R}$ such as SE or Matérn, if a basis function is defined as $k_x \triangleq K(\cdot, x)$ for $x \in \mathcal{X}$, there exists a unique Hilbert Space $\mathcal{H}$ such that

$$f(x) = \langle f, k_x \rangle_{\mathcal{H}} \quad \forall f \in \mathcal{H}, \forall x \in \mathcal{X}. \quad (10)$$

Also following property holds in $\mathcal{H}$ for $\forall x, y \in \mathcal{X}$,

$$K(x, y) = k_y(x) = \langle k_y, k_x \rangle_{\mathcal{H}} = \langle k_x, k_y \rangle_{\mathcal{H}} = k_x(y) = K(y, x) \quad (11)$$

which is called *kernel trick*.

2.3 Acquisition Function

The acquisition function encodes a criterion of potential optimality at a given point in analytic forms. Well-known acquisition functions are Probability of Improvement, Expected Improvement, GP-UCB. Illustrative comparison between these acquisition functions is provided in [1]. Recently, Predictive Entropy Search is also proposed in machine learning community.

2.3.1 *Probability of Improvement*

Probability of Improvement (PI) measures the probability of improving the current best output at a given input point. The analytic form is given by

$$\text{PI}(\mathbf{x}) \triangleq \Pr(f(\mathbf{x}) \geq \eta) = \Phi\left(\frac{\mu(\mathbf{x}) - \eta}{\sigma(\mathbf{x})}\right) \quad (12)$$

where η is the current maximum output, $\Phi(\cdot)$ is Normal Cumulative Distribution Function and $\mu(\mathbf{x}), \sigma(\mathbf{x})$ are posterior mean and posterior deviation.

PI is pure exploitation. The chosen point would improve the current optimal value with high probability, however, the improvement is prone to be small and the chosen points tend to cluster around the observed points. This results from ensemble of two factors, which are PI's preference of high value of $\frac{\mu(\mathbf{x})-\eta}{\sigma(\mathbf{x})}$ and diminishing posterior variance near the observed points in Gaussian Process. When $\sigma(\mathbf{x})$ is infinitesimal, $\frac{\mu(\mathbf{x})-\eta}{\sigma(\mathbf{x})}$ can become effectively large even with insignificant $\mu(\mathbf{x}) - \eta$. Therefore, PI would end up choosing points with small improvement and minute variance in the regions with overpopulated evaluations.

2.3.2 *Expected Improvement*

Expected Improvement (EI) takes the expectation of improvement from the current maximum output at a given input point. Unlike PI, EI does not suffer from getting stuck in narrow regions as it balances the amount of improvement and the probability of improvement. The expression is given by

$$\begin{aligned}\text{EI}(\mathbf{x}) &\triangleq \int_{\eta}^{\infty} (f(\mathbf{x}) - \eta)\mathcal{N}(\mu(\mathbf{x}), \sigma(\mathbf{x})^2) df(\mathbf{x}) \\ &= \int_{\eta}^{\infty} ((f(\mathbf{x}) - \mu(\mathbf{x})) + (\mu(\mathbf{x}) - \eta))\mathcal{N}\left(\mu(\mathbf{x}), \sigma(\mathbf{x})^2\right) df(\mathbf{x}) \\ &= (\mu(\mathbf{x}) - \eta)\Phi(Z) + \sigma(\mathbf{x})\phi(Z)\end{aligned} \quad (13)$$

where $Z = \frac{\mu(\mathbf{x})-\eta}{\sigma(\mathbf{x})}$ and $\mu(\mathbf{x}), \sigma(\mathbf{x})$ are posterior mean and posterior deviation. $\Phi(\cdot)$ is Normal Cumulative Distribution Function and $\phi(\cdot)$ is Normal Probability Density Function.

The last expression in Eq.13 shows trade-off between exploitation and exploration in EI. The first term, $(\mu(\mathbf{x}) - \eta)\Phi(Z)$, encourages large improvement $(\mu(\mathbf{x}) - \eta)$ and high probability of improvement $(\Phi(Z))$. Since $\mu(\mathbf{x})$ and $\Phi(Z)$ heavily rely on the current GP model, it can be interpreted as exploitation. On the other hand, the second term, $\sigma(\mathbf{x})\phi(Z)$, prefers high variance. Note that $\phi(Z)$ increases as variance increases. The pursuit of large variance fosters exploration over the domain since GP naturally imposes high variance on outputs for inputs in under-explored regions.

Also, convergence to the global optimum is proven for objective functions drawn from RKHS. On the assumption that hyperparameters are known, Bayesian Optimization with EI can find the optimal value with infinite evaluations [22]. Also, convergence rate is proven for fixed hyperparameters and estimated hyperparameters with Maximum Likelihood Estimator (Eq.8) [2].

2.3.3 *Upper Confidence Bound*

GP-UCB acquisition function balances exploitation and exploration in a simple manner but provides strong theoretical guarantees [21]. The acquisition function is defined as

$$\text{UCB}(\mathbf{x}) \triangleq \mu(\mathbf{x}) + \sqrt{\beta_t}\sigma(\mathbf{x}) \quad (14)$$

where $\mu(\mathbf{x}), \sigma(\mathbf{x})$ are posterior mean and posterior deviation and β_t is a function of t that balances exploitation and exploration represented by $\mu(\mathbf{x})$ and $\sigma(\mathbf{x})$.

Performance of Bayesian Optimization with GP-UCB is proven not only for objective functions that follow Gaussian Process but also functions that have low RKHS norms. Functions with low RKHS norms are smooth functions in terms of basis functions in RKHS.

When $\mathbf{x}^*$ is the global optimum, define simple regret at time T, $r_T \triangleq f(\mathbf{x}^*) - \max_{t \leq T} f(\mathbf{x}_t)$ and cumulative regret at time T, $R_T \triangleq \sum_{t=1}^{T} f(\mathbf{x}^*) - f(\mathbf{x}_t)$. Global optimality can be derived from the simple regret converging to 0 in the infinite horizon and convergence rate can be analyzed by the decaying rate of the cumulative regret.

In the original paper of GP-UCB [21], β_t is carefully chosen so that Bayesian Optimization with GP-UCB achieves sublinear cumulative regret, $R_T = o(T)$. Cumulative regret is bounded by Information Gain at selected points and then bounded by Maximum Information Gain [3]. Lastly, Maximum Information Gain is bounded by operator spectrum of the kernel yielding sublinear complexity. Sublinear regret is proven for SE kernel and Matérn kernel.

Sublinear cumulative regret leads to no-regret property, $\lim_{T\to\infty} \frac{R_T}{T} = 0$ from which the property of global optimality also holds $\lim_{T\to\infty} r_T = 0$.

GP-UCB is the most frequently used acquisition function mainly due to its simple implementation and solid theoretical guarantee. Also, GP-UCB exhibits impressing experimental results in many applications [1, 19, 20, 21].

2.3.4 Predictive Entropy Search

Predictive Entropy Search measures the reduction in uncertainty of the optimal point in the domain [7]. The acquisition function is given by

$$\text{PES}(\mathbf{x}) \triangleq H[p(\mathbf{x}_*|\mathbf{D})] - \mathbb{E}_{p(y|\mathbf{D},\mathbf{x})}[H[p(\mathbf{x}_*|\mathbf{D} \cup \{(\mathbf{x}, y)\})]] \quad (15)$$

where H is entropy and $\mathbf{D}$ represents previous evaluations. Narratively, PES quantifies the expected reduction in entropy of the optimal point $\mathbf{x}_*$ when a point $\mathbf{x}$ is chosen for next evaluation. This is new approach to evaluating potential optimality for next evaluation contrasting with other heuristics that aim to reduce cumulative regret.

However, $p(\mathbf{x}_*|\mathbf{D} \cup \{(\mathbf{x}, y)\})$ in the second term of Eq.15 is not only impossible to solve analytically in GP framework but also difficult to approximate.

By the transitive law of Mutual Information,

$$\begin{aligned} &H[p(\mathbf{x}_*|\mathbf{D})] - \mathbb{E}_{p(y|\mathbf{D},\mathbf{x})}[H[p(\mathbf{x}_*|\mathbf{D} \cup \{(\mathbf{x}, y)\})]] \\ =&MI[\mathbf{x}_*; y|\mathbf{D}, \mathbf{x}] = MI[y; \mathbf{x}_*|\mathbf{D}, \mathbf{x}] \end{aligned} \quad (16)$$

where $MI(X;Y|Z)$ is Mutual Information between X and Y given Z, PES can be re-written as

$$\text{PES}(\mathbf{x}) \triangleq H[p(y|\mathbf{D}, \mathbf{x})] - \mathbb{E}_{p(\mathbf{x}_*|\mathbf{D})}[H[p(y|\mathbf{D}, \mathbf{x}, \mathbf{x}_*)]] \quad (17)$$

where $p(\mathbf{x}_*|\mathbf{D} \cup \{(\mathbf{x}, y)\})$ is replaced with $p(y|\mathbf{D}, \mathbf{x}, \mathbf{x}_*)$.

In order to evaluate PES, $p(\mathbf{x}_*|\mathbf{D})$ and $p(y|\mathbf{D}, \mathbf{x}, \mathbf{x}_*)$ in Eq.17 are converted into tractable forms. Continuous function sampling is used for approximating $p(\mathbf{x}_*|\mathbf{D})$ [16] to sample continuous functions and obtain $\mathbf{x}_*$ per sample. In order to approximate $p(y|\mathbf{D}, \mathbf{x}, \mathbf{x}_*)$, several functional assumptions are made on f and various approximation techniques including Expectation Propagation [13] are used.

3. HIGH DIMENSIONAL BAYESIAN OPTIMIZATION

Applying Bayesian Optimization to problems with high dimensional input space is a challenging task due to its exponentially growing domain size $|\mathcal{X}|^D$. Explosive domain size causes two difficulties in Bayesian Optimization.

First, regression of the function is prone to suffer from high approximation error due to insufficient data. When each function evaluation incurs non-negligible computational time, the number of data points does not easily scale up to catch up with exponentially growing domain size. Regression function with small number of data would overly approximate the true function which in turn omits the characteristic behavior as well as promising regions in the domain [8].

Also, the number of candidates for the optimal points in the surrogate function easily outweighs the capacity of thorough search. Suppose search algorithms that find near optimal points in a finite number of iterations in one dimensional input space such as grid search, Monte Carlo, Branch and Bound. These search algorithms would incur exponential time with increasing dimension when a same number of iterations are imposed for each dimension. If run with a finite number of search for the entire domain, the search becomes superficial evaluating only a fraction of candidates, thus the performance is substantially compromised.

One way of taming the explosive domain size is to make structural assumptions on the objective function to reduce the search space efficiently. Existing methods can be categorized by functional assumptions as subspace projection and additive model.

3.1 Subspace Projection

Subspace projection assumes a linear subspace on which the function value is uniquely defined. Formally, given the objective function defined in the original domain $f : \mathbb{R}^D \to \mathbb{R}$, there exist a function $g : \mathbb{R}^d \to \mathbb{R}$ that satisfies

$$f(\mathbf{x}) = g(\Phi^\intercal \mathbf{x}) = g(\mathbf{y}), \quad \mathbf{y} \in \mathbb{R}^d \quad (18)$$

with $\Phi \in \mathbb{R}^{D\times d}$ whose columns form an orthonormal basis.

Note that usually $d \ll D$. If BO is run in $\mathbb{R}^d$ with the objective function g, it would suffer less from poor regression and exponential search space than when run in $\mathbb{R}^D$ with f.

There are two approaches to deciding the subspace to make use of the functional structure. One is to randomly decide subspace (Random Embedding) and the other is to find the true subspace Φ (Subspace learning).

3.1.1 Random Embedding

Random EMbedding Bayesian Optimization (REMBO) reduces the original domain $\mathbb{R}^D$ into $\mathbb{R}^k$ ($d < k \ll D$) by introducing an embedding matrix $A \in \mathbb{R}^{D\times k}$ whose elements are drawn from $\mathcal{N}(0,1)$ [24]. Formally, BO runs in the embedded domain $\mathbb{R}^k$ with the objective function $h : \mathbb{R}^k \to \mathbb{R}$ such that

$$h(\mathbf{y}) \triangleq f(A\mathbf{y}), \quad \mathbf{y} \in \mathbb{R}^k. \quad (19)$$

It is possible to perform BO in $\mathbb{R}^k$ with the objective function h without losing optimal points since there exists $\mathbf{y} \in \mathbb{R}^k$ such that $f(\mathbf{x}) = f(A\mathbf{y})$ for any $\mathbf{x} \in \mathbb{R}^D$. This is because projection of A into the true subspace Φ is non-degenerate with probability 1 that the linear system

$$\Phi^\intercal \mathbf{x} = (\Phi^\intercal A)\mathbf{y} \tag{20}$$

has solutions $\mathbf{y}$ almost surely for any $\mathbf{x} \in \mathbb{R}^D$.

Suppose the original domain is constrained to $\mathcal{X} = [-1, 1]^D$. For $\mathbf{x}^* \in \mathcal{X}, \mathbf{y}^* \in \mathbb{R}^k$ such that $f(\mathbf{x}^*) = f(A\mathbf{y}^*)$, it satisfies that

$$\|\mathbf{y}^*\|_2 \leq \frac{\sqrt{d_e}}{\epsilon}\|\mathbf{x}^*\|_2 \tag{21}$$

with probability of $1 - \epsilon$. Eq.21 indicates that the range in the embedded domain should be set properly in order to contain optimal points in the original domain. Space of A, spanned by its column vectors, may expand little along some directions in the basis defined by Φ. Then, changes along the directions in the original function are barely reflected on the function defined in the embedded domain. In order to compensate for such degeneration, the range should be appropriately enlarged.

3.1.2 Subspace Learning

Subspace learning finds a linear subspace represented by an orthonormal matrix $\Phi \in \mathbb{R}^{D\times k}$ $(d < k \ll D)$ by analyzing gradients at multiple points [4]. BO is run in $\mathbb{R}^k$ with the objective function $h : \mathbb{R}^k \to \mathbb{R}$ that satisfies

$$f(\mathbf{x}) = h(\Phi^\intercal \mathbf{x}) = h(\mathbf{y}), \quad \mathbf{y} \in \mathbb{R}^k. \tag{22}$$

Suppose $n(\geq k)$ points $(\xi_1, \cdots, \xi_n)$ in the original input space. Gradients on these points are given by

$$\mathcal{L} \triangleq [\nabla f(\xi_1), \cdots, \nabla f(\xi_n)] = \Phi^\intercal[\nabla h(\Phi\xi_1), \cdots, \nabla h(\Phi\xi_n)] \tag{23}$$

where $rank(\mathcal{L}) = rank(\Phi) = k$ since $\Phi \in \mathbb{R}^{D\times k}$. Therefore, if $\mathcal{L}$ is decomposed with SVD (Singular Value Decomposition), k column vectors with the largest singular values shape the same orthonormal basis with Φ.

When analytic gradients are not available, $\mathcal{L}$ is linearly approximated yielding up to second degree curvature errors. With stepsize δ, the gradient at ξ in the direction of φ is approximated by

$$\langle \varphi, \nabla f(\xi)\rangle \approx \frac{1}{\delta}\left(f(\xi + \delta\varphi) - f(\xi)\right). \tag{24}$$

However, when function evaluation is noisy, measurement of approximated gradients would entail substantial noise. Suppose Gaussian noise $\mathcal{N}(0, \sigma_n^2)$ in the evaluation. The approximated gradient has a form of

$$\begin{aligned} &\frac{1}{\delta}\left(f(\xi + \delta\varphi) + \epsilon_n - f(\xi) - \epsilon_n'\right) \\ =&\frac{1}{\delta}\left(f(\xi + \delta\varphi) - f(\xi)\right) + \frac{\epsilon_n - \epsilon_n'}{\delta} \end{aligned} \tag{25}$$

where the error term follows another Gaussian distribution,

$$\frac{\epsilon_n - \epsilon_n'}{\delta} \sim \mathcal{N}\left(0, \frac{2\sigma_n^2}{\delta^2}\right). \tag{26}$$

Thus, when the ratio of noise to step size is not negligible, the error term shadows the gradient information.

The ratio of noise to the step size can be reduced by increasing the step size or reducing the evaluation noise. Note that, however, when the step size is increased too much, gradients are poorly approximated that Φ would not be correctly recovered. Besides, we can reduce evaluation noise by evaluating the same point multiple times. However, $\mathcal{O}(\frac{1}{\delta^2})$ resamples are required to cancel out the effect of the denominator in Eq.26. If the evaluation incurs substantial calculation time, such amount of resamples would come as onerous computational burden.

Also, Dantzig Selector is suggested to retrieve the matrix $\mathcal{L}$ with as low rank as possible. Due to curvature error in gradient approximation and noise in the evaluation, $\mathcal{L}$ would have rank more than k. In that case, Dantzig Selector can effectively reduce the rank [6].

3.2 Additive Model

Additive model assumes that the function value is defined by the sum of independent sub-functions whose inputs are disjoint and constitute the original domain [10]. Mathematically,

$$f(\mathbf{x}) = f^{(1)}(\mathbf{x}^{(1)}) + f^{(2)}(\mathbf{x}^{(2)}) + \cdots + f^{(M)}(\mathbf{x}^{(M)}) \tag{27}$$

where $\mathbf{x}^{(i)} \in \mathcal{X}^{(i)}$ and $\mathbf{x} = \cup_i \mathbf{x}^{(i)}$ and $\mathcal{X}^{(i)} \cap \mathcal{X}^{(j)} = \phi$ for any i, j.

By the independent assumption on sub-functions, mean and covariance are also independent,

$$\mu(\mathbf{x}) = \mu^{(1)}(\mathbf{x}^{(1)}) + \cdots + \mu^{(M)}(\mathbf{x}^{(M)}) \tag{28}$$

$$k(\mathbf{x}, \mathbf{x}') = k^{(1)}(\mathbf{x}^{(1)}, \mathbf{x}'^{(1)}) + \cdots + k^{(M)}(\mathbf{x}^{(M)}, \mathbf{x}'^{(M)}). \tag{29}$$

When the mean function is 0, the joint distribution of $f^{(i)}(\mathbf{x}_*^{(i)})$ given the evaluation points $(\mathbf{X}, \mathbf{Y})$ can be written as

$$\begin{bmatrix} f^{(i)}(\mathbf{x}_*^{(i)}) \\ \mathbf{Y} \end{bmatrix} \sim \mathcal{N}\left(\mathbf{0}, \begin{bmatrix} k^{(i)}(\mathbf{x}_*^{(i)}, \mathbf{x}_*^{(i)}) & \mathbf{k}^{(i)}(\mathbf{X}^{(i)}, \mathbf{x}_*^{(i)}) \\ \mathbf{k}^{(i)}(\mathbf{x}_*^{(i)}, \mathbf{X}^{(i)}) & \mathbf{K}(\mathbf{X}, \mathbf{X}) + \epsilon_n^2\mathbf{I} \end{bmatrix}\right) \tag{30}$$

where $\mathbf{K}$ is a data kernel matrix and $\mathbf{k}_i$ is a cross kernel matrix in terms of variables in ith group. Consequently, the posterior distribution of $f^{(i)}(\mathbf{x}_*^{(i)})$ given the evaluation points $(\mathbf{X}, \mathbf{Y})$ is described as

$$f^{(i)}(\mathbf{x}_*^{(i)})|\mathbf{x}_*, \mathbf{X}, \mathbf{Y} \sim \mathcal{N}(\mu_{\mathbf{x}_*^{(i)}|\mathbf{X},\mathbf{Y}}, \Sigma_{\mathbf{x}_*^{(i)}\mathbf{x}_*^{(i)}|\mathbf{X}}). \tag{31}$$

where posterior mean and posterior variance are given by

$$\mu_{\mathbf{x}_*^{(i)}|\mathbf{X},\mathbf{Y}} \triangleq \mathbf{k}_{\mathbf{x}_*\mathbf{X}}^{(i)}\Delta^{-1}\mathbf{Y} \tag{32}$$

$$\Sigma_{\mathbf{x}_*^{(i)}\mathbf{x}_*^{(i)}|\mathbf{X}} \triangleq k^{(i)}(\mathbf{x}_*^{(i)}, \mathbf{x}_*^{(i)}) - \mathbf{k}_{\mathbf{x}_*\mathbf{X}}^{(i)}\Delta^{-1}\mathbf{k}_{\mathbf{X}\mathbf{x}_*}^{(i)} \tag{33}$$

with $\Delta \triangleq \mathbf{K}(\mathbf{X}, \mathbf{X}) + \epsilon_n^2\mathbf{I}$ and $\mathbf{k}_{\mathbf{x}_*\mathbf{X}}^{(i)} \triangleq \mathbf{k}^{(i)}(\mathbf{x}_*^{(i)}, \mathbf{X}^{(i)})$.

The additive acquisition function is given by

$$\mathbf{x}_t \leftarrow \cup_{i=1}^M \arg\max_{\mathbf{z}_i \in \mathcal{X}^{(i)}} \mu_{t-1}^{(i)}(\mathbf{z}_i) + \sqrt{\beta_t}\sigma_{t-1}^i(\mathbf{z}_i) \tag{34}$$

where β_t is chosen carefully to guarantee *no-regret* property. Note that the additive acquisition function is a variant of GP-UCB which is different from GP-UCB of the original function with the additive kernel,

$$\mathbf{x}_t \leftarrow \arg\max_{\mathbf{z} \in \mathcal{X}} \sum_{i=1}^M \mu_{t-1}^{(i)}(\mathbf{z}) + \sqrt{\beta_t \sum_{i=1}^M (\sigma_{t-1}^i(\mathbf{z}))^2}. \tag{35}$$

In finding the decomposition, marginal likelihood is compared to choose the most likely one. However, total combination of splitting the original domain is $\frac{D!}{(d!)^M M!}$ that considering all cases is infeasible. Instead, the author compares $\mathcal{O}(D)$ random decomposition.

However, decomposition directly relates to the functional form of the objective function, thus, significantly affects the performance. Consider an extreme case where each dimension is independent. The additive kernel has a form of

$$k(\mathbf{x}, \mathbf{x}') = \sum_{i=1}^{D} k^{(i)}(\mathbf{x}^{(i)}, \mathbf{x}^{(i)'}) \tag{36}$$

which is equivalent to

$$\langle k_{\mathbf{x}}, k_{\mathbf{x}'} \rangle_{\mathcal{H}} = \sum_{i=1}^{D} \langle k^{(i)}_{\mathbf{x}^{(i)}}, k^{(i)}_{\mathbf{x}'^{(i)}} \rangle_{\mathcal{H}^{(i)}} \tag{37}$$

where $\mathcal{H}$ is RKHS induced by the additive kernel and $\mathcal{H}^{(i)}$ is induced by a kernel for ith variable. Consequently, the function form is restricted to

$$f(\mathbf{x}) = \sum_{i=1}^{D} f^{(i)}(x^{(i)}) \qquad f \in \mathcal{H}, f^{(i)} \in \mathcal{H}^{(i)} \tag{38}$$

which does not consider any interaction between variables.

In general, independent assumption drops interaction across the groups and only counts interaction within the groups, which leads to restricting the functional form. Therefore, suitable decomposition that reflects the true interaction between dimensions is crucial to guaranteeing performance.

4. EXPERIMENTS AND ANALYSIS

We compare the original BO and high dimensional BOs (Random basis, Random embedding, Subspace learning, the additive model) with regard to *simple regret*[1]. We assume the simplest case in the additive model with the kernel given by Eq.36 where every dimension is independent.

We test the methods on widely accepted benchmark functions[2] with noise-free evaluation. For meaningful comparison, we choose three representative functions where each function satisfies assumption of subspace projection or the additive model or none. By testing on these functions, we can observe distinctive behavior of each method in terms of performance.

As in the proposed methods, GP-UCB is adopted for the acquisition function with β_t set according to the empirical values in the original papers. GP is specified with the prior mean 0 [3] and the SE kernel function (Eq.6).

SE kernel function involves 3 types of hyperparameters, namely, lengthscales, signal and noise. We fix signal and noise values and estimate only lengthscales to reduce complexity in learning hyperparameters. Signal and noise are more sensitive to tune since they have effects on all dimensions while lengthscales only affect individual dimension. We set signal and noise values to be around 10% and 1% of the range of the function. In learning lengthscales, we set the bound and find the point that maximizes the likelihood (Eq.8). Lengthscales are updated every 50 iterations to incorporate new evaluations.

When optimizing the likelihood and the acquisition function, we first use Lipschitz optimization method (DiRect [9]) and then gradient based methods[4] with the initial point set to the result of DiRect. By doing so, we can avoid getting stuck in local optimal points employing smoothness of the function and find the exact optimum point using gradient information. The number of function evaluations and iterations in DiRect are set proportional to the input dimension.

[1]The source code is available at https://bitbucket.org/woalsdnd/highdim_bo.

[2]http://www.sfu.ca/~ssurjano/optimization.html

[3]The prior mean is usually set constant given no prior knowledge about the mean function and the constant can be set to any arbitrary value without affecting the choice of next evaluation point.

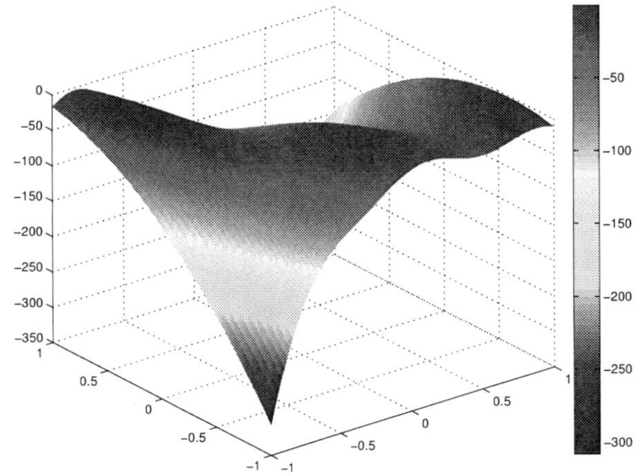

Figure 2: Illustration of Branin Hoo function. The value is negated. The function has the maximum value of -0.397887 at $\mathbf{x}^* = (-0.75221, 0.63667)$, $(0.08555, -0.69665)$ and $(0.92330, -0.67)$.

4.1 Branin Hoo function in high dimensions

Branin Hoo function is 2 dimensional function whose analytic form is given by

$$f(\mathbf{x}) = \left(x_2 - \frac{5.1x_1^2}{4\pi^2} + \frac{5x_1}{\pi} - 6\right)^2 + 10\left(1 - \frac{1}{8\pi}\right)\cos(x_1) + 10 \tag{39}$$

where input domain is restrained to $[-5, 10] \times [0, 15]$. The function is illustrated in Fig.2.

In the experiments, This 2 dimensional function is embedded in high dimensional input space after randomly rotating the axes. Then the newly generated objective function satisfies the assumption of subspace projection. Therefore, the tests on this objective function demonstrate qualitative difference between subspace projection methods and other methods. The results are shown in Fig.3.

As initial settings, a equal number of initial points to the original dimension are chosen randomly and the intrinsic dimension is set to 2 and the range is set to $\sqrt{2}$ in subspace projection methods following the choice of the original paper [24].

We can observe that subspace projection methods converge faster than the original BO and the additive model. Since the search space is reduced to lower dimensions, these methods can approach to the optimal point defined in the subspace faster than the methods that run in the original dimension. Among subspace projection methods, subspace learning achieves the best simple regret since it optimizes over the subspace close to the true one.

On the other hand, random basis hardly improves the output value. This is because some directions in the true subspace degenerate when the original input space is projected onto a random basis. In such a case, the objective function

[4]Specifically, we used fmincon with sequential quadratic programming in matlab.

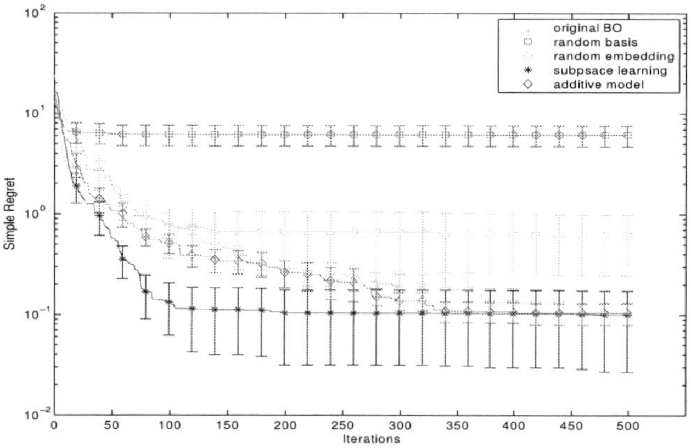

(a) Branin Hoo ($D = 10$)

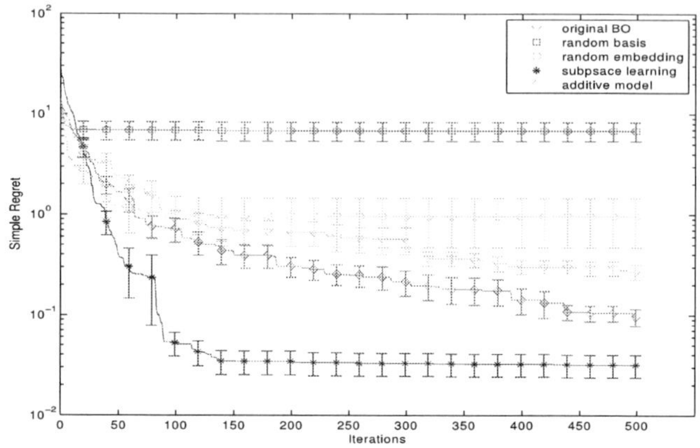

(b) Branin Hoo ($D = 20$)

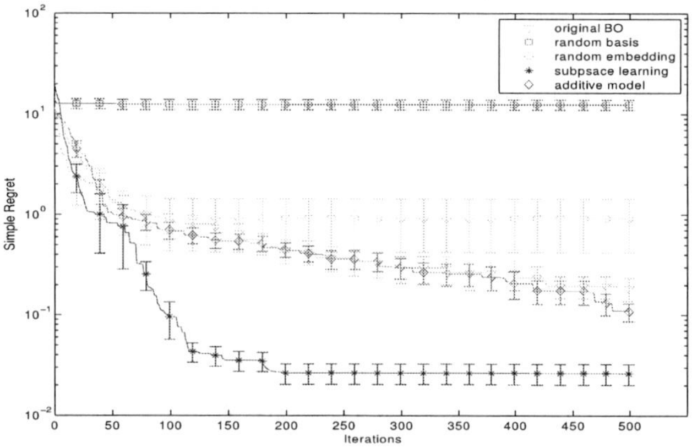

(c) Branin Hoo ($D = 50$)

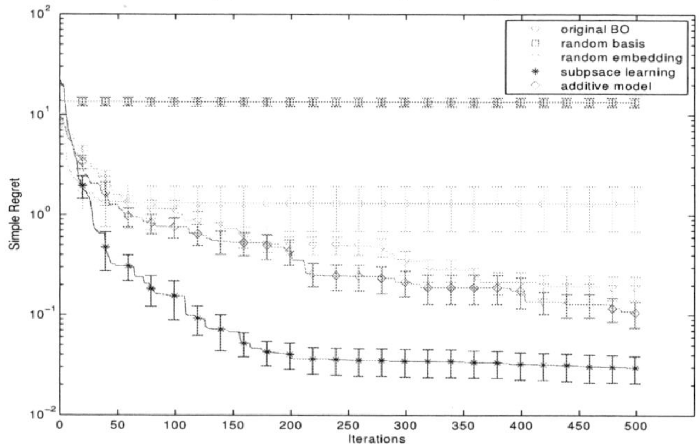

(d) Branin Hoo ($D = 100$)

Figure 3: Plots of simple regret for the different methods on Branin Hoo. Input dimension is varied to 10, 20, 50, 100 and the results are averaged over 20 runs. Error bars represent a quarter of empirical standard deviation.

after the projection incorporates little changes in the original function along the degenerated directions. The chance of degeneration increases when the original dimension is high and the intrinsic dimension is low. It can be confirmed from 3a that degeneration in both directions occurs even when the original dimension is 10 and intrinsic dimension is 2.

Also note that random embedding is outperformed by both the additive model and the original BO. Even though random embedding reaches to the optimal point defined in the embedding, that optimal point is likely suboptimal in the original objective function. The additive model and the original BO show very similar performance which suggests that the additive model does not exploit the assumption of subspace projection.

4.2 Schwefel function in high dimensions

Schwefel function is D dimensional function whose analytic form is given by

$$f(\mathbf{x}) = 418.9829D - \sum_{i=1}^{D} x_i \sin(\sqrt{|x_i|}) \tag{40}$$

where the domain is restrained to $[-500, 500]^D$. The function when $D = 2$ is illustrated in Fig.4.

Note that Schwefel function has a form of Eq.38. It means that the function resides in Hilbert space induced by the additive kernel given by Eq.37. Therefore, we witness the advantage of the additive model over subspace projection methods as the additive model does not lose information by projection of the original domain onto subspace. Also, the additive model outperforms the original BO by making use of the functional form. The result is shown in Fig.5.

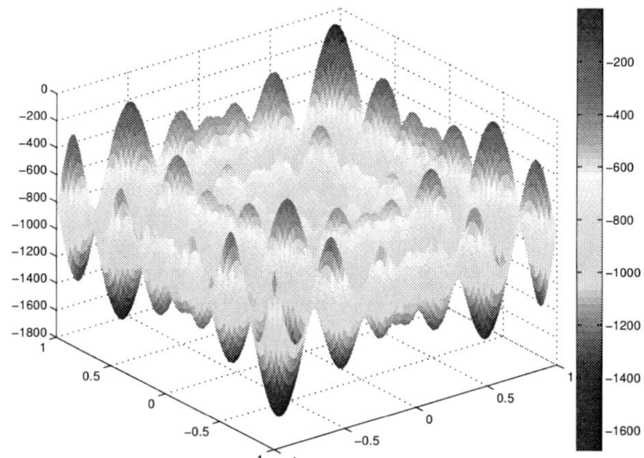

Figure 4: Illustration of Schwefel function in 2 dimensional input space. The value is negated. The function has the maximum value of 0 at $\mathbf{x}^* = (0.84194, \cdots, 0.84194)$.

In the experiments, a equal number of initial points to

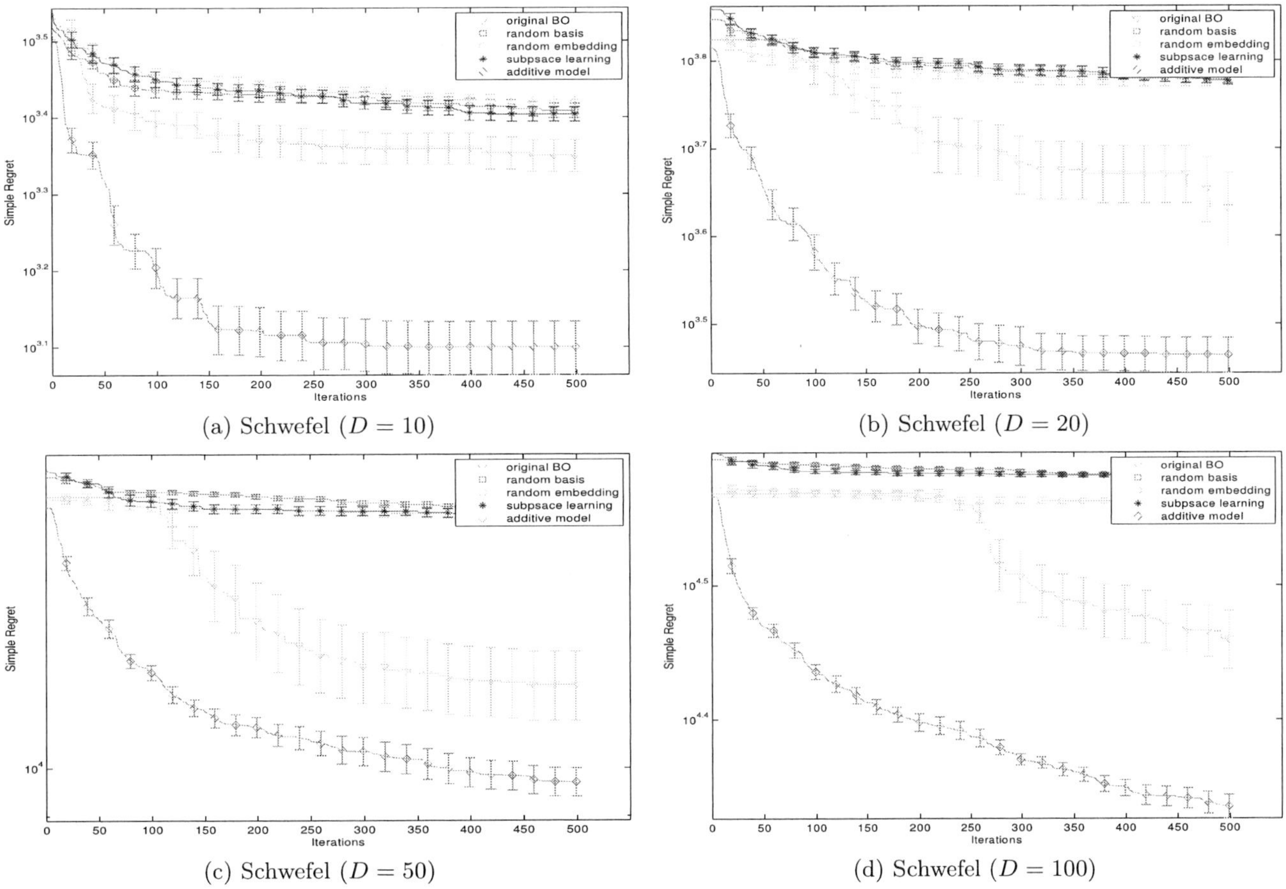

(a) Schwefel ($D = 10$)

(b) Schwefel ($D = 20$)

(c) Schwefel ($D = 50$)

(d) Schwefel ($D = 100$)

Figure 5: Plots of simple regret for the different methods on Schwefel. Input dimension is varied to 10, 20, 50, 100 and the results are averaged over 20 runs. Error bars represent a quarter of empirical standard deviation.

the original dimension are chosen randomly. In subspace projection methods, the intrinsic dimension is set to 5 and the range is set to $\sqrt{5}$ following the choice of the original paper [24].

We can confirm two interesting trends. First, all subspace projection methods (Random basis, Random embedding, Subspace learning) show little improvement in the output value. This is a natural consequence because the original domain cannot be projected to any subspace without significantly losing functional complexity and badly dropping near-optimal values. Even when projected to an arbitrary subspace, the methods only approach to highly suboptimal points no matter how the subspace is derived. Therefore, the performance for these methods is not only trivial but also similar each other.

Secondly, the additive model outperforms other methods including the original BO. Since the original BO does not assume projection of the original domain onto subspace, it improves the output value gradually. However, the additive model improves the output value faster than the original BO as the function can be efficiently captured by the additive kernel. This suggests that the additive model makes use of the functional structure.

4.3 Eggpack function in high dimensions

Eggpack function is a custom function that does not satisfy any functional assumptions introduced so far. It cannot be decomposed into multiple additive subfunctions nor projected onto the subspace. Its analytic form is given by

$$f(x) = \left(\prod_{i=1}^{D} \frac{1 - x_i}{2} \right)^{\frac{1}{D}} \left(\frac{1}{D} \sum_{i=1}^{D} \sin \frac{7}{2} \pi x_i \right) \tag{41}$$

where the domain is restrained to $[-1, 1]^D$. The function when $D = 2$ is illustrated in Fig.6.

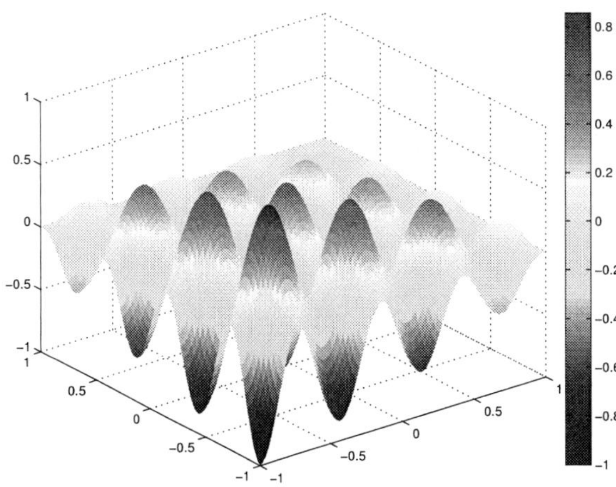

Figure 6: Illustrations of eggpack function in 2 dimensional input space. The value is negated. The function has the maximum value of 0.85716 at $x^* = (-0.72385, -0.72385)$.

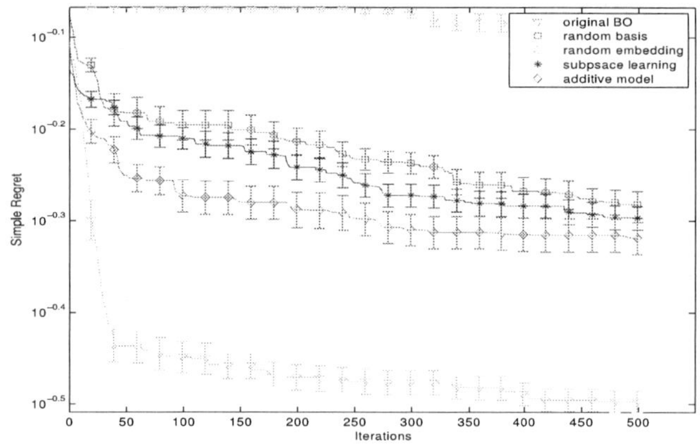

(a) simple regret ($D = 10$)

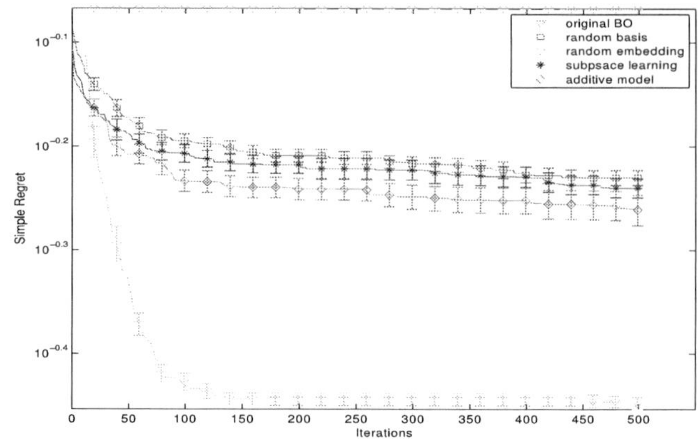

(b) simple regret ($D = 20$)

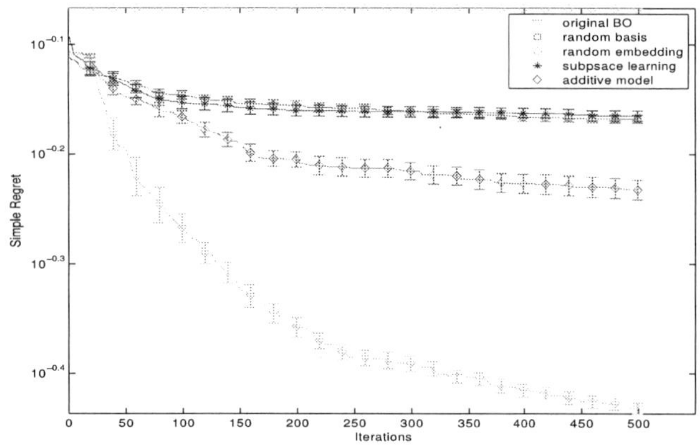

(c) simple regret ($D = 50$)

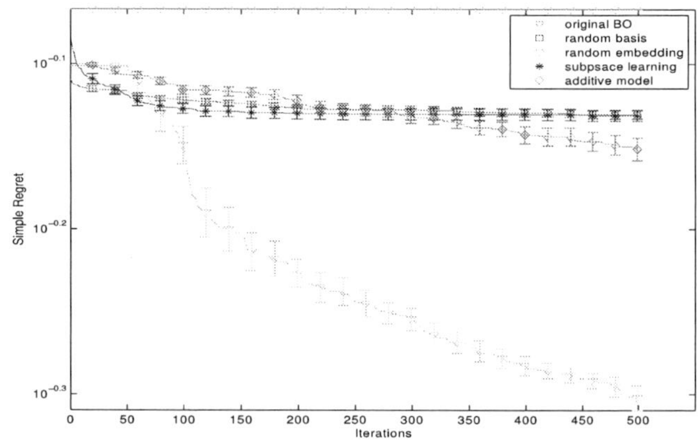

(d) simple regret ($D = 100$)

Figure 7: Plots of simple regret for the different methods on Eggpack function. The results are averaged over 20 runs. Error bars represent a quarter of unbiased standard deviation.

In experiments, intrinsic dimension for subspace projection is set to 5. The profiles of simple regret are shown in Fig.7.

First of all, the original BO shows the most superior simple regret leaving a good deal of margin with other methods in all the dimensions ($D = 10, 20, 50, 100$). Its superiority compared to other methods becomes more prominent as the dimension grows. The original BO outperforms subspace projection methods since eggpack cannot be projected onto subspace. Thus, subspace projection methods only optimize over subdomain embedded in the true objective function. Also, eggpack cannot be decomposed into summation of subfunctions without substantially losing information due to its multiplication term. Therefore, the additive model cannot approximate the function effectively.

Since there is little meaning in the true subspace, subspace learning and random basis show similar results in both simple regret and average of cumulative regret. Note that the estimated subspace by subspace learning is no better than a random guess when the true subspace does not exist. Average cumulative regret shows weak decaying curves suggesting that they only optimize over the defined subspace.

The additive model shows better performance than subspace projection methods in simple regret, however, its performance is overwhelmingly dominated by the original BO. The gap from the original BO in simple regret is greater in high dimensions. From these observation, we can conclude that the additive model performs relatively well on eggpack in low dimension, though, when dimension increases, the performance becomes similar to those of the subspace projection methods. This is reasonable since eggpack involves multiplication term which cannot be effectively approximated with the additive form. Thus, the GP model with the additive kernel fails to reflect the function sufficiently well which leads to degradation of performance in simple regret.

5. CONCLUSIONS

We presented BO as a promising way to optimizing functions that are expensive to evaluate. We also summarized high dimensional BOs and empirically tested these methods on three representative analytic functions.

We confirmed that high dimensional BOs perform well only when the functional structure of the objective function is properly exploited. When the objective function spans in subspace, subspace learning achieves the best performance converging faster than the methods. When the objective function follows the additive forms, the additive model exhibits best performance.

If a method is used for the objective function that does not satisfy the corresponding functional assumption, there is no meaningful advantage. Subspace projection methods would show little improvement on the objective function that does not satisfy the assumption of subspace projection. If the objective function does not satisfy the additive assumption, the additive model would not perform well as it fails to make use of the functional form. When the objective function satisfies neither of assumptions, the original BO would perform better than the proposed high dimensional BOs.

Therefore, knowing the functional structure of the objective function is crucial in choosing a method in high dimensional input space. By making use of the functional structure, the search space can be effectively reduced and regression model can approximate the objective function with fewer observations. Particularly, in simulations, prior knowledge in the modular architecture may provide information about relationship between different variables.

As future work, we are planning to experiment high dimensional BOs on multi-agent based traffic simulation to gain more insight in applying BO to simulation-based optimization.

6. ACKNOWLEDGMENTS

This research was supported by the National Research Foundation, Singapore through the Singapore MIT Alliance for Research and Technology's Future Urban Mobility IRG research program.

7. REFERENCES

[1] E. Brochu, V. M. Cora, and N. De Freitas. A tutorial on bayesian optimization of expensive cost functions, with application to active user modeling and hierarchical reinforcement learning. *arXiv preprint arXiv:1012.2599*, 2010.

[2] A. D. Bull. Convergence rates of efficient global optimization algorithms. *The Journal of Machine Learning Research*, 12:2879–2904, 2011.

[3] T. M. Cover and J. A. Thomas. *Elements of information theory*. John Wiley & Sons, 2012.

[4] J. Djolonga, A. Krause, and V. Cevher. High-dimensional gaussian process bandits. In *Advances in Neural Information Processing Systems*, pages 1025–1033, 2013.

[5] R. B. Gramacy and H. K. Lee. Adaptive design of supercomputer experiments. Technical report, Citeseer, 2006.

[6] T. Hemant and V. Cevher. Active learning of multi-index function models. In *Advances in Neural Information Processing Systems*, pages 1466–1474, 2012.

[7] J. M. Hernández-Lobato, M. W. Hoffman, and Z. Ghahramani. Predictive entropy search for efficient global optimization of black-box functions. In *Advances in Neural Information Processing Systems*, pages 918–926, 2014.

[8] D. R. Jones. A taxonomy of global optimization methods based on response surfaces. *Journal of global optimization*, 21(4):345–383, 2001.

[9] D. R. Jones, C. D. Perttunen, and B. E. Stuckman. Lipschitzian optimization without the lipschitz constant. *Journal of Optimization Theory and Applications*, 79(1):157–181, 1993.

[10] K. Kandasamy, J. G. Schneider, and B. Póczos. High dimensional bayesian optimisation and bandits via additive models. In *Proceedings of the 32nd International Conference on Machine Learning, ICML 2015, Lille, France, 6-11 July 2015*, pages 295–304, 2015.

[11] M. C. Kennedy and A. O'Hagan. Bayesian calibration of computer models. *Journal of the Royal Statistical Society: Series B (Statistical Methodology)*, 63(3):425–464, 2001.

[12] H. J. Kushner. A new method of locating the maximum point of an arbitrary multipeak curve in the presence of noise. *Journal of Fluids Engineering*, 86(1):97–106, 1964.

[13] T. P. Minka. Expectation propagation for approximate bayesian inference. In *Proceedings of the Seventeenth conference on Uncertainty in artificial intelligence*, pages 362–369. Morgan Kaufmann Publishers Inc., 2001.

[14] J. Mockus, V. Tiesis, and A. Zilinskas. The application of bayesian methods for seeking the extremum. *Towards Global Optimization*, 2(117-129):2, 1978.

[15] M. A. Osborne, R. Garnett, and S. J. Roberts. Gaussian processes for global optimization. In *3rd international conference on learning and intelligent optimization (LION3)*, pages 1–15, 2009.

[16] A. Rahimi and B. Recht. Random features for large-scale kernel machines. In *Advances in neural information processing systems*, pages 1177–1184, 2007.

[17] C. E. Rasmussen and C. K. I. Williams. *Gaussian Processes for Machine Learning (Adaptive Computation and Machine Learning)*. The MIT Press, 2005.

[18] J. Sacks, W. J. Welch, T. J. Mitchell, and H. P. Wynn. Design and analysis of computer experiments. *Statistical science*, pages 409–423, 1989.

[19] B. Shahriari, K. Swersky, Z. Wang, R. P. Adams, and N. de Freitas. Taking the human out of the loop: A review of bayesian optimization. *Proceedings of the IEEE*, 104(1):28, 2016.

[20] J. Snoek, H. Larochelle, and R. P. Adams. Practical bayesian optimization of machine learning algorithms. In *Advances in Neural Information Processing Systems*, pages 2951–2959, 2012.

[21] N. Srinivas, A. Krause, S. Kakade, and M. Seeger. Gaussian process optimization in the bandit setting: No regret and experimental design. In *Proc. International Conference on Machine Learning (ICML)*, 2010.

[22] E. Vazquez and J. Bect. Convergence properties of the expected improvement algorithm with fixed mean and covariance functions. *Journal of Statistical Planning and inference*, 140(11):3088–3095, 2010.

[23] J. Villemonteix, E. Vazquez, and E. Walter. An informational approach to the global optimization of expensive-to-evaluate functions. *Journal of Global Optimization*, 44(4):509–534, 2009.

[24] Z. Wang, M. Zoghi, F. Hutter, D. Matheson, and N. De Freitas. Bayesian optimization in high dimensions via random embeddings. In *Proceedings of the Twenty-Third international joint conference on Artificial Intelligence*, pages 1778–1784, 2013.

Adaptive Synchronization Interface for Hardware-Software Co-Simulation based on SystemC and QEMU

Bruno Kleinert
Universität Erlangen-Nürnberg
Martensstraße 3
91058 Erlangen, Germany
bruno.kleinert@fau.de

Simone Weiß
Universität Erlangen-Nürnberg
Martensstraße 3
91058 Erlangen, Germany
simone.weiss@fau.de

Franziska Schäfer
Universität Erlangen-Nürnberg
Fürther Straße 246b
90429 Nürnberg, Germany
franziska.schaefer@faps.fau.de

Jupiter Bakakeu
Universität Erlangen-Nürnberg
Egerlandstraße 7-9
91058 Erlangen, Germany
jupiter.bakakeu@faps.uni-erlangen.de

Dietmar Fey
Universität Erlangen-Nürnberg
Martensstraße 3
91058 Erlangen, Germany
dietmar.fey@fau.de

ABSTRACT

This paper presents a runtime reconfigurable interface for Hardware-Software Co-Simulations. We present our research project for autonomously configuring smart home networks, in which our hardware-software co-simulation is used to simulate network sensor and actuator nodes in an early development stage. The improved architecture of our connection between the SystemC hardware simulator and the virtual machine QEMU, to build the hardware-software co-simulation, is presented. We developed our adaptive simulated time synchronization interface, which keeps QEMU and the hardware simulator SystemC synchronized. We present the runtime low-latency reconfigurability of it, to adapt to frequent changes of loose and tight synchronization timing requirements.

Keywords

Hardware-software co-simulation, time synchronization, virtual machine, QEMU, SystemC, emulator

1. INTRODUCTION

Modern homes are equipped with home automation devices to make life more comfortable, save energy and support people in everyday life situations. Such devices range from temperature measurement, sensors to detect opened windows and doors, up to complex automatic illumination systems. Today, products are offered to home owners and landlords, that need to be configured and integrated into existing home automation systems by their owner. This can

SIMUTOOLS 2016, August 22-23, Prague, Czech Republic

Figure 1: Smart home "ants".

The vision of smart homes comprises technology as integral part and clever support for the inhabitants' needs through a nearly invisible presence of technology. To realize this vision, nature can serve as a role model. Ants are a good example to observe self-organization in its perfection. Every single ant gives and senses certain signals from their colleagues and knows intuitively how to act in order to achieve a common global goal which is not reachable for a single individual. The transfer of this role model to our technical world leads to the term "digital ecosystem", which includes the aspects self-organisation, scalability and sustainability [3]. Figure 1 shows a collaboration of heterogeneous entities in a smart home.

We believe such devices can configure themselves autonomously to integrate into existing home automation networks in the future. Since autonomous configuration is a subject of current research, we want to contribute to a faster and cost-saving development cycle of autonomously configuring home automation devices.

Since home automation devices are built from hardware and software, we present our hardware-software co-simulator (HW-SW co-simulator) that targets software and hardware developers of device manufacturers of home automation network components. We modified and improved an existing HW-SW co-simulator, that we previously presented to simulate hardware and software of a medical X-ray control unit

[5]. Our improved HW-SW co-simulator delivers interactive simulations, by keeping simulated time synchronization overhead between the software and hardware simulation as small as possible. At the same time, it allows configurable simulation time synchronization and accuracy. It is based on the SystemC [7] hardware simulator and the virtual machine (VM) QEMU [1], that we connect to each other by our adaptive interface, that allows to adjust simulated time synchronization according to external boundary conditions and requirements. Our adaptive interface allows latency-free reconfiguration during runtime to adapt quickly to frequently changing timing and accuracy requirements during test and verification processes.

This paper is organized as follows. In Section 2 we present the research project in which our HW-SW co-simulator is needed. Section 3 presents and discusses the previous state of our HW-SW co-simulator. We present our improved HW-SW co-simulator and our adaptive interface in Section 4. In Section 5 we describe a SystemC hardware model that we use to develop and verify our implementation, while Section 6 presents results and measurements of our work. Section 7 concludes this paper and in Section 8 we present future plans for our work.

2. MOTIVATION

In state of the art home automation networks, devices need to be configured by hand, i.e., the topology and network parameters need to be configured before the network as a whole can work as desired. Often, communication partners, i.e., sensor and corresponding actuator devices, need to be made aware of each other to execute an operation. In many cases, not only the node to be added has to be configured initially, but devices of an existing network need to be reconfigured by hand to communicate appropriately with newly added devices. The presented work is part of a research project, in which existing networks and to be added home automation devices configure themselves autonomously, to make user or manufacturer interaction needless.

The presented work of our development framework to support software and hardware developers of device manufacturers, is a virtual hardware device for simulation to save development time and costs. Its purpose is to simulate autonomous home automation network nodes with their respective hardware components. A device node is a sensor or actuator, that is built from hardware and software, often a microprocessor that executes application software and interacts with its physical surrounding. Typically, application software reads sensor data, processes it and transmits the results to communication partners that consume the refined data. In the case of an actuator node, application software processes sensor data and generated controls signals for actuators, e.g., turns on lights or controls motors of jalousies. Here we contribute our HW-SW co-simulator. It is capable to simulate models of sensor and actuator hardware, as well as the execution of application and device driver software in a virtual machine environment. It enables hardware and software developers to automate verification, but also allows interactive testing.

3. RELATED WORK

There exist other HW-SW co-simulators that we evaluated, but turned out to be unsuitable for our approach. FAUmachine [8] emulates an 64bit x86 processor and can run a co-simulation of HW described in VHDL. Its main purpose is failure analysis of systems and allows error injection, e.g., memory faults, disk faults. Though it does not allow to configure the simulated time synchronization between the emulated host computer and the VHDL simulation. Furthermore, FAUmachine can not take advantage of KVM, i.e., it can not run guest code virtualized on the host processor, which has a negative impact on execution performance.

The QEMU-SystemC project [9] sounded promising because it is based off QEMU and SystemC, but is discontinued. During the evaluation of QEMU-SystemC we discovered shortcomings that impact its usefulness. QEMU-SystemC needs to be compiled with an outdated version of the GNU Compiler Suite, otherwise it will terminate unexpectedly, due to a lot of illegal C++ code. Another shortcoming of QEMU-SystemC are unexpected terminations when KVM mode is enabled.

The gem5 simulator [2] allows precise simulations of different processors and caches and enables SystemC co-simulation. Its disadvantage results from its fine-grained simulation granularity, that makes simulation compute-intensive and makes interactive simulation impossible.

Due to the shortcomings of the above HW-SW co-simulators, we implemented our own HW-SW co-simulator. In [5] we presented an earlier stage of our HW-SW co-simulator that was limited to functional simulations. Though, hardware was described in our own XML-based language, instead of directly using SystemC to safe compilation time when hardware changes were necessary, this language added complexity for hardware developers. Furthermore, the XML-based language disallowed the use of typical C/C++ debug techniques, that led to time consuming development cycles. Also, it demanded a doubled effort, when the XML-based language needed to be extended, complex SystemC templates needed to be implemented accordingly.

The lack of simulated time synchronization disallowed testing of time-bound hardware or software components. E.g., it was impossible to use it for applications that require a hardware and/or software watchdog. Also, the Inter Process Communication (IPC) based on Linux Signals added delays in data exchange, due to inherent context switches between the QEMU and SystemC processes and the Operating System (OS).

4. HARDWARE-SOFTWARE CO-SIMULATION

This section presents our HW-SW co-simulator and our adaptive interface, that connects the SystemC hardware simulator with the virtual machine QEMU [1] and vice versa. While other co-simulators aim at precise but expensive synchronization of simulated times between both simulators [2] [8], our goal is to provide users interactive co-simulations, but still enable them to run also strongly synchronized co-simulations when boundary conditions or requirements demand precise simulated time synchronization. The latter applies to, e.g., watchdog hardware or software. Loosely synchronized high-performance co-simulations are for users who need to run interactive functional tests, which can lack hard timing requirements. This applies to, e.g., user input screens, in which case delays between inputs can not be predicted and happen at random times by nature. This can also be desirable in early stages of software development, when developers take advantage of interactive debug functionality in their software. A lack of flexibility, that allows loose synchronization but interactivity, of an adaptive interface for HW-SW co-simulation can slow down early development phases, when interactive testing is required.

4.1 Simulation, Emulation, Virtualization and Hybrid Systems

This section defines terminology that we use in this paper. For our work we need to strictly distinguish between these techniques: simulation, emulation and virtualization. There are also hybrid systems, that are a mixture of different techniques.

Simulation We use the term *simulation* when we refer to a model of something in reality. During simulation of a model, its internally and externally observable states are the same as in reality.

As there are not only outside interfaces simulated, but also the internal state, a simulation of a model reflects reality perfectly. This comes at the cost of being compute expensive. Not all virtual environments require a realistic simulation.

Emulation We use the term *emulation* when we refer to an imprecise simulation where only the behavior of the external interfaces need to correspond to the real world example.

We use emulation where a precise simulation of internal and external states is unnecessary but performance is of importance. Emulation is typically used, when user interaction and responsiveness matter, e.g., emulators for old game consoles.

Virtualization We use the term *virtualization* when we refer to the technique of executing guest software, that is executed under the supervision of a Virtual Machine Monitor (VMM), nowadays typically supported and accelerated by hardware virtualization extensions, as they can be found in modern processors by ARM, Intel and AMD.

QEMU can utilize the Linux Kernel Virtual Machine (KVM) [4] that uses hardware based acceleration found in the above mentioned processors. QEMU in KVM mode is an established technique, often found in cloud computing or on desktop computers to enable users to run different operating systems, e.g., Windows on Linux host systems.

Hybrid Systems Such systems use two or more of the above techniques at the same time, usually to improve performance and responsiveness for interactive use. Typical hybrids are Virtual Machines that virtualize the main processor, and emulate peripheral hardware, e.g., keyboard and mouse devices, graphics cards and storage controllers. QEMU is such a hybrid system, when the KVM mode is enabled, and well-known commercial hybrids are products of VMware [6].

4.2 Simulation time and simulated time

Two important kinds of time measurement for software simulation or virtual machines are simulation time and simulated time. The simulated time is the time, that passes inside simulators, emulators or virtual machine. This time is independent of the real world, e.g., a wall clock, i.e., the time needed to simulate 5 seconds can be less or more than 5 seconds.

Though, the simulation time is the time measured for the execution of a simulation to simulate a given simulated time. Depending on the simulation granularity of different simulators, there can occur magnitudes in differences of the simulation time to simulate the same simulated time among different simulators.

4.3 Emulated expansion card for QEMU

To connect a real computer to external devices, there are several interfaces available on the x86 PC platform. They fulfill different requirements, e.g., high data transfer rates, low power consumption or even comfort for users like USB connections.

Not all such scenarios apply to QEMU and its emulated buses and peripheral devices, e.g., low power consumption. But there are high speed interfaces available like the emulated PCI-Express bus, to which we connect the SystemC simulator to exchange data. For this we partly reused our previous work in [5]. We implemented our own emulated PCI-Express card for QEMU. It allows data input and output operations (I/O) via Linux IPC between the QEMU und SystemC Linux processes. In contrast to our previous implementation [5], we improved the IPC connection and use Linux shared memory to transfer data between QEMU and SystemC. Using shared memory allows us a zero-copy data exchange, to avoid I/O overhead. A positive side-effect is a slightly lower memory consumption.

Our expansion card emulates 1MiB of 32 bits width register that can be accessed via PCIe read and write operations from a guest Linux operating system. The registers are implemented as an array of uint32_t data types that resides in a Linux shared memory segment (SHM), which is shared between the QEMU and SystemC processes. Other processes can map this SHM segment into their own address space, too. Later, Section 4.5 presents, why this is necessary. Figure 7 shows in the center the SHM segment, containing the emulated registers.

Since SHM does not signal changes in data to processes that consume data from the SHM page, there needs to be mechanism to signal data changes to other processes, when it makes sense to notify the other process about the change. In our interface, data updates from the QEMU to the SystemC process are signaled via Linux Signals. When a guest system does a write access to an emulated register, our PCIe card emulation sends a Linux signal to the SystemC process, after the value in a register is changed. A corresponding signal handler in the SystemC process updates SystemC *sc_signals* of the simulated hardware device. This is necessary, since in reality hardware notices by nature when a write access is carried out to a register. Figure 7 shows the signaling mechanism on register write accesses and where data is transformed by the signal handler into SystemC data types.

Though in the opposite direction, there is no *implicit* signal sent to the QEMU process. Instead, the SystemC process expects to be *explicitly* told to send an Interrupt Request (IRQ). This needs to be triggered by the sensor or actuator model, since the developer of it knows when it makes sense to notify application software about a change. The real hardware device, from which the emulated PCIe card is derived from, works the same way: A peripheral hardware can change values in registers without notifying the OS via an IRQ. The real device has to notify a device driver in the operating system explicitly by raising an IRQ signal, which is also the case in our emulation. We implement the IRQ mechanism again via Linux IPC, so that the corresponding signal handler in the QEMU process signals an IRQ to the guest operating system. Figure 7 shows where the Linux Remote Procedure Call server is located and that it calls a corresponding function to raise an IRQ in the PCI-Express subsystem of QEMU.

To access the emulated registers, we implemented a Linux kernel driver and a user space program to read and write registers. Both are depicted as user space *Application* and the kernel space *I/O card device driver* in Figure 7. In read mode, our program must be given an address of a register to read a 32bit value from, and displays it on a command line interface In write mode, an address of a register to be written, must be given and a 32bit value that should be stored in the target register.

Our user space program communicates with our Linux device driver via the ioctl system call, which is defined on Linux systems as *int ioctl (int d, unsigned long request, ...)*, with *int d* being a file descriptor, *unsigned long request* encoding which code path in the driver should be chosen and ... being interpreted as a *void ** void pointer. The void pointer refers to a buffer that can be used to exchange data between user and kernel space. For this, our device driver presents the Linux character device /dev/iocard which can be opened and used to call valid ioctl system calls on it. When our device driver is loaded, it maps the I/O memory capable 32bit registers of the emulated registers to an unused address space. Our driver can now access the registers via the memory mapped memory area.

Figure 5 shows how register addresses and data values are exchanged between our test program and our device driver. In read mode, our driver extracts the register address from the ioctl system call buffer, and uses this address to read a 32bit value from the memory mapped area of our emulated PCIe card. In write mode, our driver extracts the register address and the 32bit value from the system call buffer, and uses this address to write the given value to the memory mapped area of our emulated PCIe card.

As discussed in Section 4.1, the design of our emulated PCIe card is a hybrid system, i.e., the PCIe bus is emulated, while the connected peripheral hardware is modeled and simulated in SystemC. This allows a high-speed simulation and interactive use of our HW-SW co-simulation, since the PCIe bus is emulated instead of being expensively modeled in SystemC. Our approach avoids a compute intensive simulation of the PCIe bus system, by connecting our I/O card by with the emulated PCIe subsystem API inside QEMU.

4.4 Synchronization of simulated times

The possibility to keep the simulated times in QEMU and the SystemC simulator synchronized is necessary for more precise simulations, when external conditions require it. Since both are different kinds of simulators, the most fine-grained achievable overall resolution of the simulated time is limited by the simulator with the coarse-grained time resolution.

$$|t_{QEMU} - t_{SystemC}| > \varepsilon$$

Figure 2: Pause condition.

While the SystemC reference simulator can work up to femtosecond resolution, QEMU operates on nanosecond resolution. Hence, our simulated time synchronization granularity is limited to a nanosecond resolution.

4.4.1 Simulated time control thread

In order to keep simulated times in QEMU and SystemC synchronized, a mechanism has to keep track of the simulated times in them. In case of a deviation, action this mechanism has to take action to restore synchronization. In our HW-SW co-simulator, this task is executed by the *simulated times control thread.* It is a POSIX thread inside the QEMU process, that queries the simulated times of QEMU and the SystemC simulator.

Since we identified use cases that do not require QEMU and SystemC to run with synchronized simulated times, e.g., when time is irrelevant to a pure functional test scenario, our simulated time control can be instructed to tolerate a user-configurable deviation (ε) of the simulated times. ε is the positive absolute value in nanoseconds of the difference of the simulated times in QEMU and the SystemC simulator. Its value is interpreted as nanoseconds, because the time resolution of QEMU is limited to a nanosecond granularity (see Section 4.4).

When the absolute deviation of the simulated times exceeds ε, action needs to be taken to get the deviation back below ε. Our HW-SW co-simulator can synchronize simulated times by pausing the simulator with advanced value of its simulated time minus ε. Figure 2 shows the computation of the pause condition for simulation partners, i.e., either QEMU or the SystemC simulator. When either QEMU or the SystemC simulator are in paused state, further simulation progress is stalled until the absolute deviation of simulated times becomes less or equal to ε. Once the pause condition does not apply anymore, simulation continues to progress in the simulation partner that previously had advanced.

4.4.2 (Re-)Synchronization of QEMU and SystemC

This section describes how we put the simulated times of QEMU and SystemC back in synchronization, when they diverge from each other. This situation occurs when the *simulated times control thread* (see Section 4.4.1) detects a deviation of the simulated times in QEMU and SystemC that is larger than ε. In QEMU, the simulated time control thread obtains the simulated time from the return value of a call of qemu_clock_get_ns(QEMU_CLOCK_VIRTUAL). From the SystemC simulator, the simulated time is obtained by the return value of a call to sc_time_stamp().value().

The simulated time control thread finds out whether one of QEMU or SystemC has progressed further ahead of the other one, and selects the one that has advanced. The control thread stops the advanced simulation partner by setting a progress lock for its simulation loop. We implemented the locks for QEMU and SystemC individually. In QEMU, we modified the main loop, to query the lock each time control

```
if (time_hw > time_sw ) {
  /* HW is faster */
  if ((time_hw - time_sw) > epsilon) {
    ptr_shm[0] = 1;
    ptr_shm[1] = 0;
  } else {
    ptr_shm[0] = 0;
    ptr_shm[1] = 0;
  }
} else {
  /* SW is faster */
  if ((time_sw - time_hw) > epsilon) {
    ptr_shm[0] = 0;
    ptr_shm[1] = 1;
  } else {
    ptr_shm[0] = 0;
    ptr_shm[1] = 0;
  }
}
```

Figure 3: Progress determination.

flow returns back from guest code to the main loop code. When the progress lock is active, the main loop skips handing back control to the guest code. Also, the main loop skips to increment the counter for the simulated time of QEMU. In this state, QEMU can not progress the simulated time, until the lock becomes unset by the *simulated time control thread*.

In the SystemC simulation, we have a different implementation to allow the *simulated time control thread* to pause the progress of the simulated time in the SystemC simulation. Since QEMU works with a coarse-grained resolution of simulated time compared to SystemC, a pause mechanism can only work on an equal or larger granularity. As for QEMU, we implement a progress lock, that is set and unset by the *simulated time control thread*. In our program that wraps around the SystemC library, in our HW simulator main loop, we have SystemC simulate user-configurable intervals of time steps in each iteration of our main loop. In each iteration, the progress lock is read and if it is set, the SystemC simulation is skipped. In this state, the HW simulation does neither progress the simulated time nor the simulation itself. Figure 6 depicts how progress of the simulated times in QEMU and SystemC is carried through by setting the progress lock to pause QEMU or SystemC, and how to make them continue by unsetting the locks.

The source code to determine the simulation partner that needs to be paused is shown in Figure 3. In the simulated time control thread, *time_hw* stores the simulated time of SystemC, while *time_sw* stores the one of QEMU. Both values are in nanoseconds. *epsilon* stores ε. *ptr_shm* is a pointer to an array in a SHM segment that is shared between QEMU and SystemC as shown in Figure 7. Index 0 in the array is the progress lock for the SystemC simulator, while index 1 is the progress lock for QEMU. The effect of setting a lock with a non-zero value and unsetting the lock with zero is depicted in Figure 6.

Figure 4 presents our modifications to the main_loop() function in QEMU.

Figure 7 shows the architecture of our adaptive coupling

```
static void main_loop(void)
{
/* ... */
#ifdef ALLOW_STOP
  int is_paused = 0;
  int get_time = 1;

  ctrl = pthread_create(&ctrl, NULL,
                 ctrl_thread, NULL);
  if (ctrl) {
    exit(-1);
  }

  rpc_srv = pthread_create(&rpc_srv,
              NULL, rpc_thread, NULL);
  if (rpc_srv) {
    exit(-1);
  }
  time_start = qemu_clock_get_ns(
               QEMU_CLOCK_VIRTUAL);
#endif
  do {
#ifdef ALLOW_STOP
    if (ptr_shm[1] == 1){
      /* Disables clock */
      pause_all_vcpus();
      get_time = 0;
      is_paused = 1;
    }
    if ((ptr_shm[1] == 0) &&
      (is_paused == 1)) {
      is_paused = 0;
      get_time = 1;
      resume_all_vcpus();
    }
#endif
/* ... */
#ifdef ALLOW_STOP
  if (get_time == 1){
    time_sw = qemu_clock_get_ns(
      QEMU_CLOCK_VIRTUAL)-time_start;
  }
#endif
  } while (!main_loop_should_exit());
}
```

Figure 4: Pausing QEMU.

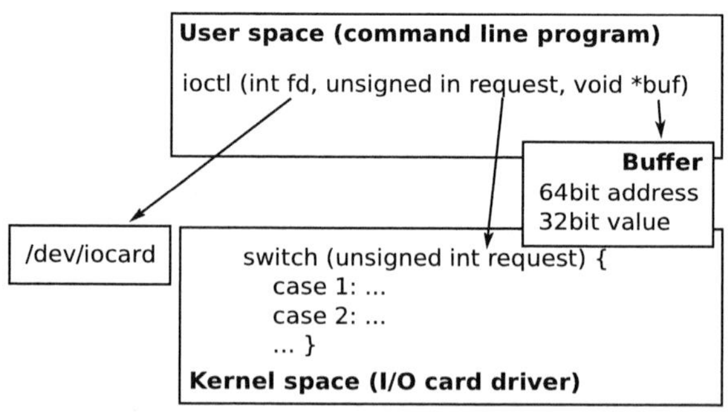

Figure 5: Data exchange with ioctl system call.

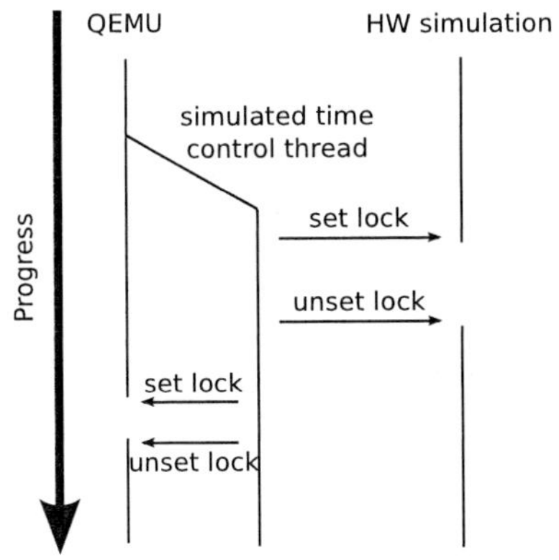

Figure 6: Simulated time control thread interaction.

between QEMU and SystemC. On the one hand, our *simulated time control thread* in QEMU reads the simulated time from the main loop of QEMU. On the other hand, the simulated time of SystemC is updated after each iteration of our simulation control loop that wraps around the *sc_start()* function in the shared memory segment. This allows the simulated time control thread to read the simulated time of the SystemC simulation, to compare the difference of both simulated times against ε. Either a user or a validation software of our research partner can not only initially set, but also re-adjust ε during a running simulation. Also, pause and continue signaling is presented that sets or unsets locks in the QEMU main loop and our simulation control loop.

4.5 Adaptive interface

In Section 4.4.2, we mentioned that the user defined tolerated deviation of simulated times ε, can also be changed during runtime to enable an adaptive interface between QEMU and SystemC to changing accuracy requirements. This Section describes our design and implementation of our adaptive interface.

In Section 4.4.1 we presented our control thread, that monitors and controls the simulated times of QEMU and the SystemC simulator via our pause mechanisms. The thread reads ε to check, if the difference of simulated times exceeds ε, which triggers a resynchronization between QEMU and SystemC.

The repeated reading of the memory that stores ε allows us to store it in the same SHM segment, that also holds the array for the emulated registers, that are described in Section 4.3. This results in the advantage, of using a passive update technique to change ε, by mapping the SHM segment into another process and change the value of the memory area that stores ε. We implemented a command line program *neweps*, which accepts a numeric parameter, interpreted as nanoseconds, that writes the user-supplied value, to set a new ε, into the SHM segment. *neweps* maps the SHM segment, into its own process local address space, and writes the new user supplied value for ε to the appropriate memory address. After that, following iterations in the *simulated times control thread*, the new value for ε is read for comparisons of simulated times. If a newly set ε is smaller than the current deviation of simulated times, the simulated time control thread will cause a resynchronization of QEMU and SystemC when it reads the updated value of ε during a following iteration. I.e., it will cause an immediate resynchronization.

Updating ε as a memory area in a polled SHM segment is inexpensive in contrast to IPC mechanisms that introduce a context switch, e.g., RPC, Linux signals or D-BUS. This allows frequent inexpensive changes of ε if external validation software needs to adapt frequently and rapidly to changing boundary conditions of tests, e.g., rapid frequent switching between timing accuracy bound and functional tests. Furthermore, our interface allows changes without having to restart running HW-SW co-simulations that need to be carried out with different parameters. Figure 7 presents the feature how ε is changed during a running simulation. An external program accesses the SHM segment that contains ε and changes its value, while the simulated time control thread can immediately access the updated value.

5. SAMPLE HARDWARE MODEL

In Section 4 we presented our modifications to QEMU to connect it to the SystemC HW simulator. In this section we present our sample SystemC hardware model, which we used to test and verify our HW-SW co-simulator. As described in Section 4.1, our hardware model completes our hybrid system by simulation.

Our sample SystemC HW describes a counter as a state machine, that can be reset, started, resumed and its current value read out via the emulated registers as shown in Figure 7. Figure 8 shows the three possible states of our sample counter.

The emulated registers are mapped to the control register of the counter as follows. The first emulated write-only register at address 0x00[1] controls the *RESET* register of our counter. The second emulated write-only register at address 0x04 controls the *RUN_ENABLE* register. The third emulated read-only register at address 0x08 is connected to the *VALUE* register of the counter. Figure 9 shows the mapping of the *RESET*, *RUN_ENABLE* and *VALUE* registers to memory mapped addresses.

Only the lowest bit of the write-only registers are used, since they control binary operations, whether the counter should be reset or if it should be in running state. The read-only value register is connected to all 32bits of the the *sc_uint <32>* value register. This is also shown in Figure 9.

I.e., writing 1 to the lowest bit at address 0x00 will put the counter into reset mode, and set the value register to zero and the *run_enable* register to 0. Writing 1 to the lowest bit at address 0x04 will cause the counter to increment the value register on each rising clock edge. One can pause the counter by writing any even value to address 0x04. The current value of the counter can be read from address 0x08. For our hybrid system, data types of C and SystemC are translated among each other during data transfers between emulation and simulation.

6. RESULTS

To verify the correctness of our HW-SW co-simulator, we used our sample hardware counter as presented in Section 5 which we ran as a co-simulation to our modified QEMU as presented in Section 4 (see Figure 7). This setup was used for all verifications and measurements presented in this

[1]To increase readability, we write 8bit addresses in this Section instead of full-length 64bit PCI-Express addresses.

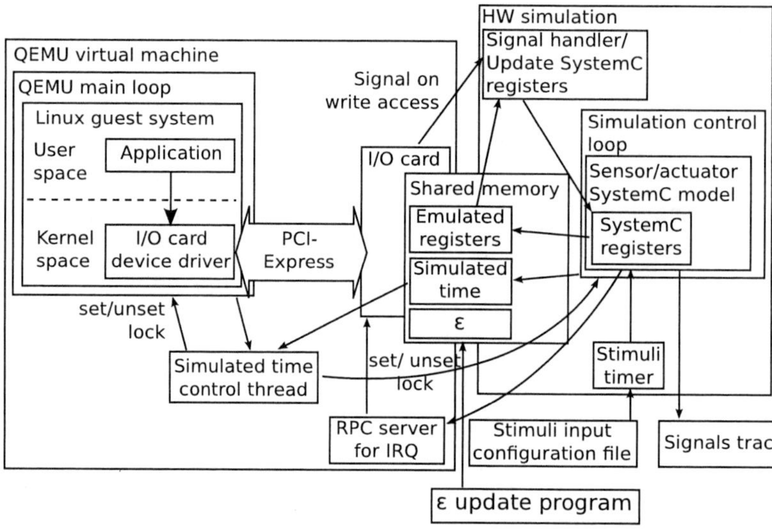

Figure 7: Architecture of our HW-SW co-simulation.

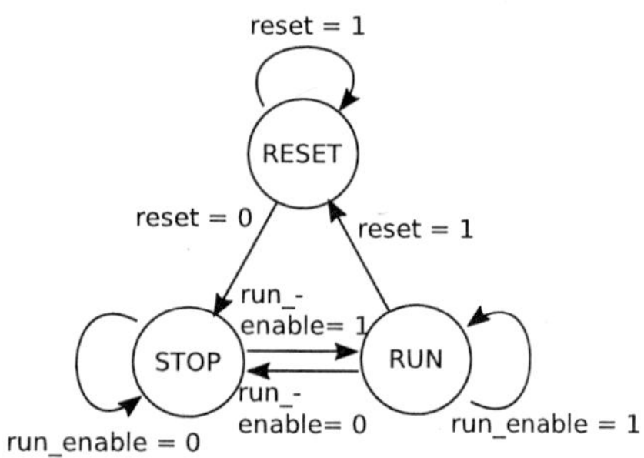

Figure 8: Counter state machine.

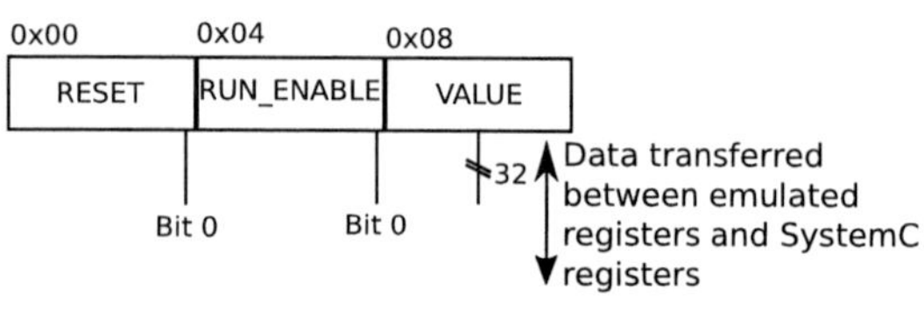

Figure 9: Control register mapping of our counter.

Section. The host computer is an Intel Core 2 processor with four cores clocked at 2,83GHz. For all measurements, QEMU was run in KVM mode, i.e., it was started with the *-enable-kvm* command line switch.

By a pure functional test by resetting, starting, stopping and reading out the value of our SystemC counter module, we could verify that our HW-SW co-simulation works correctly. We controlled the counter from the guest Linux command line by our control program (see Section 4.3). We put debug messages in our SystemC counter to proof the correct behavior of our interface between QEMU and SystemC.

In order to measure the efficiency of our HW-SW co-simulator, we measured the time it takes to transfer a datum from QEMU to SystemC. We measured the time difference between the arrival of a datum from the PCIe subsystem of QEMU and when storing the datum in a SystemC register has finished. Figure 10 shows a measurement without any pausing by the simulated time control thread, i.e., an infinite ε. 50 measurements were recorded and in average it took 0,06ms until a transmitted datum is stored in a SystemC target register. Side effects, e.g., the Linux scheduler, IRQs by external HW of the host system, influence the transmission time.

Figure 11 shows the average transmission time, when pausing is enabled by varying values of ε. This reveals a longer transmission time for smaller ε because of the overhead for pausing and resuming QEMU and SystemC.

Also, we measured the roundtrip time it takes to transfer a datum to SystemC that triggers a transmission of an IRQ back to QEMU. As we presented in Section 4.3, IRQs are emulated via RPC. Figure 12 shows the roundtrip time between sending a datum QEMU and receiving an RPC call back in QEMU. In most cases it takes 0,2ms until an RPC is received. In other cases it takes magnitudes longer, which is caused by side effects of other activities of our host system, e.g., other IRQs from external devices or desktop environment housekeeping.

Figure 13 presents average roundtrip times with pausing enabled by varying values of ε. It shows higher roundtrip times for lower values of ε. Compared to Figure 12, Figure

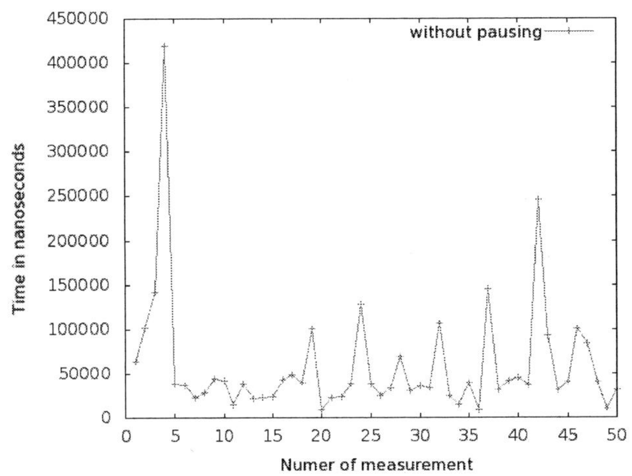

Figure 10: QEMU transferring a datum to SystemC.

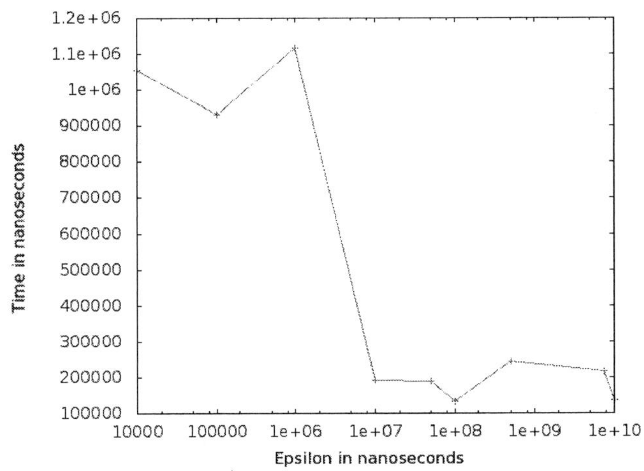

Figure 11: QEMU transferring a datum to SystemC with differing ε, average values.

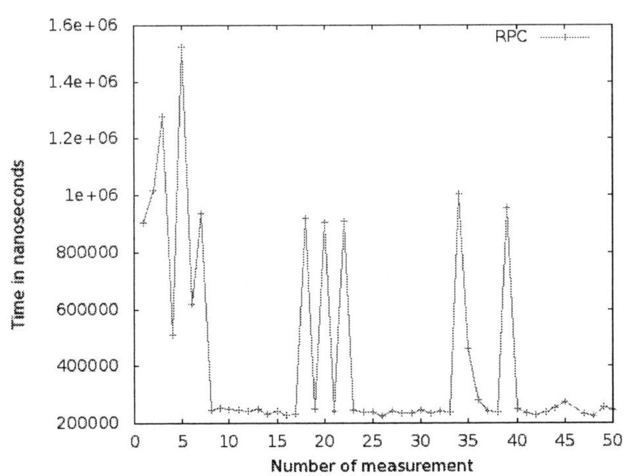

Figure 12: Measurement of RPC.

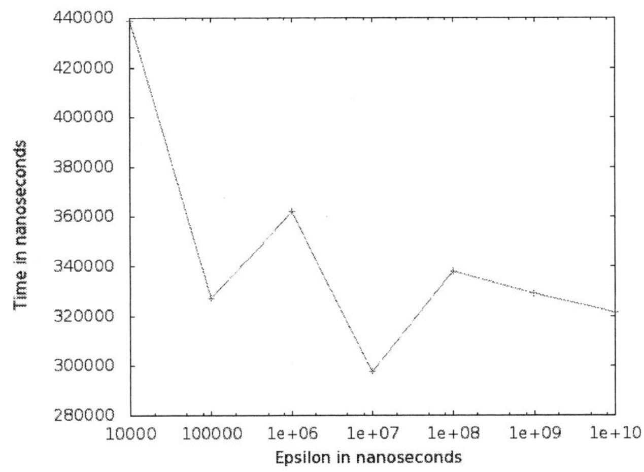

Figure 13: Measurement of RPC with differing ε, average values.

13 shows less varying roundtrip times, which is caused by the higher effect of the RPC overhead.

7. CONCLUSION

In this paper we presented our contribution to enable developers of home automation nodes to save development time by a hardware-software co-simulation in an early stage of development. In contrast to other projects, e.g., QEMU-SystemC [9] or gem5 [2], our solution targets more specific at the needs of home automation node developers, i.e., interactive performance and low latency by our developed adaptive interface between QEMU and SystemC.

Our adaptive interface allows a configurable synchronization of the simulated times in QEMU and SystemC, according to the needs of the home automation node developer or the to be simulated SystemC hardware model. Furthermore, the configuration can be adjusted during runtime. If boundary conditions or requirements of the synchronization lower or raise, the interface can be adjusted without having to restart the simulation.

Not only the user can configure and reconfigure our adaptive interface, but also software can. For use cases with automatic validation software, test supervision software can reconfigure the synchronization configuration. Also SystemC hardware models can be packaged with their own required configuration for a correct simulation.

Configuration changes to our adaptive interface are free of any latencies and take effect immediately. For automated testing this allows frequent configuration changes free of any latencies. In simulation scenarios, that require many frequent configuration changes, our adaptive interface does not affect the overall simulation time.

With a counter model in SystemC we verified the correctness of our hardware-software co-simulation and our adaptive interface between QEMU and SystemC. We also analyzed the efficiency of our adaptive interface by measuring data transfers between QEMU and SystemC, but also data roundtrips from QEMU back to QEMU. The measurements revealed a high latency in our Interrupt signaling code from SystemC to QEMU. We use Linux Remote Procedure Calls, which introduce a high latency. Despite of the latency of

Interrupt delivery, the measurements showed efficient data transmission and data roundtrip times of our design and implementation.

8. FUTURE WORK

As mentioned in Section 7, there is room for improvement in our Interrupt signaling code between SystemC and QEMU. Because of the high overhead of the server-client based architecture of Linux RPC, a lightweight solution should lower latency. A more lightweight IPC on Linux should be identified and replace the current RPC code to implement low-latency IRQ delivery.

In the current state, ε needs to be set initially on simulation start. A possibility could be found, to automatically find a reasonable value for ε when our HW-SW co-simulation is used only in an interactive scenario. Also, a continuously automatically tuned value could be possible.

9. ACKNOWLEDGMENT

This work was in part carried out in the E|Home Center project decentralized control in private residential by smart sensors and OPC UA, based on paradigms of Industry 4.0. We would like to thank the Bavarian State Ministry of Education, Science and the Arts for funding this project.

10. REFERENCES

[1] F. Bellard. QEMU, a Fast and Portable Dynamic Translator. In *USENIX Annual Technical Conference, FREENIX Track*, pages 41–46, 2005.

[2] N. Binkert, B. Beckmann, G. Black, S. K. Reinhardt, A. Saidi, A. Basu, J. Hestness, D. R. Hower, T. Krishna, S. Sardashti, R. Sen, K. Sewell, M. Shoaib, N. Vaish, M. D. Hill, and D. A. Wood. The Gem5 Simulator. *SIGARCH Comput. Archit. News*, 39(2):1–7, aug 2011.

[3] G. Briscoe and P. De Wilde. Digital ecosystems: evolving service-orientated architectures. In *Proceedings of the 1st international conference on Bio inspired models of network, information and computing systems*, page 17, 2006.

[4] A. Kivity, Y. Kamay, D. Laor, U. Lublin, and A. Liguori. kvm: the Linux virtual machine monitor. In *Proceedings of the Linux Symposium*, volume 1, pages 225–230, 2007.

[5] B. Kleinert, G. R. Rahimi, M. Reichenbach, and D. Fey. Hardware-software co-simulation for medical x-ray control units. In *Proceedings of the 8th International Conference on Simulation Tools and Techniques*, pages 305–307, 2015.

[6] P. Li. Selecting and using virtualization solutions: our experiences with VMware and VirtualBox. *Journal of Computing Sciences in Colleges*, 25(3):11–17, 2010.

[7] P. R. Panda. SystemC - a modeling platform supporting multiple design abstractions. In *System Synthesis, 2001. Proceedings. The 14th International Symposium on*, pages 75–80, 2001.

[8] S. Potyra. *Transparente und hochperformante VHDL-Cosimulation im Kontext der virtuellen Maschine FAUmachine*. PhD thesis, Universitätsbibliothek der Universität Erlangen-Nürnberg, 2013.

[9] T.-C. Yeh, G.-F. Tseng, and M.-C. Chiang. A fast cycle-accurate instruction set simulator based on QEMU and SystemC for SoC development. In *MELECON 2010 - 2010 15th IEEE Mediterranean Electrotechnical Conference*, pages 1033–1038, April 2010.

CloudEval: A Simulation Environment for Evaluating the Dynamic Cloud VM consolidation

Zhi Wang
Software College
Northeastern University China
Shenyang, Liaoning, China
yfwz100@163.com

Zhaohua Zhou
Software College
Northeastern University China
Shenyang, Liaoning, China
zhou.zh@qq.com

Shilin Jia
Software College
Northeastern University China
Shenyang, Liaoning, China
958240037@qq.com

Hao Liu
Software College
Northeastern University China
Shenyang, Liaoning, China
18202409257@163.com

Dancheng Li*
Software College
Northeastern University China
Shenyang, Liaoning, China
*Corresponding Author
Ldc@mail.neu.edu.cn

Jingde Cheng
Department of Information and Computer Sciences
Saitama University
Saitama-shi 338-8570, Japan
cheng@ics.saitama-u.ac.jp

ABSTRACT

Virtual machine(VM) scheduling algorithms optimize the energy consumption without performance degradation, where cloud providers profited greatly. However, not any algorithms performs the same. To evaluate the power efficiency of such algorithms, various scale of cloud clusters have to be maintained, which is costly and difficult. In this paper, we present a emulation software *CloudEval* to evalute the performance of migration algorithms of VMs. Comparing to previous cloud simulation environment, we addresses the evaluation of dynamic scheduling of the VMs in the cloud, by a simpler and a non-intrusive manner. Most previous cloud simulation environments encapsulate the simulation process in a close form(eg. the coupling of simulation and evaluation), which is not easy for researchers to design a VM scheduling algorithm and perform the evaluation. Besides, it suggests the clear test cases of workload and energy model, which is also important in VM scheduling algorithm evaluation.

Specifically, we address 3 aspects in the evaluation environment: the open architecture of simulation framework for algorithm/strategy design, the evaluation metrics, the simulation cases of workload and mapping of realistic cloud environment. The framework is intended to provide references for algorithm researches.

CCS Concepts

•Computing methodologies → Simulation environments; •Computer systems organization → *Cloud computing;*

Keywords

cloud computing, virtual machine live migration, performance evaluation tools

1. INTRODUCTION

The fast developing economics in cloud computing is gaining more and more attention for the energy profiling of the data center. Nowadays, as the virtualization engaged in most cloud infrastructure, the scale of data center is much larger than before. However, much of the servers are underutilized [10] [20] [16]. With the development of live migration technology of VMs [5], dynamically managing the layout of the VMs becomes possible. The dynamic scheduling of VMs is to dynamically allocate/consolidate VMs to achieve better trade-off between performance and energy consumption. Various energy conservation alogirhtms for the management of VMs is thus developped since then and proposed a concept of "Green Computing" [20]. However, by utilizing the energy-saving algorithms, the performance of the data center may be degraded by the dynamic consolidation of the VMs. One obvious reason is that VM has to be paused when migrating from the original host. Besides, the number of VM allocated in a physical host also affects the performance of the host, where VMs tend to compete for the limited resources. Notably, most algorithms tend to make the host overloaded by putting as many VMs as possible, which by turn results in a performance degradation when there's possible peak in resource utilization [16].

Evaluating the algorithm of VM dynamic scheduling requires theoretic analysis and experiments. However, setting up a large scale of machine clusters is not practical to many researchers. Basically proposed methods are evaluated in a self-constructed non-standard environment on simulation software, like matlab. It is a cheap way to verify the effectiveness of the algorithms. However, there's the risk to misleading the researcher because the complexity of the simulation environment. The scheduling of the VMs involves the scheduler of VM supervisors(on physical hosts) and the scheduler of the cloudlets or programs. Literatures make assumptions on the simplification on the simulation environment and few of them have done the experiments on the same condition. Li et al. make the first attampt to do a comprehensive evaluation of scheduling methods of VM migration for energy conservation [11]. However, the implementation detail of the experiment environemnt is omitted.

In this paper, we introduce a new emulation software to perform the evaluation on VM consolidation, based on the famous cloud infrastructure simulation software CloudSim [4]. To further describe the work, purpose of our work is addressed in the following aspects:

1. Design a Domain-Specific Language to better facilitate the process of algorithm implementation and experimental automation. To achieve this goal, we do a comprehensive survey about how authors design their VM migration strategy to carefully design the interfaces.

2. Design and maintain a consistent simulation environment for evaluating energy-efficient VMs dynamic scheduling algorithms.

3. Simplify the design of evaluation metrics for researchers who attempt to evaluate dynamic scheduling algorithms of VMs, without the knowledge of cloud simulation.

In Section 2, we will survey about simulation of cloud infrastructures. Section 3 will introduce the architecture of the cloud evaluation and the common simulation loop. Section 4 discusses the issues in simulation of the cloud and proposes the potential fixes. Later Section 5 gives a case study to evaluate a VM scheduling algorithms. Finally, Section 6 discusses the defects and suggests the future work. Finally, Section 7 gives a conclusion.

2. RELATED WORK

As CloudEval is an evaluation framework based on simulation environment, the related works will includes basis of the simulation environment, the specific-designed language as well as the foundation of the evaluation process, which build up the foundation of the framework.

As we survey about the simulation environmnt, the research of the cloud infrastructure is initiated in about 2009 closely followed by the concept of Cloud Computing suggested by Google in 2006. In the past decades, several simulation environment is proposed. Among these simulation tools, CloudSim[4] is the most comprehensive simulation environment for cloud computing at the present. After its release, many researchers extended CloudSim to many other aspects in order to do the related experiments, like NetworkCloudSim[9]. At the same time, the concept of Green Cloud is suggested. Many researchers try to optimize the cost and the energy consumption and CloudSim is extended to such fields[2]. However, many researchers just extended CloudSim to a special case and haven't do experiments on the same condition[11]. Besides, CloudSim builds around the entity and relation from the cloud infrastructure, as shown in Figure 1 . It doesn't provide guidelines to facilitate the development of evaluation metrics designs and algorithms implementation. It lacks the standard interfaces to monitor the data and formulate the evaluation reports. Our work will base on the cloud simulation concept of CloudSim, with emphasis on parts of the performance evaluation of VMs migration.

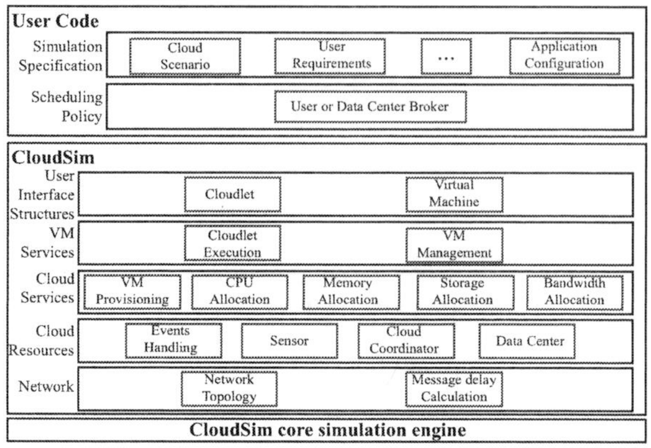

Figure 1: Layered design of CloudSim.

To distinguish from the CloudSim, we extract the important entities from the CloudSim and make our own engine and domain specific language, as shown in Figure 2. The contribution of CloudSim is the clear separation of cloud levels and the interactions of entities between each level. However, in an evaluation process, the interactions between entities is not enough. Our work will focus on the evaluation process, which is the upper layer of the CloudSim.

To the best of our knowlege, this is the first attampt to build a specifically-designed language for evaluation on CloudSim or similar simulation environment. Since CloudSim is built upon Java. In order to reuse the code, a Java-based language is selected as a basis of the design. Groovy[18] is a general-purpose programming language based on JVM with the thoughts of domain specific language design in its core. It can delegate the running context to create custom control structures and operator overloadings to build the symbolic programming[17]. With the flexibility of the syntax, a specific designed of the evaluation can be built clearly on the CloudSim and our evaluation metrics.

For evaluation metrics defined to build the evaluation process, we surveyed about many literatures[2][11][13][12]. [11] is the first attampt to sum up a comprehensive evaluation process and metrics in VM migration evaluation. It sums up most of the metrics seen in the literatures before and evaluate many algorithms at the same simulation platform. This is the attampt to build a flexible and solid foundation of the evaluation process. Therefore, as a simulation framework, we will focus on the validation of the process and the ability to extend the evaluation metrics. The validation of the simulation process is achieved by the base of CloudSim and the extension which defines the flexible interfaces to build evaluation metrics refered mostly in [11] and other works.

3. ARCHITECTURE OF THE SIMULATION

Firstly, we will demostrate the overall layer design of the architecture and how we build the simulation process with the detailed differences from CloudSim. As shown in related works, the layered design of CloudSim provides a clear seperation of cloud infrastructures. As the evaluation process of the VMs performs on migration, it mainly focus on the "Infrastructure as a Service"(IaaS) layer of the overall cloud framework, which is the basis of the "Plaftorm as a Service"(PaaS) and "Software as a Service"(SaaS) layer. In

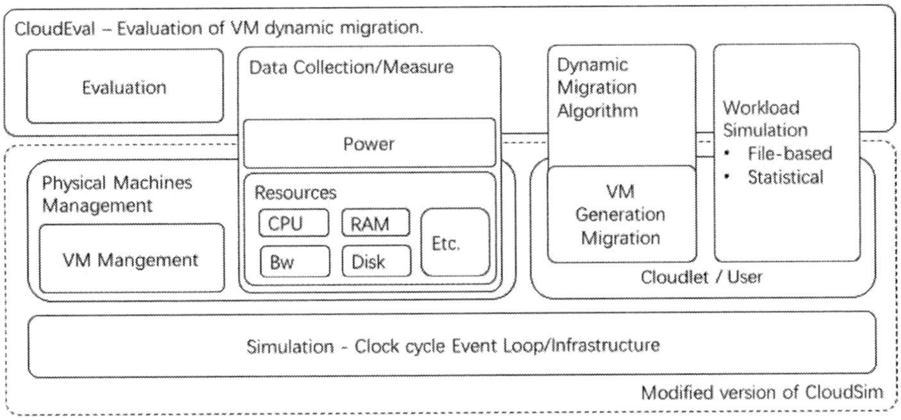

Figure 2: The architecture design.

this case, the framework won't pay much attention to the details in PaaS and SaaS layer and mostly consider them as the user activities on the underlie VM and platforms. As known from the layered design, PaaS is completely dependent by the SaaS layer. SaaS is the layer that interacted with the end user, which is the source of the workload. In this case, we model this behavior as resource usage distribution. It will be described in the Section 4.

In this case, entities of IaaS of CloudSim is adopted and collaborated in the framework. See Figure 2 for an overview of the architecture. Besides the entity foundation of CloudSim, CloudEval enhances the workload module, energy consumption module and data collection module. These models are mostly data models and should be considered as experiment parameters.To better described them, the detail of the models will be introduced in Section 4.

We also improve the design of evaluation metrics. The consideration is to define the abstract math expressions for better understanding and utilization of the metrics. Currently, with CloudSim or other simulation environment, there's no limitation on the framework so that logic of algorithm and evaluation computation are likely to be messed up in experiments, which is hard to extract the target of the metrics and reuse the metrics in other experiments. This part will be further discussed in the sub-section in 'domain specific language'.

3.1 Component Design of the System

In a functional perspective, the architecture of the simulation is loosely divided into 3 aspects: the data center definition, algorithms to evaluate, and definition of evaluation metrics. As shown in Figure 2, the data center is built upon a modified version of CloudSim. It manages the relations and interactions among cloud entities. The algorithms and evaluation are defined as the user layer of a cloud simulation environment, corresponding to CloudSim's layered design. The infrastructure layer manages the resources and update the state of the entities involved in the cloud. The algorithms manage the live scheduling of VMs over physical machines, including consolidation and live migration. The evaluation module collects data from the infrastructure and the running cycle.

Compared with figures of architecture in the CloudSim, CloudEval is simplified. Unlike the definition of 'data center' in CloudSim, the part of 'data center' is an abstract concept of whole infrastructure of CloudSim, including the physical host cluster, VMs and the user behaviors(the abstract workload). When people refer to the data center, people tend to imply the things around the data center.

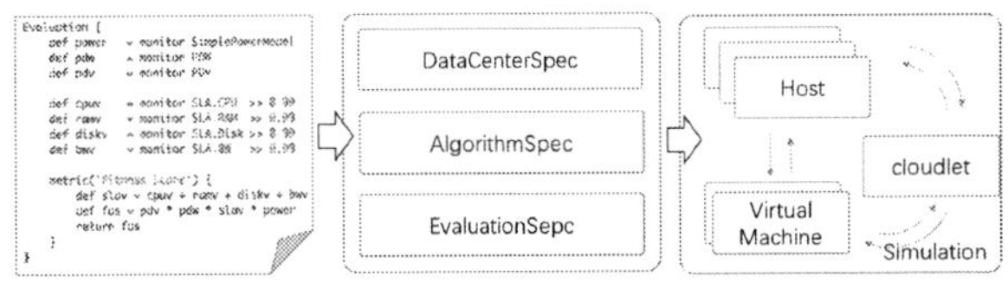

Figure 3: The execution process of DSL.

In an evaluation process, things to be considered important is the same configuration across in different experiments. Data center in this case is the evaluating object. The evaluation process is seemed as meaningful unless it is tested across the same environment under the same evaluation process. The configuration is provided to maintain the same configuration of the evaluation objects. In this case, the configuration is defined in 3 parts:

1. the scale of the data center, eg. the host clusters.
2. the scale of user behaviors. To describe the user behaviors, we further describe 2 aspects:
   (a) the workload simulation.
   (b) the VM generation strategy.
3. the evaluation part.

Specifically, VM generation strategy is important in simulating the clouds because some of the cloud providers will just provide several resources-limited fixed-size VMs regardless of the actual resources requested by the user.

3.2 The Design of Domain Specific Language

To simplify the development of algorithm evaluation, a domain specific language is introduced, via a JVM-based programming language, Groovy. It mainly includes two aspects: the specification definition of the cloud infrastructure being evaluated and the symbolic design of evaluation metrics.

In the language layer, it features:

1. Declarative blocks for defining specification of experiment, like the scale of the data center and the VM scheduling strategies. It clearly defines the border of configuration so that each part will not be confused in the experiment configuration scope.

2. Utilizing operator overloading that makes evaluation metrics convenient and consistent in a clear symbolic way and seperation from the simulation process.

3. Unified expressions in data collection and performance metrics. Monitored data is wrapped as a symbol that can be integrated into the definition of evaluation metrics.

To better describe the experiment, we give an example that illustrate the process of the whole architecture in Figure 3. As the figure said, the engine first turned the DSL into a set of specification classes where the entities envolved in the simulation is then generated. Finally, the simulation toolkit will simulate the interactions between entities and perform the evaluation.

3.2.1 Configuration of Data Center

The configuration of data center is a mapping of the CloudSim's cloud entities, representing the real entity in simulation environment. It includes the definition of the scale of host clusters, the scale of VMs and the model of resource utilization process. Most of the concepts are taken from CloudSim with some simulation consideration addressed in Section 4. It ensures that all algorithms defined in the same script will be treated as the same environment in the cloud infrustructure.

3.2.2 The Interfaces for Algorithm Implementation

To summarize the interfaces of the algorithm, we studied a wide range of scheduling methods of VM live migration and adopted literature[2][1][11] as reference. The typical process can be concluded as the following three steps: (1) determine the trigger timing of VM migration. (2) select VMs as migrated objects. (3) select hosts to place the VMs as destination. The three steps will be designed as three interfaces in CloudEval so researchers only need to implement their own new algorithm in the corresponding interface and configure the names of these new policy in the experiment script to evaluate the new policy in the simulation.

`MigratedHostPolicy` is an abstract class that represents the determination policy of VM migration timing. Determination Policy of VM Migration Timing is defined as the trigger condition of VM migration. To determine the migration time, Beloglazov et al. [2] proposed a heuristic policy based on Double-Threshold Trigger Policy (DTTP) to determine the timing of VM migration in [1], which "set upper and lower utilization thresholds for hosts and keep the total utilization of the CPU by all the VMs allocated to the host between these thresholds." Li et al. [8] also adopted Delay Trigger Policy (DTP), which judges whether current migration is reasonable by monitoring and forecasting resource utilization when upper or lower threshold is satisfied. We can see that most algorithms determined migration time by checking the status of the utilization of physical hosts. It runs every clock cycle to monitor the changes in order to prepare for the migration.

`VmSelectionPolicy` is an abstract class that represents the VM selection policy. The VM selection problem consists of defining, among the VMs in a certain host, which one should migrate to a new machine requested by a user because of the power consideration. Researchers can extend class `VmSelectionPolicy` and override the `getMigratedVms-fromHost` method to define new selection policy of migrated VM.

`VmPlacementPolicy` is an abstract class that represents the VM placement policy, which selects a suitable hosts to place the migrated hosts. Selection Policy of Destination Servers is the process of selecting idle servers as destination servers from the server list, and mapping the migrated VMs to these destination servers. In the process of placing migrated VMs on the hosts, the avoidance of cluster effect is required to be taken into account, which tries to avoid allocating excessive migrated VMs to an idle destination server. Sometimes this method will be combined in the `VmSelec-tionPolicy` but we separate the implementation of them in order to better decouple the selection and placement steps. Researchers can implement new VM placement policy by extending this class and overriding the `getNewVmPlacement` method.

For some combined VM Migration policy which optimized only one or two steps, we provide the default policy for other steps. For example, Beloglazov et al. [1] have proposed a novel combined optimization policy, which optimizes the determination policy of VM migration timing and the selection policy of migrated VM. Therefore, it is more helpful for simulation and evaluation of scheduling method of VM live migration by dividing the process of VM live migration to three steps. For a complete list of timing, literature[11] lists 11 algorithms which classify the algorithms in these two steps. The sequence diagram of the mentioned process is shown in Figure 4.

3.2.3 Symbolic Design of the Evaluation Metric

The symbolic representation of the metric calculation is the main consideration when designing these parts. The past problem of the metric definition is the coupling with simulation metrics.

To evaluate the overall performance of the energy-saving algorithms for VM live migration, many researchers proposes different metrics. Li et al. [11] sum up a comprehensive evaluation of VM scheduling algorithms for energy conservation. It considered the basic performance metrics collected from simulation process, such as migration times, violations of service level agreement, delay of executions and etc. It also considers the transformed metrics which turn the multi-objective problem into a unified single metrics, such as the PDM(performance degradation of machines), PDV(performance degradation of VMs) and fitness score. Mills et al. [14] proposes statistical analysis variables on experiment evaluation in several aspects including resource usage(workload), sucessful requests rate/latency and etc. The statistical variables are derived from the basic measured data.

To sort out the measure types, we define the two sorts of metrics:

1. Accumulative metric. Accumulative measurement is

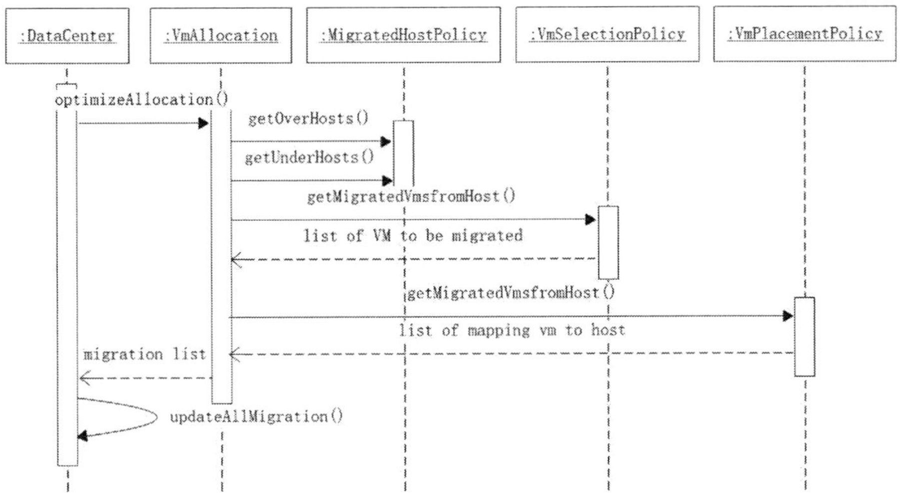

Figure 4: The sequence diagram of algorihtm interfaces.

often defined as data collection metrics, such as volation times of SLA. It collects the data from looping over the cloud resources and accumulate the needed value for later process. Such value will be wrapped into a symbolic variable for use with transformed metrics.

2. Transformed metric. Transformed measure is the combination of severalother metrics. Like the *fitness of score* [11]. It's calculated by the transformed metric itself or through the accumulative metric.

The most important part is to deal with the transformed metrics. In order not to mess up the logic, the symbolic engine overloads operators to express the metric in a mathematical way. Thus, the two types can be defined seamlessly and compute with all the types of the evaluation model in the same way.

4. CONSIDERATION OF SIMULATION

In an evaluation process, the significant part of the experiment is to maintain the same configuration across different algorithms. The evaluation process is seemed as meaningful unless it is tested under the same environment and the same evaluation process. If one cannot guarantee the same configuration, the result of the experiments is meaningless to compare. As described above, in the simulation of a data center, things will be messed up when faced with so many variables in the simulation.

In this section, we try to apply some restraints on the simulation by restraining several interfaces.

4.1 Simulation of the Clockcycle

Firstly, the data center entity, as the evaluating object, is divided into 3 parts: the overall simulation process, the workload model, and the metrics. The simulation of the clockcyle is the core of the running process. It's trivial if we can disassemble the steps into instructions. We can guarantee to disassemble running process of VM into atomic running steps and evaluate the cost when it runs every clock move. However, we couldn't guarantee that every algorithm implementation moves according to the clock cycle. To produce a possible implementation, the clock cycle is defined as an abstract period cycle.

To solve this problem, we define two clock measuring system. We define T_{clock} as the explicit clock cycle and T_{sys} as system time counter. The total running time defined as:

$$T_{running} = T_{clock} + T_{sys}$$

In every simulation, T_{clock} can be controlled. However, the real running time cannot be controlled for every machine's CPU is not always the same but we can ensure that every experiments works on the same machine with the same configuration. When the algorithm lasts for a long time, we consider the whole running of the cluster is paused.

To monitor the algorithm running, we hook two methods into Measure interface:

1. `preUpdate()`: execute before algorithm performs.

2. `postUpdate()`: execute after algorithm performs.

In this way, we can monitor the cost of algorithm itself as a metric to evaluate the algorithm.

The defect on this clock-cycle implementation will also be discussed in the defects section.

4.2 Modeling the Migration

Migrating a VM is costly. It is a resource-intensive operation which tends to impact the application performance of the migrating VM and other concurrent VMs though live VM migration is generally fast[5]. [5] points out the general migration steps performed by a typical hypervisor, which is a time-bounded iterative operation. It first performs a pre-copy process which iterative copy all the data from the source to destination. When the stop condition satisfied, it stops the VM and start the VM in destination server instantly and redirect all workload to the new VM. So it's affected by the workload and the resource usage level, as also stated in [19]. In this sense, the migration will cause an extra low resource usage on the destination. It's a typical disk-instensive operation. Besides the disk-intensive operation, the newly-added workload will also affects the running physical machine.

As surveyed in [11], the cost of migration is defined as "Performance Degradation of Migration", which symplified the model by the number of migrating VM, the data transfered, the migration time, and the degraded workload execution. They will be subject to workload and power model.

4.3 Modeling the Workload

Workload is an abstract concept of running applications in the physical machines. The modeling of workload is still a hot topic. It's defined in literatures as a stochastic process or a queue model [8] [3]. The complexity of the workload is obvious and has been discussed intensively. The workload could affect many aspects of a physical machines and even the environmental instruments, like cooling systems. And the workload is not simply a linear relation between programs generating the resource usages. The workload of two identical programs running on the one machine is different from two programs each running one machine. In this case, we don't dig deep into the details of the running programs. We consider that the nature of programs is a finite sequences of commands with the ability to recur itself so as to run infinitely. The command will be executed by CPU so it can manage all the resources controlled by CPU. In this sense, we will describe the workload model by a resources usage model which can be described by stochastic models. For further classification of features of workload, [8] gives a comprehensive survey.

In CloudSim, the workload is defined as the resource usage model in Cloudlet. It can be seen as a queue model. Every cloudlet is an application that requires the resources provided by infrastructure such as number of CPU cores. In this paper, we still adopt such simplified model and define the workload as stochastic model of resources usage. However, it will causes problem when applying such dynamic usage model of resources – the algorithm will take different actions according to its many features that haven't been covered by the model, such as burstiness. The skew of the distribution and the time of a burst in the same distribution may affect the algorithm largely, see Figure 5. We couldn't provide these constraints on workload generation model.

Another thing to mention is that the influence of workload. Firstly, the migration will cause a higher resource usage in destination machine (mainly the memory usage and disk usage). It could be a fixed cost depending on the migrating VM. Another thing to consider is that the extra copying process will have an impact on the current running applications, so it may also related to a decay on performance of current physical machine.

To maintain the consistency across experiments, two strategies are considered. The first one is giving a dynamic stochastic model controlled by distribution features of a workload. Another one is giving a file-based pre-configured model to generate the workload.

4.4 Estimating the Power

The simulation of power consumption of machines has a long history. The initial work dates back to the early 90s and new models still emerged up to now [15]. The power estimation model is widely used in many places, including CPU scaling, tasks scheduling and VMs consolidation. The difficulty of the estimation is that it is affected by so many factors. The parameters examined extensively includes the hardware resource utilization percentage, performance counter (PMC) and the hardware features such as CPU frequency. The estimation model is often obtain in a model-tunning fashion: assume an equation between power and selected parameters and train the model through collected data to calibrate the equation. Notably, PMC-based models are elaborate in the fact that not all CPU implements the power-related sensors and there seem to be more sensors than the collected data (most servers are under-utilized.) to calibrate the parameters.

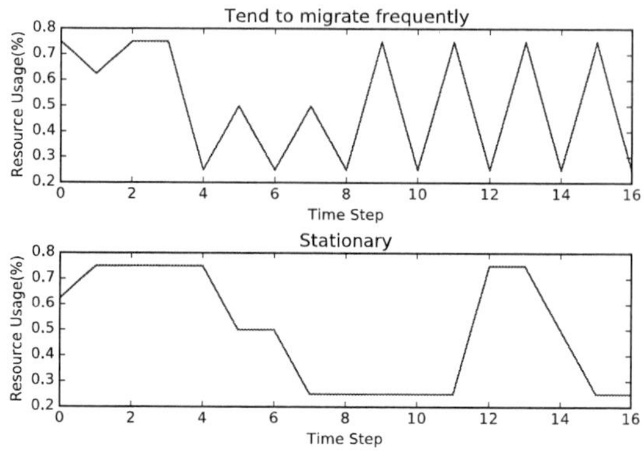

Figure 5: The workload generated from the same distribution of resource usage, performs differently in evaluation.

Some models focus on the sole host for power consumption. It's obvious that the power consumption of a host tends to depend on the resource utilization. That's the equation that's widely used by researchers, concluded in [11]:

$$P = P_{idle} + \alpha_1 u_{CPU} + \alpha_2 u_{RAM} + \alpha_3 u_{disk} + \alpha_4 u_{net} + e$$

where α_i means the parameters, $u_i \in [0, 1]$ means the resource usage percentage. It's an ideal model and assumes a linear relation among the resource utilization of hardware. The power consumption of disk and bandwidth is omitted for some of the literatures provided that the power of CPU and RAM takes more than 90% of the power in a host, as practical experiments shown in [7][11][15]. So there's another widely accepted empirical equation considering only the CPU usage:

$$P = P_{idle} + (P_{busy} - P_{idle})(2u_{cpu} - u_{cpu}^r)$$

while P_{busy} denotes the maximum power consumed by the host and r is the calibration factor minimizing the squared error of the model. It's been validated by using 'a few hundred' servers [7]. It's also compared in [15] and shows superior than PMC based model in some cases.

In reality, the relation between power and resource utilization is more than linear relation. CPU scaling is more effective than CPU utilization to estimate the power consumption. As shown in Figure 6, we did experiments to show the influence by CPU frequency. Different color indicates the different frequency level. There's a vast difference

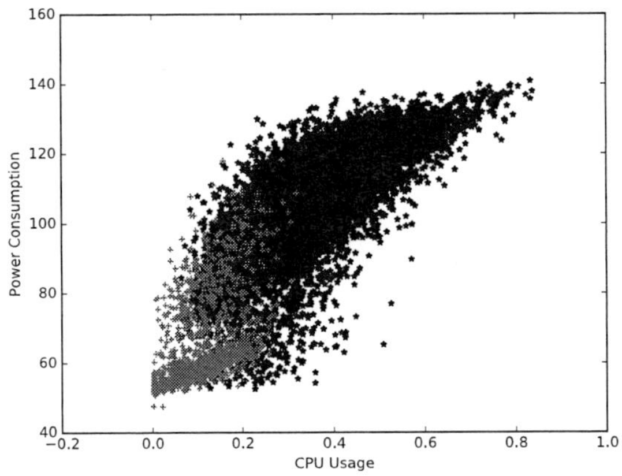

Figure 6: The scatter graph of CPU usage and power consumption.

on the same CPU usage level. The differences in power consumption on the same usage level is mainly caused by CPU frequency. Nevertheless, the fact is that high utilization of CPU tends to trigger the high frequency scaling so we can take only the CPU utilizationlevel to simplify the models. The power consumption of a data center is also affected by the environmental factors such as temperature, which is also correlated with high resource usage. A coarse-grained model with a penalty on high resources usage is also plausible.

To sum up the power estimation technique, the framework predefines the linear and non-linear equations for use with evaluation. The input parameters are the pre-defined parameters or a file describe the historical data to train for the optimal parameters. To implement a new model or modify the existing model, the framework drops the model implemented by CloudSim encompassing power model of a host. Instead, it exposes a interface taking the entire data center object for fine- or coarse-grained estimation.

5. A CASE STUDY

This section introduces a case study on evaluating two simple VM consolidation algorithms, DT-MU-PABFD and IQR-MMT-PABFD. The two name of the algorithm reflect the strategy used in the 3 steps mentioned in the algorithm sections. In the script, we defines the data center as providing a large host clusters with 700 hosts of 4 cores CPU, 4G RAM and 1000GB disk. The workload model used is a typical CPU-intensive type with random resource utilization of CPU range in [0.5, 1], RAM range in [0, 0.3], bandwidth range in [0, 0.3] and disk range in [0, 0.3].

In the algorithm part, we define two cases:

1. DT-MU-PABFD.
   (a) MigratedHostPolicy: double-threshold policy(DT) [1] - "set upper and lower utilization thresholds for hosts and keep the total utilization of the CPU by all the VMs allocated to the host between these thresholds."
   (b) VmSelectionPolicy: minimum utilization policy(MU) [12] - "select a VM to be migrated that requires the minimum CPU utilization relatively to other VMs in the host."
   (c) VmPlacementPolicy: power-awared best fit policy(PABFD) [1] - select hosts with the maximum resource as the destination for the migrated VM.

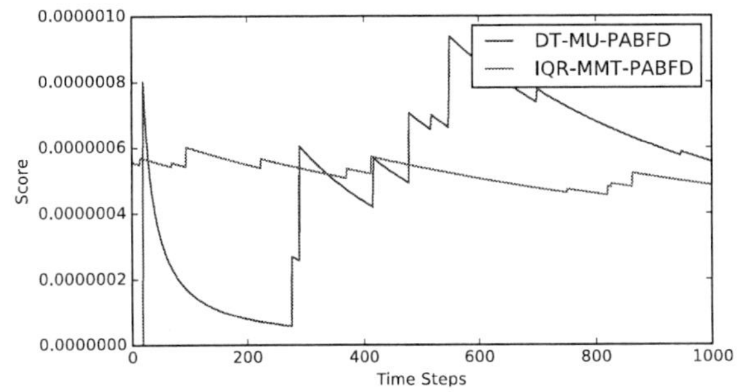

Figure 7: The simulation of PDV.

2. IQR-MMT-PABFD.
   (a) MigratedHostPolicy: interquartile range policy(IQR) - "adjust the value of the upper utilization threshold depending on the strength of the deviation of the CPU utilization."
   (b) VmSelectionPolicy: minimum utilization policy(MMT) - "select a VM to be migrated that requires the minimum CPU utilization relatively to other VMs in the host."
   (c) VmPlacementPolicy: power-awared best fit policy(PABFD) - select hosts with the maximum resource as the destination for the migrated VM.

In evaluation metric definition, we have the following definition:

1. Power measuring. It adopts a linear model with predefined factors considering the linear relation with resources utilization percentage.

2. Performance Degradation of VMs (PDV). The total migration times.

3. Performance Degradation of Workload (PDW). The delayed response time for workload execution.

4. SLA. The violation times of SLA, defined in a symbolic way. The overall SLA is also defined as $SLA = SLA_{cpu} + SLA_{ram} + SLA_{disk} + SLA_{net}$

5. Fitness Score. The value represents the trade-off between performance and power consumption. It's defined in by the following equation:

$$S_{fit} = PDV \times SLAV \times Power$$

   It's a simplified equation derived from [11].

From the code below, we can see that the configuration is presented in a declarative manner with the knowledge of the simulation layer.

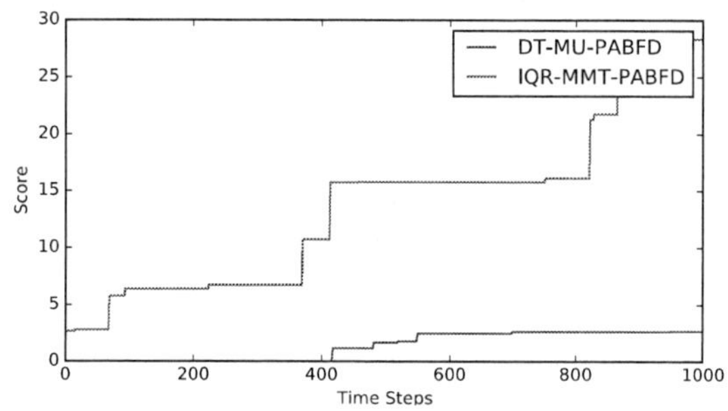

Figure 8: The simulation of fitness score.

From Figure 7, we can clearly see the fluctuation of the simulation and know how they changes under different algorithms. Figure 8 shows that the fitness score of DT-MU-PABFD is better than the other and we can infer that the combination strategy of DT-MU-PABFD performs better in the experiment.

6. DISCUSSIONS

When preparing such an environment, we present the following problems with performance evaluation in VM scheduling:

1. Evaluation on a real host cluster or data center is expensive.
2. Maintenance of a standard host cluster tends to be difficult. It is affected by so many variables.
3. No mature toolkit addressing the simulation issues on VM consolidation evaluation.

As mentioned before, most of the issues have been considered in the above. For the last issues, we have studied some of the works, like [4] and [2]. The work mentioned is impressive. However, both of the work before still lacks the consideration of the following issues: no limitation or tracking of algorithm running time. The algorithm being evaluated runs parallel with the VMs. However, the fact is that the algorithms is part of the workload. If we modeled the clockcycle or a small period, the algorithm should be divided into a small period and run once at a time. To some extent, we put a penalty on long run time of the algorithm.

6.1 Scallability

Another issue is the scalability of the framework. Though different size of host clusters and workload model is scalable, the algorithms written in the framework is running at a centralization manner. It lacks of the ability to track algorithms running distributedly, eg. running at every VMs and track the resources utilization every time instead of tracking after a determined clock cycle. Such conditions are left for researchers to maintain so as to ensure fairness of the comparison. The scalability of the algorithm and the framework should be further improved.

6.2 Extensibility

The toolkit is based on the famous CloudSim with the modification on the simulation loop. The extensibility of the toolkit is obvious. What has to concern is that the framework lacks the simulation of network activity. At present, network activity of CloudSim is not ported into the toolkit for the complexity of the network topology. The cost of data transfered in network is considered part of migration cost. In the simulation, the network is modeled as an ideal network with short distance between machines. As shown in [6], the migration cost mainly concerns the bandwidth and the size of consumed RAM. However, further work on network topology is necessary if the data center is complex and data transfered cannot be ignored.

7. CONCLUSIONS

In this paper, we introduce the simulation-based evaluation framework for algorithms of power-efficient VM scheduling. It's built on top of CloudSim, with the consideration of workload and power simulation in addition. The work present a solution of the following aspects:

1. A simulation environment for evaluation of VMs scheduling algorithms.
2. The consideration and pre-defined environmental variables to facilitate the development of the experiment environment.
3. A domain specific language for evaluation metrics design and algorithm implementation.

The simulation toolkit has been used in research of performance evaluation of the scheduling strategies. As Section 6 said, it's still a coarse-grained framework for performance evaluation. The simulation of clock cycle is still a major problem when simulating the algorithm. The cost of the migration, power and other factors should also be mentioned. Further research on workload model, power model and the simulation of algorithm running at bytecode level should be undertaken to improve the whole experimental environment in the future.

8. ACKNOWLEDGMENTS

This work was supported by the National Natural Science-Foundation of China (Grant Nos.61300019), the Research Fund for Online Education of MOE (Grant No. 2016YB125).

9. REFERENCES

[1] Anton Beloglazov, Jemal Abawajy, and Rajkumar Buyya. Energy-aware resource allocation heuristics for efficient management of data centers for cloud computing. *Future Generation Computer Systems*, 28(5):755–768, 2012.

[2] Anton Beloglazov and Rajkumar Buyya. Optimal online deterministic algorithms and adaptive heuristics for energy and performance efficient dynamic consolidation of virtual machines in cloud data centers. *Concurrency and Computation Practice and Experience*, 24(13):13971420, 2012.

[3] Dario Bruneo. A stochastic model to investigate data center performance and qos in iaas cloud computing systems. *Parallel and Distributed Systems IEEE Transactions on*, 25(3):1, 2013.

[4] Rodrigo N Calheiros, Rajiv Ranjan, Anton Beloglazov, César AF De Rose, and Rajkumar Buyya. Cloudsim: a toolkit for modeling and simulation of cloud computing environments and evaluation of resource provisioning algorithms. *Software: Practice and Experience*, 41(1):23–50, 2011.

[5] Christopher Clark, Keir Fraser, Steven Hand, Jacob Gorm Hansen, Eric Jul, Christian Limpach, Ian Pratt, and Andrew Warfield. Live migration of virtual machines. In *Proceedings of the 2nd conference on Symposium on Networked Systems Design and Implementation - Volume 2*, pages 273–286, 2005.

[6] W. Dargie. Estimation of the cost of vm migration. In *The 23rd International Conference on Computer Communications and Networks (ICCCN 2014)*, pages 1–8, 2014.

[7] Xiaobo Fan, Wolf Dietrich Weber, and Luiz Andre Barroso. *Power provisioning for a warehouse-sized computer*. ACM, 2007.

[8] Dror G. Feitelson. *Workload Modeling for Performance Evaluation*. Springer Berlin Heidelberg, 2002.

[9] S. K. Garg and R. Buyya. Networkcloudsim: Modelling parallel applications in cloud simulations. In *IEEE International Conference on Utility and Cloud Computing, Ucc 2011, Melbourne, Australia, December*, pages 105 – 113, 2011.

[10] Dzmitry Kliazovich, Pascal Bouvry, and Samee Ullah Khan. Simulation and performance analysis of data intensive and workload intensive cloud computing data centers. *Optical Networks*, pages 47–63, 2013.

[11] D. Li, W. Wang, Q. Li, and J. Cheng. A comprehensive evaluation of scheduling methods of virtual machine migration for energy conservation. *IEEE Systems Journal*, pages 1–12, 2015.

[12] Dancheng Li, Wei Wang, Quanzuo Li, and Donglin Ma. Study of a virtual machine migration method. In *2013 International Conference on Advanced Cloud and Big Data (CBD)*, pages 27–31, 2013.

[13] Gerg Lovász, Florian Niedermeier, and Hermann De Meer. Performance tradeoffs of energy-aware virtual machine consolidation. *Cluster Computing*, 16(3):481–496, 2013.

[14] K. Mills, J. Filliben, and C. Dabrowski. Comparing vm-placement algorithms for on-demand clouds. In *IEEE International Conference on Cloud Computing Technology and Science, Cloudcom 2011, Athens, Greece, November 29 - December*, pages 91–98, 2011.

[15] Christoph Mobius, Waltenegus Dargie, and Alexander Schill. Power consumption estimation models for processors, virtual machines, and servers. *Parallel and Distributed Systems, IEEE Transactions on*, 25(6):1600–1614, 2014.

[16] Eduardo Pinheiro, Ricardo Bianchini, and Enrique V. Carrera. Load balancing and unbalancing for power and performance in cluster-based systems. *Department of Computer Science Rutgers University*, 2015.

[17] Groovy Team. Domain specific languages in groovy. http://groovy-lang.org/dsls.html.

[18] Groovy Team. The groovy programming language. http://groovy-lang.org.

[19] Yangyang Wu and Ming Zhao. Performance modeling of virtual machine live migration. pages 492–499, 2011.

[20] Andrew J Younge, Gregor Von Laszewski, Lizhe Wang, Sonia Lopez-Alarcon, and Warren Carithers. Efficient resource management for cloud computing environments. In *Green Computing Conference, 2010 International*, pages 357–364. IEEE, 2010.

A Non-Blocking Priority Queue for the Pending Event Set

Romolo Marotta, Mauro Ianni, Alessandro Pellegrini and Francesco Quaglia
romolo.marotta@gmail.com, mianni@dis.uniroma1.it, pellegrini@dis.uniroma1.it, quaglia@dis.uniroma1.it
DIAG – Sapienza, University of Rome

ABSTRACT

The large diffusion of shared-memory multi-core machines has impacted the way Parallel Discrete Event Simulation (PDES) engines are built. While they were originally conceived as data-partitioned platforms, where each thread is in charge of managing a subset of simulation objects, nowadays the trend is to shift towards share-everything settings. In this scenario, any thread can (in principle) take care of CPU-dispatching pending events bound to whichever simulation object, which helps to fully share the load across the available CPU-cores. Hence, a fundamental aspect to be tackled is to provide an efficient globally-shared pending events' set from which multiple worker threads can concurrently extract events to be processed, and into which they can concurrently insert new produced events to be processed in the future. To cope with this aspect, we present the design and implementation of a concurrent non-blocking pending events' set data structure, which can be seen as a variant of a classical calendar queue. Early experimental data collected with a synthetic stress test are reported, showing excellent scalability of our proposal on a machine equipped with 32 CPU-cores.

CCS Concepts

•Theory of computation → Data structures design and analysis; Shared memory algorithms; •Computing methodologies → Discrete-event simulation;

1. INTRODUCTION

Parallel Discrete Event Simulation (PDES) is a well known method to speedup the execution of large/complex discrete event models [9]. The core concept it relies on is the partitioning of the model into different simulation objects, interacting via cross-scheduling of events. Multiple threads take care of concurrently executing events bound to the objects, and the trajectories of the state updates of different objects is driven by synchronization protocols (e.g. [6, 15]) aimed at

SIMUTOOLS 2016, August 22-23, Prague, Czech Republic

Most of the historical proposals along the path of devising/building efficient PDES platforms are based on the notion of "assignment" of objects to threads. In particular, each thread running within the PDES system is in charge of handling the execution of a subset of the simulation objects, by also managing the corresponding pools of their pending events in isolation (with respect to the execution of other threads). In this scenario, load balancing has been supported by periodically migrating objects (and their associated event pools) across threads according to different policies [18, 5, 10, 3]. Still, the objects and their pools are accessed in isolation by threads after any rebalance operation takes place.

However, the advent and large diffusion of shared-memory multi-core machines led to a shift in the design of PDES environments. In particular, the rising approach is to slide towards a share-everything paradigm, where the binding between threads and objects has (as an extreme) a lifetime equal to the processing of individual events. Examples of PDES platforms adhering to this paradigm have been envisaged in, e.g., [21, 7, 13, 8]. With this organization, event pools are no longer accessed by threads in isolation, rather in a shared mode. This is done in order to assign the highest priority pending events (i.e., those with lower timestamps) destined to whichever simulation object to any thread that has already finished processing its last assigned one. Multiple threads becoming free can therefore poll some shared event pool to extract the lowest-timestamp event concurrently. Additionally, they can concurrently access the pool to post newly-scheduled events resulting from the processing activities at the involved objects.

Although the problem of optimizing the performance of event-pool data structures has been long studied in the literature, most of the solutions are tailored for isolated (non-concurrent) accesses. In fact, the issue of optimizing event pools' management in face of concurrent accesses in PDES systems has only recently attracted attention by the research community (see, e.g., [11]) even though concurrent data structures for managing (ordered) sets have been proposed [12, 22] long before.

In this paper we present a non-blocking (lock-free) concurrent pending events' pool data structure, and its management logic, which also shows an amortized $O(1)$ time complexity. The latter feature is not provided by existing proposals like non-blocking (skip)lists [12, 22], which pay a linear (or at least logarithmic) cost for insertion operations. Our proposal is suited for conventional hardware since its only requirement from the underlying ISA (Instruction Set

Architecture) is the support for atomic Compare-and-Swap (CAS) operations, which is commonly found in off-the-shelf processors. As an example, such a support is offered by the Compare-and-Exchange (CMPXCHG) machine instruction in x86 processors.

We release our non-blocking pending events' set as free software[1], and we report in this article a preliminary performance study showing excellent scalability of our proposal when tested on top of a 32-core HP ProLiant machine. The tests have been carried out under synthetic workloads which, as we will discuss, are anyhow representative of stress scenarios one may expect when employing a shared events' pool within PDES systems.

2. RELATED WORK

Optimized event set data structures have been the object of several studies in the literature. One main thread of research has been devoted to time-complexity optimization to manage sequential insertions and extractions, namely when a single thread manages the pool of events in isolation. The seminal article in [4] presents the Calendar Queue, a timestamp-ordered data structure based on multi-lists, each one associated with a well-defined time bucket. It offers amortized constant time insertion of events with generic timestamps and constant time extraction of the event with the minimum timestamp. The Ladder Queue [23] is a variant of the Calendar Queue which is more suited for contexts with skewed distribution of the timestamps of the events to be managed. Compared to the Calendar Queue, the Ladder Queue entails a dynamic splitting of an individual bucket in sub-intervals (hence sub-lists of records) if the number of elements associated with it exceeds a given threshold. This is not supported by the Calendar Queue, which instead requires to resize the overall data structure, rather than a single bucket. The LOCT Queue [19] is an additional variant which allows to reduce the actual overhead for constant time insertion/extraction operations thanks to the introduction of a compact hierarchical bitmap indicating the status of any bucket (empty or not). As hinted, none of these proposals has been devised for concurrent accesses. Therefore, their usage in scenarios with workload sharing (hence event-pool sharing) across multiple threads would require global locking to serialize the accesses. As also discussed in [11], this would be detrimental to scalability.

A few studies, such as [2], have attempted to provide queuing data structures enabling parallel accesses. These have been based on the partitioning of the data structure and on fine-grain locking approaches, only blocking a portion of the data structure upon performing an operation. However, the intrinsic scalability limitations of locking still make these proposals unsuited for large levels of parallelism. In fact, as shown in [20], they can reveal effective for parallel machines with relatively small counts of CPU-cores.

Non-blocking management of sets has also been studied, and there exist various proposals such as non-blocking linked lists [12] or the skip-list [22]. However, these solutions do not allow executing all the operations (either an insertion or an extraction) in constant time. In particular, non-blocking linked lists pay a linear cost for ordered insertions while the skip-list pays logarithmic cost for this same operation. Given that algorithms in the non-blocking class may suffer from abort/retries caused by concurrent conflicting accesses to some portion of the data structure, aborting operations that may entail non-constant time can be significantly adverse to performance. We note that the likelihood of conflicts can be expected to increase for larger thread counts and for frequent accesses to the shared pool. The latter aspect highlights the risk for reduced effectiveness in PDES applications with finer grain events, where threads may spend a significant portion of their lifetime in the management of housekeeping tasks (like the management of the shared pool).

To the best of our knowledge, the work in [11] is the first to propose a non-blocking events' set data structure with constant time operations. This proposal is a variant of the Ladder Queue, where the elements are always bound to the correct bucket, but the bucket list is not ordered. Constant time is achieved since the extraction from an unordered bucket returns the first available element, which not necessarily corresponds to the one with the minimum timestamp. In other words, this variant is based on a partial ordering of elements, which allows to get rid of the costly guarantee of returning the lowest-timestamp event upon extractions. In fact, this proposal has been devised for PDES systems relying on speculative processing, where unordered extractions leading to causal inconsistencies within the simulation model trajectory are recovered (in terms of their effects on the simulation model trajectory) via proper rollback/recovery mechanisms. However, still for speculative PDES, some recent results [7, 21] have shown the relevance of delivering event records from the shared pool in correct order, as a means to build synchronization schemes able to exploit alternative forms of recoverability standing aside of the traditional Time Warp protocol [15].

Last, the recent proposal in [13] explores the idea of managing a shared pool concurrently by relying on Hardware Transactional Memory (HTM) support, currently available on few processors by major vendors. Insertions and extractions are run as HTM-based transactions, hence concurrently in non-blocking mode. However, the level of scalability of this approach is limited by the level of parallelism in the underlying HTM-equipped machine, which still appears modest. Also, HTM-based transactions can abort for several reasons, not only because of conflicting concurrent accesses to a same portion of the data structure. As an example, they can abort because of conflicting accesses to the same cache line by multiple cores, which might be adverse to PDES with (very) large data set.

Compared to literature results, our proposal is the unique that jointly offers: i) non-blocking concurrent accesses, ii) amortized constant time operations, iii) total order while managing timestamped event records, and iv) independence on specific hardware support.

3. THE NON-BLOCKING QUEUE

3.1 Basics

Given that we target amortized constant time for any operation, our non-blocking priority queue (NBPQ) is based on a multi-list data structure, inspired to the basic ideas underlying the Calendar Queue and its variants. Moreover, this strategy allows confining concurrent potentially-conflicting accesses to a same individual list, thus fully avoiding conflicts when concurrently accessing different lists. The time

[1] https://github.com/HPDCS/NBPQ

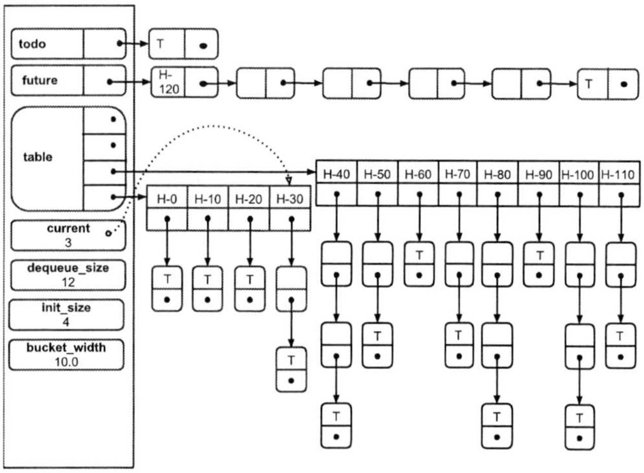

Figure 1: The NBPQ data structure.

axis is subdivided into equal slots and each list, that we also refer to as bucket, is associated with a particular time slot $[a, b)$. Each bucket keeps events with timestamp $T \in [a, b)$. The length of time slots is called *bucket width* and generally should change over time in order to control the average number of items per bucket. Similar considerations can be made for the number of buckets, which should be variable in order to cover a well-suited interval of time, depending on the locality of the events and its variation over time.

In our solution we explicitly focus on the second point since changing the bucket width would mean changing the strategy for referring buckets. In a fully non-blocking approach this should be done while still enabling lock-free accesses according to the old strategy up to the point in time where the new one is finalized. This type of approach will be the objective of future work we plan to carry out. In any case, the reshuffle operation changing the bucket size in our current version of the NBPQ can be executed as a critical section, which would lead to very reduced intrusiveness along time if executed infrequently, with respect to normal insertion/extraction operations on the queue (which are the ones whose concurrency needs to be optimized). Also, the selection of the new bucket size can be inherited, in terms of policy, from already existing solutions, a few of which are PDES-oriented such as [19]. Clearly, avoiding the resize of the bucket at all leads to the scenario where the amortizing factor for the cost of the queue operations is not directly controllable, and purely depends on the distribution of event records across the different buckets. Performance implications by this scenario will be analyzed in Section 4.

A representation of our NBPQ data structure is provided in Figure 1. The buckets are arranged in a dynamic array `table` in order to allow accesses based on indices. The queue uses the following variables: `current` stores the index of the bucket which contains the minimum timestamp; `init_size` is the initial number of buckets in the queue; `bucket_width` is the width of a bucket, i.e., the length of the time interval covered by each bucket.

Since each bucket covers a fixed interval of time, at start-up the whole set of lists covers a time interval equal to $[0, \texttt{bucket\_width} \cdot \texttt{init\_size})$. In order to be able to keep events with timestamp in the interval in $[\texttt{bucket\_width} \cdot \texttt{init\_size}, +\infty)$, we use two overflow stacks, pointed by `future` and `todo`. A variable `enqueue_size` is used to represent the left limit of the covered timestamps in $[\texttt{bucket\_width} \cdot \texttt{init\_size}, +\infty)$. Also, a variable `dequeue_size` keeps the right limit of the time interval covered by all buckets. `todo` is initially set to `null`. At start-up, we have `dequeue_size` = `enqueue_size`. The organization of our queue and its initialization are shown in Algorithm 1.

Algorithm 1 NBPQ object.

```
NBPQueue {
    pointer<Stack> future;
    pointer<Stack> todo;
    pointer<HarrisSet> table[32];
    integer current;
    integer dequeue_size;
    integer init_size;
    double bucket_width;
}
procedure NBPQUEUE(integer size, double width)
    new ←NBPQueue()
    new.todo ←Stack(0)
    new.future ←Stack(size)
    new.init_size ← size
    new.dequeue_size ← size
    new.bucket_width ← width
    return new

Stack {
    pointer<Node> top;
    pointer<Node> replica;
    integer enqueue_size;
}
procedure STACK(integer index)
    new ←new Stack()
    new.top ← null
    new.enqueue_size ← index
    return new
```

Along its lifetime, our NBPQ works according to the following rules: (a) dequeue operations return an event with timestamp in the interval $[0, \texttt{dequeue\_size} \cdot \texttt{bucket\_size})$; (b) the stack pointed by `future` contains events with timestamps in the interval $[\texttt{enqueue\_size} \cdot \texttt{bucket\_size}, +\infty)$; (c) enqueue tasks can only decrease `current`[2], while dequeue tasks can only increase `current`.

Upon enqueueing an event e with timestamp T_e the index is computed as $i_e = \left\lfloor \frac{T_e}{\texttt{bucket\_width}} \right\rfloor$. If $i_e <$ `enqueue_size`, the event is inserted into the corresponding i_e-th bucket (in sorted manner if the bucket is not empty), otherwise it is pushed to `future`. Finally if $i_e \leq$ `current`, to cope with concurrent manipulations of `current`, the index of the current minimum is updated.

On the other hand, the DEQUEUE procedure checks that the bucket at index `current` is not empty. In this case the first node of the list is removed and then returned, otherwise `current` is incremented by one and the check is repeated until a non-empty bucket is found or the value of `current` is equal to `dequeue_size`. If the last condition is true and `future` is empty, we can return `null` (the queue keeps no events). Conversely, if the overflow structure has some items, it contains the new minimum. Thus we have to move items from `future` into the array. The first step consists in doubling the number of buckets in the

[2]Differently from a classical Calendar Queue, insertion of events with timestamps smaller than the minimum one in the queue are allowed, due to the concurrent nature of the data structure.

Algorithm 2 Augmented Treiber's Stack algorithm.

```
procedure TRYPUSH(Node n)
    tmp ← top
    n.next← tmp
    return ¬ISMARKED(tmp) ∧ CAS(&top, tmp, n)

procedure DENYPUSH()
    repeat
        tmp ← top
    until ISMARKED(tmp) ∨ CAS(&top, UNMARK(tmp), MARK(tmp))
```

queue[3]. At this point a new enqueue of an event e', such that $i_{e'} \leq 2 \cdot$ enqueue_size, could be served by a new allocated bucket. To allow this without blocking, we store the current `future` in a temporary storage `todo` and we exchange the overflow structure with a new one, that covers timestamps in $[2 \cdot$ bucket_width $\cdot$ enqueue_size$, +\infty)$. Clearly the new **future** has an enqueue_size that is twice as the previous one. Now new enqueues can be served coherently, while dequeues have to move every event from `todo` into `table`. When `todo` is empty, dequeue_size is doubled and dequeues can restart from current = dequeue_size. At this point we have restored the initial condition dequeue_size = enqueue_size.

As a final note, although for space constraints we cannot provide a formal proof, our solution is correct with respect to the *linearizability* property [14].

3.2 The NBPQ Algorithm

Our NBPQ algorithm relies on a few baseline lock-free data structures, namely Harris' Sorted Linked List [12] and Treiber's Stack [24], to which we have added features suited for our purposes, as we explain below.

Harris' Sorted Linked List. In order to support events with equal timestamps, we have slightly modified the SEARCH routine of the non-blocking linked list by Harris in a way similar in spirit to what is done in [17], so as to retrieve a right node such that it has a key greater than or equal to the search key. Anyhow, we have left the capability to invoke the original search by adding a parameter that allows to switch between the two versions. In particular, given a search key k, SEARCH(k, $<$) calls the original version which returns a right node with key greater than or equal to k. On the contrary, a right node with timestamp strictly greater than k is obtained by using SEARCH(k, $\leq$).

Treiber's Stack. A major change to the original data structure algorithm has been put in place by adding the new DENYPUSH procedure, which prevents any enqueue from succeeding. This is achieved by marking the `top` field as it is done the for logical deletion in the Harris' list. After that DENYPUSH completes, any push attempt fails to add an event and only pops are allowed. Consequently, we have defined a TRYPUSH routine that tries to insert a node into the stack with a `CAS` only if the `top` field is not marked and it returns true if and only if the swap succeeds. This allows us to ensure that pop and TRYPUSH cannot alternate each other after a completed DENYPUSH. Finally, our stack maintains the left limit of the time interval that it covers in the enqueue_sizevariable. The complete stack algorithm, along with our modifications, is shown in Algorithm 2.

[3]As we shall discuss, the NPBQ exposes an API for the notification of a newly-computed commit horizon T for the simulation, so that the queue can simply shift the minimum time it keeps to T, and recover memory for obsolete buckets. This avoids that doubling operations eventually lead to unbounded growth of the NBPQ data structure.

Algorithm 3 Non-blocking ENQUEUE.

```
procedure ENQUEUE(event e)
    index ← ⌊newNode.t / bucket_width⌋
    newNode ← new node(e)
    INSERT(newNode, index)
    FLUSHCURRENT(index)

procedure INSERT(node newNode, integer index)
    repeat
        tmp ← future
        tmpSize ← tmp.enqueue_size
        if index ≥ tmpSize ∧ tmp.TRYPUSH(newNode) then
            return
    until index < tmpSize
    bucket ← table[h1(index)][h2(index)]
    repeat
        ⟨leftNode, rightNode⟩ ← bucket.SEARCH(newNode.t, ≤)
        newNode.next ← rightNode
    until CAS(&leftNode.next, rightNode, newNode)

procedure H1(integer index)
    tmp ← (ibsr(index) − ibsr(init_size) + 1)
    return tmp & (-(index ≥ init_size))

procedure H2(integer index)
    return index & (~ ( (index ≥ init_size) << ibsr(index)))

procedure FLUSHCURRENT(integer n)
    repeat
        old ← current
        ind ← old >> 32
        if n > ind then
            return
    until CAS(&current, old, (n << 32) | ABAMARK())
```

3.2.1 Queue Operations

The ENQUEUE operation (Algorithm 3) is split into two phases. The first one consists in connecting the new node to the structure. The INSERT routine first retrieves the `future` stack and then checks enqueue_size in order to discover where the node has to be connected. If it is lower than or equal to the linear index i of the event to be inserted, computed as $i = \lfloor \frac{timestamp}{\texttt{bucket\_width}} \rfloor$, then INSERT attempts to connect the new item to the stack with a TRYPUSH and returns whether it succeeds, otherwise it restarts from the beginning. The try-loop ends when either the TRYPUSH succeeds or the condition $i <$ enqueue_size is true. In this case we compute the location of the i-th bucket and we insert the node using the augmented search of the Harris' Sorted Linked List. This guarantees that events with same timestamps are managed in FIFO order[4]. At this point the insertion phase is completed and the event is connected either to `future` or to `table`. The second phase guarantees that `current` points to, or precedes, the bucket containing the minimum. This is done by the FLUSHCURRENT procedure that tries to exchange the `current` variable with a `CAS` until either it succeeds or i is strictly greater than the current value of `current`.

[4]The expansion operation which shall be discussed later might hamper the FIFO ordering. This ordering could be anyhow preserved by resorting to a per-node counter which is atomically incremented upon a push operation on the Treiber's stack.

Algorithm 4 Non-blocking DEQUEUE.

```
procedure DEQUEUE()
    while true do
        oldCur ← current
        index ← oldCur >> 32
        min ← table[h1(index)][h2(index)]
        ⟨_, right⟩ ← SEARCH(min.t, min, <)
        newCur ← current
        if newCur ≠ oldCur ∧ (newCur >> 32) ≤ index then
            continue
        candidate ← right
        rNext ← right.next
        if cand ≠ tail then
            isNotMarked ← ¬ISMARKED(rightNext)
            casRes ← CAS(&cand.next, rNext, MARK(rNext))
            if isNotMarked ∧ casResult then
                return cand.event
            else
                continue
        index ← index + 1
        tmpSize ← dequeue_size
        if index = tmpSize then
            tmpFut ← future
            eSize ← tmpFut.enqueue_size
            if tmpSize = eSize ∧ tmpFut.next= null then
                return null
            if ¬EXPANDARRAY(tmpSize) then
                continue
        CAS(&current, oldCur, (index << 32) | ABAMARK())
```

The DEQUEUE operation (Algorithm 4) searches for the minimum in the bucket corresponding to `current`. This is done by resorting on the standard search offered by Harris' List, invoked as SEARCH(`bucket_width` · `current`, <). This ensures that the left node is always the head of the list, while the right node has the minimum key in the bucket. Once the minimum is identified, DEQUEUE restarts if `current` is concurrently updated by another thread, otherwise it tries to logically remove the right node by marking it with a `CAS`. If it succeeds, DEQUEUE completes and returns after searching again for the minimum in the bucket in order to remove marked nodes. However, the bucket might be empty and the right node might be `tail`. Now four cases are possible:

1. `current` < `dequeue_size` − 1;
2. `current` = `dequeue_size` − 1, while `future` is empty and its `enqueue_size` is equal to `dequeue_size`;
3. `current` = `dequeue_size` − 1, while `future` is non-empty and its `enqueue_size` is equal to `dequeue_size`;
4. `current` = `dequeue_size` − 1 and `future` is such that `enqueue_size` ≠ `dequeue_size`.

Case 1 implies that the next time interval is covered by `table`, thus the next bucket is the candidate to search for the minimum. This is achieved by incrementing `current` with a `CAS` and restarting the operation. Case 2 means that we have passed all the buckets in `table` which cover the interval [0, `dequeue_size` · `bucket_width`) and no items are stored in the overflow data structure associated with the time interval [`dequeue_size` · `bucket_width`, $+\infty$), thus we can safely return `null` to indicate that the queue is empty. Case 3 occurs when `current` points to the last bucket in `table` and, at the same time, `future` is non-empty. It means that `table` can be expanded and every item in `future` can be inserted into appropriate buckets. We thus invoke the EXPANDARRAY routine, that returns true if `dequeue_size` is doubled at the ending of its invocation. If it returns false, then we restart from the beginning, otherwise we are sure that `table` covers the next time interval and we can increment `current` with a `CAS`. Independently of the result of this `CAS`, we restart from the beginning. Case 4 allows to detect whether an expansion is already occurring, thus EXPANDARRAY is executed in order to help in the expansion operation. Finally DEQUEUE completes only if it succeeds to mark a node or it meets the empty condition (case 2).

Algorithm 5 The EXPANDARRAY routine.

```
procedure EXPANDARRAY(oldSize)
    tmpFut ← future
    if tmpFut.enqueue_size = oldSize then
        newBlock ← new array[oldSize]
        if ¬ CAS(&table[h1(oldSize)], null, newBlock) then
            release newBlock
        tmpTodo ← todo
        if tmpTodo.enqueue_size < oldSize then
            CAS(todo, tmpTodo, tmpFut)
        CAS(future, tmpFut, new future(2 · oldSize))
    tmpTodo ← todo
    tmpTodo.DENYPUSH()
    while UNMARK(todo.next) ≠ null do
        top ← UNMARK(todo.next)
        copy ← COPY(top)
        while true do
            if successful insertion of copy in table as invalid then
                break
            else if a replica n of top is found then
                RELEASE(copy)
                copy ← n
                break
        CAS(&top.replica, null, copy)
        if top.replica≠ copy then
            retry-loop to mark copy
        retry-loop to validate top.replica
        CAS(&todo.next, top, MARK(top.next))
    CAS(&dequeue_size, oldSize, 2 · oldSize)
    return oldSize < dequeue_size
```

The EXPANDARRAY operation (Algorithm 5) has two goals: extending `table` and moving the elements from the overflow structure to `table`. The first step takes place only if `enqueue_size` associated with the current `future` is equal to `dequeue_size` of the invoking queue. Before moving nodes, we verify that the `enqueue_size` associated with `future` is equal to the `dequeue_size` read when the operation is started. This avoids that two expansions can occur simultaneously. The expansion of the array is performed by allocating the new required block and connecting it to the first level array with a single-shot `CAS`, because the old value is `null`. Before the stack could be emptied, we have to communicate to all threads that an expansion phase is taking place. This is done by making `todo` point to the current future with a single-shot `CAS`. The exchange is performed only if `enqueue_size`, stored in the stack currently pointed by `todo`, is strictly lower than `dequeue_size` seen when DEQUEUE is invoked. This avoids that `todo` is reset to its initial condition, while other threads are moving events. Now `table` is capable of storing items in an increased interval of time, but this information is not published yet. Thus we exchange `future` with a new stack such that its `enqueue_size` is equal to 2 · `dequeue_size`. Since the size of the array is always increasing, it is guaranteed that exactly one `CAS` can successfully update `future`, because new expansions cannot occur until `dequeue_size` is updated. When the new stack is installed, ENQUEUE sees a wider `table` than DEQUEUE. After that this condition is met, the stack referred by `todo` can be emptied with a sequence of consecutive pops, but we have to invoke DENYPUSH first. Preventing TRYPUSH from succeeding allows us to reach a stable condition in which the stack is empty. In fact, we have ensured that a very slow thread cannot push an event after the stack is detected as empty. Finally, when this condition is verified, the current `dequeue_size` is doubled with a single-shot `CAS`, restoring the condition `enqueue_size` = `dequeue_size`.

During a pop operation, a thread-local copy c of the top node of the stack is inserted into `table`, flagged as to be validated. Then, the original copy's `replica` field is atomically updated with the address of c using a `CAS`. After that, the unique copy corresponding to `replica` is validated, and the original node can be removed from the stack. In this way we avoid that a slow thread can copy into `table` an event which had already been dequeued.

3.2.2 Garbage Collection

The problem of releasing memory buffers is non-trivial in the context of non-blocking data structures. In particular, since we rely on Harris's non-blocking list, the extraction of an event from the NBPQ initially entails marking it as no longer valid. But the actual unlink from the list and the free operation of the buffer need to be carried out subsequently. However, at any time interval, it is not trivial to discover whether a thread operating on event buffers is still keeping a valid reference to the corresponding memory areas (e.g. for list traversing).

To cope with this issue, we have adopted the following strategy to realize a garbage collector which can be used to safely reclaim event buffers. Whenever an event is extracted from the queue, it is connected to a thread-private list, so that a reference to its memory buffer is never lost. Contextually, we expose an ad-hoc PRUNE(BOUND) API which accepts a timestamp value as its argument. It is therefore the responsibility of the overlying software level to properly invoke the PRUNE() function, whenever it determines that a set of events up to a certain timestamp value are safe to be deleted (since the threads within the simulation engine are working on successive buckets). PRUNE() simply scans the list of disconnected events `free()`'ing buffers associated with a timestamp $T < \lfloor \frac{bound}{\texttt{bucket\_width}} \rfloor \cdot \texttt{bucket\_width}$. This can be safely done without any synchronization, due to the thread-separate nature of the recollection lists where the event buffers are placed after extraction. Although this way of reclaiming memory requires an explicit interaction with the software exploiting the NBPQ, this is somehow coherent with the nature of simulation systems relying on pending event sets, e.g., because of periodical revaluation of the commitment horizon of the whole simulation.

4. EXPERIMENTAL RESULTS

We tested our proposal using a multi-thread program in which each thread repeatedly enqueues or dequeues an event with a given probability P_E and P_D respectively, such that $P_E + P_D = 1$. Each thread maintains a local variable `local_time` representing the timestamp of the last dequeued event. We tested with three different probability distributions of the timestamp increment (starting from `local_time`) of newly-scheduled events—uniform, triangular and exponential. Additionally, for each distribution we considered different mean inter-arrival time values $\mathbb{E}[T] \in \{1, 10, 50\}$. Table 1 provides the definition of these distributions. Relying on different distributions allowed us to assess our proposal when considering different patterns of the binding between event timestamps and NBPQ buckets. Also, continuous access by the threads to the event pool leads our tests to represent stress cases where the scalability (and performance) of some overlying multi-thread PDES engine would be essentially limited by the scalability while managing the fully-shared event pool. In other words we make our tests independent of any strategy (e.g. conservative vs optimistic) used to actually process the events and to keep causality across the simulation objects. Further, we make our tests not biased in terms of reduction of contention in the access to the shared pool depending on the granularity of the event-processing routine—the routine we run upon the extraction of an event from the pool only entails the generation of other events to be immediately injected in the pool.

PROBABILITY DISTRIBUTION	FORMULA
Uniform (U)	$2\mathbb{E}[T]\cdot\texttt{rand}$
Triangular (T)	$\frac{3\mathbb{E}[T]}{2}\cdot\sqrt{\texttt{rand}}$
Exponential (E)	$-\mathbb{E}[T]\cdot\ln(\texttt{rand})$

Table 1: Probability distributions used in evaluation tests and their formula given the mean value $\mathbb{E}[T]$.

All the tests have been run on a 32-core HP ProLiant machine running Linux (kernel 2.6) equipped with 64 GB of RAM. The number of threads running the test-bed program has been varied from 1 to 32. Each test ends when the total number of performed operations (which is independent of the number of employed threads) reaches a given threshold $\#OPS = 1280000$. This guarantees that for every thread count we worked with the highest concurrency degree (no thread is ever switched off before the ending condition is reached). Our NBPQ is initialized with a `bucket_width` equal to 1 and `init_size` is set to 32768. The PRUNE routine (which garbage collects obsolete buckets) is invoked periodically every 5000 completed operations. We also run the same experiments with a single ordered linked-list (LList) and a traditional Calendar Queue (CalQueue), both protected via a classical global spinlock to guarantee atomicity of concurrent manipulations. In these configurations, the invocation of the memory allocator for acquiring new event buffers is placed outside of the lock-based critical section, thus the critical section only entails actual data structure manipulations. CalQueue is set up with a maximum number of buckets equal to 32768.

In each run we sampled the $CPUtime$ parameter, that is the sum of time spent by each thread both in user mode and kernel mode. Since the employed machine was executing only our test-bed multi-thread program (and the operating system), $CPUtime$ captures the fact that in a blocking algorithm (say the tested global lock based approaches to manage the event pool) a thread actively waits in order to eventually acquire the spinlock. The throughput has been then evaluated as $\frac{\#OPS}{CPUtime}$.

In a first test settings (test 1) we configured an equal probability for ENQUEUE and DEQUEUE operations, say $P_D = P_E = 0.5$. Although the expected average size of the queue is zero, it is not empty all the time, allowing us to capture the base cost of our algorithm and the resilience to performance degradation potentially caused by inadequate bucket width (or the gain in case of adequate sizing). In Figure 2 we show the measured $CPUtime$ values for all the

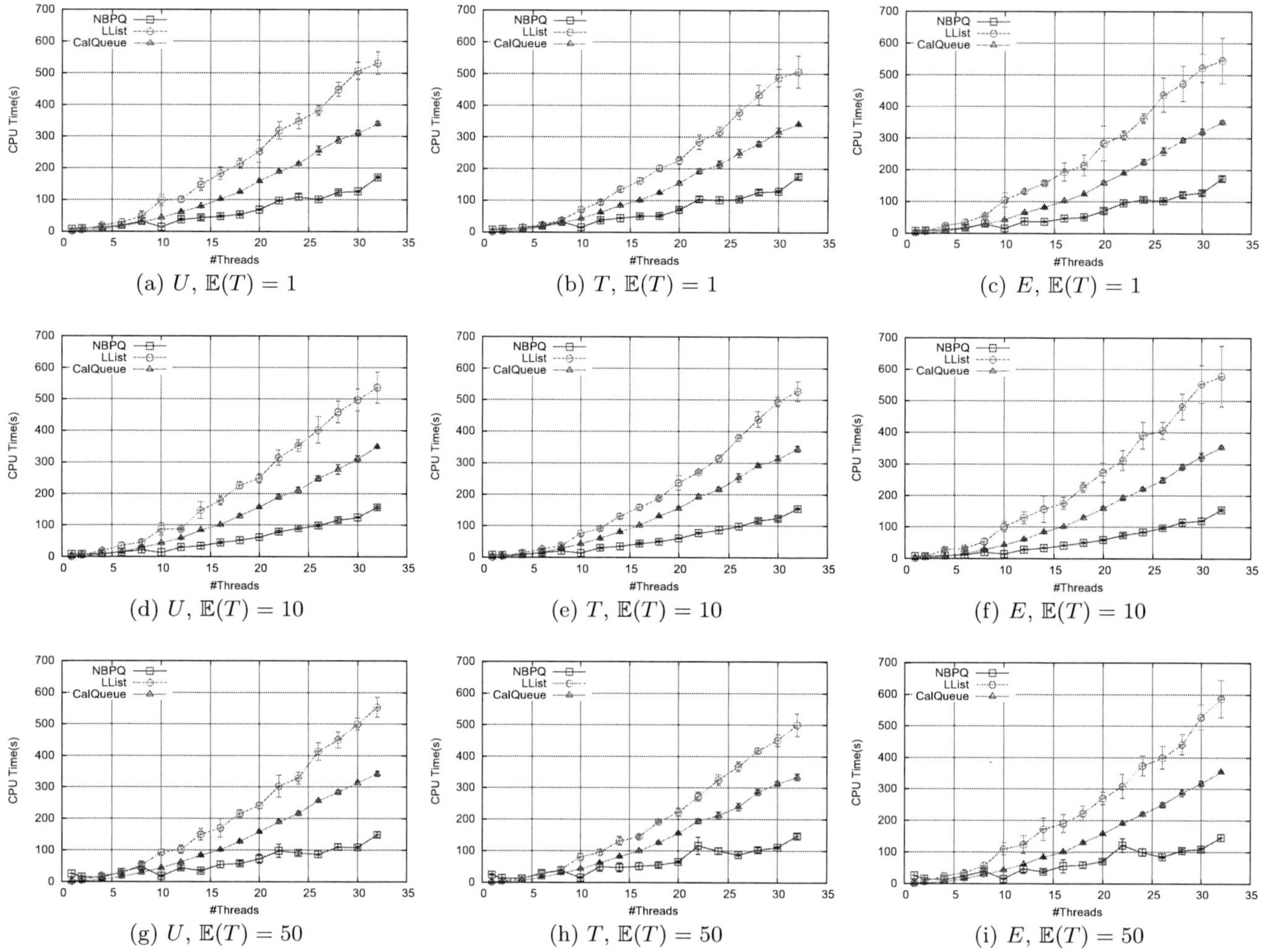

(a) U, $\mathbb{E}(T) = 1$ (b) T, $\mathbb{E}(T) = 1$ (c) E, $\mathbb{E}(T) = 1$

(d) U, $\mathbb{E}(T) = 10$ (e) T, $\mathbb{E}(T) = 10$ (f) E, $\mathbb{E}(T) = 10$

(g) U, $\mathbb{E}(T) = 50$ (h) T, $\mathbb{E}(T) = 50$ (i) E, $\mathbb{E}(T) = 50$

Figure 2: CPU times for test 1.

tested configurations of timestamp increment distributions and their mean values. LList and CalQueue both appear not to be affected by the selected settings, which is due to the fact that the queue contains no more than few elements at any time. Thus, the computation steps performed by LList for managing the event records are a few, while CalQueue is slightly more efficient thanks to its indexed access that spreads events in multiple buckets, reducing the number of items to be traversed per insertion. This leads to advantages over LList for large thread counts, since the global lock protected critical section lasts less time. However, the main advantages in performance (thanks to better scalability) are achieved exactly with the employment of non-blocking concurrent accesses as provided by NBPQ. Overall, our algorithm performs better than the alternatives because ENQUEUE operations are both fast and non-blocking, while the number of empty buckets is non-critical for DEQUEUE operations.

We note that detecting the queue emptiness is an operation somehow expensive in our solution, since it requires the scan of the whole `table`. This explains why our algorithm shows similar performance in all the tested configurations. In order to verify this hypothesis, we have repeated the tests with 32 threads and `init_size` equal to 2. This ensures that the `current` index is close to `table`'s size most of the time, thus detecting an empty queue requires fewer buckets to be traversed. This allowed achieving a speed-up ranging from 1.3x to 1.6x. The improvement is not larger since, with this settings, we moved contention from `current` to the Treiber's Stack pointed by `future` or `todo`. A solution to detect the queue emptiness more efficiently could be to use a counter updated with a `fetch&add` instruction, a strategy we plan to explore as future work.

In a second test settings (test 2) we pre-populated the event set and compared the steady state behavior of the global lock-protected CalQueue with the one of NBPQ. As discussed in [20], for the considered timestamp increment distributions, the steady state access time is reached after a number of operations that is five times the queue size. Thus we imposed $P_D = 0.3$ and $P_E = 0.7$ for the 30% initial part of execution of the test, achieving an expected queue size of about 153600, and $P_D = P_E = 0.5$ for the remaining 760000 operations. In Figure 3 we show how the performance of CalQueue is still not relevantly affected by the used timestamp increment distributions (images from left to right) and their respective mean values (from top to

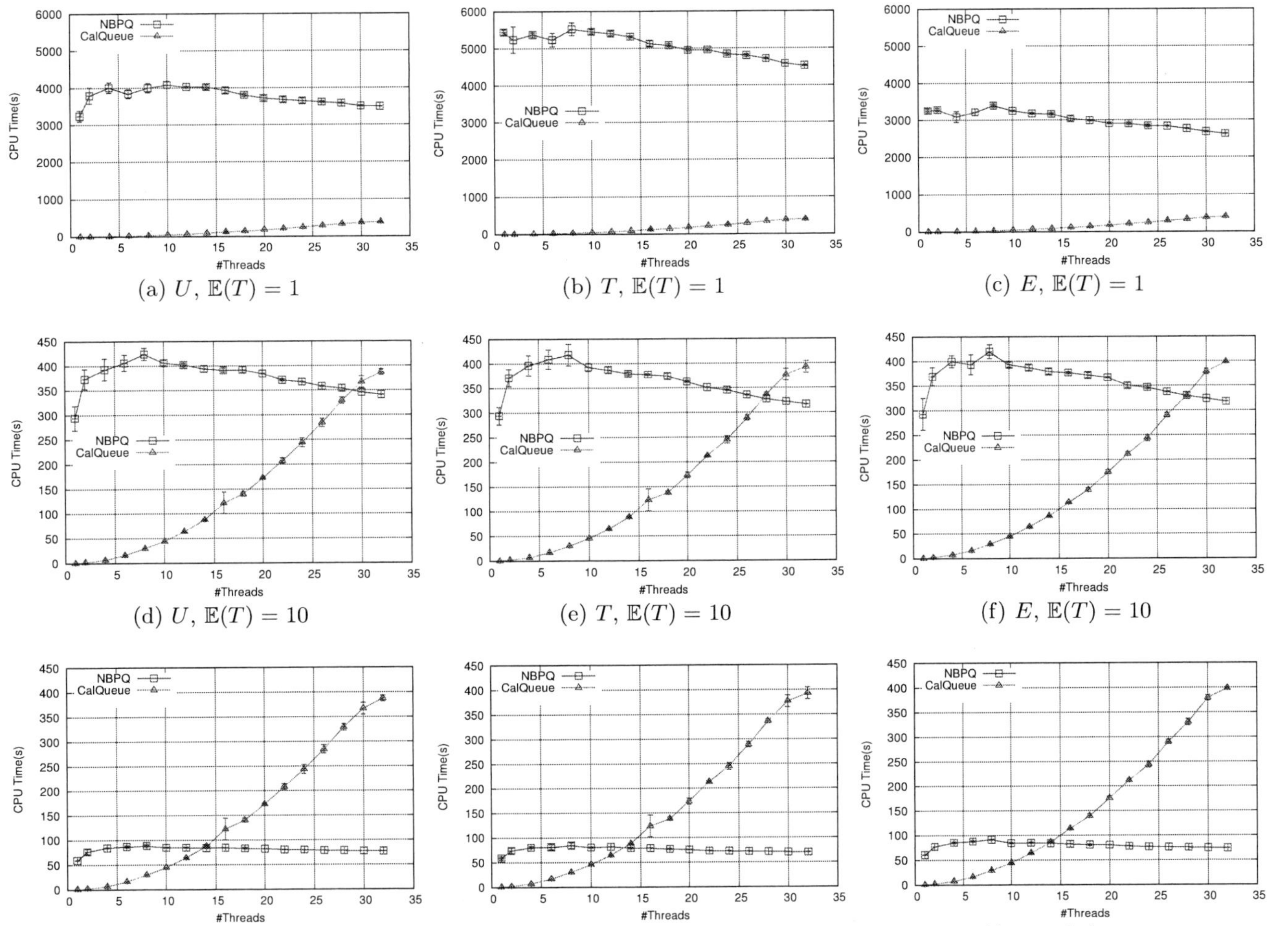

(a) U, $\mathbb{E}(T) = 1$ (b) T, $\mathbb{E}(T) = 1$ (c) E, $\mathbb{E}(T) = 1$

(d) U, $\mathbb{E}(T) = 10$ (e) T, $\mathbb{E}(T) = 10$ (f) E, $\mathbb{E}(T) = 10$

(g) U, $\mathbb{E}(T) = 50$ (h) T, $\mathbb{E}(T) = 50$ (i) E, $\mathbb{E}(T) = 50$

Figure 3: CPU times for test 2.

$\mathbb{E}[T]$	$\frac{BucketWidth_{NBPQ}}{BucketWidth_{CQ}}$
1	≈ 15000
10	≈ 1200
50	≈ 200

Table 2: Relative bucket size values.

bottom), due to its capability to resize the array and the bucket width, a capability not yet offered (in non-blocking fashion) by our proposal. In fact this leads to an access time that is constant with respect to the queue size.

NBPQ shows degraded performance when running with with $\mathbb{E}[T] = 1$ (Figure 3(a), 3(b) and 3(c)), since we did not rely on bucket resize in this experiment, and a single bucket becomes the container of half of the pending events, leading to spending 99.9% of the execution time in the ENQUEUE operation. However, a ten times smaller bucket width (Figures 3(d), 3(e) and 3(f)) leads to an execution time that is comparable with the one offered by CalQueue, while a fifty times finer grain bucket makes our non-blocking algorithm definitely outperform the rival in all the test cases (Figures 3(g), 3(h) and 3(i)). These results prove that, even if non-blocking scaling of the bucket size is not yet supported by our approach, running the scaling within a critical section would still lead to a big potential for higher scalability of our solution, with respect to the global lock-protected CalQueue. Also, the flat behavior of the response time of NBPQ (even with suboptimal bucket size) is a clear indication of its potential for higher scalability (say at thread counts much larger that 32) compared to CalQueue.

In Table 2 we show the average ratio between the bucket width of our NBPQ proposal ($BucketWidth_{NBPQ}$) and the bucket width of CalQueue at steady state ($BucketWidth_{CQ}$), just depending on its dynamical resize. A value of this ratio close to 1 means that the statically-selected bucket size used in NBPQ is close to the well suited value dynamically recomputed by the CalQueue algorithm. When this ratio is about 1000:1, the performance of the two queueing data structures under high contention (larger thread counts) is comparable. This is an interesting result, still indicating that, in order to achieve scalability with a non-blocking queue based on calendars, it is not mandatory to guess an optimal width of the bucket. In fact, we only need that buckets are short enough

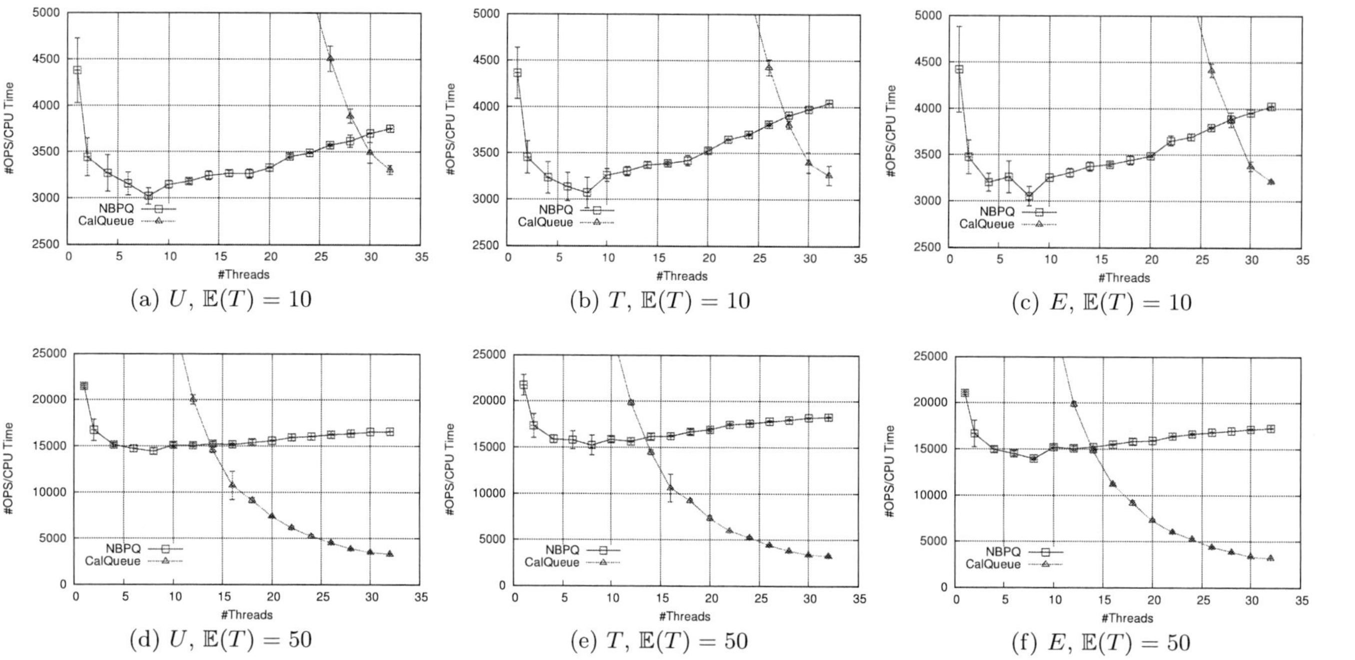

Figure 4: Thread throughput for test 2.

to guarantee fast ENQUEUE operations. However, given that we use non-blocking lists, these can be up to 1000 times longer than the counterpart blocking alternatives.

Still reasoning about the ability of NBPQ to efficiently handle longer lists in the buckets, let us assume to have p threads in the system. When one thread is accessing the global lock-protected CalQueue for a time interval k, the other $p-1$ threads could be waiting for the access the same amount of time k. Thus the average access time of each thread is $O(p \cdot k)$. Ideally, in order to provide a non-blocking priority queue as fast as the blocking CalQueue we can spend up to $O(p \cdot k)$ time per operation, thus we could choose a bucket p times wider than the optimal size. However, given that our experiments have been run with up to 32 threads, the ideal ratio among the buckets size in the two scenarios (blocking vs non-blocking) is significantly lower than the one we measured. The reason for this discrepancy stands in the usage of spinlocks, which have been shown to make threads in a critical section run slower by a factor that depends on actual contention [1]. Hence, when we have $p-1$ threads that are spinning, the thread holding the lock runs $O(p)$ times slower. It means that a thread completes an operation after $O(p^2 k)$ time. Thus to reach a comparable execution time with p threads, our non-blocking algorithm can run up to $O(p^2)$ times slower, which is achieved just when processing many more elements in the ENQUEUE operation.

In other words increasing the per-thread work for ENQUEUE operations is not a dramatic choice provided that we can handle more ENQUEUE operations at a time and these are in buckets that do not contain the minimum. DEQUEUE operations are not significantly affected by the bucket width, which only determines the length of the scan to find the next non-empty bucket. Indeed, a DEQUEUE from a non-empty bucket consists in trying a `CAS` on the first unmarked node, but in case of an unsuccessful exchange we can restart from the beginning of the bucket. On the contrary, the search for a non-empty bucket takes advantage from an increased width, because it allows DEQUEUE operations to scan a lower number of buckets. Moreover, even if NBPQ executes as fast as CalQueue, it still takes advantage from the absence of adverse effects caused by spinlocking. In fact, as shown in Figures 4(a), 4(b) and 4(c), the per-thread throughput is increased, still suggesting how NBPQ could exploit more processors if available. On the contrary, a bucket 200 times larger than the optimum makes the throughput of each thread stable (see Figures 4(d), 4(e) and 4(f)), showing that our algorithm is working at its maximum capability.

5. CONCLUSIONS AND FUTURE WORK

In this paper we have presented NBPQ, a non-blocking implementation of a priority queue for the pending event set, explicitly targeting PDES systems organized according to the multi-threaded paradigm and where the workload distribution among the threads is (fully) driven by the share everything model. Our proposal allows multiple concurrent threads to perform enqueue/dequeue operations on the pending event set without the need for using locking primitives. From our experimental assessment, our proposal looks promising under various execution (i.e., event generation/extraction) patterns and for different scaling levels.

Future work is planned along multiple directions. On the one hand, as mentioned, we plan to devise a more efficient way to detect the queue emptiness, by relying on the atomic `fetch&add` primitive. On the other hand, we plan to extensively test our implementation on real environments, such as the PDES platforms in [7, 16, 21] oriented to workload share across worker threads, and with real world applications. Finally, we plan to design a non-blocking technique to allow the resize of the bucket width at runtime, thus enabling its dynamical adaptation to variations in the events' timestamps generation pattern. This would lead to a priority queue that is scalable (an already achieved target) and which is able to provide optimized performance in face of different workloads.

Acknowledgements

Mauro Ianni and Alessandro Pellegrini are also working with Value Up S.r.l., an InResLab partner. This work is partially supported by the WFDA: "Wait-Free Synchronization Algorithms in High Performance Data Processing on Multi-Core Environments" project funded with the support of MISE research funds.

6. REFERENCES

[1] T. E. Anderson. The performance of spin lock alternatives for shared-memory multiprocessors. *IEEE Transactions on Parallel and Distributed Systems*, 1(1):6–16, 1990.

[2] R. Ayani. LR-Algorithm: concurrent operations on priority queues. In *Proceedings of the 2nd IEEE Symposium on Parallel and Distributed Processing*, SPDP, pages 22–25, Dallas, TX, USA, 1990. IEEE Computer Society.

[3] A. Boukerche and S. K. Das. Dynamic load balancing strategies for conservative parallel simulations. In *Proceedings of the 11th Workshop on Parallel and Distributed Simulation*, PADS, pages 20–28, 1997.

[4] R. Brown. Calendar queues: a fast O(1) priority queue implementation for the simulation event set problem. *Communications of the ACM*, 31(10):1220–1227, 1988.

[5] C. D. Carothers and R. M. Fujimoto. Efficient execution of Time Warp programs on heterogeneous, NOW platforms. *IEEE Transactions on Parallel and Distributed Systems*, 11(3):299–317, 2000.

[6] K. M. Chandy and J. Misra. Distributed simulation: A case study in design and verification of distributed programs. *IEEE Transactions on Software Engineering*, SE-S5(5):440–452, 1979.

[7] D. Cingolani, A. Pellegrini, and F. Quaglia. RAMSES: Reversibility-based agent modeling and simulation environment with speculation support. In *Proceedings of the 3rd Workshop on Parallel and Distributed Agent-Based Simulations*, PADABS, pages 466–478, Vienna, Austria, 2015. LNCS, Springer-Verlag.

[8] T. Dickman, S. Gupta, and P. A. Wilsey. Event pool structures for PDES on many-core Beowulf clusters. In *Proceedings of the 2013 ACM SIGSIM conference on Principles of advanced discrete simulation*, pages 103–114. ACM Press, 2013.

[9] R. M. Fujimoto. Parallel discrete event simulation. *Communications of the ACM*, 33(10):30–53, 1990.

[10] D. W. Glazer and C. Tropper. On process migration and load balancing in Time Warp. *IEEE Transactions Parallel Distrib. Syst.*, 4(3):318–327, 1993.

[11] S. Gupta and P. A. Wilsey. Lock-free pending event set management in time warp. In *Proceedings of the 2014 ACM SIGSIM conference on Principles of advanced discrete simulation*, PADS, pages 15–26. ACM Press, 2014.

[12] T. Harris. A pragmatic implementation of non-blocking linked-lists. In J. Welch, editor, *Distributed Computing*, volume 2180, pages 300–314. Springer Berlin/Heidelberg, 2001.

[13] J. Hay and P. A. Wilsey. Experiments with Hardware-based Transactional Memory in Parallel Simulation. In *Proceedings of the 3rd ACM Conference on SIGSIM-Principles of Advanced Discrete Simulation*, SIGSIM-PADS, pages 75–86, New York, New York, USA, 2015. ACM Press.

[14] M. P. Herlihy and J. M. Wing. Linearizability: a correctness condition for concurrent objects. *ACM Transactions on Programming Languages and Systems*, 12(3):463–492, 1990.

[15] D. R. Jefferson. Virtual Time. *ACM Transactions on Programming Languages and System*, 7(3):404–425, 1985.

[16] D. E. Martin, T. J. McBrayer, and P. A. Wilsey. WARPED: A Time Warp simulation kernel for analysis and application development. In *Proceedings of the 29th Hawaii International Conference on System Sciences. Volume 1: Software Technology and Architecture*, HICSS, pages 383–386. IEEE Computer Society, 1996.

[17] A. Pellegrini, S. Peluso, F. Quaglia, and R. Vitali. Transparent speculative parallelization of discrete event simulation applications using global variables. *International Journal of Parallel Programming*, apr 2016.

[18] S. Peluso, D. Didona, and F. Quaglia. Supports for transparent object-migration in PDES systems. *Journal of Simulation*, 6(4):279–293, nov 2012.

[19] F. Quaglia. A low-overhead constant-time lowest-timestamp-first CPU scheduler for high-performance optimistic simulation platforms. *Simulation Modelling Practice and Theory*, 53:103–122, 2015.

[20] R. Rönngren and R. Ayani. A comparative study of parallel and sequential priority queue algorithms. *Transactions on Modeling and Computer Simulation*, 7(2):157–209, 1997.

[21] E. Santini, M. Ianni, A. Pellegrini, and F. Quaglia. Hardware-Transactional-Memory based speculative parallel discrete event simulation of very fine grain models. In *Proceedings of the 22nd International Conference on High Performance Computing*, HiPC, 2015.

[22] H. Sundell and P. Tsigas. Fast and lock-free concurrent priority queues for multi-thread systems. *Journal of Parallel and Distributed Computing*, 65(5):609–627, 2005.

[23] W. T. Tang, R. S. M. Goh, and I. L. Thng. Ladder queue: An O(1) priority queue structure for large-scale discrete event simulation. *Transactions on Modeling and Computer Simulation*, 15(3):175–204, 2005.

[24] R. K. Treiber. Systems programming: coping with parallelism. Technical report, IBM US Research Centers, Yorktown, San Jose, Almaden, US, 1986.

Implement Domain Name System (DNS) on network simulator-3

Implement RFC 1035 on ns-3

Janaka Wijekoon
Dept. of Computer Science,
Faculty of Science and Technology
Keio University
Yokohama, Japan
janaka@west.sd.keio.ac.jp

Hiroaki Nishi
Dept. of Systems Design Engineering,
Faculty of Science and Technology
Keio University
Yokohama, Japan
west@sd.keio.ac.jp

ABSTRACT

This paper proposes to implement a domain name system (DNS) module to network simulator-3 (ns-3). The ns-3 is one of the well-known Internet simulators that provides the ideal simulation environment for network research. Despite its advantages, the ns-3 is not yet possesses a module to simulate DNS, which is an essential module required for Internet-oriented simulations. To this end, this paper implements a DNS module for ns-3 according to the design notes provided in RFC 1035. Moreover, this paper presents the implementation notes of the proposed ns-3 DNS module including its class structures, protocol message structures, name server application development, and host-to-IP resolver development. The proposed ns-3 DNS module is evaluated in terms of host-to-IP mapping, recursive DNS resolution, DNS cache management, and internationalized domain name support.

CCS Concepts

•General and reference → Computing standards, RFCs and guidelines; •Networks → Naming and addressing; Network servers; *Network simulations;*

Keywords

DNS; ns-3; DNS Implementation

1. INTRODUCTION

The Internet protocol stack consists of notations, e.g. IP addresses, that are used to direct users to servers [1]. However, such notations are not in a human readable format. At the early ages, the mapping between human-readable host addresses to IP addresses was dealt by sharing host-to-IP address mapping lists among the hosts. But, maintaining one master list for such mappings became hard to manage. Therefore, sharing host-to-IP address mapping lists eventually evolved to Domain Name System (DNS) [10, 16].

SIMUTOOLS 2016, August 22-23, Prague, Czech Republic

users to map human-readable host names to IP addresses [2, 16], and to redirect the users to the best replica servers [10, 18].

The DNS is a distributed and a hierarchical naming system that distributes the naming information among a large number of servers located on the Internet [2, 16]. When an application needs to translate a hostname into an IP address, the application soon becomes a client of the naming system and requests the host-to-IP mapping from a name server. The name server looks up its cache for the requested name and replies the cosponsoring IP address to the client if available. Otherwise, the server becomes a temporary client of another name server; the server sends request messages to other name servers until it finds the cosponsoring IP address and returns it to the original requester [16].

The study [5] provides live statistics of the Internet usage, and the statistics show that more than 40% of the world population has an Internet connection today. Also, Casteleyn et al. showed that rich internet applications (RIA) have been a subject to experiment since 2002 [12]. Furthermore, it incurs that RIA's designs, methods, and methodologies are the major topics of the research communities that are studying on. However, it is impractical to conduct experiments directly on the Internet because the Internet is the largest production-scale network. Therefore, network simulation software is a vital tool for developing, testing, debugging, and evaluating network protocols and services. Thus, in [11], Carniro pointed out that ns-2 [14] is the most used simulator among network researchers, and eventually, ns-3 [6] deprecated the ns-2 for more realistic simulations of network protocols.

ns-3 is a discrete-event simulator [6]. ns-3 supports most generic real-world packet structures, and the packets are serialized and deserialized as they traverse the network stack similar to the Linux network stack [7]. ns-3 emulates physical network cards using `ns3::NetDevices` and the `ns3::NetDevices` possess both IP and MAC addresses. Two `ns3::NetDevices` are connected using `ns3::Channel`, which represents a network communication medium (wired or wireless) links [3]. Furthermore, ns-3 supports both IPv4 and IPv6 addressing schemes. Hence, these features make ns-3 an ideal network simulator that provides a more realistic and real-world-like simulation environment.

Despite its advantages, ns-3 is relatively a new simulator and new models are currently being developed and incorporated into ns-3 distributions [15, 17, 21, 22]. It is important that ns-3 support DNS because ns-3 was introduced to simulate real-network-like simulations. However, thus far ns-3 does not comply with a DNS module, and thereby it limits the ability to simulate and analyze Internet-related network topologies such as Content Delivery Networks (CDNs) [18]. To this end, this paper proposes to imple-

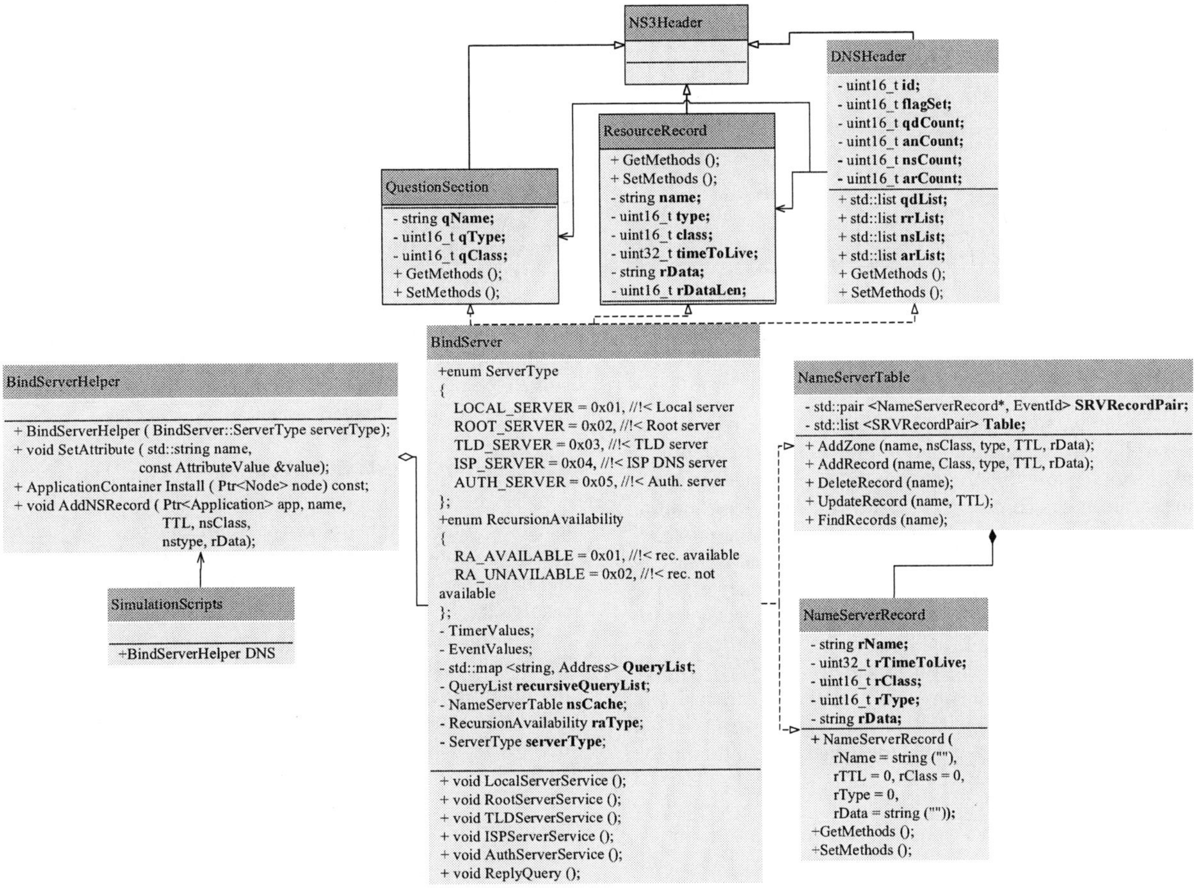

Figure 1: Class diagram

ment a DNS module for ns-3. The DNS module is implemented according to the design notes provided in RFC 1035 [16]. The implemented DNS module supports: 1) host-to-IP mapping, 2) generic DNS header structures, 3) recursive name server resolutions, 4) automatic name server resolution according to the time-to-live (TTL) values, and 5) internationalized domain names (IDNs) [2]. This paper is the first attempt of introducing the DNS module to ns-3 according to our best knowledge.

The remainder of the paper is organized as follows: Section 2 elaborates the implementation notes including the class diagram, messaging, name server cache, and name server algorithm. Section 3 provides the additional modifications required to the existing ns-3 modules, e.g. application, to support the proposed DNS module. Section 4 reports the obtained results followed by concluding the paper in Section 5.

2. IMPLEMENTING THE DNS MODULE ON NS-3

This section elaborates the implementation notes of the proposed ns-3 DNS module. Figure 1 illustrates the class diagram of the proposed DNS module and, its interaction with the ns-3 simulator is illustrated in Figure 2. The implemented DNS module can be segregated as follows: 1) class overview, 2) DNS message headers, 3) name server caching, 4) name server implementation and resolving algorithm, and 5) implementing ns-3 DNS helper class.

2.1 Class overview

As presented in Figure 1, the DNS module consists of seven classes. Subsequently, this sections explains each class in detail.

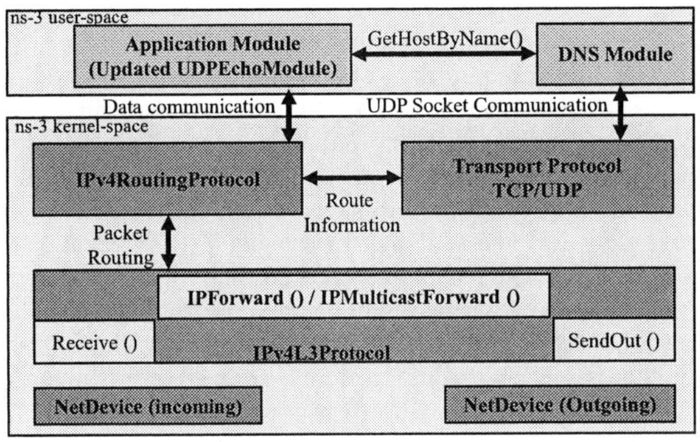

Figure 2: Overview of the implementation [8]

BindServer is the main class that combines other six classes together and, it provides the name server functions to ns-3. As Figure 1 displays, *BindServer* class defines five types of name servers: 1) root, 2) Top-level Domain (TLD), 3) Internet Service Provider (ISP), 4) Authoritative, and 5) local. Each name server is designed as a method of this class. Therefore, *BindServer* class executes a method that works for the relevant service according to the configuration parameters passed from a simulation script. A detailed explanation of how to configure and start a name server is provided in Section 3.2.

BindServer class further provides options to enable recursive DNS resolution. If the recursive resolution is configured to a name server, e.g. local DNS, that particular name server then recursively

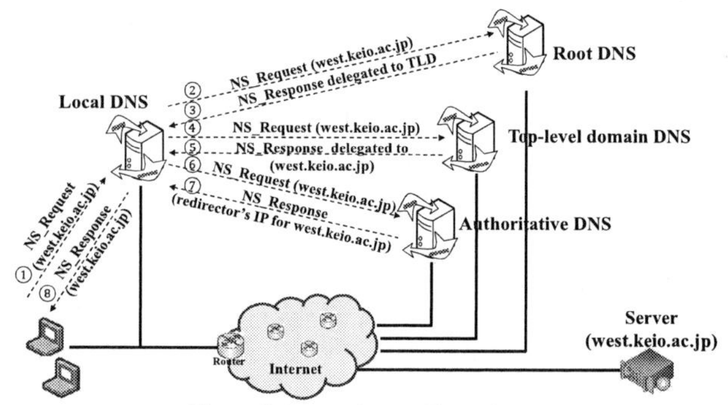

Figure 3: Recursive DNS resolution

queries rest of the name servers until it receives the IP address for the requested host name as illustrated in Figure 3. Subsequently, a name server should store the original requester that made the host-to-IP request during the name server performs recursive resolution. Therefore, *BindServer* class maintains a c++ map structure, *recursiveQueryList*, to store the IP addresses of the original requesters and the originally requested query names. When the name server resolves the IP address for a query stored in the *recursiveQueryList*, the server replies the relevant IP address to the original requester and removes the relevant record from *recursiveQueryList*. Moreover, the *BindServer* class maintains an object of *NameServerTable* class as the name server cache, which is named as *nsCache*.

BindServerHelper class is mainly designed to configure the DNS module through ns-3 simulation scripts similar to the conventional ns-3 modules [8]. Consequently, the *BindServerHelper* class provides methods to add a name server to a ns-3 node, initialize a name server, set the attributes of the name server, and to add *resource-records* to the name server.

NameServerRecord class provides attributes and methods that are required to cache *resource-records*. As displayed in Figure 1, the *NameServerRecord* class has attributes to store *name*, *TTL*, *class*, *type*, and *resource-data* of a *resource-record*. In addition, this class provides methods to `Get` and `Set` each attribute separately. Given that the c++ string variables support Unicodes, string values were used to define the *name* attribute. This approach enables the ns-3 DNS module to support IDNs. Nevertheless, the *resource-data* attribute is also defined using a string value instead of an IP address. The reason is that, according to [16], a *resource-record*, i.e. a host address, might be an IP address or a canonical name (CNAME) for an another server. Technically, this approach enable the ns-3 DNS module to store *resource-records* regardless the type of the record, e.g. IPv4, IPv6, or a character string.

NameServerTable class is used to implement the *nsCahce* of each name server. Primarily this class maintains a c++ list that stores the `cached-records` in an organized table structure. Each `cached-record` has two attributes: an object of the *NameServerRecord* and an ns-3 event. The *NameServerRecord* attribute has the actual reference to the *resource-record*, whereas the ns-3 event is prudently uses for automatic cache management. For an example, the ns-3 event attribute can be programmed to remove `cached-records` from *nsCache* after expiring the TTL time.

Furthermore, the *NameServerTable* class provides methods to `Add`, `Update`, and `Delete` `cached-records` from a name server. In addition, this class provides various `Find` methods for effective cache management. `Find` methods are designed to match either entire *name* or a partial *name* of a `cached-record` depending on the application and the requirement. For an example, a `Find` method can be used to match either exactly a given text "`west.keio.ac.jp`", or to match partial text such as "`.jp`" with a `cached-record` that has "`west.keio.ac.jp`" as the *name*.

QuestionSection, ***ResourceRecord***, and ***DNSHeader*** classes are implemented by inheriting the `ns3::header` class in order to use `Serialize` and `Deserialise` methods provided by ns-3. All class structures are designed according to the design notes provided in [16]. However, as previously mentioned, the attributes *qName* and *name* of *QuestionSection* class and *ResourceRecord* class respectively were defined using c++ string vales to enable Unicode support for the proposed ns-3 DNS module. Moreover, the *DNSHeader* class maintains four c++ lists to add *questions*, *recourse-records*, *ns-records*, and *additional-records* to a DNS header. This method is carefully implemented to the ns-3 DNS module in order to reduce the number of headers required to resolve DNS. `Get` and `Set` methods were implemented in each class to access the attributes individually.

2.2 Header structures

DNS messages consist of requests and responses. Requests are obviously questions to convert a *host-name* into an IP address. The response contains either an IP address of the requested *host-name* or yet a *name-record* of another name server which can be used to resolve the IP address of the *host-name*. A request might contain multiple questions, and so responses may include multiple answers. The header structures were prudently designed by directly inheriting the design notes from RFC 1035 [16] to provide such obligatory provisions. The implemented header structures are presented in Figures 4, 5, 6, and 7.

The *question section header* presents in Figure 4 was designed as follows: the *QNAME* filed was designed using a c++ string value to support UTF-8 encoding. Therefore, ns-3 DNS implementation supports host names that has characters other than ASCII. Both *QTYPE* and *QCLASS* attributes were defined as 16 bit unsigned integer variables. `Get` and `Set` methods were implemented to manage each attribute individually.

The *resource record header* presents in Figure 5 was also implemented according to the RFC 1035. Both *RDATA* and *NAME* fields were implemented using c++ string values. Rest of the attributes were implemented using 16-bit unsigned integer values. `Get` and

```
                                1  1  1  1  1  1
  0  1  2  3  4  5  6  7  8  9  0  1  2  3  4  5
+--+--+--+--+--+--+--+--+--+--+--+--+--+--+--+--+
/                                               /
/                     QNAME                     /
+--+--+--+--+--+--+--+--+--+--+--+--+--+--+--+--+
|                     QTYPE                     |
+--+--+--+--+--+--+--+--+--+--+--+--+--+--+--+--+
|                     QCLASS                    |
+--+--+--+--+--+--+--+--+--+--+--+--+--+--+--+--+
```

Figure 4: Question section [16]

```
                                1  1  1  1  1  1
  0  1  2  3  4  5  6  7  8  9  0  1  2  3  4  5
+--+--+--+--+--+--+--+--+--+--+--+--+--+--+--+--+
/                                               /
/                      NAME                     /
+--+--+--+--+--+--+--+--+--+--+--+--+--+--+--+--+
|                      TYPE                     |
+--+--+--+--+--+--+--+--+--+--+--+--+--+--+--+--+
|                     CLASS                     |
+--+--+--+--+--+--+--+--+--+--+--+--+--+--+--+--+
|                                               |
|                      TTL                      |
+--+--+--+--+--+--+--+--+--+--+--+--+--+--+--+--+
|                   RDLENGTH                    |
+--+--+--+--+--+--+--+--+--+--+--+--+--+--+--+--+
/                     RDATA                     /
/                                               /
+--+--+--+--+--+--+--+--+--+--+--+--+--+--+--+--+
```

Figure 5: Resource record [16]

```
                                1  1  1  1  1
  0  1  2  3  4  5  6  7  8  9  0  1  2  3  4  5
+--+--+--+--+--+--+--+--+--+--+--+--+--+--+--+--+
|                      ID                       |
+--+--+--+--+--+--+--+--+--+--+--+--+--+--+--+--+
|QR|   Opcode  |AA|TC|RD|RA|   Z    |   RCODE   |
+--+--+--+--+--+--+--+--+--+--+--+--+--+--+--+--+
|                    QDCOUNT                    |
+--+--+--+--+--+--+--+--+--+--+--+--+--+--+--+--+
|                    ANCOUNT                    |
+--+--+--+--+--+--+--+--+--+--+--+--+--+--+--+--+
|                    NSCOUNT                    |
+--+--+--+--+--+--+--+--+--+--+--+--+--+--+--+--+
|                    ARCOUNT                    |
+--+--+--+--+--+--+--+--+--+--+--+--+--+--+--+--+
```

Figure 6: DNS header [16]

```
+---------------------+
|       Header        |
+---------------------+
|     Question (s)    | The question for the name server
+---------------------+
|      Answer(s)      | RRs answering the question
+---------------------+
|      Authority      |
|      Record(s)      | RRs pointing toward an authority
+---------------------+
|      Additional     |
|      Record(s)      | RRs holding additional information
+---------------------+
```

Figure 7: DNS message [16]

Set methods were implemented to mange each attribute individually.

The *DNS header* presents in Figure 6 was designed as follows: all attributes were defined as 16-bit unsigned integer values (see Figure 1). The *OPCODE*, *RCODE* and other bit operators were defined as a single variable, *flags*, and the bits were set using bitwise operations. The Get and Set methods were implemented to manage each attribute separately. Since the RFC 1035 explains the *DNS header* attributes in detail, this document does not provide detailed explanation of each attribute; further information can be found in [16].

As shown in Figure 7, a DNS message consists of five sections: *header*, *questions*, *answers*, *authority-records*, and *additional-records*. The *header* section is always present in a DNS message [16]. In addition, all *resource-records* including *questions*, *answers*, *authority-records*, and *additional-records* should be attached to the *header* section according to the requirement. As presented in Figure 1, four c++ lists were used in the DNS *header* presented in Figure 6 to add multiple records for each *resource-record* type. Moreover, methods Add, Delete, Clear, and Get were implemented to manage each type of *resource-record* separately. Let us consider the following scenario for further explanation.

Let us assume a client required to find the IP address of "west.keio.ac.jp." The client creates and sends a request message by adding a *question* to the DNS *header* as follow: DnsHeader.AddQuestion (QuestionHeader). The AddQuestion method automatically increment the *QDCOUNT* of the DNS header. When the name server received the question, and if it possesses the required IP address, the name server then adds an *answer* to the DNS *header* by calling the following method: DnsHeader.AddAnswer (ResourceRecordHeader). The AddAnswer method increments the *ANCOUNT* of the DNS header. Suppose that the name server further needs to add an another *CNAME* to the DNS *Header*. That can be done by calling DnsHeader.AddARecord (nsRecord); method and this method eventually increments the *NSCOUNT* of the DNS header. The name server attaches the DNS *Header* to a ns-3 packet structure by calling the following method: Packet->AddHeader (DnsHeader), after adding all relevant *resource-records*. Finally, the name server forwards the *DNS Message* to the requester by using the UDP socket created on port number 53 [1,16]. Note that, in this implementation, an assumption has been made that the effective size of a DNS message does not exceed the maximum transfer unit (MTU) of a particular link, hence, the packets will not fragmented en route.

2.3 DNS caching module

The DNS caching module consists of two sub modules. The first sub module is cached-record, which is implemented using *NameSeverRecord* class. As previously stated, cached-record module provides the attributes to store *resource-records* in a name server (see Figure 1). In particular this module has five attributes *name*, *class*, *type*, *TTL* and *resource-data* to store the properties of the *resource-records*.

The *name* attribute stores the human readable host address such as west.keio.ac.jp. The *class* attributes intended to store the type of the network the cached-record is about. There are two classes presented in the internet; the value 1 indicates "The Internet" and the value 255 indicates "Any Class" as explained in [1]. The *type* attribute denotes the classification of the cached-records. For an example, the type value 1 denotes that the cached-record is a host address or type value 2 denotes that the cached-record is about an authoritative name server. The

```
Time delay = Seconds (TTL) + Seconds (m_rng
    ->GetValue (0.0, 5.0));
EventId removeEvent = Simulator::Schedule (
    delay, &SRVTable::DeleteRecord, this,
    newEntry);
m_recordsTable.push_front (std::make_pair (
    newEntry, removeEvent));
```

Figure 8: Add a new cache record

TTL value indicate, in seconds, how long a cached-record will remain in the *nsCache* as a valid record. The *resource-data* describes the mapped address for the *name* field. The format of this varies according to the *type* and the *class* of the *resource record*. For an example, *resource-record* will be an IP address if the *class* is value 1 and *type* is value 1, whereas the *resource-data* will be a name if the *class* is value 1 and *type* is value 5.

The second sub module, *nsCache*, is developed using the *NameServerTable* class. This class primarily provides a c++ list structure to maintain the cached-records in an organized manner. The *nsCache* maintains two attributes, one is an object of the cahced-record and the other one is an object of an ns3::event. As previously stated, the ns3::event attribute is used for automatic cache management. Eventually, the *nsCache* table looks as follows:

|name|class|type|TTL|resource-recod||<ns3::event>|

The steps given in Figure 8 are used to add new cached-records to the *nsCache*. As the figure explains, bind server first creates a new entry by passing the necessary attributes to *NameSeverRecord* class. Then, the bind server schedules an ns3::Event to call DeleteRecord method after TTL seconds. Finally, it makes a pair of objects above and pushes the pair to the *nsCache*.

Technically, the DNS module provides two methods to add cached-records to the *nsCache*. The first method is to add cached-records by calling the AddNSRecord method defined in the *BindServerHelper* class. A detailed explanation can be found in Section 2.5. The next method is to add cached-records when a name server learns a new *resource-record* from the recursive DNS resolution process.

The caching module provides an Update method to update both *TTL* values and *resource-data* values. Moreover, the caching module provides various Find methods (See Figures 9, 10, and 11). All Find methods were developed to match either a partial or a full string values. In general, the Find methods were implemented by using string matching methods provided in c++ string class because both *name* and *resource-data* attributes were stored using c++ string variables. A detailed explanation can be found in Section 2.4.

2.4 Implementing name servers

One of the main features of the DNS is autonomy of the system. The system is designed to add name servers to a hierarchy of name servers without contacting any authority or a central body [1]. Thus, each name server contains information that links the name servers up and down of the hierarchy. Whenever a particular name server receives a *name* to resolve, the server automatically contacts the relevant name servers within the hierarchy and finds the IP address that matches the received *name*. Finally, the name server replies the IP address to the original requester.

The ns-3 name server module is implemented using the *BindServer* class to provide this autonomy (see Figure 1). As previ-

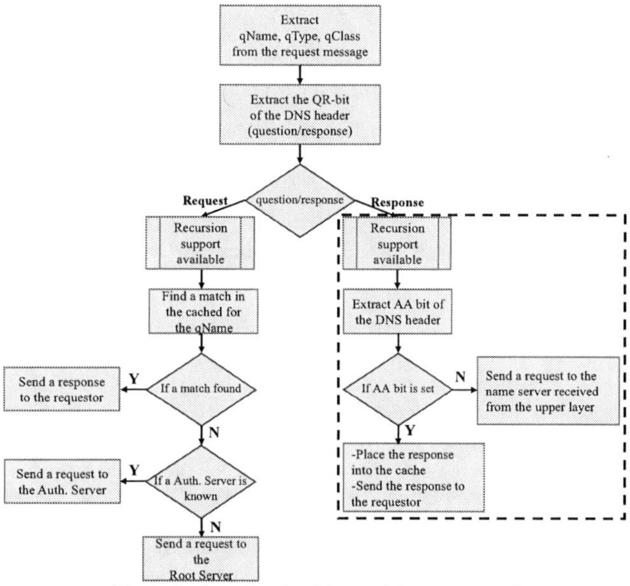

Figure 9: Steps involved in resolving a name [1]

ously mentioned, the DNS module supports five types of name servers: 1) Root, 2) Top-level Domain, 3) ISP, 4) authoritative, and 5) Local. Each server has three basic components: a communication module, a service module, and a caching module. The communication module is simply developed using a UDP socket bound to the UDP PORT number 53. The communication module accepts DNS messages, i.e. requests and responses, and forwards the messages to other name servers or sends reply messages to the original requester. As previously explained, the caching module is the *nsCache* that explained in Section 2.3. Furthermore, the name server module provides methods to the *BindServerHelber* class; the *BindServerHelber* class is used to setup ns-3 DNS module using simulation scripts. In particular, the name server module provide attributes: `ServerAddress`, `ServerNetMask`, `RootServerAddress`, `NameServerType`, and `RecursiveSupport` to set via ns-3 simulation scripts. Detailed explanation about configuring a name server can be found in Section 3.2.

Technically, the proposed DNS module maintains separate services for each above mentioned name server types. However, fundamental implementation of each service assumes the algorithm presented in Figure 9. As shown in the figure, when a name server receives a DNS message, the server exacts the question header using following method `questionList = DnsHeader.GetQuestionList ()` and retrieves the *name*, *type*, and *class* of the DNS request. After that, the server checks whether the DNS message is a request or a response. If the corresponding message is a request message, the server checks for `cached-records` that match the received *name*. Code segments provided in Figures 10 and 11 are used to find the cached records from the *nsCache*. If a `cached-record` is found, the server replies the query using the method explained in Section 2.2.

Otherwise, if the `RecursiveSupport` is enabled, the name server checks for an authoritative server that can use to find the IP address for the received *name*. If a *resource-record* record is found in the *nsCache*, the server then sends a DNS query message to the authoritative server and waits for the response. Otherwise, the name server sends a DNS request message to the Root name server to find the Top-level domain name server and the Authoritative name server. However, note that if the `RecursiveSupport` is not

```
SRVTable::SRVRecordI
SRVTable::FindARecord (std::string name,
    bool &found)
{
  SRVRecordI foundRecord;
  bool retValue = false;

  for (SRVRecordI it = m_recordsTable.begin
    (); it != m_recordsTable.end (); it ++)
  {
    if (it->first->GetRecordName () == name)
    {
      foundRecord = it;
      retValue = true;
      break;
    }
  }
  found = retValue;
  return foundRecordl;
}
```

Figure 10: Find a cached-record matches entire query name

```
SRVTable::SRVRecordI
SRVTable::FindARecordMatches (std::string
    name, bool &found)
{
  SRVRecordI foundRecord; // An iterator
  bool retValue = false;
  std::size_t foundAt = 0;

  for (SRVRecordI it = m_recordsTable.begin
    (); it != m_recordsTable.end (); it ++)
  {
    foundAt = name.find (it->first->
    GetRecordName ());
    if (foundAt == std::string::npos)
    {
      continue; }
    else
    {
      foundRoute = it;
      retValue = true;
      break; }
  }
 found = retValue;
 return foundRoute;
}
```

Figure 11: Find a cached-record matches a part of a queried name

enabled and the name server is unable to find a `cached-record` in its *nsCache*, the name server replies the question by setting the `RCODE = 3`, which indicates `Name Error`.

The section separated by a dotted line of Figure 9 is only implemented in the local name server. An assumption has been maid that the `RecursiveSupport` was always enabled in the local name server. According to the Figure, local name server inspects the message for the `AA-bit` using `DnsHeader.GetAAbit ()` method when the local name server received a response message. If the `AA-bit` is set, the server then stores the DNS record in its *nsCache* and sends a DNS reply message to the original requester. Or else, the Local name server forwards the DNS request to the name server that is specified in the received DNS response message. Otherwise, the local name server also replies the question by setting the `RCODE = 3`, if the local name server is not configured with `RecursiveSupport`.

Both Root and Top-level Domain (TLD) name server services were implemented by assuming no recursion support as well as both servers do not send DNS query messages. Thus, those two services only reply the requests. Therefore, the communication modules of these servers were implemented by deprecating the DNS querying process. The ISP and the Authoritative name server services were implemented to support two methods. The first method is to find `cached-records` in the *nsCache* that matches exactly same as the *name* mentioned in the *question header*. For an example, the method explained in Figure10 is implemented to find a `cached-record`, which exactly matches the *name* of DNS query message.

If such record is found, the name server then creates a DNS response message by setting the `AA-bit` and replies the requester. In general, Such replies are always returned to the local name server because the local name server recursively queries the other available name servers (see Figure 3). Therefore, if the local name server receives a DNS response message that has `AA-bit` enabled, the local name server then caches the received *resource-record* and replies the record the original requester.

The next method is to find a *resource-record* of an authority name server for the *name* mentioned in the *question header*. Suppose that the *name* is `west.keio.ac.jp` and the server has a `cached-record` of `.ac.jp`. In that case the server uses the the method explained in Figure11 to retrieve the `cached-records` from *nsCache*. When the name server found such records, the server creates a DNS response message and replies the requester without setting the `AA-bit`. As previously mentioned, suppose that the local name server receives that record. In that case, the local name server caches the received *resource-record* and sends a DNS request to the server mentioned in the *resource-record*.

2.5 Implementing DNS helper

The DNS helper module is implemented by using the *BindServerHelper* class. The helper module instantiates a *BindServer* object and adds it to an `ns3::Node` object in order to work as a name server. Therefore, the constructor method, `BindServerHelper::BindServerHelper (BindServer::ServerType serverType)`, is implemented to accepts the server type; the constructor method creates an instance of a name server according to the passed server type, e.g. *ROOT* or *TLD*. Moreover, the helper module provides the method provided in Figure 12 to add *name-server* records to the *nsCache* via the simulation script. Consequently, the helper module leverages the ns-3 attributes to allow users to control the parametrization of the DNS module, and thus, provides methods to manage the ns3 DNS module.

3. ADDITIONAL CONFIGURATIONS REQUIRED TO THE NS-3

```
void
BindServerHelper::AddNSRecord (Ptr<
    Application> app, std::string name,
    uint32_t TTL, uint16_t nsClass, uint16_t
     type, std::string rData)
{
  app->GetObject<BindServer> ()->AddZone (
    name, TTL, nsClass, type, rData);
}
```

Figure 12: Adding name-server records

This section states the additional configurations and modifications required to run DNS module on the ns-3. The additional configurations can be categorized into three parts: 1) the changes made to the application module, 2) changes made to the "waf" build system, and 3) write simulation scripts to use both newly introduced DNS module and the modified application module.

3.1 Configuring the application module

The DNS resolving process is invoked by calling `gethostbyname` function in the Linux socket API. However, none of the existing `ns3::Application` modules are capable of resolving DNS before contacting the data servers. Therefore, a similar method to `gethostbyname` was implemented in the ns-3 to invoke DNS resolution when necessary. In this study, several modifications were made to the `UdpEchoClient::StartApplication (void)` method in order to call the implemented `GetHostbyName` method because this study assumed the `UdpEchoClient` as the client application for the experiments. The `gethostbyname` can be used in any client application by calling the `GetHostbyName` method presented in Figure 13 from any `StartApplication (void)` method, i.e., starting point of any ns-3 application.

The `UdpEchoClient::StartApplication (void)` method was updated as follow. Initially an UDP socket has been created and bound it to the UDP port number 53, which is the DNS port given in [16]. Also, a receive call-back function was set by invoking the following method: `m_dnsSocket->SetRecvCallback (MakeCallback (&UdpEchoClient::ResolveDns, this))`.

```
void
UdpEchoClient::GetHostByName (std::string
   name)
{
  if (m_enableDNS)
  {
    if (!m_dnsResolved)
    {
      Ptr<Packet> requestRR = Create<Packet>
     ();

      DNSHeader nsHeader;
      nsHeader.SetId (1); //FIXME (random no)
      nsHeader.SetQRbit (1);
      nsHeader.SetOpcode (0);
      nsHeader.SetAAbit (0);
      nsHeader.SetTCbit (0);
      nsHeader.SetRDbit (0);
      nsHeader.SetRAbit (0);
      nsHeader.SetRcode (0);
      nsHeader.SetZcode ();

      QuestionSectionHeader nsQuery;
      nsQuery.SetqName (m_url);
      nsQuery.SetqType (1);
      nsQuery.SetqClass (1);

      nsHeader.AddQuestion (nsQuery);
      requestRR->AddHeader (nsHeader);
      m_dnsSocket->SendTo (requestRR, 0,
   InetSocketAddress (m_localDnsAddress,
   53));
    }
    m_dnsResolved = true;
  }
}
```

Figure 13: Implemented GetHostbyName method

Finally, the `GetHostbyName` method was called to invoke the DNS resolution.

The `GetHostbyName` method is presented in Figure 13. The `GetHostbyName` method creates a DNS header and sets the necessary attributes. After that it adds a DNS query to the DNS header by setting the *name* attribute as the intended URL, i.e. `west.keio.ac.jp`. Finally, it adds the DNS header to a `ns3::Packet` and sends it to the configured local DNS server.

When the client receives the DNS response form the Local DNS server, the client obtains the resolved IP address by calling the `m_peerAddress = Ipv4Address (answerList.begin ()->GetRData ().c_str ())` method. Also, the client retrieves the TTL value by calling `m_ttlValue = answerList.begin ()->GetTimeToLive ()` method. After that, the client starts downloading data from the resolved IP address. Meanwhile, the client invokes `m_resolveDnsEvent = Simulator::Schedule (Seconds (m_ttlValue), &UdpEchoClient::GetHostByName, this, m_url)` method in order to reschedule an `ns3::event` to resolve the DNS after expiring `m_ttlValue`.

The `UdpEchoClient` module has been updated by introducing `EnableDNS`, `SetLocalDNS`, and `SetClientID` attributes to enable DNS resolution via a simulation script. In addition, from the view point of ns-3 system, the module name "'dns'" was added to the `<ns3Dir>/src/applications/wscript` file and solved the ns-3 module dependency problem. That is done by modifying the `module` command as follow: `module = bld.create_ns3_module('applications', ['internet', 'config-store', 'stats', 'dns'])`. The ns-3 DNS module was tested with ns-3.21 and ns-3.24, and however, above explanation assumes the latest ns-3 version, ns-3.24.

3.2 Writing a simulation with DNS support

This section elaborates the necessary steps that are involved in writing a simulation script to resolve DNS and download data from content servers. The simulation script is written by assuming the WIDE networks topology which is presented in Figure 15.

Figure 14 presents a sample simulation script, which uses both updated application and newly introduced DNS modules. As explained in the Figure 14, the `BindServerHelper` method is used to create a name server by passing the `ServerType` parameter to the constructor, i.e. `ROOT_SERVER`. After that, the `ServerAddress` attribute is used to set an IP address for the catered name server. As previously explained, the *resource-records* were added to the name server by using the `AddNSRecord` method. Finally, a client module is created by using the `UdpEchoClientHelper` class; client is created by passing the local name server's IP address to the constructor of the `UdpEchoClientHelper`. The `EnableDNS` attribute is then set to call the `GetHostbyName` method. After that, `client1.SetUrl (appClient.Get(0), "west.keio.ac.jp")` method is used to set the URL, which the client should resolve in order to download the intended content.

```
#include "ns3/dns-module.h"

using namespace ns3;
NS_LOG_COMPONENT_DEFINE ("DNSExample");

int
main (int argc, char *argv[])
{
// Step 1. Create nodes for routers, servers
   , DNS servers, and clients
// Step 2. Create links among routers,
   clients, servers and DNS servers
// Step 3. Create channels and add them to
   the links
// Step 4. Create the Internet stack and
   routing, i.e. list routing
// Step 5. Assign IP address to the links
// Step 6. Create and set-up name servers

// Set-up Root DNS by adding .com, .jp, .net
   TLDs
BindServerHelper rootNs (BindServer::
    ROOT_SERVER);
rootNs.SetAttribute ("SetServerAddress",
    Ipv4AddressValue (rootDNS->GetObject<
    Ipv4> ()->GetAddress (1, 0).GetLocal ())
    );
ApplicationContainer appsRoot = rootNs.
    Install (rootDNS);

// Add TLDs to the Root server
serverAddress = "";
std::stringstream rootDNSAddress;
rootDNSAddress << tldDNS->GetObject<Ipv4> ()
    ->GetAddress (1, 0).GetLocal ();
serverAddress = rootDNSAddress.str ();
rootNs.AddNSRecord (appsRoot.Get (0),
          ".jp"          /*domain name*/,
          86400          /*TTL*/,
          1              /*class*/,
          1              /*type*/,
          serverAddress  /*r_record*/);
// Configure rest of the name servers

// Step 7. Create and set-up clients with
   DNS support
// Pass Local name server address to the
   helper class
UdpEchoClientHelper client1 (localDNS->
    GetObject<Ipv4> ()->GetAddress (1, 0).
    GetLocal (), 9, true);
client1.SetAttribute ("EnableDNS",
    BooleanValue (true));
ApplicationContainer appClient = client1.
    Install (c1);
client1.SetUrl (appClient.Get(0), "west.keio
    .ac.jp");
}
// Step 8. Set UDP echo server and the
   necessary attributes
// Step 9. Run the simulation
}
```

Figure 14: Sample simulation script

4. EXPERIMENTS AND RESULTS

Several experiments were carried to evaluate the proposed DNS module in terms of host-to-IP mapping, recursive name server resolution, Internationalized DNS resolution, and configuring an authoritative name server to work as a load balancer. The simulations were conducted by using the topology presented in Figure 15, which is implemented according to the WIDE network's topology information. WIDE network is an operational testbed network for WIDE Project, and further information can be found in [9].

Simulations were carried out using ns-3.24 version; ns-3.24 was installed on a computer that is configured with an Intel i7-2600 CPU, 8Gb of memory, and CentOS 6.7 (Final). Five name servers were configured namely, root, top-level domain, ISP, authoritative, and local, according to the hierarchy displayed in Figure 3. Moreover, three content servers were used, and those servers

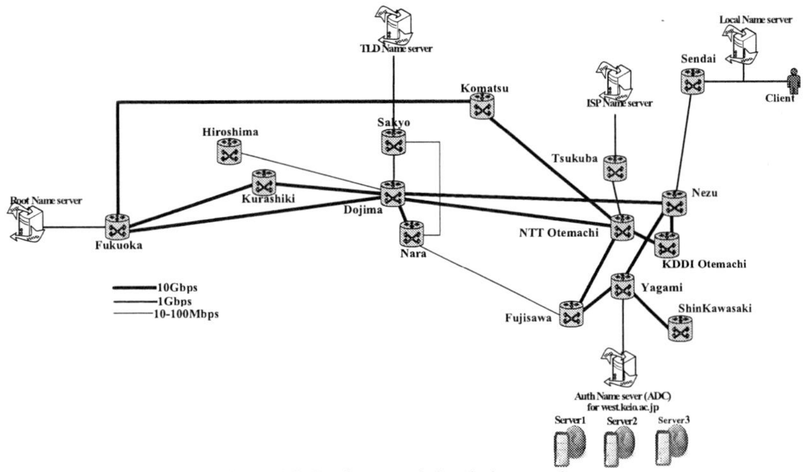

Figure 15: Implemented simulation topology

were attached to the "Yagami" router. Each server was configured by the name of `<servername>.west.keio.ac.jp`.The *resource-records* about those servers were manually added to the authoritative name server by using the method explained in Figure 14. Furthermore, the authoritative name server was configured as a load balancer, and the content servers were accessed via the load balancer as explained in [13]; the results are reported in Section 4.4. Since ns-3 still does not have a module to simulate HTTP traffic streaming scenarios, the experiments performed in this study used packet based simulation scenarios. However, following experiments sufficiently addresses the behaviour of the implemented ns-3 DNS module because the DNS resolution is independent of the application layer protocols.

Note that the following results were obtained by using static TTL values. For an example, the TTL values of the *resource-records* that stored in the local name server were 25 s. Furthermore, the local DNS server was configured with recursive resolution support. The client, which is placed at "Sendai", was configured to request two host addresses: 1) `west.sd.keio.ac.jp` and 2) はじめよう.みんな.jp in order to simulate full functionality of the implemented DNS module. Also, the client was configured to contact the local DNS when calling the function `GetHostbyName`. Figure 15 illustrates the server, client and name server placements.

4.1 Basic host-to-IP mapping

The client was configured to contact the local name server and resolve the IP address of `west.keio.ac.jp` for this experiment. The received DNS response message is printed at the client and the output is given in Figure 16. The output illustrates the DNS header including query, answer, and additional sections. According to the figure, the local name server replied the resolved server address as `server1.west.keio.ac.jp`, and the IP address as `172.16.10.1`, to the client. Moreover, the message displays the TTL value, class, type, and the data length. Also, it is notable that the DNS resolution time is about 0.012 s according to the output displays in Figure 16. The DNS resolution time depends on number of steps the local DNS server contacts other high level DNS servers, i.e., TTL value of the cached DNS records, and the network state such as link delays and congestion. According to the Figure 16, it can concluded that the implemented ns-3 DNS module successfully resolved the host-addresses to IP address as explained in RFC 1035 [16].

```
Waf: Entering directory `/root/Desktop/ns-allinone-3.24/ns-3.24/build'
Waf: Leaving directory `/root/Desktop/ns-allinone-3.24/ns-3.24/build'
Build commands will be stored in build/compile_commands.json
'build' finished successfully (2.300s)
———— [ Time: 225.14s client started resolving DNS ] ————
DNS header ID: 1
 Flags: 32896
 Questions: 1
 Answers: 1
 Authority RRs: 0
 Additional RRs: 0
Queries
 west.keio.ac.jp: type 1, class 1
Answers
 server1.west.keio.ac.jp: type A, class IN, addr 172.16.10.1
  Name: server1.west.keio.ac.jp
  Type: 1
  Class: 1
  Time to Live: 25
  Data length: 11
  Address: 172.16.10.1
———— [ Time: 225.152s client resolved DNS] ————
```

Figure 16: Host name to IP address mapping

4.2 Recursive resolution

The recursive DNS resolution scenario was simulated according to the scenario explained in Figure 3. As stated previously, the

```
Waf: Entering directory `/root/Desktop/ns-allinone-3.24/ns-3.24/build'
Waf: Leaving directory `/root/Desktop/ns-allinone-3.24/ns-3.24/build'
Build commands will be stored in build/compile_commands.json
'build' finished successfully (2.300s)
———— [ Time: 200s client started resolving DNS ] ————
DNS header ID: 1
 Flags: 1024
 Questions: 1
 Answers: 1
 Authority RRs: 0
 Additional RRs: 3
Queries
 west.keio.ac.jp: type 1, class 1
Answers
 server3.west.keio.ac.jp: type A, class IN, addr 172.16.10.1
  Name: server3.west.keio.ac.jp
  Type: 1
  Class: 1
  Time to Live: 25
  Data length: 11
  Address: 172.16.10.1
Additional RRs
 .jp: type A, class IN, addr 98.139.183.1
  Name: .jp
  Type: 1
  Class: 1
  Time to Live: 86400
  Data length: 12
  Address: 98.139.183.1
Additional RRs
 .ac.jp: type A, class IN, addr 192.54.93.1
  Name: .ac.jp
  Type: 1
  Class: 1
  Time to Live: 86400
  Data length: 11
  Address: 192.54.93.1
Additional RRs
 .keio.ac.jp: type A, class IN, addr 206.190.36.1
  Name: .keio.ac.jp
  Type: 1
  Class: 1
  Time to Live: 86400
  Data length: 12
  Address: 206.190.36.1
———— [ Time: 200.14s client resolved DNS] ————
```

Figure 17: Recursive name server resolution

local name server was configured with recursive resolution. Thus, when a client contacts the local name server, and a cached record is not found in *nsCache*, the local name server contacts either Root or TLD name servers to resolve the query. Note that the *nsCaches* of all servers except Root and TLD name servers were flushed in order to obtain the results.

Moreover, all name servers were configured to add the resource records to the answer section of a DNS message without deleting the existing answers. Finally, when the authoritative name server receives a DNS message, the authoritative name server first removes all the existing answers added to the answer section. Then the authoritative name server adds those answers to the addition section of the DNS message. After that, the authoritative name server adds the IP address mapped to the queried *name* to the answer section of the DNS message. Therefore, the DNS message contains the actual IP address that the client should contacts and traces of the answers given by root, TLD, and ISP name servers to the local name server. Finally, when the client receives the reply, the client printed the DNS header.

The obtained header output is presented in Figure 17. According to the figure, the total DNS resolving process consumed about 0.14 s. The client sent a DNS query message to the local name server to resolve the `west.keio.ac.jp`. According to the Figure 17, the local name server contacted the root, TLD, ISP and Authoritative name servers because the local name server does not possess the IP address for `west.keio.ac.jp`. Subsequently, the hierarchy of the servers added `.jp`, `.ac.jp`, and `.keio.ac.jp` to the DNS message respectively. Thus, those servers also added the IP addresses that the local name server should contact for resolving the hostname. Finally, the authoritative name server added `server3.west.keio.ac.jp` as the server name and `172.16.10.1` as the IP address that the client should contact in order to download the data.

4.3 Internationalized domain names

Reference [4] incurs that Internationalized Domain Names (IDNs) permit the people to use domain names in their native languages. Furthermore, IDNs allow that the domain names have characters beyond the letters (a to z), digits (0 to 9) and hyphen (-) because novel DNS implementations support Unicode encoding. Moreover, [4] states that, in the year 2014, 22% of the Chines population used IDNs in their Internet accesses. Therefore, as previously stated, the ns-3 DNS module was designed and implemented with Unicode support to store IDNs. Subsequently, several domain names such as `.jp`, `.みんな.jp` and `はじめよう.みんな.jp` were configured into the TLD, ISP, and the authoritative name servers respectively. The client was then configured to call `GetHostbyName` and resolve the IP address for the `はじめよう.みんな.jp`. The header information is printed when the client received the DNS response message. The output is displayed in Figure 18.

```
Waf: Entering directory `/root/Desktop/ns-allinone-3.24/ns-3.24/build'
[1428/2521] Compiling src/dns/examples/dns-example.cc
[2479/2521] Linking build/src/dns/examples/ns3.24-dns-example-debug
Waf: Leaving directory `/root/Desktop/ns-allinone-3.24/ns-3.24/build'
Build commands will be stored in build/compile_commands.json
'build' finished successfully (3.685s)
────────── [ Time: 200s client started resolving DNS ] ──────────
DNS header ID: 1
 Flags: 1024
 Questions: 1
 Answers: 1
 Authority RRs: 0
 Additional RRs: 2
Queries
 はじめよう.みんな.jp: type 1, class 1
Answers
 はじめよう.みんな.jp: type A, class IN, addr 206.190.36.1
   Name: はじめよう.みんな.jp
   Type: 1
   Class: 1
   Time to Live: 25
   Data length: 12
   Address: 206.190.36.1
Additional RRs
 .jp: type A, class IN, addr 98.139.183.1
   Name: .jp
   Type: 1
   Class: 1
   Time to Live: 86400
   Data length: 12
   Address: 98.139.183.1
Additional RRs
 .みんな.jp: type A, class IN, addr 192.54.93.1
   Name: .みんな.jp
   Type: 1
   Class: 1
   Time to Live: 86400
   Data length: 11
   Address: 192.54.93.1
────────── [ Time: 200.115s client resolved DNS] ──────────
```

Figure 18: Internationalized Domain Names (IDNs) resolution

As the figure illustrates, the implemented ns-3 DNS module is capable of storing, transmitting, and resolving IDNs. This means that the implemented ns-3 DNS module successfully resolves IDNs, which contains both Japanese and English characters in the *name*. The figure further proves that the implemented DNS module can handle `names` that contains both ASCII and Unicode characters. Moreover, the ns-3 DNS module is capable of storing both ASCII and Unicode characters together in a `name` and `resource-data` sections of DNS messages. The recursive resolution process consumed about 0.115 s.

4.4 Configuring a server as a load balancer

In this experiment, the authoritative name server was configured to work as a load balancer module according to the explanation given in [13]. Consequently, the authoritative name server was configured as application delivery controller (ADC) and the ADC was programmed to send the contact server names to the clients when they are querying host addresses. This method is implemented in CDNs, and thus, the purpose of this experiment is to test the basic CDN end-user redirection process [20] using the implemented ns-3 DNS module.

Three data servers were used for the experiment and the *resource-records* of those data servers were added to the authoritative name server using the method explained in Figure 14. Furthermore, the TTL values were set in both local name server and the client accordingly; very short TTL values were set to expire the cached records of the local name server by the time that the client contacts the local name server. Therefore, local name server

```
Waf: Entering directory `/root/Desktop/ns-allinone-3.24/ns-3.24/build'
Waf: Leaving directory `/root/Desktop/ns-allinone-3.24/ns-3.24/build'
Build commands will be stored in build/compile_commands.json
'build' finished successfully (2.317s)
────────── [ Time: 300.178s client started resolving DNS ] ──────────
DNS header ID: 1
Queries
 west.keio.ac.jp: type 1, class 1
Answers
 server2.west.keio.ac.jp: type A, class IN, addr 172.16.10.1
   Name: server2.west.keio.ac.jp
────────── [ Time: 300.191s client resolved DNS] ──────────
────────── [ Time: 325.191s client started resolving DNS ] ──────────
DNS header ID: 1
Queries
 west.keio.ac.jp: type 1, class 1
Answers
 server1.west.keio.ac.jp: type A, class IN, addr 172.16.10.1
   Name: server1.west.keio.ac.jp
────────── [ Time: 325.205s client resolved DNS] ──────────
────────── [ Time: 350.205s client started resolving DNS ] ──────────
DNS header ID: 1
Queries
 west.keio.ac.jp: type 1, class 1
Answers
 server3.west.keio.ac.jp: type A, class IN, addr 172.16.10.1
   Name: server3.west.keio.ac.jp
────────── [ Time: 350.216s client resolved DNS] ──────────
────────── [ Time: 375.216s client started resolving DNS ] ──────────
DNS header ID: 1
Queries
 west.keio.ac.jp: type 1, class 1
Answers
 server2.west.keio.ac.jp: type A, class IN, addr 172.16.10.1
   Name: server2.west.keio.ac.jp
```

Figure 19: DNS as a load balancer module

contacts authoritative name server at each time the client contacts the local name server. When the authoritative name server receives a DNS request message, the authoritative name server replies the query with the actual server name that the client should contact. Round robin algorithm was used for the DNS load balancing because the round robin algorithm is the basic load balancing method used in DNS systems.

When a client received a DNS response message, the DNS response message was printed at the client and the output is displayed in Figure 19. As depicted in Figure 19, the client receives a new server address at each time the client was resolving DNS. Nevertheless, it is notable that the server addresses are changed according to the round robin algorithm. However, the IP address of each name server record is same, `172.16.10.1`. That is because, as explained in [13], when an ADC is used for server load balancing, the ADC works as a reverse proxy server. Thus, it always returns the IP address of the reverse proxy server and the reverse proxy server forwards the traffic based on the URL.

Above reported results confirm that the proposed DNS module can be configured to the ns-3 as other generic modules. Furthermore, the proposed DNS module is capable of working as explained in RFC 1035 [16]. Moreover, the proposed DNS module can be used to simulate Internet applications such as CDN end-user redirection and server load balancing.

5. CONCLUSIONS

This paper proposed and implemented a DNS module to the ns-3. The DNS module is implemented according to the design notes provided in RFC 1035 [16]. The proposed DNS module supports following features: 1) host-to-IP mapping, 2) recursive name server resolutions, 3) generic DNS header structures, 4) automatic name server resolution according to the time-to-live (TTL) values, and 5) internationalized domain names.

Several experiments were conducted to analyze the behavior of host-to-IP mapping, recursive resolution, and IDN resolution. The results showed that the proposed DNS module works as a standard DNS module, and it can be used to simulate the Internet-based simulations on the ns-3. The results further confirmed that the modifications made to both applications and the "waf" system allowed to use the ns-3 DNS module without any malfunctions. Moreover, the test results shows that the proposed DNS module can be configured as load balancer module as well.

However, for the experiment purposes, only static TTL values were used on both name servers and the content servers. Thus, in [20], a novel method is proposed to calculate and set TTL values according to the states of a content server, e.g. a load of the server. Consequently, this study will further continue to analyze the behavior of CDNs in terms of using such dynamic TTL values. The source code of the implemented DNS module can be found in [19], and we welcome suggestions, further developments, and modifications for the future improvements of ns-3 DNS module.

6. ACKNOWLEDGMENTS

This work was partially supported by funds of SECOM Science and Technology Foundation, MEXT Scholarship for Research Students, Keio University Doctorate Student Grant-in-Aid Program, and the Keio University KLL Ph.D. Research Grant Program.

7. REFERENCES

[1] Chapter 2 - the internet protocol. In A. Farrel, editor, *The Internet and Its Protocols*, The Morgan Kaufmann Series in Networking, pages 23 – 77. Morgan Kaufmann, Burlington, 2004.

[2] Chapter 4 - traditional internet applications. In D. E. Comer, editor, *Computer Networks and Internets*, pages 49 – 79. Pearson, 6th edition, 2014.

[3] Emulation overview. https://goo.gl/ruuat4, Accessed:2016/Mar.

[4] Internationalized domain names. https://goo.gl/FdnHju, Accessed:2016/Mar.

[5] Internet live stats. http://goo.gl/EzIAer, Accessed:2016/Mar.

[6] Ns-3 network simulator 3. https://goo.gl/621U1M, Accessed:2016/Mar.

[7] Packets. https://goo.gl/inA6WA, Accessed:2016/Mar.

[8] Routing overview. https://goo.gl/k4IWxq, Accessed:2016/Mar.

[9] Wide network topology diagram. http://two.wide.ad.jp/, Accessed:2016/Mar.

[10] T. Callahan, M. Allman, and M. Rabinovich. On modern dns behavior and properties. *SIGCOMM Comput. Commun. Rev.*, 43(3):7–15, July 2013.

[11] G. J. Carneiro. Ns-3 network simulator 3. https://goo.gl/v9rd15, Accessed:2016/Mar.

[12] S. Casteleyn, I. Garrig'os, and J.-N. Maz'on. Ten years of rich internet applications: A systematic mapping study, and beyond. *ACM Trans. Web*, 8(3):18:1–18:46, July 2014.

[13] Citrix. Citrix netscaler global server load balancing primer: Theory and implementation. https://goo.gl/QvI5Va, Accessed:2016/Mar.

[14] DARPA. The network simulator - ns-2. http://goo.gl/hvuiPy, Accessed:2016/Mar.

[15] A. R. A. Kumar, S. V. Rao, and D. Goswami. Ns3 simulator for a study of data center networks. In *Parallel and Distributed Computing (ISPDC), 2013 IEEE 12th International Symposium on*, pages 224–231, 2013.

[16] P. Mockapetris. Domain names - implementation and specification. https://goo.gl/GNVpBY, Accessed:2016/Mar.

[17] H. Narra, Y. Cheng, E. K. Çetinkaya, J. P. Rohrer, and J. P. G. Sterbenz. Destination-sequenced distance vector (dsdv) routing protocol implementation in ns-3. In *Proceedings of the 4th International ICST Conference on Simulation Tools and Techniques*, SIMUTools '11, pages 439–446, 2011.

[18] E. Nygren, R. K. Sitaraman, and J. Sun. The akamai network: A platform for high-performance internet applications. *SIGOPS Oper. Syst. Rev.*, 44(3):2–19, Aug. 2010.

[19] J. Wijekoon. Dns-for-ns3. https://goo.gl/PCDI7w, Accessed:2016/Mar.

[20] J. Wijekoon, E. Harahap, K. Takagiwa, R. Tennekoon, and H. Nishi. Effectiveness of a service-oriented router in future content delivery networks. In *Ubiquitous and Future Networks (ICUFN), 2015 Seventh International Conference on*, pages 444–449, 2015.

[21] J. Wijekoon, R. Tennekoon, E. Harahap, and H. Nishi. Service-oriented router module implementation on ns-3. In *Proceedings of the 7th International Conference on Simulation Tools and Techniques*, SIMUTools '14, 2014.

[22] J. Wijekoon, R. Tennekoon, E. Harahap, and H. Nishi. Introducing a distance vector routing protocol for ns-3 simulator. In *Proceedings of the 8th International Conference on Simulation Tools and Techniques*, SIMUTools '15, pages 38–46, 2015.

Modeling and Prediction of Software-Defined Networks Performance using Queueing Petri Nets

Piotr Rygielski
Institute of Computer Science
University of Würzburg,
Germany
piotr.rygielski
@uni-wuerzburg.de

Marian Seliuchenko
Dept. of Telecommunication
Lviv Polytechnic National
University, Ukraine
m.seliuchenko@gmail.com

Samuel Kounev
Institute of Computer Science
University of Würzburg,
Germany
samuel.kounev
@uni-wuerzburg.de

ABSTRACT

Using various modeling and simulation approaches for predicting network performance requires extensive experience and involves a number of time consuming manual steps regarding each of the modeling formalisms. Descartes Network Infrastructure (DNI) is a data center network performance modeling approach that addresses this challenge by offering multiple performance models but requiring to use only a single modeling language. In this paper, we thoroughly extend DNI to support new networking paradigms like, among others, Software-Defined Networking (SDN) and Network-Function Virtualization (NFV). Additionally, we demonstrate how SDN-based networks can be modeled using DNI and how are they transformed later into Queueing Petri Nets (QPN) using a model-to-model transformation. In the analysis of the performance prediction accuracy, we show that automatically generated QPN models represent the performance of heterogeneous SDN hardware with maximal prediction accuracy error of 12%.

CCS Concepts

•**Networks** → **Network performance modeling;** *Network simulations;* •**Hardware** → Networking hardware;

Keywords

performance modeling, software-defined networking, data center networks, meta-modeling

1. INTRODUCTION

Performance modeling and prediction approaches help system operators to analyze data center performance at the system's design-time and during operation. Nowadays, data centers are becoming increasingly big and dynamic due to the common adoption of virtualization technologies. Virtual machines, data, and services can be migrated on demand be-

SIMUTOOLS 2016, August 22-23, Prague, Czech Republic

enforcing service-level agreements. This high level of complexity makes an accurate and timely performance analysis a challenging problem [6]. Furthermore, the network infrastructures shift towards virtualization with emergence of such paradigms as Software-Defined Networking (SDN) and Network Functions Virtualization (NFV).

In our research, we focus on the modern network infrastructures of virtualized data centers that leverage SDN or NFV technologies. The network infrastructures in such environments introduce several new challenges for performance analysis. Some examples of such challenges include the growing density of modern virtualized data centers (increasing amount of network end-points), the high volume of intra-data-center traffic (having its source and destination within the same data center), or the new traffic sources introduced in the management layer of virtualized environments (e.g., migration of virtual machines). For SDN and NFV paradigms, new performance-related challenges emerge as the classical hardware-based networking is now tightly bound to software running on commodity servers (e.g., applications in the SDN Controller in SDN-based networks, or virtualized network functions in NFV setups).

Data center networks can be represented in multiple performance modeling formalisms, for example, domain-specific simulation models, stochastic Petri nets, queueing networks, and stochastic process algebras. The modeling with a given performance model requires understanding of its formalism and the usual modeling steps. Thus, specific knowledge and experience with multiple modeling formalisms are required in order to benefit from the variety of their characteristics. Usually, such knowledge and experience is missing or it is limited to a single modeling formalism.

In [16], we proposed an initial modeling approach that requires to model the network using a high-level descriptive language named DNI (Descartes Network Infrastructures). DNI is a generic network modeling formalism and contains elements familiar to any network operator. That approach allows to use multiple various modeling and analysis approaches without requiring in depth expertise in the respective modeling formalisms. Using the descriptive DNI model as a basis, we provide model-to-model transformations to automatically generate predictive performance models without requiring the operator to have expertise in any of them. Network models that are built using DNI modeling language can be automatically transformed to various predictive models. In this paper we present new, substantial changes to the architecture of the DNI Meta-model and its model-to-model transformations.

1.1 Motivation

Software-Defined Networking and Network Functions Virtualization slowly become ubiquitous in nowadays networks. Most of the networking hardware vendors offer SDN-enabled devices and software solutions to bring more programmability into networks and move the network design from the hardware layer to the software tier. However, new networking paradigms impose a new way of the network workload processing and thus enable new performance bottlenecks that may originate from the software in contrast to the purely hardware-related sources of the performance degradation in the classical networks. Moreover, to enable support for SDN, the hardware vendors need to redesign their equipment by adding new processing workflows. This may lead to the emergence of new performance-influencing factors that were not present in the classical network architectures.

Many authors support the need to investigate the performance of SDN setups in a more throughout manner including the hardware and the software aspect of a network. In [8], the authors investigate various performance-related parameters of an SDN network. The authors note that "performance bottleneck may be located in the existing switches, and the flow table entry installation delay is a pressing issue." This statement is confirmed by the authors of [11] who investigated control planes of three hardware SDN switches and observed that hardware is still not mature enough for the performance to be repeatably predicted, because "each switch under test has many quirks which result in unexplained performance changes." They conclude that "the switch performance is difficult to predict—a single rule can degrade the update rate of a switch by an order of magnitude". The authors stress high diversity of the performance of the switches. The statements are amplified by the authors of [12], who stress the diversity of switch capabilities and behaviors what makes network harder to understand and control. They observe that rules may be shifted between flow tables in the switch. In some switches rules may be rejected whereas on other, rules may be installed into the software or the hardware flow table. In contrast to this, the authors of [5] find out that building an SDN switch emulator is possible as "an appropriately calibrated emulation infrastructure can approximate the behavior of the switches."

Many other authors (e.g., [7, 4]) focus on the data-plane of an SDN setup and identify possible bottlenecks in the SDN controllers. In this paper, we do not focus on the SDN controller aspect, although the SDN controllers and the modeling of their performance is supported in DNI. In evaluation of this paper, we analyze proactive networks scenarios, i.e., such a state of the network, where all SDN flow rules are already installed in the switch.

Many SDN-related performance factors cannot be ignored and the performance modeling approaches should take them into consideration despite of the challenges stated in related work. This constitutes the main incentive for the substantial extension of the DNI modeling approach.

1.2 Contributions

The main contributions of this paper are the following. (i) We present new, substantial changes to the architecture of the DNI meta-model. The newly introduced modeling entities enable modeling of modern network infrastructures (such as SDN, NFV) and load balancing scenarios (load balancing in the sense of both: using multiple network paths and multiple software entities as destinations) while still supporting the classical data center network architectures and virtualization technologies (e.g., VLAN, tunneling) at a high level of abstraction. (ii) Furthermore, we show how the newly introduced modeling entities are transformed from the descriptive DNI model into the predictive QPN models. (iii) We evaluate the automatically generated predictive models with respect to their performance prediction accuracy in three scenarios where we compare the QPN performance predictions against performance measurements of three heterogeneous SDN-enabled HP switches. We show how different switch characteristics can be modeled in DNI and how well the QPN simulation can represent the throughput of the switches. Finally, we discuss the results and describe technical challenges.

1.3 Novelty

The novelty of our approach can be characterized by the following aspects. First, we propose an original descriptive performance modeling language—DNI—capable of modeling modern network virtualization infrastructures based on SDN and NFV paradigm. Additionally, we offer automatic transformation to performance predictive models for performance prediction so the DNI models can be transformed and solved with a single mouse click. Second, thanks to the technology-independence of the DNI modeling language, our approach can be used for modeling novel networking technologies and custom protocols without limiting its scope to a single technology. Third, DNI is the first descriptive model to support all switching modes of an SDN-enabled switch: native, *software SDN switching mode*, *hardware SDN switching mode*, and the reactive SDN scenarios with the *packet_-in–flow_mod* message exchange between the switch and the SDN controller. Moreover, the generic character of DNI, the modeling of the virtualization, and the support for the modeling of the software layers allows to model NFV setups where parts of the network functions are offered by commodity servers. Finally, we have characterize the most relevant performance aspect of four heterogeneous SDN-enabled switches that served as a validation case study for DNI and QPN simulation.

1.4 Organization

The rest of this paper is organized as follows. In Section 2, we introduce the foundations of SDN, briefly reviewing the related work on SDN performance prediction approaches. In Section 3, we introduce our approach to performance modeling and prediction. In Section 4, we present the DNI meta-model and its novel features. In Section 5, we present the *DNI-to-QPN* model transformation, whereas in Section 6, we evaluate the automatically generated simulation models using four heterogeneous switches in three scenarios. We present future work directions and conclude in Section 7.

2. FOUNDATIONS AND RELATED WORK

In this section, we briefly introduce the most relevant aspects of the SDN-based networks, including, so called, the *software-* and the *hardware SDN switching mode*. Moreover, we briefly review the related work on performance modeling of SDN and NFV-based networks.

2.1 SDN Performance Foundations

Software-defined networking (SDN) assumes separation of the data plane and the control plane. In the data plane, a switch forwards the packets, whereas in the control plane, algorithms make decisions where the packets should be forwarded to. The control plane is implemented using an SDN controller that is a special software running in a commodity server. The controller makes the forwarding decisions which are later stored in switch forwarding tables.

The forwarding tables contain forwarding rules that define behavior of the switch. The packets arriving to the switch are matched against the table entries and once a match is found, the programmed action is executed (e.g., forward, modify, drop packet). If a matching rule cannot be found, a *packet_in* message is sent to the controller so that it can react and decide what to do with the packet—we will refer to this as the *reactive SDN switching*. The controller calculates the decision and sends a *flow_mod* message to the switch to modify the table. If the controller preconfigures the switches and installs the forwarding rules beforehand, we speak of the *proactive SDN switching*. The flows installed by the controller remain in the table for the time defined in the *timeout* parameter (where 0 means no timeout). The communication between the switch and the controller is usually realized with the OpenFlow protocol.

The rules saved in the switch can be exact-match (all match fields are specified explicitly) or wildcard-match (some fields are wildcarded). Exact match rules are stored in the BCAM memory (binary content-addressable memory), whereas the wildcard rules are saved in the TCAM (ternary content-addressable memory) that allows each cell to have three states: 1, 0, and $*$. TCAM is usually power hungry and expensive [11]. The rules that do not fit to the hardware flow tables (i.e., implemented using hardware memory chips, either in BCAM or TCAM) are placed in the switch SDRAM—so called software flow table. Placement of the rules in the software or hardware flow tables influence the switching performance significantly (as we show in Section 6). If a packet is matched against a rule from the hardware switching table, we observe the *hardware SDN switching mode*, whereas if the matched rule is placed in the switch SDRAM, we refer to the *software SDN switching mode*, which is usually slower than the hardware one. Moreover, a rule placed in a given flow table can be later moved (promoted) to another, which may be implement using a faster memory chip. Finally, various switch models provide various performance characteristics of the flow table implementations. More information about SDN and OpenFlow foundations can be found in [14].

2.2 Related Work on Performance Models of SDN-based Networks

There is a large body of existing work on performance modeling of communication networks. However, only several cover SDN and NFV-based networks and even less work put focus on a whole network (i.e., including server virtualization and software), as opposed to, for example, [7], where only parts of a network are modeled.

The topic of performance of SDN-based networks attracts many researchers and some aspects were already investigated in the literature. However, various authors usually focus on selected parts of SDN networks so they miss the overall picture of the system (e.g., they focus on the control path, data path, or a controller [11, 5, 2]), or model an SDN network too coarsely [7]. The relatively young concept of SDN resulted in multiple heterogeneous hardware products that offer the support for the OpenFlow protocol. This variety resulted in different implementations and thus the offered performance may differ among the vendors, switch models, or even among the versions of the same switch model.

Jarschel et al. [7] model an SDN switch using two queues (M/M/1-S and M/GI/I-S) and thus specify two processing paths (with and without the controller) with different performance. The selection of the controller and non-controller path is modeled in a probabilistic manner. Unfortunately, the software SDN switching mode, which involves CPU and SDRAM processing on a switch, is not modeled making the results applicable only to a switch with unlimited BCAM/TCAM capacity. Similar work was conducted by Azodolmolky et al. [1], where the authors propose an analytical performance model similar to the one proposed by Jarschel et al. The authors validate the model against results that were obtained in the literature and do not investigate any real hardware on their own.

In the NFV-related literature, the authors of [19] claim that many performance problems in the modern NFV testbeds are located in the software of the virtualized network function. This implies that the analysis of the software performance needs to be taken into account to accurately predict the performance of an NFV-based network. Influence of the server virtualization on the ClickOS router was the main focus in [13]. The authors analyzed software-emulated networking hardware and found out that a network function that is virtualized may increase switching latencies and decrease switching capacity. This has a visible influence on the performance of an NFV-based network.

In the contrast to the related work, we do not limit our focus to selected parts of the system but treat the data center as a whole (including the software architecture using the Descartes Modeling Language (DML) [10]). By widening the modeling scope, we represent the system at a higher level of details as we aim to provide a *good-enough* performance prediction in a timely manner for run-time capacity planning purposes. Moreover, the DNI meta-model presented in Section 4 is the first descriptive performance model capable of modeling SDN and NFV-based network infrastructures.

3. APPROACH TO MODELING AND PERFORMANCE PREDICTION

The wide variety of performance models makes it challenging to select the proper models and learn them extensively to model the performance accurately. Model-based approaches assume that there exists a single descriptive model and all predictive models are derived automatically using model transformations. The general performance prediction process based on model-to-model transformations is presented in Figure 1a. A model of a real network is built and stored in a descriptive form with performance annotations, whereas the transformations to predictive models are automated and can deliver as many different predictive performance models as many model transformations are available. The prediction results can be used to further refine the descriptive models (the dashed line in Fig. 1a).

We divide the area of performance models as shown in Figure 1b. We intentionally exclude the simulation models

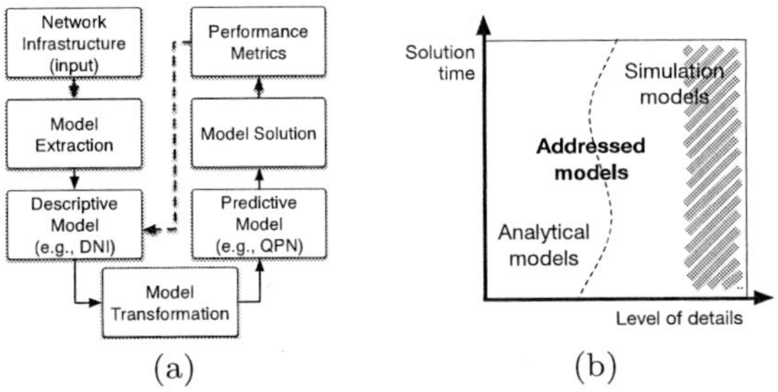

Figure 1: (a) Process of performance prediction based on model-to-model transformations. (b) Abstract division of predictive models into analytical and simulation models. Models with very fine modeling granularity (gray area) are not in our scope.

with high level of details (striped area in Fig. 1b) because they require specifying too many low level input parameters and usually do not model the infrastructure in an end-to-end manner (e.g., due to their complexity and size). However, we do not question the applicability of those models and their high prediction accuracy; we recommend using them when the modeling accuracy is required to be maximized.

Using our model-based approach, we address the medium and low-detailed predictive models (the non-stripped area in Fig. 1b) that can be generated automatically using model transformations. Among the addressed predictive models, we consider models with various level of detail (respectively prediction accuracy) and with different model solution time. Using automatic model generation methods enables us to pick the proper model according to the given situation: quick but less detailed solution or longer simulation providing more accurate predictions. We call this the *flexible performance prediction* because by modeling the infrastructure once, one can freely pick the suitable predictive model or even use multiple models in parallel.

The modeling approach we propose is based on a meta-model for modeling network infrastructures in virtualized data centers. This meta-model, which we refer to as Descartes Network Infrastructure (DNI) meta-model, is part of our broader work in the context of the *Descartes Modeling Language* (DML)![10], an architecture-level modeling language for modeling Quality-of-Service and resource management related aspects of modern dynamic IT systems, infrastructures and services. The DNI meta-model has been designed to support describing the most relevant performance influencing factors that occur in practice while abstracting fine-granular low-level protocol details.

In our approach, instances of DNI meta-model are automatically transformed to predictive stochastic models (e.g., stochastic simulation models) by means of model-to-model transformations. The approach supports the implementation of different transformations of the descriptive DNI models to underlying predictive stochastic models (by abstracting environment-specific details, transformations to multiple predictive models are possible), thereby providing flexibility in trading-off between the overhead and accuracy of the analysis. In this paper, we present one of the model transformations, which generates the predictive models automatically. In Section 4, we present the redesigned DNI meta-model and the DNI-to-QPN model transformation.

4. MODELING NETWORK INFRASTRUCTURES USING DNI

In this Section, we present the new DNI meta-model designed to model data center SDN- and NFV-based networks for performance prediction purposes. Later, in Section 5, we demonstrate how do we transform the DNI models to QPNs.

Since its last version (*DNIv2*) [16], the DNI meta-model was redesigned and extended to support SDN, NFV, and load-balancing scenarios (e.g., Equal-Cost Multi Path Routing (ECMP)). We use the DNI meta-model to describe a network infrastructure. The DNI meta-model—initially presented in the work-in-progress paper [17] (*v1*) and later extended in [16] (*v2*)—is intended to describe the common network components in an abstract manner. In this section, we present the new aspects of the DNI model (*DNIv3*).

The DNI meta-model covers three main parts of every data center network infrastructure: network structure, network traffic and network configuration. The network structure is intended to model the structure (topology) of the network. The meta-model for network structure contains entities such as nodes and links connected through network interfaces. Nodes can be nested to represent server virtualization. We describe the performance-relevant parameters of every performance-relevant element in the model. The DNI network structure meta-model is presented in Figure 2.

We characterize the network nodes as `end` (e.g., virtual machine, server) and `intermediate` (e.g., switch, router), because their roles (and thus the way they influence the performance) are different. An intermediate node represents a node that only forwards the traffic between its ports; an end node usually represents a server or a virtual machine that is a traffic generator, traffic sink, or both. Moreover, a node can be both end and intermediate simultaneously that enables modeling NFV scenarios where commodity servers serve as network devices. A node that is neither `End` nor `Intermediate` is assumed to have no influence on the performance and is usually used in the model to reflect the topology of the network.

Nodes can host other nodes (e.g., VM). In the transformations, we currently support only one level of virtualization (i.e., no VMs in a VM), but the modeling formalism does not prohibit multi-level virtualization. `Nodes` are connected using `Links` and `NetworkInterfaces` that have their respective performance descriptions. Any DNI entity missing a performance description is assumed to offer infinite performance—the element in the model has purely descriptive role.

Additionally, a `Node` can be either `SDN` or `Common` (`IType`). Common nodes are described by their `Performance` (end or intermediate respectively), whereas the SDN nodes with the`PerformanceSdnNode` that exclusively defines their performance in SDN modes: `software-` or `hardware SdnSwitchingPerformance` as some devices offer only one mode while other support modes simultaneously. The decision how a flow is processed (using nonSDN, software, or *hardware SDN switching mode*) depends on the `SdbFlowRules`. An `SdnFlowRule` defines probabilities (see Fig. 4) for a given `Flow` on a given `Node` to be processed using the SDN controller (reactive scenarios), *software SDN*, or the *hardware SDN* switching mode.

The `SdnController` is a special type of a `CommunicatingApplication` that represents software deployed on an `End`

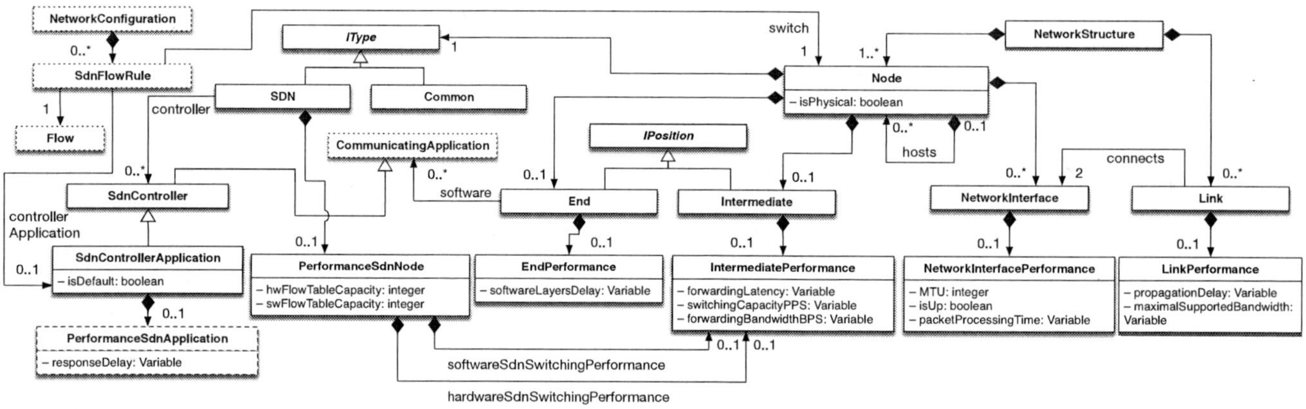

Figure 2: Structure of the DNI meta-model including SDN-related elements. Dashed entities represent in a compact manner elements offered by DML [10], dotted ones represent briefly other parts of DNI.

node. The `SdnController` hosts `SdnControllerApplications` that are responsible for processing the traffic forwarded to the controller. An `SdnControllerApplication` applies delay to the switching process and installs the rules in the switch. Unfortunately, installing the rule cannot be modeled directly in DNI (the model cannot be changed during solving) and the rule installation needs to be expressed using the probabilities located in the `SdnFlowRule` entities.

In the DNI meta-model, network traffic is generated by `TrafficSources` that are deployed on end nodes. Each traffic source generates traffic `Flows` that have exactly one source and possibly multiple destinations. Flows can be composed in a `Workload` that defines how each flow is generated (e.g., with sequences, loops, or branches). Flows are described using the amount of transferred data in the `GenericFlowTraffic` entity. The traffic description proposed in this paper covers all possible open workloads including traffic sources, sinks, and traffic profile characteristics. The meta-model and its transformations can be systematically extended to support other flow descriptions, e.g., [3]. The traffic meta-model is presented graphically in Figure 3.

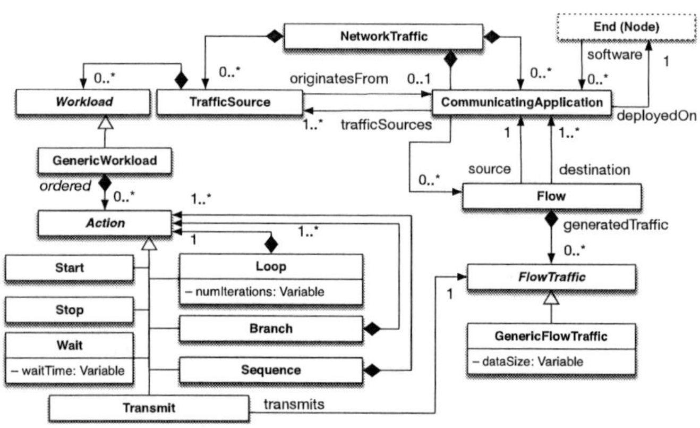

Figure 3: Traffic representation of the DNI meta-model. Dotted boxes represent other DNI entities.

The `NetworkConfiguration` contains information about SDN configuration, routes (paths), protocols and protocols stacks. We use this information to calculate the paths in the topology graph and to coarsely estimate the overheads introduced by the protocols. In DNI, we describe a snapshot of the currently used routes in the system, disregarding if the system uses static or dynamic routing. The protocols are described by a set of generic parameters such as, MTU (maximal transfer unit) and overheads introduced by the data unit headers. We depict the configuration meta-model in Figure 4.

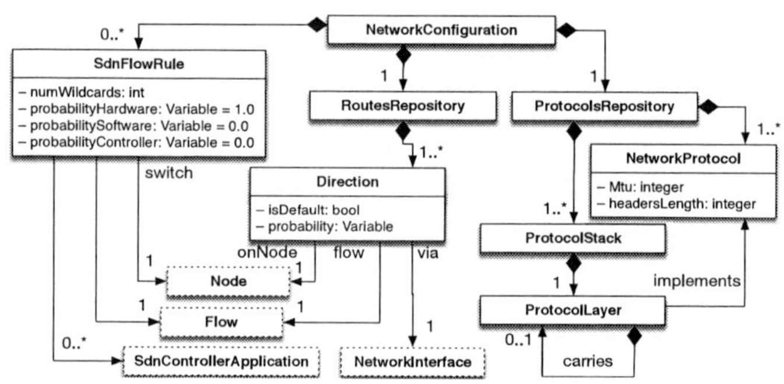

Figure 4: Configuration representation of the DNI meta-model. Dotted boxes represent other DNI entities.

In the meta-model, a path between two nodes is defined as a set of `Directions`. Each `Direction` defines via which network interface on a given node, the given `Flow` should be directed. Additionally, a `probability` of taking this path is given, so that load-balancing can be modeled. The modeling approach allows to define a network-path load-balancing (node A and B are connected using multiple network paths) and destination application load-balancing (for flows having multiple destinations the ratio of traffic division is defined using the `probability` parameter).

5. TRANSFORMATION DNI TO QPN

An instance of the DNI meta model is a descriptive model of a network. To conduct performance analysis, the instance (the DNI model) must be transformed into a predictive model. In this section, we describe the transformation that transforms a DNI model into a QPN model, which can be simulated using the *SimQPN* simulator. The *SimQPN*

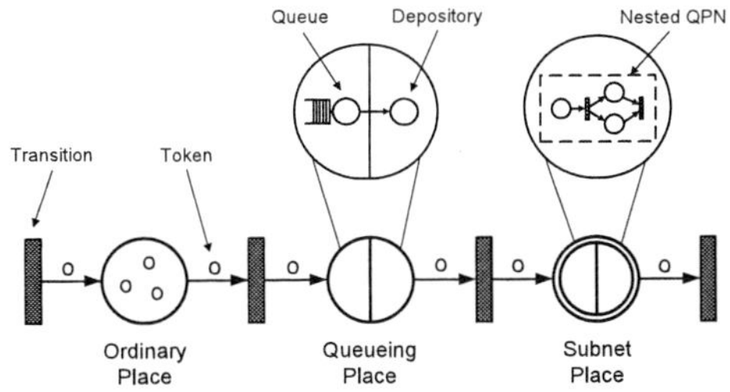

Figure 5: Notation used in QPN diagrams. Excerpted from [9].

simulator is a part of QPME (Queueing Petri Net Modeling Environment) [18]. The graphical notation used for QPNs in this section is summarized in Figure 5.

The transformation has it origins in [15], however due to the substantial changes in the DNI meta-model (added support for SDN and NFV), large part of the transformation was reimplemented. In this Section, the DNI entities are written in `verbatim` font face, whereas QPN entities in *cursive*. All transitions presented in this paper are immediate transitions. The only source of delays in the model are the queueing places.

The procedure of the transformation begins with building the QPN's topology. For each `Node`, a subnet place is created. To reflect the topology, the subnets are connected with links that are represented by two transitions—for sending and receiving respectively. The internal structure of the subnet representing a `Node` is depicted in Figure 6a. All incoming tokens are placed in the *input-place* first. Next, they are forwarded to the queueing places that represent receive queues of the network interfaces (*port-#-rx*). The *traversing-transition* has two tasks: (a) deleting the tokens that end in this node, (b) passing the traversing tokens to the *traversingTraffic* place. No tokens are passed to the traffic sources (exception: SDN controller) as the transformation supports only open workloads. Next, the *sdn-transition* gathers the traversing tokens and the tokens generated in the traffic sources and forwards them into the *switching* place or the *sdnSwitching* subnet based on the type of the node—for a `Common` node, all tokens go via *switching* place, for `SDN` via *sdnSwitching*. Graphically, we depict it in Figure 6b.

Once the switching delay is applied in the *switching* or the *sdnSwitching* place, the tokens are directed to the proper *port-#-rx* and leave the `Node`. We discuss the internal structure of two parts in more details: *sdnSwitching* subnet, and the *routing-transition* for load-balancing scenarios.

The *sdnSwitching* subnet groups entities responsible for switching in SDN `Nodes`. We depict its internal structure in Figure 7. Two separate subnets (*hw-* and *swSdnSwitching*) handle the traffic switched in the *hardware-* and *software SDN switching mode* respectively. The `SdnFlowRule` probabilities are mapped on to the firing weights represented by parameters *A, B, C* in the Figure. The internal structure of the *switching* (in Fig. 6a), *hw-* and *swSdnSwitching* (Fig. 7) is identical and implements the node forwarding performance as given by equation $forwarding\_delay = latency + max(capacity, bandwidth)$.

The in the third processing mode all packets are passed to the controller. This is represented using the *buffer* and *toController* places. The traffic tokens (color t) directed to the SDN controller are forwarded to the *toController* place. Next, the *controller-tr* transition issues a new token with *packet_in* message (color p) and forwards it via *output* place to the node where the controller is deployed. At the same time, the traffic token (color t) is deposited in the *buffer* until the controller responds. When the controller responds with a *flow_mod* token (color f), the traffic token is released form the buffer and switched using *hwSdnSwitching*.

The *SdnController* subnet—depicted in Figure 8a—is responsible for receiving the *packet_in* tokens and issuing a *flow_mod* reply. The *SdnController* subnet is a special type of a traffic source located in a node. The tokes arriving to the controller are delayed twice. First, the delay of the controller itself and the delay of the respective *controllerApp* that represent internal controller components programmed by SDN developers.

For scenarios with load-balancing the *routing-transition* is organized differently. The transition (as depicted in Fig. 6a) is replaced by multiple transitions, each with a single mode but different firing weight. The firing weight represents relative firing frequency of the transition, so that it can properly represent load-balancing ratios. An example of SDN switching and "60/40" load-balancing is depicted in Figure 8b. In this example, the tokens consumed from the *sdnSwitching* place are interchangeably deposited to port *port-1-tx* and *port-2-tx* with probabilities 0.6 and 0.4 respectively.

More information about the transformation can be obtained by looking at the examples and its source code online. The transformation with example models are available publicly in our git repository[1]. The validation of the automatically-generated QPN simulation model is presented in Section 6.

6. VALIDATION

In this section, we validate the approach by comparing the performance predicted by the generated QPN models against their respective physical hardware setups. We analyze the prediction accuracy and focus mainly on the new SDN capabilities of DNI.

Although the modeling capabilities of DNI and QPN are large, in this Section, we focus on simple topologies and relatively simple workloads but use heterogeneous SDN hardware that differs in almost every SDN performance aspect. We conduct three experiments to investigate the factors that influence the switching performance the most: switching latency and switching capacity. We limit the validation to proactive SDN scenarios (no traffic is forwarded to the SDN controller), as the controller has no influence on the performance heterogeneity of the switches.

6.1 Testbed

Our testbed consists of two servers connected with a switch. The servers are exchanging data over the network organized in a dumbbell topology. In the experiments, we replace the switch with other models to investigate their heterogeneity and its influence on the performance characteristics. We present the set of available switches and their brief performance characteristics in Table 1. All switches used in the experiment support OpenFlow protocol in version at least 1.0. All connections are $1Gbps$ copper cables.

[1]DNI resources: http://descartes.tools/dni

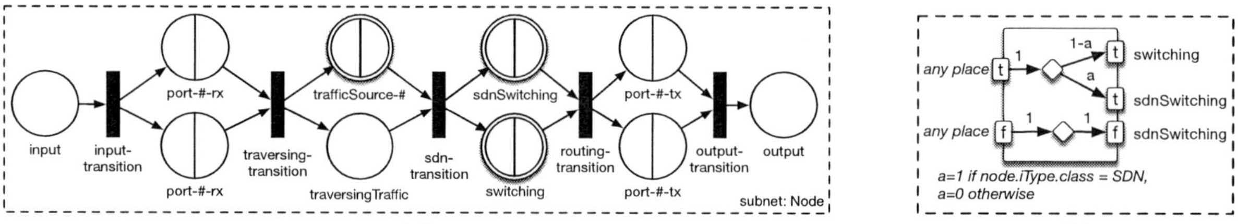

Figure 6: (a) QPN representation of DNI's `Node`. (b) Modes of the *sdn-transition*. Token colors: *t* traffic, *f* flow_mod. A mode (diamond-shape) consumes tokens of a given color and quantity from the preceding places and deposits tokens with defined color and quantity to the succeeding places.

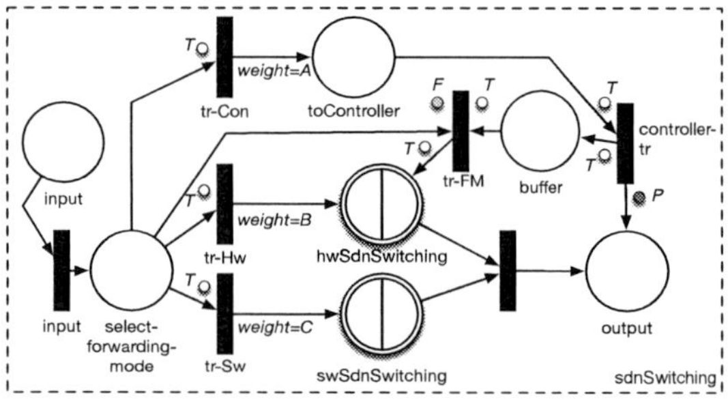

Figure 7: QPN representation of SdnSwitching subnet. A, B, C are numeric parameters. T, F, P denote *traffic*, *flow_mod*, and *packet_in* colors.

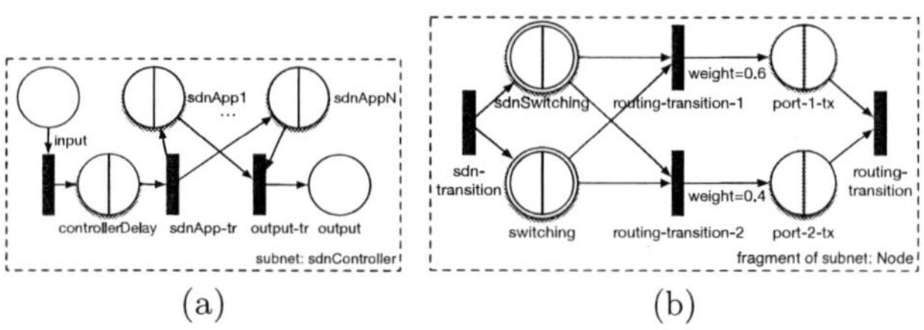

Figure 8: QPN representation of (a) `SdnController`, (b) `Node` with load-balancing.

Switch models named 5130 and 5700 (Comware product line) run under control of a different operating system than the two 2920 and 3500 (ProVision product line). The Comware switches support only hardware SDN switching whereas ProVision support both, hardware and software modes. According to the data sheets, the switches are heterogeneous not only to their data plane performance but also built-in control plane hardware. The 2920 for example runs a Tri-Core ARM1176 processor at 625 MHz and uses 512 MB SDRAM memory; the 3500 is an older model and is equipped with a Freescale PowerPC 8540 processor at 666 MHz and 256 MB DDR SDRAM. The vendor specify the Comware switches as follows: 1000MHz CPU and $2GB$ SDRAM memory for the 5700 and $1GB$ for the 5130.

6.2 Experiment Setup

The two commodity servers handle the traffic using *iperf* tool. A separate server runs the HP VAN SDN Controller but this has no influence on the measurements as we do not

Table 1: Performance specification of switches.

Switching in native mode (source: vendor datasheet)			
Model	**Capacity**	**Throughput**	**Latency**
HP 2920 (J9726A)	92.2 $Mpps$	128 $Gbps$	$< 3.3\mu s$
HP 3500 (J8692A)	75.7 $Mpps$	101.8 $Gbps$	$< 3.4\mu s$
HP 5700 (JG898A)	714.2 $Mpps$	960 $Gbps$	$< 1.5\mu s$
HP 5130 (JG932A)	96.0 $Mpps$	128 $Gbps$	$< 5.0\mu s$
Switching in SDN Software mode ($\approx$ empirical estimation)			
HP 2920	2 $Kpps$	≈ 14 $Mbps$	$\approx 340\mu s$
HP 3500	10 $Kpps$	≈ 63 $Mbps$	$\approx 90\mu s$

investigate reactive rule-insertion scenarios. The testbed is controlled from an experiment controller that is connected over a separate, isolated network to not interfere with the experiment traffic.

Every experiment starts with a configuration of the SDN flow tables. The rules forcing a specific behavior are pushed to the switches over the SDN Controller. We use wildcard matching rules with defined source and destination IP addresses, as the ProVision switches do not support SDN switching using MAC addresses. As default action for a matching rule, we set "output to port". The rule timeout is set to 0, so the rules are never removed by the switch. For Provision switches, matching against the software flow rules is achieved with filling the hardware flow table with dummy rules (rules that can never be matched) as long as the hardware flow table capacity is reached, so the next rule is automatically installed into slower software flow table.

6.3 Heterogeneity in SDN Support

As shown in [11], the capacity of hardware flow tables varies from 750 to 2000 rules so the probability of filling the hardware table completely is non-negligible and should be considered in the analysis. Our observations complement the results of [11]; we observe the following maximal capacities of the hardware flow tables: 460 for the 2920, $381 - 1526$ for the 3500, $384 - 512$ for the 5130, and $512 - 640$ for the 5700. The Comware switches offer an additional memory allowing for matching exclusive against the MAC and IP addresses with capacities 16000 and 65535 rules for 5130 and 5700 respectively. The rest of the observations about switches heterogeneity are abstracted in this paper as they have no or little influence on the data-plane performance.

6.4 Experiment 1: Maximal Throughput

In the first experiment, we measure the maximal throughput achieved for each switch in the available SDN modes;

Table 2: **Maximal throughput in hardware (HW) and software (SW) SDN switching mode for various switch models and the QPN simulation.**

Switch model	2900 HW	2900 SW	3500 HW	3500 SW	5700 HW	5130 HW
Throughput [$Mbps$] measured	942	14	941	63	941	941
Throughput [$Mbps$] QPN simulation	951	14.1	951	62.3	951	951

the Comware switches in hardware and the ProVision in *hardware-* and *software SDN switching modes*. We measured the maximal throughput of the using the values delivered by *iperf* benchmark tool using TCP as the transport protocol.

We simulate the scenario by building a DNI model using the parameters from Table 1. The parameters for the *software SDN switching mode* (switching latency) were estimated as the official data sheets do not specify them. The maximum switch capacity was acquired from the operating system of the switches, whereas the switching latency was determined empirically. The constructed DNI model was later transformed using the model transformation presented in Section 4 and the resulting QPN model was solved using *SimQPN*. The measured (real) and predicted (simulated) results are presented in Table 2. Additionally, we measure and predict the native (non-SDN) switching throughput. The values were identical to the SDN switching in the *hardware SDN switching mode*.

The predicted results truly depict the measured performance. The variations of the predicted maximal throughput hold within 1% relative difference for the *hardware SDN switching mode* (and the not shown native switching). The throughput reported for *software SDN switching mode* of the 2920 and 3500 switches was bound by two parameters: maximum switching capacity expressed in packets per second (pps) and the switching latency that aggregates multiple internal latencies in the switch that we abstract in DNI (e.g., flow table lookup).

Taking the 3500 switch as an example, we can calculate the upper bound of the switching throughput (assuming switching latency= 0) using the default IP packet size (MTU=1500B) multiplied by maximal switching capacity $10Kpps$ resulting in $120Mbps$. The constant switching latency of $\approx 90\mu s$ added to each packet resulted in maximal throughput of $63Mbps$ that fits the observed performance of the switch 3500. For the 2920 the switching delay consisted of $1/2000pps = 500\mu s$ plus additionally $\approx 340\mu s$ per packet. Higher switching latencies in the *software SDN switching mode* were confirmed by the end-to-end ping measurements where the setup with the 3500 switch resulted in about $0.65ms$ whereas for 2920 the pings were higher $2.07ms$. Unfortunately, the end-to-end ping delay cannot be easily mapped to the respective switching latencies, but the difference of the values obtained for the different switches shows that the switch 2920 in *software SDN switching mode* is about three times slower than 3500. The real switching latencies are difficult to measure at the microsecond scale without a dedicated measurement hardware, so we will use the approximated values in the experiments. In Section 6.5 and 6.6, we demonstrate the performance metric values for other switching latencies.

Table 3: **Throughput for the 3500 switch depending on the packet size in three switching modes: SDN software (SW), SDN hardware (HW), and non-SDN.**

IP MTU	1500	1200	900	600	300	128
Real Hardware HP 3500yl						
	Throughput $Mbps$					
non-SDN	941	927	904	859	720	315
SDN Hardware	941	927	904	859	716	316
SDN Software	62.4	54.7	41.3	23.3	11.1	4.11
QPN Simulation: Software SDN switching						
Switching latency	Throughput $Mbps$					
$80\mu s$	65.77	51.92	38.58	25.25	11.91	4.8
$90\mu s$	62.32	49.18	36.55	23.92	11.28	4.55
$100\mu s$	59.2	46.72	34.72	22.72	10.71	4.32
QPN Simulation: Hardware SDN switching						
$3.3\mu s^*$	951	944	934	913	645	260
* Value obtained form the hardware data sheet						

6.5 Experiment 2: Packet Size

In the second experiment, we investigate more the *software SDN switching mode* of the 3500 switch. In this experiment, we varied the packet size that was emitted by the *iperf* tool (parameter *-M*) and observed the maximal throughput offered by the switch in the native, the *hardware-*, and the *software SDN switching mode*. We modeled the selected packet sizes in DNI using the `NetworkProtocol.mtu` parameter and simulated the transformed model assuming the performance characteristics of the 3500 estimated as described in Section 6.4.

Although the *iperf* with parameter *-M* sets TCP segment size (MSS: Maximal Segment Size), the switch observers the IP packets as the switching of Ethernet frames is not supported in the *hardware SDN switching mode* in this model. We set the maximum MTU (MTU: Maximum Transfer Unit) to 1500B and decrease it every 300B concluding with the minimal value of 128B (protocol limitation). The results are presented in Table 3.

The results of the SimQPN simulation of *software SDN switching mode* include additional data the presents the predicted behavior of the switch (and also the sensitivity of the DNI model) for other switching latencies. We observe that the simulation properly represents the measured values. Only for low MTU values the performance for hardware SDN switching reported by simulation was underestimated. This may be caused by the fact, that DNI represented the full protocol stack (TCP/IP/Ethernet) and the additional overhead of the Ethernet frame was also the part of the switching in the simulation, whereas the real switch has decapsulated the IP packet and conducted L3-switching (what is usually not expected in the switching). In the end, the switch has processed about 14 bytes less per packet (11% less for MTU=128) than in the simulation.

In the *software SDN switching mode* the throughput was underestimated by maximally 12% for 900B and latency $90\mu s$. Additionally, we show how similar switching latencies influence the reported throughput as the precise measurement of the real switching latency was impossible. The value used in other experiments ($90\mu s$) was marked in bold.

6.6 Experiment 3: Switching Capacity

In the third experiment, we focus on the switching capacity and its influence on the performance of the ProVision switches in the *software SDN switching mode*. Using the operating system of the switch, we lowered the switching capacity stepwise and analyzed the offered performance. The operating system of the Comware switches does not support neither limiting of the switching capacity nor the *software SDN switching mode*.

6.6.1 Switch 2920

The 2920 switch in the *software SDN switching mode* offers maximal switching capacity of 2000 packets per second. We varied the value of the maximal switching capacity parameter to investigate the throughput curve of the switch and the curve predicted by the QPN simulation. Additionally, we investigated selected values of switching latencies to present the modeling alternatives. The results are depicted in Figure 9.

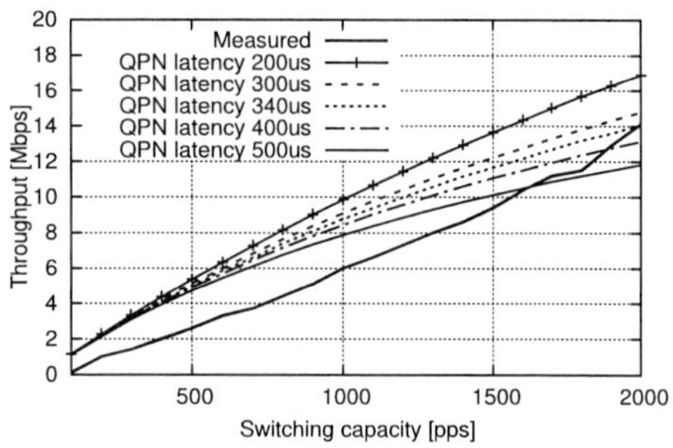

Figure 9: Throughput of the 2920 switch in the *software SDN switching mode* for variable switching capacity.

The throughput curves presented in Figure 9 represent the measured performance less accurately than in the previous experiments—the prediction errors reach even $\approx 100\%$ relatively (for $340\mu s$ and $500pps$). The switching latency in the DNI model was calibrated to $340\mu s$ to properly represent the throughput at the maximal switching capacity of $2000pps$. The worse fit of the model for other capacities can be explained as follows. First, the switch in the *software SDN switching mode* demands more CPU (up to 100%) and the CPU is not modeled in DNI. Second, the switch's CPU conducted also other operations during the experiment (logging, SDN counters update) that influenced its load but were not possible to control or disable. Finally, the *software SDN switching mode* received only 20% of the resources available to the 3500 switch so offering maximal throughput of $14Mbps$ must impose that the switch is incapable of using this mode efficiently. The DNI model could include more performance influencing factors to capture such situations better, but we intentionally abstract them out to keep the generic character of the model while accepting possible inaccuracies to some degree.

6.6.2 Switch 3500

The 3500 switch in the *software SDN switching mode* offers maximal capacity of 10000 packets per second. Similarly to the switch 2920, we varied the value of the maximal switching capacity and switching latency. The results are depicted in Figure 10. In this experiment, the QPN model represented the switch performance better than for the 2920 switch. The throughput curve grows nearly linearly and the

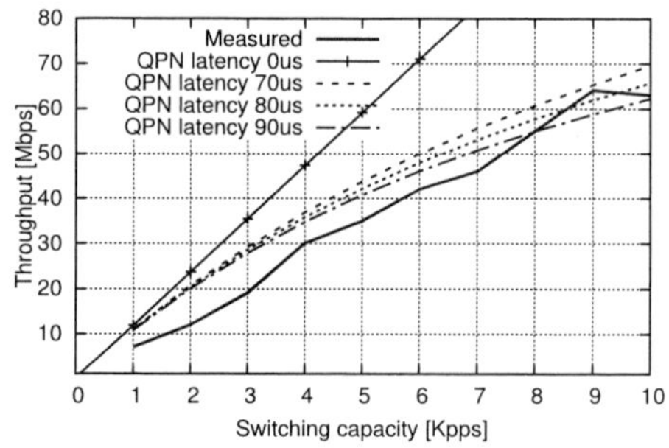

Figure 10: Throughput of the 3500 switch in the *software SDN switching mode* for variable switching capacity.

incline is properly represented using the switching latency between 80 and $90\mu s$. Based on the measurements, we observe, that the CPU of the 3500 switch has more processing power, although it has similar frequency and half of the memory size compared to the 2920.

6.6.3 Conclusions: Software SDN Switching

The experiments with the performance in the *software SDN switching mode* lead to the following conclusions. First, the throughput in the *software SDN switching mode* is low—about 10 to 70 times lower than the throughput in the *hardware SDN switching mode*. Second, the behavior of the switch in the software mode is challenging to predict as it depends on the switch's CPU that is difficult to observe and model accurately. Third, the capacity of hardware flow table in the investigated switches is limited and can be easily reached for complex SDN scenarios (e.g., SDN QoS provisioning based on customer class). The probability of placing a rule in the software flow table cannot be neglected as the performance penalty is high. Moreover, some switches (e.g., 5130, 5700) do not offer *software SDN switching mode* and report an error if the hardware flow table is full. Finally, DNI is the first model to support the modeling of the SDN performance in the *software SDN switching mode*, although it does not support modeling of the switch internal architecture (CPU) and the prediction accuracy for the 2920 switch could be further optimized. All in all, the *software SDN switching mode* should be avoided in general as the performance penalty is high.

7. CONCLUSION

In this paper, we presented a redesigned generic model-based approach to network performance prediction. We introduced the modeling entities allowing to represent SDN, NFV and load-balancing scenarios without limiting the DNI's ability to represent end-to-end data center network scenarios including server virtualization and even software architectures (when used with DML). Furthermore, we presented the *DNI-to-QPN* model transformation, so that the descriptive DNI models can be automatically transformed into QPN simulations and solved.

We characterized four models of SDN-enabled switches and validated the prediction capabilities of DNI in three challenging scenarios. We showed that the transformation works correctly and the prediction accuracy is good for run-time prediction purposes. We stress that the presented predictions were obtained through an automatically generated simulation model from a high-level descriptive model where most low-level details were abstracted, so the prediction errors are acceptable to some degree.

The previous version of *DNI* (*v2*) could be transformed into five predictive models (two additional are currently under development). As part of our future work, we will update the remaining model transformations to support the *DNIv3*, i.e., SDN, NFV and load-balancing scenarios. Finally, we aim to provide more transformations to models with different granularities to enable *flexibility* in performance prediction of virtualized networks, so that simulation at different level of details can be used depending on the required accuracy and time constraints.

8. REFERENCES

[1] S. Azodolmolky, R. Nejabati, M. Pazouki, P. Wieder, R. Yahyapour, and D. Simeonidou. An analytical model for software defined networking: A network calculus-based approach. In *Global Communications Conference (GLOBECOM 2013)*, pages 1397–1402. IEEE, Dec 2013.

[2] A. Bianco, R. Birke, L. Giraudo, and M. Palacin. OpenFlow Switching: Data Plane Performance. In *IEEE International Conference on Communications (ICC 2010)*, pages 1–5, May 2010.

[3] A. J. Field, U. Harder, and P. G. Harrison. Network Traffic Behaviour in Switched Ethernet Systems. In *MASCOTS 2002, 10th IEEE International Symposium on Modeling, Analysis, and Simulation of Computer and Telecommunications Systems*, pages 32–42, 2002.

[4] A. Gelberger, N. Yemini, and R. Giladi. Performance Analysis of Software-Defined Networking (SDN). In *IEEE 21st International Symposium on Modeling, Analysis Simulation of Computer and Telecommunication Systems (MASCOTS)*, pages 389–393, Aug 2013.

[5] D. Y. Huang, K. Yocum, and A. C. Snoeren. High-fidelity switch models for software-defined network emulation. In *Proceedings of the Second ACM SIGCOMM Workshop on Hot Topics in Software Defined Networking*, HotSDN '13, pages 43–48, New York, NY, USA, 2013. ACM.

[6] N. Huber, M. von Quast, M. Hauck, and S. Kounev. Evaluating and Modeling Virtualization Performance Overhead for Cloud Environments. In *Proc. of the 1st Int. Conf. on Cloud Computing and Services Science*, pages 563–573, 2011.

[7] M. Jarschel, S. Oechsner, D. Schlosser, R. Pries, S. Goll, and P. Tran-Gia. Modeling and Performance Evaluation of an OpenFlow Architecture. In *23rd International Teletraffic Congress (ITC 2011)*, San Francisco, CA, USA, 2011.

[8] X. Kong, Z. Wang, X. Shi, X. Yin, and D. Li. Performance evaluation of software-defined networking with real-life isp traffic. In *IEEE Symposium on Computers and Communications (ISCC)*, pages 541–547, July 2013.

[9] S. Kounev, K. Bender, F. Brosig, N. Huber, and R. Okamoto. Automated Simulation-Based Capacity Planning for Enterprise Data Fabrics. In *4th International ICST Conference on Simulation Tools and Techniques*, pages 27–36, 2011.

[10] S. Kounev, N. Huber, F. Brosig, and X. Zhu. Model-Based Approach to Designing Self-Aware IT Systems and Infrastructures. *IEEE Computer Magazine*, 2016.

[11] M. Kuzniar, P. Peresíni, and D. Kostic. What You Need to Know About SDN Flow Tables. In *Proceedings of the 16th International Conference on Passive and Active Measurement*, pages 347–359, 2015.

[12] A. Lazaris, D. Tahara, X. Huang, E. Li, A. Voellmy, Y. R. Yang, and M. Yu. Tango: Simplifying SDN Control with Automatic Switch Property Inference, Abstraction, and Optimization. In *Proceedings of the 10th ACM International on Conference on Emerging Networking Experiments and Technologies*, CoNEXT '14, pages 199–212, New York, NY, USA, 2014. ACM.

[13] J. Martins, M. Ahmed, C. Raiciu, V. Olteanu, M. Honda, R. Bifulco, and F. Huici. ClickOS and the Art of Network Function Virtualization. In *Proceedings of the 11th USENIX Conference on Networked Systems Design and Implementation*, pages 459–473. USENIX Association, 2014.

[14] N. McKeown, T. Anderson, H. Balakrishnan, G. Parulkar, L. Peterson, J. Rexford, S. Shenker, and J. Turner. Openflow: Enabling innovation in campus networks. *SIGCOMM Comput. Commun. Rev.*, 38(2):69–74, 2008.

[15] P. Rygielski and S. Kounev. Data Center Network Throughput Analysis using Queueing Petri Nets. In *34th IEEE International Conference on Distributed Computing Systems Workshops. 4th International Workshop on Data Center Performance, (DCPerf 2014)*, pages 100–105, 2014.

[16] P. Rygielski, S. Kounev, and P. Tran-Gia. Flexible Performance Prediction of Data Center Networks using Automatically Generated Simulation Models. In *Proceedings of the Eighth EAI International Conference on Simulation Tools and Techniques (SIMUTools 2015)*, August 2015.

[17] P. Rygielski, S. Zschaler, and S. Kounev. A metamodel for Performance Modeling of Dynamic Virtualized Network Infrastructures (Work-in-progess paper). In *Proc. of the 4th ACM/SPEC Int. Conf. on Performance Engineering*, pages 327–330. ACM, 2013.

[18] S. Spinner, S. Kounev, and P. Meier. Stochastic Modeling and Analysis using QPME: Queueing Petri Net Modeling Environment v2.0. In *Proc. of the 33rd Int. Conf. on Application and Theory of Petri Nets and Concurrency*, pages 388–397. Springer, 2012.

[19] W. Wu, K. He, and A. Akella. Perfsight: Performance diagnosis for software dataplanes. In *Proceedings of the 2015 ACM Conference on Internet Measurement Conference*, IMC '15, pages 409–421, New York, NY, USA, 2015. ACM.

An Application of SMC to continuous validation of heterogeneous systems *

Alexandre Arnold[1], Massimo Baleani[2], Alberto Ferrari[2], Marco Marazza[2], Valerio Senni[2], Axel Legay[3], Jean Quilbeuf[3], Christoph Etzien[4]

[1] AIRBUS,
[2] ALES - UTSCE,
[3] Inria
[4] OFFIS

ABSTRACT

This paper considers the rigorous design of Systems of Systems (SoS), i.e. systems composed of a series of heterogeneous components whose number evolves with time. Such components coalize to accomplish functions that they could not achieve alone. Examples of SoS includes (among many others) almost any application of the Internet of things such as smart cities or airport management system.

Dynamical evolution of SoS makes it impossible to design an appropriate solution beforehand. Consequently, existing approaches build on an iterative process that takes its evolution into account. A key challenge in this process is the ability to reason and analyze a given view of the SoS, i.e. verifying a series of goals on a fixed number of SoS constituents, and use the results to eventually predict its evolution.

To address this challenge, we propose a methodology and a tool-chain supporting continuous validation of SoS behavior against formal requirements, based on a scalable formal verification technique known as Statistical Model Checking (SMC). SMC quantifies how close the current view is from achieving a given mission. We integrate SMC with existing industrial practice, by addressing both methodological and technological issues. Our contribution is summarized as follows: (1) a methodology for continuous and scalable validation of SoS formal requirements; (2) a natural-language based formal specification language able to express complex SoS requirements; (3) adoption of widely used industry standards for simulation and heterogeneous systems integration (FMI and UPDM); (4) development of a robust SMC tool-chain integrated with system design tools used in practice. We illustrate the application of our SMC tool-chain and the obtained results on a case study.

*Research supported by the European Community's Seventh Framework Programme [FP7] under grant agreement no 287716 (DANSE)

SIMUTOOLS 2016, August 22-23, Prague, Czech Republic

Keywords

Systems of systems, statistical model checking, FMI, tool-chain, simulation.

1. INTRODUCTION

Context and challenges.

A System of Systems (SoS) is a large-scale, geographically distributed set of independently managed, heterogeneous Constituent Systems (CS). Those entities are collaborating as a whole to accomplish functions/goals that could not be achieved otherwise by any of them, if considered alone [26]. Those goals can either be global to the system, or local to some of its constituents. Constituent Systems are loosely coupled and pursue their own objectives, while collaborating for achieving SoS-level objectives. An SoS adapts itself to its environment through (1) an evolution of the functions provided by its Constituent Systems and (2) an evolution of its architecture. A typical example of an SoS is the Air Traffic Management System of an airport, which coordinates incoming and outgoing aircraft as well as ground-based vehicles and controllers. Such an SoS may evolve in order to accommodate a larger number of passengers, difficult climatic conditions or a modification in the laws regarding security.

Misbehaviors of the functions provided by an SoS can be dangerous and costly. Therefore, it is important to identify a set of analysis and tools to verify that the SoS implementation meets functional and non functional requirements and correctly adapts to changes of the environment during any phase of the design and operation life-cycle. The manager of a SoS should be able to run these analysis in order to take decisions regarding the evolution of the SoS. The main characteristics of an SoS have been long debated since [26]. Nevertheless, one of the key characteristics of an SoS is *dynamical evolution*, that is, the fact that Constituent Systems may evolve, leave, fail, or be replaced.

In fact, dynamical evolution of SoS makes it impossible to design an appropriate solution beforehand. Consequently, the design flow of a SoS is reiterated multiple times during the operation of the SoS, in order to adapt to its evolutions. As a summary, SoS rigorous design methodologies thus introduce two major challenges. The first one is to check whether a given view of the system (i.e. a fixed number of components) is able to achieve a mission. The second challenge is to exploit the solution to the first challenge in an engineering methodology that permits dynamical evolution of the system in case new missions are proposed, in case the environment has changed, or in case the current view cannot achieve the mission. This design approach has been followed by the DANSE project which developed a new SoS design and operation methodology [15].

Contributions.

This paper focuses on Challenge one described above, that is to reason on a given view of the system. A corner stone to solve the challenge is to develop a usable language for expressing formal requirements independent from the number and identity of CSs and thus from the architectural choices.

In this paper, we propose Goal Contract Requirement Language (GCSL). This is a very expressive pattern-based language to specify requirements on an SoS and its CSs. The language uses an extension of OCL to express constraints independent of the view such as : "the total fire area (over a set of districts) is smaller than 1 percent of the total area of the districts.". By combining those constraints with temporal patterns, we express timing requirements on the behaviors of the view. For instance, the GCSL formula "always [SoS.itsDistricts.fireArea→sum()<0.01∗SoS.itsDistricts.area →sum()]" checks that the above constraint is verified at any point of the simulation. A first version of GCSL was introduced in [27]. In this paper we propose additional patterns for expressing properties about the amount of time during which a given predicate remains satisfied. We show that GCSL is powerful enough to capture most of SoS goals and emergent behaviors proposed by our industry partners. The reader shall observe that the language can methodologically be extended to capture more requirements on demand.

The second main difficulty is to detect emergent behaviors and verify the absence of undesired ones. This requires a suitable verification technique. A first solution would be to use formal techniques such as model checking. Unfortunately, both the complexity and the heterogeneous nature of the constituent systems prevent this solution. To solve this problem, we rely on Statistical Model Checking (SMC) [37]. SMC works by monitoring executions of the system, and then use an algorithm from the statistics in order to assess the overall correctness. Contrarily to classical Validation techniques, SMC quantifies how close the view is from achieving a given mission. This information shall latter be exploited in the reconfiguration process.

The objective of the paper is not to improve existing statistical algorithm, but rather to expand the SMC verifier Plasma [9] which proposes several algorithms such as Monte Carlo or hypothesis testing. In order to implement an SMC algorithm for SoS, one has to propose a simulation approach for heterogeneous components as well as a monitoring approach for GCSL requirements. While a GCSL monitor is easily obtained by translating GCSL to Bounded Temporal Logic (BLTL) as in [6], simulating SoS requires that one defines a formal representation for SoS constituents. In this work, we exploit the Functional Mock-up Interface (FMI) [33] standard as a unified representation for heterogeneous systems. In recent years, the development of DESYRE, a new simulator, provided us joint simulation for FMI/FMU. One of the main contributions of the paper is a full integrated tool-chain between the statistical model checker Plasma [9], FMI/FMU, and DESYRE. This tool-chain is, to the best of our knowledge, the first one that offers a full SMC-based approach for the verification of complex heterogeneous systems.

The third main difficulty of our work is to make sure that the technology will be accepted by practitioners, both in terms of usability and in terms of seamless integration with existing industrial practice and tools. Our first contribution provides a solution for expressing requierements. However, we need a language to specify the system itself. In this paper, we propose to support wide-spread industry standards for SoS. This is done by exploiting UPDM [34] for SoS architecture design and the FMI standard for constituent systems. We build on Rhapsody which is a tool used to describe UPDM views, that we enrich with probability distribtutions. The latter capture uncertainty on the environment so that the verification accounts for predictions on environment's evolution. We then integrate the Constituent Systems behavioral models with the UPDM architecture through the FMI standard. By exploiting our SMC tool chain, we thus provide the full integration of our SMC-based tool for FMI/FMU within Rhapsody.

Our approach has been illustrated on a firefighting SoS, at the scale of a city. The constituent systems are the districts of the city, the cars, the firemen, the fire stations and the central command center. We show how our tools are used to model the architecture and the constituents systems of the SoS. The architecture indicates how the Constituent Systems cooperate to provide an emergent behavior, namely the extinction of the fires. Using our tool chain, we evaluate the probability of this emergent behavior.

Structure of the paper.

The paper is organized as follows. In Section 2 we provide a summary of the Statistical Model Checking approach adopted in our tool-chain. Following this, in Section 3 we introduce the GCSL formal language for specifying formal requirements on SoS and CSs behavior. Finally, we discuss in Section 4 the SMC tool-chain and its integration with existing industrial tools for System design. This tool-chain is demonstrated on an industrial case study in Section 5, where we show its application to a Fire Emergency Response system designed in DANSE [2], modeling a complex SoS that manages fire emergencies in a large city.

2. BACKGROUND ON STATISTICAL MODEL CHECKING

Analyzing Systems of Systems requires a careful choice of the verification technique to use. A first solution would be to use model checking. However, this formal approach often requires an input written in a dedicated language, which conflicts with industry acceptance. Even if a complete model were made in a suitable language, analysis would not be feasible because of the very large size of SoSs and its heterogeneous nature. Therefore, we rely on Statistical Model Checking (SMC), which is a trade off between testing and model checking. SMC works by simulating the system and verifying properties on the simulations. An algorithm from the statistic area exploits those results to estimate the probability for the system to satisfy a given requirement.

The quantitative results provided by SMC is richer than a Boolean one. Indeed, if the system does not satisfy the requirement, a Boolean tool returns "not satisfied" without any evaluation of the probability of a correct behavior.

In order to apply SMC, one has to assume that the behavior of the system is governed by a stochastic semantic, that is the choice of the next state in an execution depends on a probability distribution. This hypothesis shall not be seen as a drawback. Indeed, most of SoS do make stochastic assumptions on their external environment or on their hardware. In case no distribution is known, one relies on the uniform distribution which has the maximal entropy.

In the rest of this section, we first present the BLTL logic used to express properties on system's executions. Then, we present some statistical algorithms used by the SMC engine.

2.1 BLTL Linear Temporal Logic

In this paper, we focus on requirements of SoS that can be verified on bounded executions. This assumption is used to guarantee that the SMC algorithm will terminate. The bounded hypothesis shall not be viewed as a problem. Indeed, like it is the case in the testing world, it is sufficient to consider that the system has a finite live time.

DEFINITION 1. *Given a set of variables V and their domain $\mathcal{D}$, a state σ is a valuation of the variables, that is $\sigma \in \mathcal{D}^V$. A trace τ is a sequence of states and timestamps $(\sigma_0, t_0), \cdots, (\sigma_k, t_k)$, where $\forall i \quad t_i \in \mathbb{R}^+ \wedge t_i < t_{i+1}$.*

We present here BLTL, a variant of LTL [30] where each temporal operator is bounded. Properties of SoS will be expressed in GCSL, that instantiates to BLTL (see Section 3). The core of BLTL is defined by the following grammar, where the time subscript t is interpreted as an offset from the time instant where the sub-formula is evaluated:

$\varphi ::= \mathtt{true} \mid \mathtt{false} \mid p \in AP \mid \varphi_1 \wedge \varphi_2 \mid \neg\varphi \mid \varphi_1 \, \mathtt{U}_{\leq t} \, \varphi_2 \mid \mathtt{X}_{\leq t}\varphi$

Here, AP is a set of atomic predicates defined in Section 3.2. In our case, an atomic predicate depends on the past states. The temporal modalities $\mathtt{F}$ (the "eventually") and $\mathtt{G}$ (the "always") can be derived from the "until" $\mathtt{U}$ as $\mathtt{F}_t\varphi = \mathtt{true}\, \mathtt{U}_{\leq t}\, \varphi$ and $\mathtt{G}_t\varphi = \neg\mathtt{F}_t\neg\varphi$, respectively. The semantics of BLTL is defined with respect to finite traces τ. We denote by $\tau, i \models \varphi$ the fact that a trace $\tau = (\sigma_0, t_0), \cdots, (\sigma_\ell, t_\ell)$ satisfies the BLTL formula φ at point i of execution. The meaning of $\tau, i \models \varphi$ is defined recursively:

$\tau, i \models \mathtt{true}$ and $\tau, i \not\models \mathtt{false}$;
$\tau, i \models p$ if and only if $p(\tau, i)$ (cf. Subsection 3.2);
$\tau, i \models \varphi_1 \wedge \varphi_2$ if and only if $\tau, i \models \varphi_1$ and $\tau, i \models \varphi_2$;
$\tau, i \models \neg\, \varphi$ if and only if $\tau, i \not\models \varphi$;
$\tau, i \models \varphi_1 \mathtt{U_t} \varphi_2$ if and only if there exists an integer $j \geq i$ such that (i) $t_j \leq t_i + t$, (ii) $\tau, j \models \varphi_2$, and (iii) $\tau, k \models \varphi_1$, for each $i \leq k < j$;
$\tau, i \models \mathtt{X}_{\leq t}\varphi$ if and only if $\tau^k, 0 \models \varphi$ where $k = \min\{j > i \mid t_j > t_i + t\}$ and $\tau^k = ((s'_0, t'_0), \cdots, (s'_{\ell-k}, t'_{\ell-k}))$ with $s'_i = s_{i+k}$ and $t'_i = t_{i+k}$;

Typically, a monitor, such as in [17], is used to decide whether a given trace satisfies a given property.

2.2 Statistical Model Checking

Given a stochastic system $\mathcal{M}$ and a property φ, SMC is a simulation-based analysis technique [37, 32] that answers two questions: (1) **Qualitative :** whether the probability p for $\mathcal{M}$ to satisfy φ is greater or equal to a certain threshold ϑ or not; (2) **Quantitative :** what is the probability p for $\mathcal{M}$ to satisfy φ. In both cases, producing a trace τ and checking whether it satisfies φ is modeled as a Bernoulli random variable B_i of parameter p. Such a variable is 0 ($\tau \not\models \varphi$) or 1 ($\tau \models \varphi$), with $Pr[B_i = 1] = p$ and $Pr[B_i = 0] = 1 - p$. We want to evaluate p.

Qualitative Approach.

The main approaches [36, 32] proposed to answer the qualitative question are based on *Hypothesis Testing*. In order to determine whether $p \geq \vartheta$, we follow a test-based approach, which does not guarantee a correct result but controls the probability of an error. We consider two hypothesis: $H : p \geq \vartheta$ and $K : p < \vartheta$. The test is parameterized by two bounds, α and β. The probability of accepting K (resp. H) when H (resp. K) holds is bounded by α (resp. β). Such algorithms sequentially execute simulations until either H or K can be returned with a confidence α or β, which is dynamically detected. Other sequential hypothesis testing approaches exists, which are based on Bayesian approach [22].

Quantitative Approach.

In [18, 23] Peyronnet et al. propose an estimation procedure to compute the probability p for $\mathcal{M}$ to satisfy φ. Given a *precision* ϵ, Peyronnet's procedure, which we call *PESTIM*, computes an estimate p' of p with *confidence* $1-\delta$, for which we have: $Pr(|p'-p| \leq \epsilon) \geq 1-\delta$. This procedure is based on the *Chernoff-Hoeffding bound* [19], which provides the minimum number of simulations required to ensure the desired confidence level.

The quantitative approach is used when there is no known approximation of the probability to evaluate, i.e. to obtain a first approximation. This method is useful when the goal of the analysis is to have a idea on how well the model behaves. On the contrary, the qualitative approach determines whether the probability is above a given threshold, with a high confidence and in a minimal number of simulations.

3. TIMED OCL CONSTRAINTS FOR SOS REQUIREMENTS

The challenge in promoting the use of formal specification languages in an industrial setting is essentially to provide a good balance between expressiveness and usability. In this section we present the requirements language, called GCSL (Goal and Contract Requirement Language). The full GCSL language specification, as well as the details of translation of the GCSL *patterns* into BLTL, can be retrieved in [3]. In this section we focus on providing a brief recap of the language and illustrate why it is appropriate to define SoS and CSs requirements. We also discuss an explicit contribution of this paper to GCSL.

3.1 A Survey of GCSL

A GCSL contract is a pair of Assume/Guarantee assertions denoting requirements on SoS and CSs inputs and outputs, respectively. Contracts allow us to decompose requirements and perform local or global verification on need. Assertions are built upon GCSL natural-language patterns, some of which are shown in Figure 1. GCSL patterns are inspired by and extend the Contract Specification Language (CSL) patterns [1], developed in the SPEEDS European project. These natural-language based requirements have their formal semantics defined by translation into corresponding BLTL formulas, enabling the application of SMC. To simplify the specification of properties of complex systems and architectures, GCSL integrates the Object Constraint Language (OCL) [35], a formal language used to describe static properties of UML models. OCL is an important means to improve the expressiveness and usability of GCSL patterns. Using OCL we can describe properties about types of CS in the SoS architecture, while being independent of their actual number of instances and, thus, defining requirements that are adaptable to the natural evolution of the SoS, without the need of rewriting them.

To show the expressiveness of GCSL, consider the following simple example (based on Pattern 12 from Fig. 1):

```
SoS.its(CriticalComponent) → forAll(cc |
  whenever
    [ cc.its(TempSensor) → exists(ts | ts.temp > cc.threshold) ]
   occurs,
    [ cc.connected(CoolingFan) → exists(f | f.on) ]
   occurs within [ 1 min, 5 min ] )
```

This architecture-abstract requirement says that if any CS of type CriticalComponent has one of *its* TempSensor measuring at time t a temperature that is higher than the threshold set by the *specific* CriticalComponent (the threshold may be different for distinct components) then one of the CoolingFan connected to *that component* should be switched on within the $[t+1\ \text{min}, t+5\ \text{min}]$ time frame. This property does not depend on a concrete architecture or on the number of the mentioned CSs. It can be used as a requirement for any SoS that integrates the mentioned CSs types.

The idea of mixing OCL and temporal logic originates from the need of specifying static and dynamic properties of object-based systems. In [14, 39] OCL has been extended with CTL and (finite) LTL, respectively, without support for real-time properties. The work in [16] is more similar to ours and it is based on ClockedLTL, a real-time extension of LTL. ClockedLTL is slightly more expressive than BLTL, because it allows unbounded temporal operators, whereas BLTL is decidable on a finite trace.

Patterns provide a convenient way to represent frequently occuring and well-identified schemes, while avoiding errors due to the complexity of the underlying logic. The methodology developed during the DANSE project prescribes to have a library of patterns [3] that captures the most relevant temporal constraints for the considered domain. In the rest of this section we are going to discuss a number of these pre-defined patterns. The expressiveness of BLTL, jointly with OCL, makes the patterns library easily extensible to cover future, domain-specific needs.

Figure 1 shows some of the behavioural patterns of GCSL (all the patterns can be found in [3]). Patterns 2 and 3 are typical *safety* properties, where Ψ denotes an argument where an OCL property can be used to describe a state of the SoS. The translation of pattern 2 into BLTL states that the atomic property Ψ should be true at every real-time instant within simulation end time k. Pattern 3 is translated similarly. Pattern 8 shows the joint use of events counting (the n indicates a number of occurrences triggering the pattern) within a real-time interval, such as [*3.2 seconds*, *25.7 minutes*]. Its translation relies on the BLTL operator *occ* and, even if it does not involve any temporal operator, it cannot be decided on a single state but it needs to be checked across the entire trace. In this case we have no explicit mentioning of the simulation time k but we have the overall constraint on all patterns requiring a, b to have appropriate values ($a \leq b \leq k$). Pattern 12 is used to express a *liveness* property which is triggered by an initial condition Ψ_1 occurring at time t and discharged by a following condition Ψ_2 occurring within the interval $[t+a, t+b]$ that is *relative* w.r.t. the time t of occurrence of Ψ_1. Its translation into BLTL underlines a number of important aspects of this pattern. First, the pattern is verified on the entire simulation up to time $k-b$. This is needed because if a condition Ψ_1 occurs at $k-b$, we need to have enough remaining time (actually b) to verify whether either it is discharged by a condition Ψ_2 (making the pattern true) or not. As a consequence, a condition Ψ_1 occurring after time $k-b$ would not require any following discharging condition. Second, on the occurrence of a condition Ψ_1 the pattern requires a shift to time a (as close as possible, depending on the actual states produced by simulation) which is indicated by the next operator $X_{\leq a}$. From that point onwards, we can check for the occurrence of the condition Ψ_2 in the remaining interval using $F_{\leq b-a}$.

3.2 Contribution to GCSL

Before illustrating the new patterns, we enrich the set of atomic predicates of BLTL with adequate timing operators.

On extending BLTL.

Usually atomic predicates describe properties of system states, e.g. by comparing a variable with a constant. We propose here an extension where atomic predicates also depend on the past (i.e. from states before the current one). In particular, we are interested in measuring the amount of time during which a given atomic predicate has been true. The syntax for our predicates is as follows:

$$AP ::= \texttt{true} \mid \texttt{false} \mid AP \circ AP \mid Nexp \bowtie Nexp$$
$$Nexp ::= \texttt{\#Time} \mid \texttt{Id} \mid \texttt{Constant} \mid dur(AP) \mid occ(AP, a, b) \mid Nexp \pm Nexp$$

Here, $\circ$ contains the usual boolean connectors , $\pm$ the usual arithmetic operators and $\bowtie$ the usual comparison operators. Given a trace $\tau = (\sigma_0, t_0), \cdots, (\sigma_k, t_k)$ and a step i, our predicates are interpreted as follows:

$[[\texttt{true}]](\tau, i) = \texttt{true}$ and $[[\texttt{false}]](\tau, i) = \texttt{false}$;
$[[\#Time]](\tau, i) = t_i$ is the simulation time at step i;
$[[\texttt{id}]](\tau, i) = \sigma_i(\texttt{id})$ is the value of var $\texttt{id}$ at step i;

Operators and comparisons have their usual semantics;

$$[[dur(p)]](\tau, i) = 0, \quad \text{if } i = 1,$$
$$[[dur(p)]](\tau, i) = dur(p)(\tau, i-1), \quad \text{if } i > 1 \land \neg[[p]](\tau, i-1),$$
$$[[dur(p)]](\tau, i) = dur(p)(\tau, i-1) + t_i - t_{i-1}, \quad \text{otherwise.}$$

$$[[occ(p, a, b)]](\tau, i) = \sum_{a \leq t_j \leq b} \mathbf{1}_{\{\texttt{true}\}}([[p]](\tau, j))$$

The *dur* function computes the amount of time during which the predicate p has been true since the beginning of the trace. The $\#Time$ notation returns the simulation time at the current point. The *occ* function computes the number of steps in which a predicate holds within the given time bound. For instance, $\texttt{G}_{\leq t}(dur(UP) > 0.9 \cdot \#Time)$ is true iff for every step between 0 and t, the amount of time during which UP holds is at least 90% of the elapsed time.

On monitoring extended BLTL.

In order to support the new $\#Time$ and *dur* constructs, we extend the atomic predicates available in BLTL. Concerning the $\#Time$ variable, we first recall that each state in a trace contains a timestamp, according to Definition 1. In-

ID	Pattern	(below, k is the simulation time and $a < b \leq k$)
2	always [Ψ]	$G_{\leq k}(\Psi)$
3	whenever [Ψ_1] occurs [Ψ_2] holds	$G_{\leq k}(\Psi_1 \rightarrow \Psi_2)$
	...	...
8	[Ψ_1] occurs at most n times during [a,b]	$occ(\Psi_1, a, b) \leq n$
	...	...
12	whenever [Ψ_1] occurs [Ψ_2] occurs within [a,b]	$G_{\leq k-b}(\Psi_1 \rightarrow X_{\leq a} F_{\leq b-a} \Psi_2)$
13	always during [a,b], [Ψ] has been true at least [e] % of time	$G_{\leq b}(\#Time < a \vee dur(\Psi) \geq (\frac{e}{100} * \#Time))$
14	at [b], [Ψ] has been true at least [e] % of time	$F_{\leq b}(dur(\Psi) \geq \frac{e}{100} * b)$

Figure 1: GCSL Patterns extract and their BLTL translations, with $\Psi, \Psi_1, \Psi_2 \in$ *OCL-prop*, $a, b \in \mathbb{R}$, $e \in$ *OCL-expr*

deed, this value is necessary for verifying patterns involving time bounds. At a given state, each predicate is evaluated by replacing $\#Time$ by the timestamp of that state. The predicate $dur(\phi)$ is evaluated by accumulating the amount of time during which the predicate ϕ evaluates to true, according to its semantics defined above.

On GCSL extension.

We are now ready to present our new contribution to GCSL, that is patterns 13 and 14. Those patterns are suitable for expressing safety and reliability constraints, such as the availability of a SoS. As shown in Figure 1, the BLTL translation of these patterns relies on the novel $\#Time$ and dur. Pattern 13 checks that, at each simulation point during $[a,b]$, the amount of time during which Ψ has been seen to be true so-far is at least $e\%$ of the currently elapsed simulation time. We use the operator *dur* to accumulate the overall time during which Ψ is true, and we compare the accumulated value with the required portion of the current simulation time, extracted with the operator $\#Time$, at each simulation point. Pattern 14 checks that, at time $[b]$ the amount of time during which Ψ has been seen to be true is at least the required portion of b.

Figure 2 shows a (simplified) portion of the grammar defining the OCL integration within the GCSL atomic properties (indicated by *OCL-prop*). Properties are constructed using usual boolean operators ($\circ$) and basic arithmetic comparisons ($\bowtie$) between expressions. Attributes of Constituent Systems can occur in properties or expressions and can be accessed by using their *Fully Qualified Name* (*FQN*), such as SoS.Sensor03.isOn.

OCL propositions can describe properties about sets of Constituent Systems that are unknown at requirements-definition time. These sets are left undetermined because (1) the requirements may apply to several variant architectures of the same SoS and (2) the SoS architecture may evolve during the SoS life-cycle. Indeed in [26] one of the five SoS-specific properties of a complex system is that the number and type of systems participating to a SoS may change over time. Ideally, the specifications of the system should remain independent of the number and type of CSs, which is exactly what OCL provides as a feature within GCSL. In order to support properties that are *parametrized* by the SoS architecture, GCSL provides the quantifiers forAll and exists that allow us to instantiate properties over *finite* collections (*OCL-coll*) of Constituent Systems (the *var* ranges over these collections and occurs in the *OCL-prop* which is the scope of the quantifier). A corner case of quantification is provided by the set operators empty and notempty that simply return a truth value after testing the emptiness of the collection. Standard OCL allows to concatenate object names (here indicated as *csName*) by the "."-containment relation, until reaching an *attribute*. In GCSL we add (1) another (weak) containment operator (**its**) that allows to navigate the systems hierarchy in terms of CSs *types* and (2) an operator (**connected**) that allows to navigate the *neighborhood* of a CS, again in terms of *types*.

Quantifiers occur also in expressions (*OCL-expr*) and allow to aggregate the values of (equally-typed) attributes. E.g. the simple expression

(SoS.its(Sensor).temp $\rightarrow$ sum( ))/(SoS.its(Sensor) $\rightarrow$ size( ))

can be used to compute the average temperature in a SoS independently of the number of CS of type Sensor.

Since BLTL does not interpret the OCL syntax (except for *FQN*), the translation from GCSL to BLTL is done once the architecture is fully known and fixed. OCL operators can be nested and their elimination is performed by induction over the structure of the formula in an outside-in fashion. Conceptually, this can be done by repeated application of three steps: (1) resolution of the outermost OCL collections (that is, replacing a collection with a *finite* set of *FQN*), which eliminates its and connected operators, (2) elimination of the universal (existential) quantifiers, replaced by the corresponding conjunctions (disjunctions) of the instantiated scopes, (3) elimination of the remaining operators by replacement with corresponding Boolean or arithmetic expressions, and (4) recursion on new outermost OCL collections. Termination of this procedure is trivially proved. In practice, this procedure is reiterated each time the SMC analysis is called in order to capture every architecture change.

4. SMC TOOL-CHAIN

This Section describes the tool-chain we have set-up to address the challenges listed in the introduction. The tool-chain has been adopted by the industry partners of the DANSE Project project, that are CARMEQ, IBM, EADS, and Thalès. The core of our SMC tool-chain is composed of three main tools: IBM Rhapsody is the tool implementing the UPDM language, DESYRE is the tool providing the joint simulation engine for SMC and PLASMA [9] is the tool providing the SMC analysis engine. A SoS model consists of a model of the architecture and a model of each Constituent System. Our choice is to use UPDM to describe the architecture, that is the interconnection between the instances of Constituent Systems. In order to encompass heterogeneity of the CSs model, our only requirement is that they comply with the Functional Mock-up Interface (FMI) [33]. Additional modeling and simulation tools like for example Modelica, JModelica, Dymola, Rhapsody and

OCL-prop	::=	**true** | **false** | *FQN* | **not** *OCL-prop* | *OCL-prop* $\circ$ *OCL-prop* | *OCL-expr* $\bowtie$ *OCL-expr* | *OCL-coll* $\rightarrow$ **forAll(** *var* | *OCL-prop* [*var*] **)** | *OCL-coll* $\rightarrow$ **exists(** *var* | *OCL-prop* [*var*] **)** | *OCL-coll* $\rightarrow$ **empty()** | *OCL-coll* $\rightarrow$ **notempty()**
OCL-expr	::=	*FQN* | *OCL-coll* $\rightarrow$ **sum()** | *OCL-coll* $\rightarrow$ **size()** | ...
OCL-coll	::=	*attribute* | *csName* | **its(***type***)** | **connected(***type***)** | *OCL-coll* . *OCL-coll*

Figure 2: Simplified OCL fragment for GCSL Atomic Properties, with $\circ \in \{\wedge, \vee, \rightarrow, \leftrightarrow\}$ and $\bowtie \in \{>, \geq, =, <, \leq\}$.

Simulink/StateFlow or any tool exporting models to FMI 1.0 can be seamlessly integrated with this core tool-chain thanks to our choice to adopt that standard. The remaining of this Section describes our core SMC tool-chain.

4.1 Describing SoS Architecture in IBM Rhapsody

UPDM, or Unified Profile for DoDAF[1] and MoDAF[2] [34], is a modeling language based on UML 2 standardized by the Object Management Group (OMG) in 2012. Profiles, such as UPDM, extend the UML meta-model in order to model specific systems. A profile basically includes additional modeling elements that are frequently used in that domain. IBM Rational Rhapsody [20] is a model-based system engineering environment implementing industry-standard languages such as UML, SysML and UPDM.

The SoS architecture is specified in Rhapsody by using UPDM, extended with a new profile enabling pseudo-random number generation according to uniform, normal or custom probability distributions. More precisely, this profile provides additional functions for constituent systems to which it is applied. These additional functions can be used inside constituent systems model whenever a random value is needed, for instance to model a sensor input, the waiting time before the occurrence of an event, or to make global hypotheses on the environment for future predictions.

Rhapsody provides a Java API for integration with external tools. We developed a Java Exporter Plug-in to translate informations from the UPDM SoS architecture model to a format intelligible by DESYRE, the joint simulation engine.

4.2 Performing Joint Simulation in DESYRE

Joint simulation capabilities are provided by DESYRE [27], a simulation framework based on the SystemC standard and its discrete-event simulation kernel. Inputs to DESYRE are the SoS architecture exported from Rhapsody and the Functional Mock-up Units (FMUs) associated to CS types. Joint simulation of several FMUs, that are units complying with the FMI standard, is implemented by a Master Algorithm (MA), with two alternatives. In *co-simulation*, each FMU embeds its own ODE solver and computes autonomously the evolution of its continuous-time variables. In *model exchange*, the MA is in charge of computing evolution of continuous-time variable. In general the implementation of a Master Algorithm (MA) is not a trivial task having to guarantee: (1) correctness of the composition according to the model(s) of computation (MoC) of both the host environment and the constituent FMUs, (2) termination of the integration step and (3) determinism of the composition. Challenges related to the implementation of Master Algorithms for model composition, have been extensively addressed in the literature. In [25] the authors define the operational and denotational semantics of the (hierarchical) composition of Synchronous Reactive (SR), Discrete Event (DE), and Continuous Time (CT) models. Termination and determinacy properties of MA for co-simulation are addressed in [10].

[1]Department of Defense Architecture Framework

[2]Ministry of Defence Architecture Framework

Algorithm 1 DESYRE FMI MA for DANSE.

```
Input: simStartTime, simEndTime, maxIntStep;
1: simTime = simStartTime;
2: isCT = determineIfCT();
3: for all cs ∈ csList do
4:    csEvt = cs.initialize(simTime);
5:    if (csEvt ≠ ∅); then
6:       evtQueue.addEvt(cs.getID(), csEvt);
7:    end if
8:    if (((evtQueue.getClosestEvtTime()−simTime) > maxIntStep) and isCT) then
9:       evtQueue.addEvt(cs.getID(), maxIntStep);
10:   end if
11: end for
12: while (simTime ≤ simEndTime and not(simStopEvt)) do
13:   simTime = getSimTime();
14:   while (not(isSoSFixPtReached())) do
15:      for all cs ∈ csList do
16:         cs.updateDiscrState(simTime);
17:      end for
18:   end while
19:   for all cs ∈ csList do
20:      cs.updateContState(simTime);
21:   end for
22:   evtQueue.updateEvts();
23:   simTime = evtQueue.getClosestEvtTime();
24:   waitNextActivationEvt();
25: end while
```

4.2.1 DESYRE *Master Algorithm*

Within the context of the DANSE project a specific FMI Master Algorithm has been developed in DESYRE to address the unique needs of Systems of Systems simulation and SMC. The main focus is on simulation efficiency due to SoS model complexity and large observation (i.e. simulation) time span (up to several years) and to support large number of runs (tens or hundreds of thousands) as required by SMC analysis. The MA builds on a set of assumptions that are typically satisfied by the CS models used within the DANSE context. The choice of a MA for model exchange rather than co-simulation provides us with full control of the overall integration algorithm. The MA assumes that none of the FMUs contains *direct feed-through* i.e. FMU output does not depend on the value of its inputs at the current simulation time, removing the need for a causality analysis during the fixed point computation at each step.

Lines 1 to 11 in Algorithm 1 represent the initialization phase, while lines 12 to 25 describe the SoS system simulation loop. The algorithm determines the time synchronization instants for the different FMUs composing the SoS model. Time synchronization points represent those time instants in which (1) the different FMUs are executed, (2) the generated outputs are propagated among their interfaces (line 16) and (3) FMU continuous state is updated (line 20). Synchronization points are calculated based on time events,

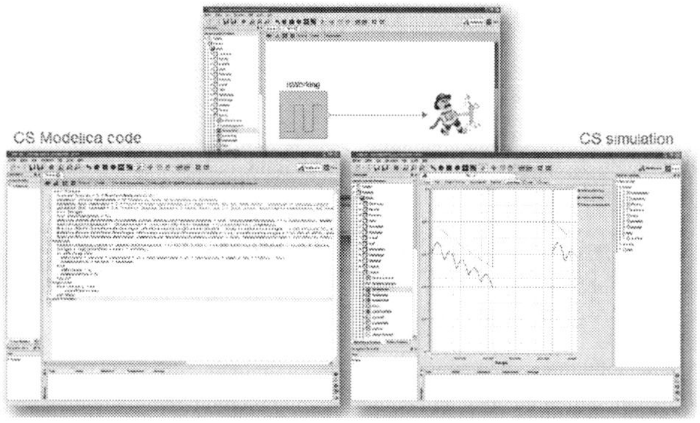

Figure 3: CS behaviour modelled in other tools (e.g. OpenModelica)

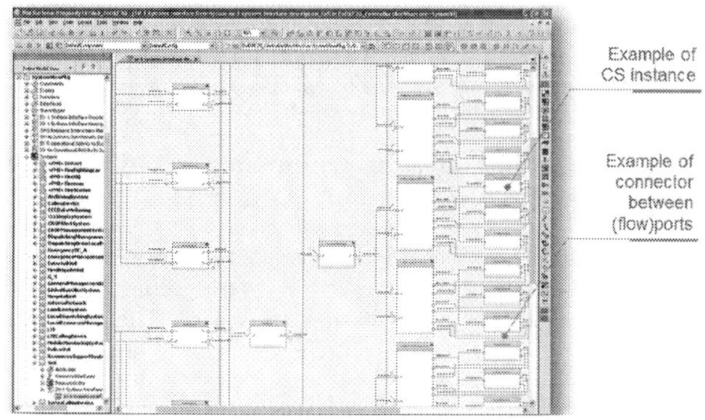

Figure 4: SoS architecture in Rhapsody

state events and step events notified by the different FMUs [33].

4.3 SMC Analysis in PLASMA

PLASMA is a tool for performing SMC analysis. Contrary to existing tools, PLASMA offers a modular architecture which allows to plug new simulators and new input languages on demand. This architecture has been exploited to verify systems and requirements from various languages/specific domains such as systems biology [13], a train station [11], or an autonomous robot [12].

The core of PLASMA is thus a set of SMC algorithms, which includes those presented in Subsection 2.2 as well as more complex ones [9]. This core is completed by two types of plug-ins, that are controlled by the SMC algorithm. First, the simulator plug-ins which implements an interface between PLASMA and a dedicated simulator to produce traces from a dedicated input language on demand. Second, there is a checker plug-ins that verify whether a finite trace satisfy a property.

In this paper we extended the facilities of PLASMA as follows. First, we built a new plug-in between PLASMA and DESYRE in order to produce traces from FMI-FMU model. Second, we used the BLTL checker plug-in that we enrich with the two new primitives *dur* and *#Time* in order to monitor those traces and report the answer to the SMC algorithm. As a last implementation effort, we also implemented a compiler from GCSL to BLTL.

5. A CASE STUDY

This section illustrates the application of our technology to a concept alignment example that was defined for the DANSE Project. This case study has the particularity to embed all the difficulties of the case studies proposed by EADS, THALES, and CARMEQ that, for confidentiality reasons, cannot be described in this paper.

5.1 Modeling

We modeled an emergency response SoS for a city fire scenario in UPDM. The city is partitioned into 10 districts, and we focus on a few fire-fighting constituent systems (CS). We consider the following CSs: the Fire Head Quarter (FireHQ), the Fire Stations, the Fire Fighting Cars and the Fire Men. The behavior of the CSs has been modeled in several FMI-compliant authoring tools. For example, the FireMan has been modeled in OpenModelica (as shown in Figure 3) which is an open-source multi-domain modeling tool based on the Modelica language. Other CSs have been modeled using Rhapsody state-charts. The CSs rely on the new UPDM profile to include probabilistic behavior. For instance, each District models occurrences of fires by randomly choosing the time before the next fire according to a exponential distribution. The time before a fire is reported to the head quarter is also randomly chosen. We remind the reader that the objective of this work is not to learn the probability distribution itself (this has to be done via observations), but rather to show that it is conceptually possible to incorporate such information within the model.

The SoS integrated architecture was built by instantiating the CSs and by specifying how to connect them through an Internal Block Diagram, shown in Figure 4. The SoS architecture is exported to DESYRE using a DANSE-specific exporter plug-in. Each CS behavioral model is exported from the corresponding authoring tool into FMUs, according to the FMI standard. This enables the DESYRE platform to simulate the whole SoS model and to plot some selected variables – see Figure 5 for an illustration.

The simulation is parameterized by its duration, expressed in the time of the model. For our experiments, we choose to simulate 10 000s of execution. Since our model of computation is event based, the computation time needed for running this simulation depends on the number of events occurring during the simulation. Whenever there are few events, such as in the top of Figure 5, the simulation takes a few seconds. In that case, there is no event between two pikes, corresponding to two fires that are very quickly extinguished. Simulations involving more events, such as the one at the bottom of the Figure, require a few dozen of seconds to complete. In that case, fires are not extinguished and the time between two events is kept small to describe the evolution of the fire.

5.2 Expressing Goals of the SoS

Our main objective is to check that the fire area remains small enough. In order to define "small enough" independently of the number of components, we require that the fire is less than a given percentage of the total area.

In our model, each district has two variables of interest, its area and the fire area.

Our first formulation states that the fire area is *always* less than X percent of the total area. The total fire area is

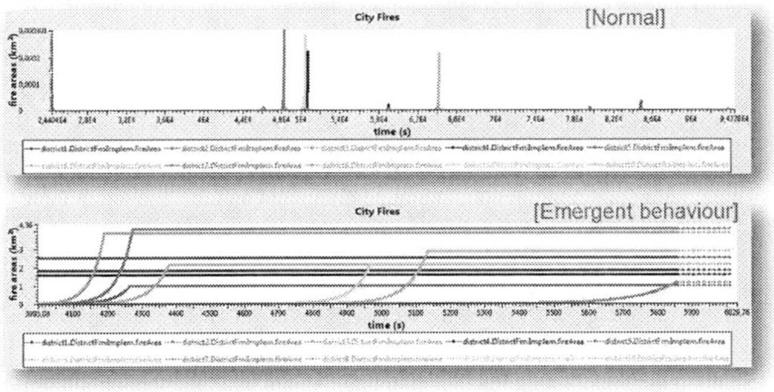

Figure 5: Simulation results in DESYRE

the sum of the fire area in each district, which can be expressed in GCSL by `SoS.itsDistricts.fireArea->sum()`. We define Pattern 1 as follows:

always [SoS.itsDistricts.fireArea $\rightarrow$ sum()
$< (X/100)*$SoS.itsDistricts.area $\rightarrow$ sum()]

As Pattern 1 might be too strong, we propose an alternative formulation. More precisely, we allow the fire area to exceed $X\%$ of the total area, but no more than 10% of the time. For technical reasons, we define Pattern 2 as the negation of the above property, namely:

at [10000], [SoS.itsDistricts.fireArea $\rightarrow$ sum()
$> (X/100)*$SoS.itsDistricts.area $\rightarrow$ sum()]
has been true at least [10] % of time

Pattern 2 is true whenever the fire area is above the threshold for more than 10% of the time, that is when the SoS behaves incorrectly. As we want the probability that the system behaves correctly, we have to compute the probability of the complementary event. This is done by subtracting the probability that Pattern 2 holds from 1.

5.3 Unwanted Emergent Behaviors Detection and Evaluation

One of the challenges in SoS design is the detection and analysis of unwanted emergent behaviour. In our case, simulation allowed us to detect an (undesired) emergent behaviour which is depicted in the lower part of Figure 5. Our analysis of this emergent behaviour is the evaluation of the probability of its occurrence. The first step is to define a GSCL pattern that characterizes the absence of the emergent behaviour. One key characteristic of this behaviour is that fires spread over entire districts. We assume that the emergent behaviour does not occur if there is no area where the fire has taken the whole district. This is specified in Pattern 3:

always [SoS.itsDistricts $\rightarrow$ forAll(district |
district.fireArea $<$ district.area)]

5.4 Analysis and Discussions

In this section, we use SMC to compute an estimate of the probability for Pattern 1, 2 and 3 to hold. We use the *PESTIM* method which is parameterized by an allowed error ϵ, and a confidence $1-\delta$. We chose an error of 0.1 and a confidence of 99% ($\delta = 0.01$), which requires 265 simulations traces. These traces are obtained by running stochastic simulations of the model. The length of a simulation is set to 10000s. We present the analysis results and time for Pattern 1 in Table 1. The analysis result is an estimation of the probability that Pattern 1 holds, based on the 256 traces.

Table 1: Probability that fire is always smaller than X percent of the total area during 10000 seconds.

X	Probability	Analysis Time
1	0.98490566	0:34:23
0.1	0.954716981	0:39:54
0.01	0.966037736	0:31:03
0.001	0.939622642	0:36:14
0.0001	0.603773585	0:28:49
0.00001	0.350943396	0:25:23

As expected, the probability that the fire remains smaller than $X\%$ of the total area increases when X increases. Indeed, "the fire area remains smaller than $X\%$ of the total area" implies that "the fire area remains smaller than $Y\%$ of the total area" for any $Y \geq X$. However, the probability returned is an approximation, with an error up to 0.1 with a confidence of 99%. Therefore, the fact that the probability decreases from 0.96 to 0.95 when X increases from 0.01 to 0.1 is not significant. Indeed, the difference between the two values is less than the error. On the contrary, the difference between the probabilities obtained for $X = 0.0001$ and $X = 0.001$ are significant since they are more than twice the error. In our model, the total area is about 23 square kilometers. Therefore the two last lines of the table correspond to respectively an area of 23 and 2.3 square meters.

Table 2: Probability that fire area is smaller than X percent of the total area at least 90% of the time.

X	Probability	Analysis Time
1	0.954716981	00:40:05
0.1	0.981132075	00:34:25
0.01	0.966037736	00:43:22
0.001	0.977358491	00:42:37
0.0001	0,973584906	00:42:59
0.00001	0,996226415	00:37:25

In order to obtain the probability presented in Table 2, we subtract from 1 the probability that Pattern 2 holds. We obtain the probability that the fire is smaller than X percent of the total area for at least 90% of the time (over 10000s). Again, since for each value of X we ran a different set of simulations, it is not clear that the probability that the pattern holds increases when X increases. With this more permissive definition, we see that even small fires have a low probability to stay on for more that 10% of the simulation time. By comparing with Table 1, we can conclude that frequently occurring fires (i.e. very small ones) are quickly extinguished, because the probability of the last two lines are significantly higher in Table 2.

Finally, we evaluate the probability to obtain the unwanted emergent behavior depicted in Figure 5, that is the probability that Pattern 3 holds. The returned result is 0.9622, which means that the probability that the contract holds is between 0.8622 and 1 with a confidence of 99%.

We showed here how our tool chain is used to evaluate whether a given pattern holds. By evaluating the probability of Pattern 1, 2 and 3, we were able to discover that small fire occur often (last two lines of Table 1) but are not likely to last long (last two lines of Table 2). Finally, the emergent behavior occurs with a probability between 0 and 0.14, which explains why Pattern 1 and Pattern 2 do not occur with a probability of 1. This problem could be resolved by studying the causes of the emergent behavior and evolving the SoS to avoid it, for instance by adding more fire fighting cars.

At this level of analysis, a precision of 0.1 is sufficient to obtain a good general idea about the probability that each of the patterns occur. In general, using SMC requires to find the appropriate trade-off between the required precision and the time available for the analysis and subsequent re-engineering.

Our Patterns are independent on the actual number of components. Indeed, adding constituent systems such as districts or cars, even if they have a new behavior, do not require specifying new patterns. The analysis is still possible on the modified SoS model.

In the framework of the DANSE project, Industrial Partners built models of their SoS under analysis. SMC and other methods provided them a higher confidence in their models [4]. More precisely, one Partner verified Mean Time Between Failures (safety) requirements in an Air Traffic Control case study. Another Partner verified sufficient water availability (robustness to failures) in a water distribution system of national scale.

6. CONCLUSION, FUTURE WORK AND RELATED WORK

This paper proposes a full tool-chain for the rigorous design of Systems of Systems via formal reasoning and Statistical Model Checking.

Recent work promotes simulation techniques as the principal way to perform SoS analysis. In [38] the authors use discrete event specification (DEVS) concepts and tools to support virtual build and test of systems of systems. Their MS4-Me environment enables modeling and simulation (M&S) of SoS by allowing the user to specify constituent systems' behavior in terms of a so-called Constrained Natural Language. The tool is implemented in Eclipse and employs Xtext, Eclipse Modeling Framework and the Graphical Modeling Project.

Recent work in [31] provides an overview of the underlying theory, methods, and solutions in M&S of systems of systems, to better understand how modeling and simulation can support the Systems of Systems engineering process. However, simulation is an incomplete analysis and it is not able to assess the likelihood of the simulated behaviors. This is not acceptable from the point of view of SoS analysis, as it does not provide to the designer sufficient confidence of correctness. Other approaches to verification of complex systems are based on exhaustive formal analysis, such as model checking, or simulation-based formal analysis, such as run-time monitoring. Industrial model checking techniques [8] are not adequate to the complexity and dynamicity of SoS. Run-time monitoring does not seem to be adequate to the context of SoS, where failures detection should provide a likelihood estimate of the failure and sufficient time for devising failure-avoidance corrections. In this perspective, a very promising approach to provide sufficient coverage of the SoS behavior while keeping the analysis cost low is based on Statistical Model Checking (SMC) [37]. SMC is a simulation-based formal analysis providing an estimate of the likelihood of requirement satisfaction and a tunable level of confidence in the accuracy of analysis results.

Some frameworks, such as BIP [7] or Reo [5] allow the user to describe architecture of systems using alternative composition operators. Both these frameworks theoretically permit composition of heterogeneous system, by including existing code into the components. However, they provide no standard such as FMI/FMU allowing to compile a particular component independently of the architecture, which make them unsuitable for an industrial environment. They both include a stochastic extension [29, 28], which is not part of the core framework.

Contracts for reasoning about heterogeneous systems are presented in [24]. However, these contracts are considered at a very abstract level, and thus are not as useful as FMI/FMU from an industrial point of view.

Future Work.

Our objective is to improve our solution by exploiting rare-event techniques [21] that would allow us to detect rare emergent behaviors with a minimal amount of simulations. Our second future work is to automatize the relationship between the outcome of SMC and the reconfiguration process, in order to automatically find an architecture satisfying sufficiently the GCSL contracts.

7. REFERENCES

[1] Speeds (2008): D2.5.4: Contract Specification Language. Public deliverable, Available at http://speeds.eu.com/downloads/D_2_5_4_RE_Contract_Specification_Language.pdf, 2008.

[2] Vv. Aa. D3.3.2 - Concept Alignment Example description. Technical report, DANSE deliverable, 2013.

[3] Vv. Aa. D6.3.3 - GCSL Syntax, Semantics and Meta-model. Public deliverable, DANSE deliverable, 2015.

[4] Vv. Aa. DANSE Final Report. Technical report, DANSE deliverable, 2015.

[5] FARHAD ARBAB. Reo: a channel-based coordination model for component composition. *Mathematical Structures in Computer Science*, 14:329–366, 6 2004.

[6] A. Arnold, B. Boyer, and A. Legay. Contracts and behavioral patterns for sos: The EU IP DANSE approach. In K.G. Larsen, A. Legay, and U. Nyman, editors, *Proc. 1st Workshop on Advances in Systems of Systems (AiSoS) 2013*, volume 133 of *EPTCS*, pages 47–66, 2013.

[7] Ananda Basu, Marius Bozga, and Joseph Sifakis. Modeling heterogeneous real-time components in BIP. In *Fourth IEEE International Conference on Software Engineering and Formal Methods (SEFM 2006), 11-15 September 2006, Pune, India*, pages 3–12, 2006.

[8] J.L. Boulanger. *Industrial Use of Formal Methods.* John Wiley and Sons, 2012.

[9] B. Boyer, K. Corre, A. Legay, and S. Sedwards. Plasma lab: A flexible, distributable statistical model checking library. In *QEST'13*, pages 160–164, 2013.

[10] D. Broman, C. Brooks, L. Greenberg, E.A. Lee, M. Masin, S. Tripakis, and M. Wetter. Determinate composition of fmus for co-simulation. In *Proc. of the 11th ACM Int. Conference on Embedded Software*, EMSOFT '13, pages 2:1–2:12. IEEE Press, 2013.

[11] Quentin Cappart, Christophe Limbrée, Pierre Schaus, Jean Quilbeuf, Louis-Marie Traonouez, and Axel Legay. Verification of interlocking systems using statistical model checking. submitted to IFM2016.

[12] Alessio Colombo, Daniele Fontanelli, Axel Legay, Luigi Palopoli, and Sean Sedwards. Efficient customisable dynamic motion planning for assistive robots in complex human environments. *JAISE*, 7(5):617–634, 2015.

[13] Alexandre David, Kim G. Larsen, Axel Legay, Marius Mikucionis, Danny Bøgsted Poulsen, and Sean Sedwards. Statistical model checking for biological systems. *STTT*, 17(3):351–367, 2015.

[14] D. Distefano, J.P. Katoen, and A. Rensink. On a temporal logic for object-based systems. In S.F. Smith and C.L. Talcott, editors, *4th International Conference on Formal Methods for Open Object-Based Distributed Systems (FMOODS) 2000*, volume 177 of *IFIP Conference Proc.*, pages 305–325. Kluwer, 2000.

[15] L. Mangeruca et al. D4.3 - DANSE Methodology V2. Technical report, DANSE deliverable, 2013.

[16] S. Flake and W. Müller. Past- and future-oriented time-bounded temporal properties with OCL. In *2nd International Conference on Software Engineering and Formal Methods (SEFM 2004)*, pages 154–163. IEEE Computer Society, 2004.

[17] Klaus Havelund and Grigore Rosu. Synthesizing monitors for safety properties. In *Tools and Algorithms for the Construction and Analysis of Systems, 8th International Conference, TACAS 2002, Held as Part of the Joint European Conference on Theory and Practice of Software, ETAPS 2002, Grenoble, France, April 8-12, 2002, Proceedings*, pages 342–356, 2002.

[18] T. Hérault, R. Lassaigne, F. Magniette, and S. Peyronnet. Approximate Probabilistic Model Checking. In *VMCAI*, pages 73–84, 2004.

[19] W. Hoeffding. Probability inequalities. *J. of the American Statistical Association*, 58:13–30, 1963.

[20] IBM. Rhapsody.

[21] Cyrille Jégourel, Axel Legay, and Sean Sedwards. Importance splitting for statistical model checking rare properties. In *Computer Aided Verification - 25th International Conference, CAV 2013, Saint Petersburg, Russia, July 13-19, 2013. Proceedings*, pages 576–591, 2013.

[22] SumitK. Jha, EdmundM. Clarke, ChristopherJ. Langmead, Axel Legay, André Platzer, and Paolo Zuliani. A bayesian approach to model checking biological systems. In Pierpaolo Degano and Roberto Gorrieri, editors, *Computational Methods in Systems Biology*, volume 5688 of *Lecture Notes in Computer Science*, pages 218–234. Springer Berlin Heidelberg, 2009.

[23] S. Laplante, R. Lassaigne, F. Magniez, S. Peyronnet, and M. de Rougemont. Probabilistic abstraction for model checking: An approach based on property testing. *ACM TCS*, 8(4), 2007.

[24] ThiThieuHoa Le, Roberto Passerone, Uli Fahrenberg, and Axel Legay. A tag contract framework for heterogeneous systems. In Carlos Canal and Massimo Villari, editors, *Advances in Service-Oriented and Cloud Computing*, volume 393 of *Communications in Computer and Information Science*, pages 204–217. Springer Berlin Heidelberg, 2013.

[25] Edward A Lee and Haiyang Zheng. Leveraging synchronous language principles for heterogeneous modeling and design of embedded systems. In *Proceedings of the 7th ACM & IEEE international conference on Embedded software*, pages 114–123. ACM, 2007.

[26] M.W. Maier. Architecting principles for systems-of-systems. *Systems Engineering*, 1(4):267–284, 1998.

[27] A. Mignogna, L. Mangeruca, B. Boyer, A. Legay, and A. Arnold. Sos contract verification using statistical model checking. In K.G. Larsen, A. Legay, and U. Nyman, editors, *Proc. 1st Workshop on Advances in Systems of Systems (AiSoS) 2013*, volume 133 of *EPTCS*, pages 67–83, 2013.

[28] Young-Joo Moon, Alexandra Silva, Christian Krause, and Farhad Arbab. A compositional model to reason about end-to-end qos in stochastic reo connectors. *Science of Computer Programming*, 80, Part A:3 – 24, 2014. Special section on foundations of coordination languages and software architectures (selected papers from FOCLASA'10), Special section - Brazilian Symposium on Programming Languages (SBLP 2010) and Special section on formal methods for industrial critical systems (Selected papers from FMICS'11).

[29] Ayoub Nouri, Saddek Bensalem, Marius Bozga, Benoît Delahaye, Cyrille Jégourel, and Axel Legay. Statistical model checking qos properties of systems with SBIP. *STTT*, 17(2):171–185, 2015.

[30] A. Pnueli. The temporal logic of programs. In *Proc. of the 18th Annual Symposium on Foundations of Computer Science*, SFCS '77, pages 46–57, Washington, DC, USA, 1977. IEEE Computer Society.

[31] L.B. Rainey and A. Tolk. *Modeling and simulation support for system of systems engineering applications.* Wiley, Jan 2015.

[32] K. Sen, M. Viswanathan, and G. Agha. Statistical model checking of black-box probabilistic systems. In *CAV*, LNCS 3114, pages 202–215. Springer, 2004.

[33] Vv.Aa. FMI standard specification. Modelica association, https://www.fmi-standard.org/, 2012.

[34] Vv.Aa. UPDM 2.0 formal specification. OMG, http://www.omg.org/spec/UPDM/2.0/, 2012.

[35] Vv.Aa. OCL language specification. OMG, http://www.omg.org/spec/OCL/, 2014.

[36] H.L.S. Younes. *Verification and Planning for Stochastic Processes with Asynchronous Events.* PhD thesis, Carnegie Mellon, 2005.

[37] H.L.S. Younes and R.G. Simmons. Statistical probabilistic model checking with a focus on time-bounded properties. *Inf. Comput.*, 204(9):1368–1409, 2006.

[38] B.P. Zeigler. *Guide to Modeling and Simulation of Systems of Systems - User's Reference.* Springer Briefs in Computer Science. Springer, 2013.

[39] P. Ziemann and M. Gogolla. OCL extended with temporal logic. In M. Broy and A.V. Zamulin, editors, *5th Conference on Perspectives of Systems Informatics (PSI) 2003*, volume 2890 of *LNCS*, pages 351–357. Springer, 2003.

Influence of Processing Delays on the VoIP Performance for IEEE 802.11s Multihop Wireless Mesh Networks – Comparison of ns-3 Network Simulations with Hardware Measurements

Christopher Hepner
hepner@hs-ulm.de

Steffen Moll
stmoll@mail.hs-ulm.de

Roland Muenzner
muenzner@hs-ulm.de

Institute of Communication Technology
University of Applied Sciences Ulm, Germany

ABSTRACT

An IEEE 802.11 [1] Multihop Wireless Mesh Network (WMN) can be set up based on the amendment for mesh networking IEEE 802.11s [2]. Such a network allows the relaying of communication data such as VoIP over several hops. In this work the influence of processing delays on the VoIP performance will be presented. The processing delay will be estimated by a testbed setup and included in the network simulator. The ns-3 mesh model is validated and compared to the actual IEEE Standard 802.11-2012 [1]. To this end a Voice over IP (VoIP) communication link is validated in a linear chain topology of several nodes and in the use case of a disaster recovery scenario.

CCS Concepts

•**Networks → Network simulations; Network performance analysis; Network measurement;**

Keywords

ns-3; IEEE 802.11s; VoIP; Medium Access Control

1. INTRODUCTION

After the occurrence of a disaster such as an earthquake, tsunami or hurricane most of the communication infrastructure is usually destroyed or not working due to loss of power. However, one of the main needs for rescuers – which are mostly volunteers during the first hours – is a functional communication infrastructure. We have shown in a previous work [3] that a wireless mesh network (WMN) based on IEEE 802.11s – which is set up by non damaged legacy, mesh capable and battery powered devices still available in the disaster region – seems to be sufficient to provide network focus thereby was on enhancing the lifetime of the Disaster Recover System (DRS) in order to bridge the time until professional rescue teams with their communication equipment will arrive while still keeping a network connectivity providing essential communication needs, especially Voice over IP (VoIP) and low rate data services. The performance of the proposed lifetime enhancement algorithm in [3] has been validated by a network simulation in ns-3 of VoIP calls between individual rescuers and validated according to the VoIP requirements shown in [4]. Thereby packet loss should be no more than 1 percent, one-way latency (mouth to ear) should be no more than 150 ms and average one-way jitter should be targeted at less than 30 ms. The simulation results showed that for a VoIP communication link of two Wireless Mesh Stations (MSTAs) for all observed scenarios with different node densities more than 90% of successful calls could be achieved. Dropped calls, however, were caused almost only due to packet loss while packet delay and jitter were very low which might not cover the real hardware performance whereas the quality of service (QoS) is dependent on both loss and delay. As most network simulators ns-3 focuses on accurate modeling of the MAC- and higher layer protocols. However, the actual simulation model in ns-3 lacks of the modeling of appropriate processing delays which are added in each Mesh Station (MSTA) due to the software execution time and scheduling mechanism of tasks in the CPU. So far the introduced delay in the network simulation is caused only by the MAC-layer protocol and duration of the transmission itself. The lack of modeling processing delays is also causing some other issues in the network simulation which are discussed in more detail in section 3. However the setup of complex large-scale testbed measurements would be very time-consuming, expensive and in some cases even not possible. Network simulations, however, allow the fast simulation of complex scenarios with reproducible results and easy change of settings, protocols and environment. The accuracy of the simulation results is always dependent on the accuracy of the simulation models and level of simulation detail which is also a trade-off between the development of accurate, but complex models and simulation time while all aspects of reality can never be included.

In this work we validate the network simulation by means of simplified testbed measurements. Thereby the introduced processing delay is estimated by the measurement of up to five MSTAs which are placed to form a linear chain topology

SIMUTOOLS 2016, August 22-23, Prague, Czech Republic

in our lab. In this arrangement it will be possible to measure the delay which is added by each hop. The estimated processing delay will be included in the network simulations which leads finally to more accurate results of the network simulations even in complex scenarios.

2. RELATED WORK

Most of research present (e.g. [5],[6],[7]), addressing VoIP in WMN are focusing on the capacity of the mesh network in terms of a maximum number of calls while still having sufficient QoS. In the use case of a disaster recovery system, however, we are interested in low rate data services and a low number of VoIP calls in the WMN providing still sufficient QoS over a maximum number of hops. The analysis presented in the existing work is based on testbed measurements, analytical models as well as simulation. [5] focuses on call admission control and different routing strategies based on available capacity or call statistics. The capacity utilization model and call admission decisions presented in [5] are evaluated on an experimental testbed based on six identical Dell laptops running Linux 2.6.15, and using Atheros 802.11a/b/g cards and madwifi driver while routing was evaluated in ns-2. [6] showed that the number of calls supported in a 15 node mesh setup – while each node has a 802.11b 2 Mbps link – is reduced from 8 calls in a single hop scenario to one call after 5 hops in their testbed. By providing a multihop aggregation mechanism, which has been also validated by ns-2 simulations, the available capacity could be increased. [7] determined the maximum number of supported calls in an experimental WMN testbed, based on Mesh Routers running DD-WRT Linux software, at different hop counts. After 5 hops only one call was possible with sufficient performance by using 11Mbps links between the Mesh Routers. Let us emphasize that non of the previously mentioned papers used the amendment for wireless mesh networking IEEE802.11s in their testbeds, but IP-layer based routing algorithms. An estimation of the processing delay and determination of a maximum number of hops was also not part of their research.

Some papers (e.g. [8],[9],[10]) propose analytical models based on Markov chains, initially proposed by Bianchi [11], to compute the throughput performance of the IEEE 802.11 distributed coordination function (DCF). Those papers focus mainly on saturated throughput which is not applicable in our case. [8] analyzed the saturation performance of the IEEE 802.11e Enhanced Distributed Channel Access (EDCA) throughput and in addition also the performance of delay, and delay jitter. [9] presented analytical formulas also for the throughput and access delay in non-saturated mode, which are obtained and verified by ns-2 simulations. Recently [10] analyzed the end-to-end throughput and delay for a IEEE 802.11 string topology multi-hop network using a Markov chain model. All previously mentioned papers account delay in terms of the access delay which means the time from when a data frame at the transmit station starts contending for the channel to the time the data reaches the MAC layer of the receiver. However the introduced processing delay of real hardware is not included in these models.

([12],[13],[14]) analyzes the performance of VoIP in WMN by simulative approaches. [12] presented the simulation results of a VoIP WMN based on simulations with Qualnet. In their simulations average one way delay increased linearly up to 7 mesh nodes. However after 7 mesh nodes the delay increases abruptly which is not further explained in their paper. In [13] the performance of VoIP by using three different routing protocols is presented in the context of IEEE 802.11s. Thereby the HWMP protocol was implemented in ns-2. [14] evaluates the Enhanced Distributed Channel Access mechanism by simulation of topologies which considered different types of delay sensitive applications such as VoIP. The results presented in [14] showed that QoS is not guaranteed in an IEEE 802.11s WMN since EDCA fails to categorize different types of applications into suitable QoS classes.

However, the presented simulation based research (e.g. [12],[13],[14]) doesn't account for hardware induced processing delays resulting from software execution time and kernel scheduling. Recently [15] proposed a methodology to extract service models from real multithreaded Operating Systems (OSs) by means of instrumentation and tracing. A proof of concept implementation, of service models for IP forwarding, derived from a Google Nexus One and Nokia N900 smartphone, in ns-3, showed the possibility to account for the overhead of protocol processing. [16] developed a simulation model in ns-3 for packet processing via the Linux network stack. They have analyzed the Network Interface Control (NIC) driver and NAPI (New API) as part of the OS and have modeled and simulated the NIC driver and NAPI mechanism by extending their ns-3 resource management module. Currently this model only simulates the latency introduced by software and does not consider realistic DMA (Direct Memory Access) or other hardware components which may introduce additional latencies. Their measurement setup was based on a Debian live Linux distribution and ixgbe NIC driver. However, these models are not part of the current ns-3 release as the state of this paper and the instrumentation and development to achieve models which are applicable for several states of system utilization as presented in [15] is quite cumbersome. We use a more simplified approach whereby we focus on the estimation of a maximum number of hops possible for a single VoIP connection by including an appropriate processing delay, estimated for a single state of utilization from our testbed measurements, in the network simulation.

3. VALIDATION OF THE WIFI AND MESH MODEL IN NS-3

The network simulator ns-3 (release ns-3.24 used in this work) is a packet-based, discrete-event network simulator which consists of a wifi and mesh module according to the WLAN standard IEEE 802.11. Most research addressing the validation of the ns-3 WIFI network simulation models focus on the validation of the physical layer and channel models, e.g. [17], however still some inaccuracies might be present. Recently we have analyzed the physical layer performance ([18] and [19]) and published recommended changes to the ns-3 error rate models in order to make them more reliable. In order to improve the credibility of the network simulation [20] validates the IEEE 802.11 MAC layer model by means of measurements in the EXTREME testbed. It is also stated in [20] that, while in general there is a good qualitative agreement between simulator and testbed, in several cases there were noticeable quantitative differences. However, this might not only be due to an inaccurate ns-3 implementation, but even more likely due to rather a non-standard behavior of some commercial cards which are aimed on performance enhancement.

The ns-3 802.11s mesh module was initially developed by [21] and was based on the IEEE 802.11s Draft Standard 3.0 (2009). Recently this module has been updated by us in [22] making it more compliant to the actual IEEE Standard 802.11-2012 [1]. The mesh module is using the low layer MAC and PHY functionality of the wifi module (e.g. DCF, PHY, Channel) and adds the required upper layer functionality (e.g. MeshWifiInterfaceMac, MeshPointDevice, MeshL2RoutingProtocol). To the best of our knowledge there is no other validation of the current ns-3 mesh model present. The ns-3 wifi model is on ongoing development, however due to the open source nature still some inaccuracies might be present.

The actual simulation model in ns-3 lacks of the modeling of appropriate processing delays which are added by each WLAN module due to software execution time and the scheduling mechanism of tasks in the CPU. In ns-3 the actual packet processing time of the Mesh Stations (MSTAs) is exactly zero and the hybrid wireless mesh protocol is highly sensitive to this fact causing an unrealistic behavior or even doesn't work at all (see bug reports 912, 1465 and 1605 [23]). One rather striking explanation of this sensitivity is the following. One MSTA is sending a broadcast Path Request (PREQ) message. Two or more MSTAs, which are located at exactly the same distance to the sending MSTA are receiving this packet. The received packet goes immediately through all the MSTA and to their outgoing wifi-queues. All received packets are forwarded immediately (backoff is not calculated, because there was no previous concurrency in the network). Packets are colliding and because of the broadcast mechanism packet loss is not recognized (broadcasts are not acknowledged). In this specific case a path can never be established by the routing protocol.

According to the DCF access procedure described in [1] a MSTA achieves immediate access to the medium when the MSTA determines that the medium is idle for greater than or equal to a DIFS (DCF interframe space) or AIFS[i] (arbitration interframe space) period in case of EDCA. However, this is not the case in the described example as the packet goes immediately to the outgoing wifi-queue. Therefore backoff should be performed (this has been also discussed in ns-3 bug report 555). Winlab Rutgers [24] proposed a patch for ns-3.16 in order to change the DCF manager to fix this issue. However, this patch has not been included in ns-3 so far and is still under discussion.

3.1 Mesh validation by linear chain topology

The behavior of the ns-3 WIFI MAC protocol in conjunction with the mesh model will be analyzed in a simple forwarding scenario by setting the Mesh Stations in a linear chain topology with up to five MSTAs (see Fig. 1). Every node has connection to its direct neighbors one hop away. However, it has to be recognized that every node 2 hops away is a hidden node to the respective node.

The time introduced by each additional hop can be estimated by performing a ping from the first to the last MSTA

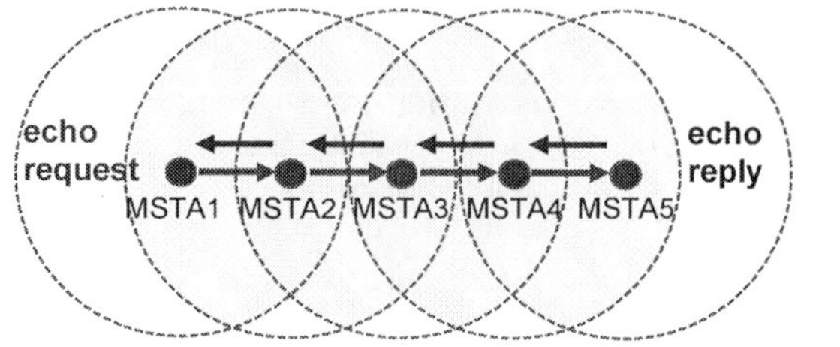

Figure 1: Schematic of the Mesh Station setup as linear chain topology.

of the chain. Thereby ping is operating by sending an Internet Control Message Protocol (ICMP) echo request to the target MSTA and waiting for an ICMP echo reply. This simulation setup will be used for the validation by comparing the results with those achieved by measurements shown in section 4. In order to simplify the simulation model, a fixed transmission radius has been chosen by using the RangePropagationLossModel. In this case each MSTAs establishes a Peer Link only to its direct neighbors. The reactive on-demand mode of the hybrid wireless mesh protocol (HWMP) is used in order to establish a route between MSTA1 and the rightmost MSTA of the chain and the round-trip-time (RTT) is determined for each configuration by the used ping.

The ping is performed with an interval of 20 ms and 222 bytes of payload. Tab. 1 shows the protocol and header lengths of the packets for the ns-3 simulation and testbed measurements. The payload in the ns-3 simulation has been adjusted to meet the packet size of the testbed measurements. The differences arise from the radiotap header which is not used in the ns-3 simulation and the Mesh Address Extension subfield of the Mesh Control Field which is present in the measurements, however not implemented in ns-3. The duration of the packets t_p can be calculated by Eq. (1):

$$t_p = 16\mu s + 4\mu s + \left\lceil \frac{16\text{bit} + b \cdot 8\frac{\text{bit}}{\text{byte}} + 6\text{bit}}{N_{\text{DBPS}}} \right\rceil \cdot 4\frac{\mu s}{\text{Sym}} = 424\mu s \quad (1)$$

N_{DBPS} is the number of data bits per OFDM symbol. b is the size of the PLCP (physical layer convergence procedure) Service Data Unit (PSDU). Assuming Binary Phase Shift Keying (BPSK) with Coderate 1/2 (datarate 6 MBits/s), N_{DBPS} equals 24 bits. With a packet size of 300 bytes this finally leads to a packet duration of $t_p = 424\,\mu s$. The duration of an Ack packet t_{ack} with length 16 bytes thereby is 44 μs.

3.2 Simulation results

Fig. 2 shows the histogram of round-trip-times for the configurations with 2, 3, 4 and 5 MSTAs. In each configuration 100 simulation runs have been performed with different seeds. In each simulation run with a duration of the ping of 60 sec, 3000 ICMP packets are sent resulting in 300.000 packets per configuration. The configuration with 2 MSTAs shows a single peak at 0.951 ms. This time can be calculated as shown in Fig. 3. The echo request from MSTA1 is received at MSTA2 after the packet duration t_p. After receipt, the echo reply is immediately generated and forwarded to the outgoing queue. However, after receipt an

Table 1: Packet compilation

Protocol	ns-3 Length (Bytes)	testbed Length (Bytes)
Radiotap Header v0	not used	38
IEEE 802.11 QoS Data	42	54
Logical-Link Control	8	8
IPv4	20	20
ICMP	8	8
Payload	222	172
Packetsize b	300	300

Ack will be sent after a Short Interframe Space (SIFS) and the echo reply will be sent after the Arbitration Interframe Space (AIFS). When operating in the 5 GHz band aSIFS-Time equals to 16 μs. AIFS is dependent on the used access category (AC) and can be calculated by AIFS = SIFS + AIFSN[AC] $\cdot$ aSlotTime. With the default access category best effort (AC_BE) and AIFSn[AC_BE] = 3, AIFS equals to 43 μs. As mentioned before backoff is not performed and the size of the contention window (CW) is zero. The total duration thus equals to $2t_p + \text{SIFS} + t_{ack} + \text{AIFS} = 0.951$ ms. The total duration of the configurations with 3, 4 and 5 MSTAs can be calculated similarly while each hop adds $2t_p + 2\text{SIFS} + 2t_{ack} + 2\text{AIFS} = 1.054$ ms. The propagation delay which is in the range of ns is neglected in these simplified calculations. As can be seen in Fig. 2 this simplified calculation which does not include any backoff does not exactly match the simulation results. However, in the actual ns-3 implementation for the configuration with 3 to 5 MSTAs backoff is performed only once, leading to 16 equally spaced slots separated by the slot time of 9 μs. This is a result of the non standard conform simulator implementation. Backoff should be calculated at every forwarding attempt except for the first MSTA.

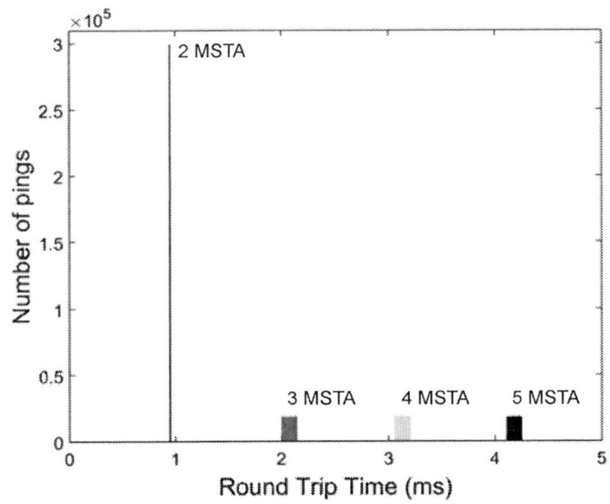

Figure 2: Histogram of round-trip-times for the network simulation setups of chains with 2, 3, 4 and 5 MSTAs.

The patch proposed by Winlab [24] initially developed for ns-3.16 with the change of the DCF-manager shows the expected results (see Fig. 4). Backoff is calculated at every forwarding attempt except for the first MSTA.

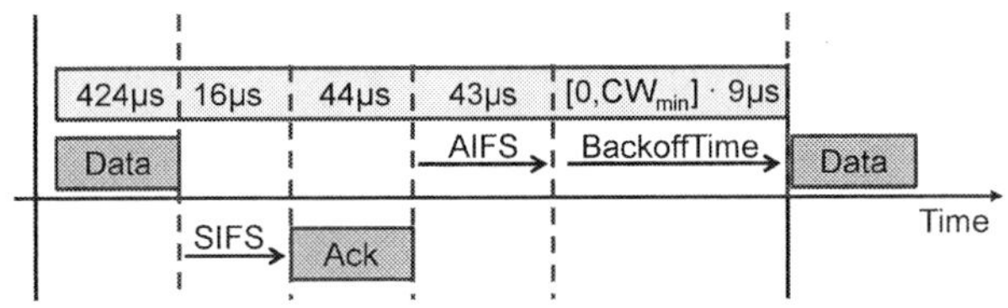

Figure 3: One hop duration.

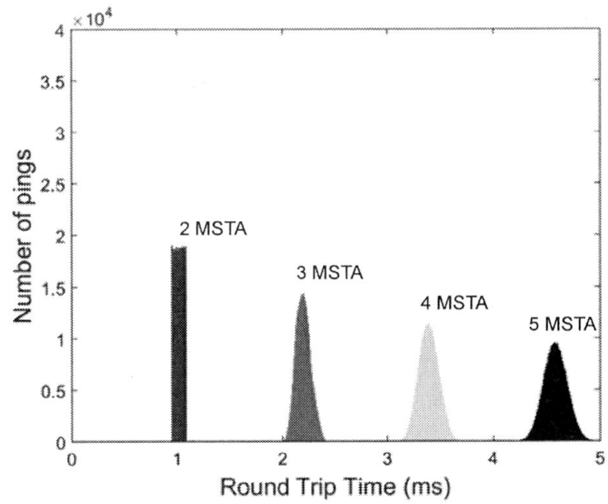

Figure 4: Histogram of round-trip-times for the network simulation setups of chains with 2, 3, 4 and 5 MSTAs and the change in DCF-manager for correctly taking the required backoff into account.

The results shown so far count for a minimum delay per hop caused by the MAC protocol. However, in real environments packet loss is likely to happen due to interference and propagation in the wireless medium. Lost packets, however, will result in retransmissions and in an increase of delay and jitter. A lost packet thereby is recognized by a missed Ack at the transmit MSTA. According to [1] the MSTA shall wait for an ACKTimeout interval, with a value of aSIFSTime + aSlotTime + aPHY-RX-START-Delay, which starts at the end of the data transmission. For an OFDM PHY with 20 MHz channel the ACKTimeout equals to 50 μs. The time introduced per retransmission is shown in Fig. 5 and is calculated by ACKTimeout + AIFS + BackoffTime + t_p. Thereby BackoffTime is calcualated by Random() $\cdot$ aSlotTime. A random integer is drawn from a uniform distribution over the interval [0,CW], where CW is an integer within the range of values of the PHY characteristics between aCWmin and aCWmax [1]. Assuming AC_BE with the values of aCWmin=15 and aCWmax=1023, the backoff time for the first retransmission is in the interval $[0, 31] \cdot$ aSlotTime. After each retransmission the CW value is increased by sequentially ascending integer powers of 2, minus 1. Therefore the delay of the first retransmission is in the interval $[517, 796]\,\mu$s.

A ns-3 simulation has been set up by adjusting the Signal-to-Noise ratio to the effect that the resulting packet suc-

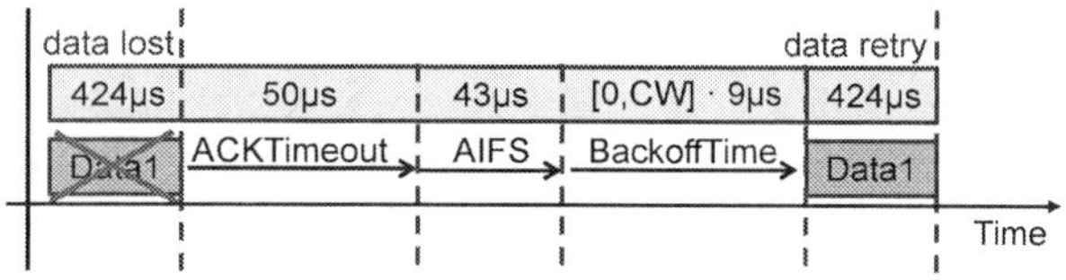

Figure 5: One hop duration – data packet lost.

cess rate (PSR) of the packets with size b equals to 90%. Fig. 6 shows the result of the ns-3 simulation of the Histogram with round-trip-times for the configuration with 2 MSTAs. As described previously, at the first transmission no backoff is performed. For the first retransmission, however, backoff is calculated leading to 32 equally spaced slots separated by the slot time of 9 μs. However, the delay with an interval of $[542, 821]\,\mu$s is not as expected. The difference of 25 μs is a result of an inaccurate implementation in ns-3 which has been also discussed in Bug 761. ns-3 calculates the ACKTimeout interval by SIFS$+t_{\text{ack}}+$aSlotTime$+$Def_max_prop_delay $= 75.66\,\mu$s which explains the difference of about 25 μs.

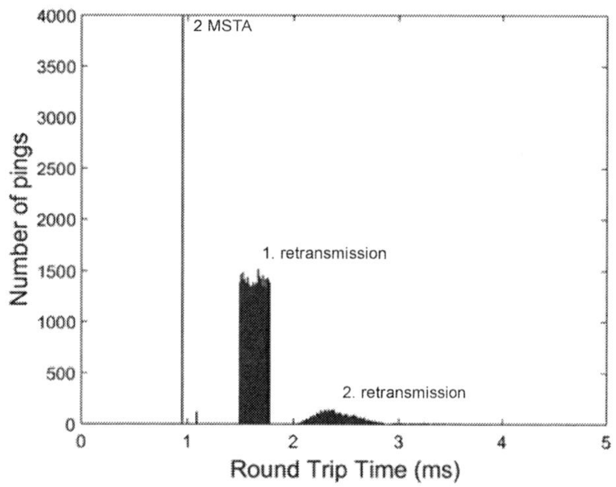

Figure 6: Histogram of round-trip-times for the setup with 2 MSTAs and PSR 90%.

4. ESTIMATION OF PROCESSING DELAY

In this section the processing delay which is added at each hop in a linear chain topology is estimated based on the measurement of the round-trip-time in our testbed. Four scenarios have been measured with 2, 3, 4 and 5 MSTAs respectively. After each measurement run one MSTA is added at the end of the chain.

4.1 Testbed setup

The measurement setup is based on up to five WLAN modules which have been placed in our lab. These WLAN modules have been developed by us together with the SME *embedded wireless GmbH* during the FP7 research project CHAMELEON (Project reference: 286510). Thereby the focus of this research project was the development of a cost-effective, fast-to-deploy, low-power and flexible video surveillance system that automatically combines images from multiple cameras to create a 180° panoramic view and a low-power, small size IEEE802.11a/g/n Wireless LAN card for wireless installation scenarios. Each WLAN module consists of an QCA9344 System-on-Chip (SoC) which allows dual-band (2.4/5 GHz) operation with up to two spatial streams (Fig. 7). The QCA9344 SoC consists of a 74Kc MIPS processor with a high single thread performance operating at up to 533 MHz. The open-source GNU/Linux distribution for embedded devices OpenWrt [25] is installed on each of the modules with the Version Chaos Calmer (SVN release 45514). Each module is configured as Mesh Station with the same mesh ID and channel based on the WLAN-Stack mac80211. By default, each MSTA automatically attempts to create peer links with MSTAs with the same mesh ID and channel. In order to keep the scenario simple, 802.11a is set as hardware mode and only Channel0 of the WLAN module is used.

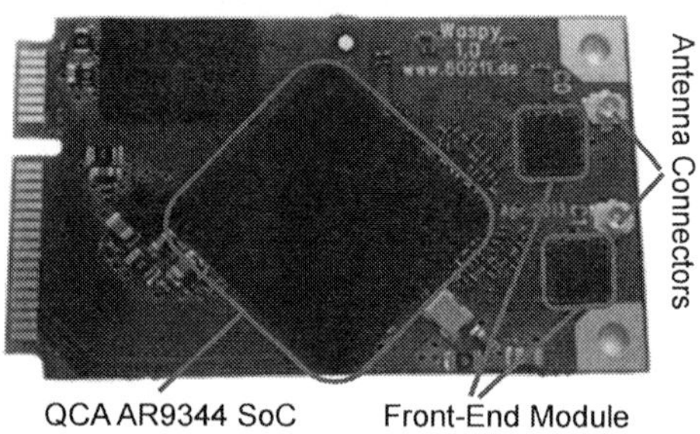

Figure 7: WLAN Module based on QCA AR9344 SoC.

The modules are placed in the lab to model a linear chain topology (Fig. 1). During the measurements it was ensured that each module has only an established peer link to its direct neighbors. However, interference between adjacent neighbors could not be completely avoided due to the wireless propagation environment. The maximum possible datarate was adjusted to 6 Mbits/s (BPSK with coderate 1/2) on each of the modules. The round-trip-time for each of the scenarios is measured by performing a ping from the first to the last WLAN module of the chain. The ping was repeated 60.000 times for each configuration and was performed with an interval of 20 ms and 172 bytes of payload. Tab. 1 shows the protocol and header length of the packet.

4.2 Measurement results

Fig. 9 shows the histogram of the round-trip-time in ms of the setups with 2, 3, 4 and 5 MSTAs. The measured RTTs are recorded with a resolution of 10 μs. For 2 MSTAs a dedicated peak of the round-trip-time can be seen. This can be explained as shown in Fig. 8. The processing delay is higher than SIFS $+ t_{\text{ack}} +$ AIFS and the MSTA achieves immediate access to the medium because the MSTA determines that the medium is idle for greater than or equal to AIFS, backoff thus is not calculated. The Jitter of the round-trip-times is a result of the scheduling mechanism of the kernel. The wireless network interface device (WNIC) is implemented as SoftMAC. This means that the MAC-layer is essentially implemented in software. Only time critical parts such as the distributed coordination function and Rx/Tx-State Machine are implemented in hardware. In order to compare these results with those obtained by the ns-3 simulation as a first step a single processing delay based on the measurement results will be calculated.

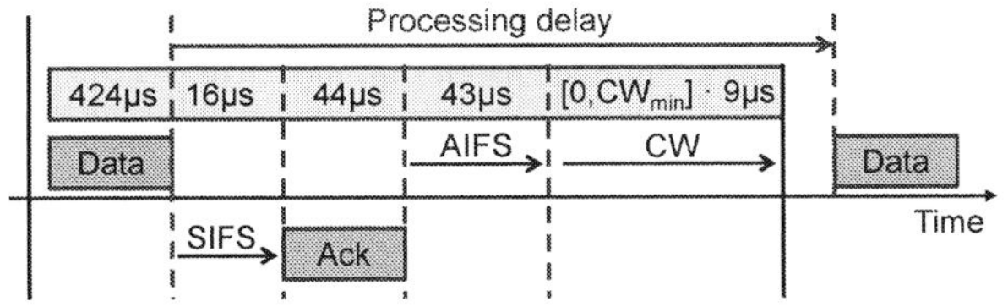

Figure 8: One hop duration with processing delay.

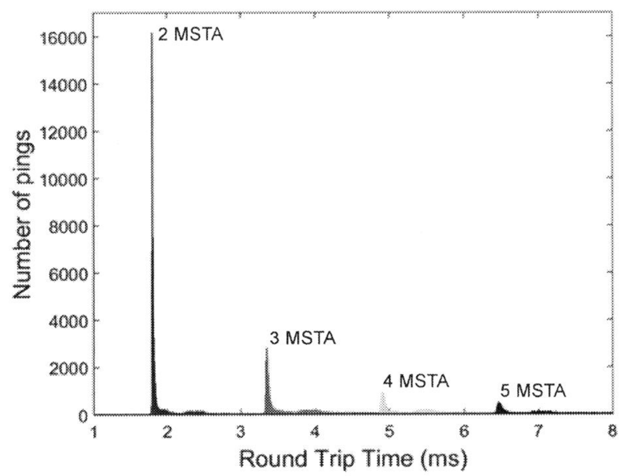

Figure 9: Histogram of round-trip-times for the measurement setups of chains with 2, 3, 4 and 5 MSTAs.

The ICMP echo request or reply are generated at the first or last MSTA respectively. In the intermediate nodes only the MAC and PHY-layer are involved by forwarding the particular messages. In order to estimate a processing delay per hop a differentiation between end nodes and intermediate nodes is needed. The modules rely on the same Hardware/Software configuration and workload. Therefore it is assumed that the software execution time is the same in each of the modules, however, dependent on the actual state of the CPU because of time sharing with other tasks. The additional processing amount which occurs by the generation of the ICMP echo request and reply messages has to be considered at the end nodes. The round-trip-time is composed of the packet duration t_{p}, the processing delays of the MAC and PHY t_{pd} and the processing delay of the IP and ICMP processing t_{pd2}. However, it is not possible to distinguish between the processing caused by the preparation of the echo request or reply message within the performed measurements. Therefore these processing delays will be equally weighted.

The following calculation of the processing delays is based on the schematic shown in Fig. 10. From the measurement results (Fig. 9) a single round-trip-time for one hop $\mathrm{RTT}_1 =$ 1.8 ms and for two hops $\mathrm{RTT}_2 = 3.35$ ms can be extracted. By using Eq. (2) and solving for t_{pd} and t_{pd2} with $t_{\mathrm{p}} =$ $424\,\mu s$, the processing delay t_{pd} can be estimated to $175.5\,\mu s$ and $t_{\mathrm{pd2}} = 62.5\,\mu s$.

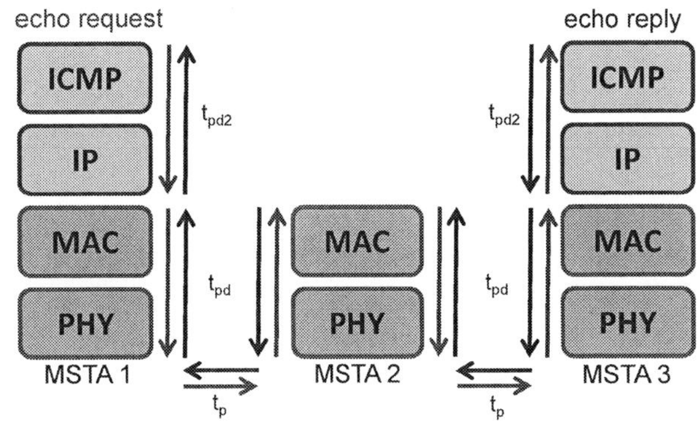

Figure 10: Breakdown of processing delays in the OSI model.

The calculation of the round-trip-time for one hop and for n hops is shown in Eq. (2).

$$\begin{aligned} &1\,\mathrm{Hop}: \mathrm{RTT}_1 = 2t_p + 4t_{pd} + 4t_{pd2} \\ &\mathrm{n\,Hop}: \mathrm{RTT}_n = 2n \cdot t_p + 4n \cdot t_{pd} + 4t_{pd2} \end{aligned} \qquad (2)$$

4.3 Network simulation validation

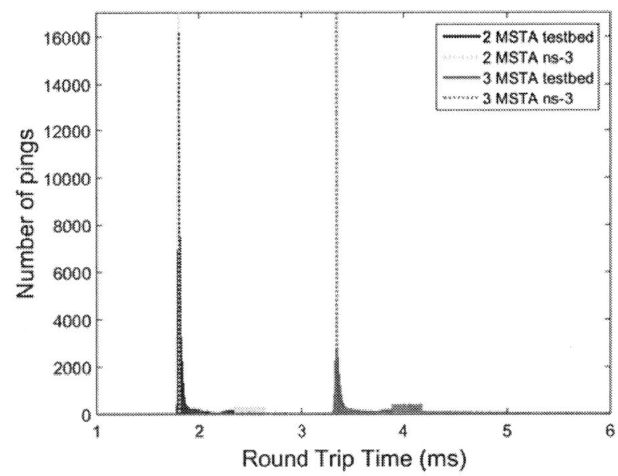

Figure 11: Histogram of round-trip-times for the measurement setups of chains with 2 and 3 MSTAs and corresponding ns-3 simulation with processing delay.

The accuracy of the estimated processing delay $t_{\mathrm{pd}} =$ $175.5\,\mu s$ can be validated by including a single processing delay in the ns-3 simulation. Fig. 11 shows the simulation results with the same setup as described in section 3.1 with a single processing delay of $2t_{\mathrm{pd}} = 351\,\mu s$ of the configuration with 2 and 3 MSTAs. The delay has been included in the mesh wifi-mac-interface in order to delay the packets before sending them to the outgoing wifi-queue. As shown in Fig. 6 the PSR is adjusted to 90% which results also in a certain amount of retransmissions. The offset $4t_{\mathrm{pd2}} = 250\,\mu s$ has been included in the simulation results as additional delay. In principle the simulation result fits to the main peak of the measurement results. The RTT which can be associated with the first set of retransmissions is higher in the simulation than in the accomplished measurements. One reason is the inaccurate calculation of the ACKTimeout as described in section 3.2. However, the delay in ns-3 is slightly higher than expected which for the time being can not be explained.

The performance of the scheduling and service execution of the single thread MIPS processor might be modeled by a M/G/1 processor sharing queue. As a simplification we modeled in a first experiment only the Poisson arrival process. The distribution of the RTTs as shown in the measurements is therefore modeled by a Poisson distribution with $\lambda = 2$ and mean value $335\,\mu s$. The simulation result compared to the measurements of the configuration with 2 MSTAs is shown in Fig. 12. The simulation results shown in Fig. 12 are plotted with the same resolution of $10\,\mu s$ as obtained by the recorded measurements. The poisson distribution models the first part of the distribution of the round-trip-times, however, the exponentially decaying profile is not considered. The spreading of RTTs of the set of the first retransmission is similar than the measurements beside the delay shift as already mentioned.

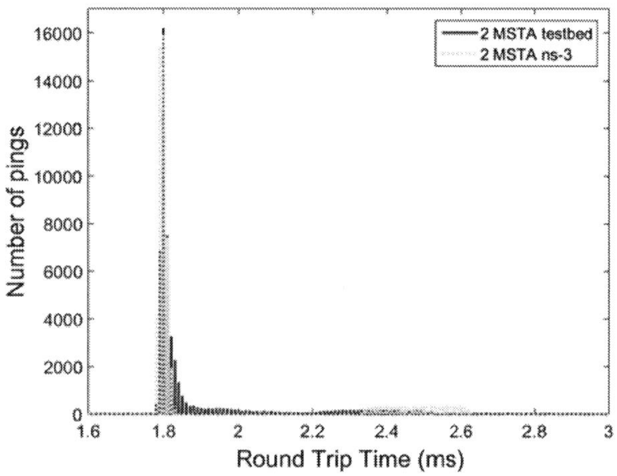

Figure 12: Histogram of round-trip-times for the measurement setups of chains with 2 MSTAs and corresponding ns-3 simulation with processing delay and Poisson distribution.

5. NETWORKSIMULATION OF VOIP COMMUNICATION LINKS WITH PROCESSING DELAY

Based on the results presented in the previous section a VoIP communication link will be simulated in the linear chain topology. The simulation results with the introduced processing delay distribution will be compared with the ns-3 standard implementation in terms of the end-to-end delay and packet loss. Compared to the simulations with ICMP the VoIP simulation is characterized by two individual data streams competing for the channel access. Due to the hidden node problem, which is fundamental in the linear chain topology, collisions may occur resulting in delay and packet loss. In the second part of this section the results originally presented in [3] will be validated with the current release ns-3.24 and the processing delay distribution proposed here. As there is no VoIP communication model in ns-3, the communication link is modeled as two individual UDP data streams. A G.711 VoIP codec at the default packetization rate (50 pps) is assumed and a new VoIP packet is generated every 20 ms. The payload of each VoIP packet is 160 bytes. With the IEEE 802.11 QoS-Data, LLC, IP, UDP, and RTP headers (42 + 8 + 20 + 8 + 12 bytes) included, this packet becomes 250 bytes in length. As there is no RTP protocol in ns-3, the corresponding header is added as additional payload such that the total payload is set to 172 bytes in the simulation.

5.1 VoIP in linear chain topology

5.1.1 Simulation setup

The duration of the connection is 60 sec during which 3000 UDP packets are sent for both data streams. For each number of hops the simulation was repeated 100 times with different seeds. The relevant simulation parameters are shown in Table 2. The IEEE 802.11s standard does not define the way of closing peer links, however, the ns-3 mesh model implemented two ways of doing this [21]. Links can be closed due to beacon loss and due to packet loss. If one of the parameters exceeds the threshold the link shall be closed. However, the default values of the ns-3 model MaxBeaconLoss=2 and MaxPacketFailure=2 are way to stringent. A closed link in the linear chain topology leads to a considerable number of lost packets and significant delay because of the additional peer link establishment process which is again carried out after a closed link. Therefore we have increased these values and guarantee that a link in the chain is always be established in our simulations.

Table 2: Simulation Parameters in ns-3

802.11s Peer Link	
MaxBeaconLoss	200
MaxRetries	3
MaxPacketFailure	200
MaxNumberOfPeerLinks	32
802.11s HWMP Protocol	
HWMPmaxPREQretries	5
UnicastPreqThreshold	10
UnicastDataThreshold	10
Communication Link	
Connections	2 Nodes (bidirectional)
tx rate	68.8 kbps payload
Packetization Interval	20 ms
Voice Payload in Bytes	172
Duration of Connection	60 sec
Transport Protocol	UDP

5.1.2 Simulation results

Fig. 13 shows the result of the simulation in ns-3 for different configurations for an ascending number of up to 20 hops. For each configuration the median of the delay and the minimum/maximum error-bounds in ms of the two UDP data streams from the leftmost MSTA (01) to the rightmost MSTA (02) of the linear chain are shown. The results obtained with the processing delay distribution (dashed line) are compared with the standard setup in ns-3 without processing delay (solid line). The simulation results with processing delay shows the expected increase in delay by ascending number of hops. The dotted line shows the simulation result with a PSR of 90% and the dash-dotted line for a PSR of 70% respectively. The adjusted PSR results in an increased number of retransmissions due to the loss of packets and therefore an increase in end-to-end delay. The error-bounds indicate that even for a large number of hops, the QoS requirement of VoIP (end-to-end delay < 150 ms) is not violated for all packets. Only with the maximum number of 20 hops some packets exceed this constraint while the medial value is still low.

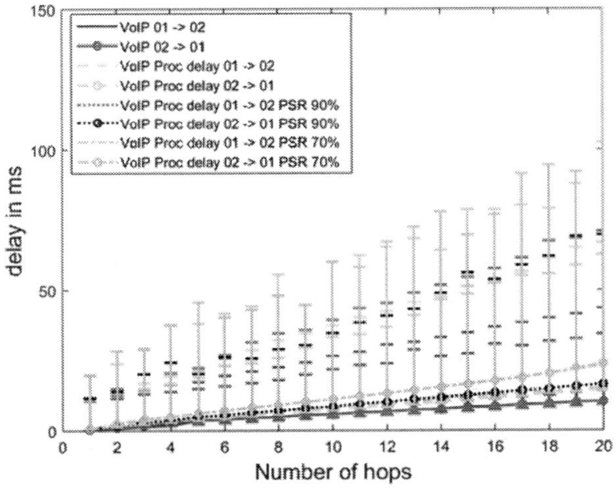

Figure 13: End-to-End delay of simulation setups of chains with 1 to 20 hops.

Fig. 14 shows the medial packetloss and error-bounds of the 100 simulation runs. Beside the configuration with PSR = 70% packetloss is almost zero. With a PSR of 70% the medial packet loss is still below 1% for 20 hops, however, the error-bounds indicate that some simulation runs exceed this threshold. The presented results show that according to the constraints of delay and packet loss a transmission of up to 20 hops with sufficient QoS might be possible even for a PSR of 70%.

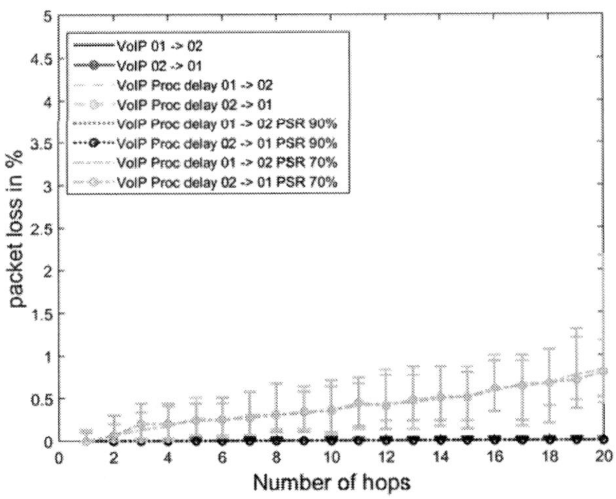

Figure 14: Packet loss of simulation setups of chains with 1 to 20 hops.

5.2 VoIP in disaster area

The proposed lifetime enhancement algorithm (LEA-DRS) presented in [3] allows to switch of devices that are not needed, especially in order to save the remaining energy in the batteries for a later usage when the initially switched on devices run out of battery, while still keeping a sufficient coverage in the disaster region. A network simulation validates the performance of VoIP calls between two individual rescuers in the thinned out mesh network. It has been shown in [3] that the reduced set of nodes while some nodes are in a sleep mode thereby even shows better network performance because of a reduced congestion in the thinned out network. The simulations presented in this work are based on the initial configuration of 102 MSTAs which are randomly placed in an area of 250 m · 250 m (see Fig. 15).

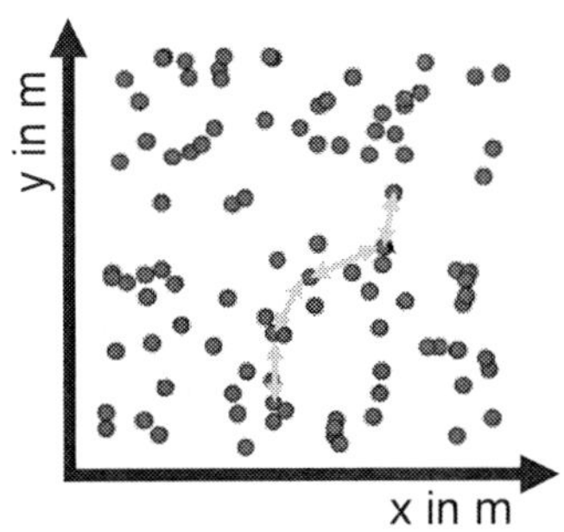

Figure 15: ns-3 setup with 102 MSTAs.

5.2.1 Simulation setup

Two nodes are arbitrarily chosen as communication partners for the validation of a communication link. The simulations have been carried out with 100 simulation runs for each configuration. Table 3 shows the relevant simulation parameters. The VoIP call starts randomly for each simulation run within a time interval from 5 to 35 sec after the beginning of the simulation and has a duration of 120 up to 180 sec. The WMN operates at a single frequency channel. At the beginning of the simulation each MSTA is setting up a peer link to all its neighboring MSTAs according to the peer link management protocol. After the establishment of all peer links, which is realized within a few seconds after the beginning of the simulation, the DRS network is assumed to be established. It should be noted, that in a dense network some of the nodes might interfere with each other and not all peer links can be established resulting in a less connected network.

5.2.2 Simulation results

Tab. 4 shows the simulation results for latency, jitter and packet loss of the connection and Fig. 16 the probability of a successful call. A successful call thereby is assumed if the requirements for latency, jitter and packet loss are met for both of the individual data links. A call is dropped if one of the three conditions is not fulfilled. The initial configuration obtained from [3] is repeated here with the actual release ns-3.24. However, compared to the results obtained from [3] a significant performance degradation of about 10% is observed. In ns-3.24 the Data packet format was changed from plain Data to QoS Data according to the standard which was wrong in the implementation of the mesh mod-

Table 3: Simulation Parameters in ns-3

Simulation Environment	
Area A	250 m · 250 m
Propagation Model	RangePropgationLoss
Max Range	60 m
Number of MSTA	102
Communication Link	
Connections	2 Nodes (bidirectional)
tx rate	68.8 kbps payload
Packetization Interval	20 ms
Voice Payload in Bytes	172
Start Time	[5 sec,35 sec]
Stop Time	[155 sec,185 sec]
Duration of Connection	2 - 3 min
Transport Protocol	UDP

ule. Due to the change, the MAC-header increases by 2 bytes because of the QoS Control field. However, recently we found out that this degradation is due to a bug in the ns-3 simulator. The degradation is caused by the detection of false duplicates in MacRxMiddle which results finally in a higher packet loss of the communication link (see also bug 2326 [23]). A possible workaround is to use the calculation of sequence numbers as used by non-QoS STAs whereby the sequence numbers are calculated from a single modulo-4096 counter, starting at 0 and incrementing by 1, for each MAC service data unit (MSDU). Configuration a) shows the simulation results with the proposed workaround and similar performance compared to the previously obtained results. The only difference in the simulation is the changed packet size because of the used QoS Data packets. Configuration b) shows the simulation results with the included processing delay distribution. Despite the higher delays Configuration b) shows even better performance. The reason is the non standard conform implementation of the DCF access procedure in ns-3. On each forwarding attempt a STA achieves immediate access to the medium and no backoff is performed which results in a higher probability of packet collisions. In configuration b) each forwarding attempt is under the influence of the used processing delay distribution and transmission attempts at the same time of different data streams is much more unlikely. All previously shown simulation results are using the IEEE 802.11e access category best effort (AC_BE) as default. However, IEEE 802.11e specifies four access categories which allow the prioritization of data traffic among others. In configuration c) we have used the access category for Voice traffic (AC_VO). This results in a change of AIFSN=2, CWmin=3 and CWmax=7. However, the result obtained by config. c) shows a heavy degradation in performance leading to only 24% of successful calls. The reason is the change of CWmin which leads to only four backoff slots in the first transmission attempt and therefore to a higher probability of collisions. Therefore it turned out that the parameters of AC_VO are not useful in a multihop scenario for VoIP communication.

6. CONCLUSIONS

In this work we have shown the validation of the ns-3.24 mesh model also in conjunction with the IEEE 802.11 MAC of the ns-3 wifi model of wireless multihop networks. The network simulations have been validated by a testbed setup in our lab which was based on up to five IEEE802.11a/g/n WLAN modules. We have shown a novel approach in order to estimate the processing delay occurring in the WLAN modules in a forwarding scenario of a linear chain topology by measuring the round-trip-time and deriving a processing delay distribution. We have extended the network simulator by a model of these processing delays and used for the performance estimation of VoIP communication links over multiple hops. The presented results show that according to the constraints of delay and packet loss a transmission of up to 20 hops with sufficient QoS might be possible even for a dedicated packet error rate of 30%. Further we have validated the network simulation results of a previous work [3] with the current release of the network simulator ns-3.24. Even though we expected higher delays and therefore higher packet loss with our processing delay model the results showed even better performance because of the non standard conform implementation of the DCF access procedure in the current ns-3 release. We have also shown that the IEEE 802.11e access category for Voice traffic (AC_VO) shows a significant performance degradation and is not useful in wireless multihop networks as shown in this work. The presented model is valid only for the specified settings. Different packet size and packet interval may result in different processing delay distributions which are also dependent on the used hardware.

Table 4: Simulation Results

	avg. Delay < 150 ms	avg. Jitter < 30 ms	packet loss < 1%
Init. Config. ns-3.22	100%	100%	93%
Init. Config. ns-3.24	100%	100%	84%
Configuration a)	100%	100%	91%
Configuration b)	100%	100%	96%
Configuration c)	100%	99%	24%

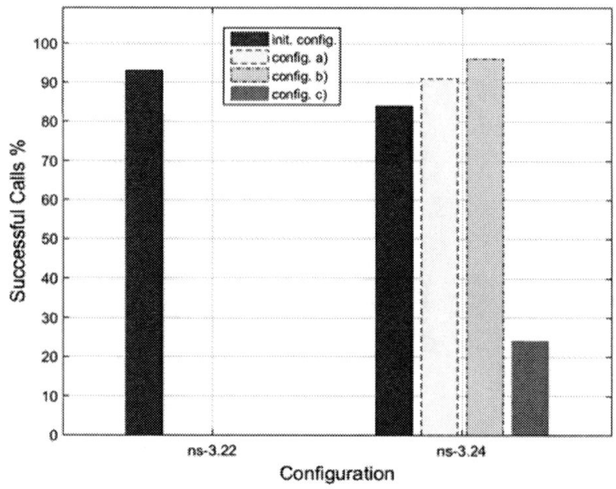

Figure 16: Successful calls in % depending on the configuration.

7. REFERENCES

[1] IEEE Computer Society, "Part 11: Wireless LAN Medium Access Control (MAC) and Physical Layer (PHY) Specifications," *IEEE Std 802.11*, 2012.

[2] ——, "IEEE Std 802.11s," *Amendment 10: Mesh Networking*, Sept 2011.

[3] C. Hepner and R. Muenzner, "Lifetime enhancement of Disaster Recovery Systems based on IEEE 802.11s Wireless Mesh Networks," *The IEEE WiMob 2015 Workshop on Emergency Networks for Public Protection and Disaster Relief*, 2015.

[4] T. Szigeti and C. Hattingh, *End-to-End QoS Network Design: Quality of Service in LANs, WANs, and VPNs.* Cisco Press, 2004.

[5] A. Kashyap, S. Ganguly, S. R. Das, and S. Banerjee, "VoIP on Wireless Meshes: Models, Algorithms and Evaluation," *INFOCOM 2007, 26th IEEE International Conference on Computer Communications*, 2007.

[6] D. Niculescu, S. Ganguly, K. Kim, and R. Izmailov, "Performance of VoIP in a 802.11 Wireless Mesh Network," *In Proceedings of IEEE INFOCOM 2006. 25th IEEE International Conference on Computer Communications*, 2006.

[7] D. van Geyn, H. Hassanein, and M. S. El-Hennawey, "Voice Call Quality Using 802.11e On A Wireless Mesh Network," *The 5th IEEE International Workshop on Performance and Management of Wireless and Mobile Networks (P2MNET) Zuerich, Switzerland*, 2009.

[8] C. l. Huang and W. Liao, "Throughput and delay performance of ieee 802.11e enhanced distributed channel access (edca) under saturation condition," *IEEE Transactions on Wireless Communications*, vol. 6, no. 1, pp. 136–145, Jan 2007.

[9] H. Zhang, R. Zhao, and Z. Gao, "Performance analysis of the 802.11 with a new model in nonsaturated conditions," in *Information Networking and Automation (ICINA), 2010 International Conference on*, vol. 1, Oct 2010, pp. V1–344–V1–349.

[10] K. Sanada, N. Komuro, and H. Sekiya, "End-to-end throughput and delay analysis for ieee 802.11 string topology multi-hop network using markov-chain model," in *Personal, Indoor, and Mobile Radio Communications (PIMRC), 2015 IEEE 26th Annual International Symposium on*, Aug 2015, pp. 1697–1701.

[11] G. Bianchi, "Performance analysis of the ieee 802.11 distributed coordination function," *IEEE Journal on Selected Areas in Communications*, vol. 18, no. 3, pp. 535–547, March 2000.

[12] D. D. Prasad and R. Goyal, "Performance study of Voice in Wireless Mesh Network," *International Journal of Emerging Technology and Advanced Engineering*, 2013.

[13] A. Ksentini and O. Abassi, "A comparision of VoIP Performance Over Three Routing Protocolls for IEEE 802.11s-based Wireless Mesh Networks (WLAN Mesh)," *MobiWac'08 Proceedings of the 6th ACM international symposium on Mobility management and wireless access*, 2008.

[14] M. Zogkou, A. Sgora, P. Chatzimisios, and D. Vergados, "EDCA mechanism and mobility support evaluation in IEEE 802.11s WMNs," *Special Session on Recent Advances in Broadband Access Networks*, 2014.

[15] S. Kristiansen, T. Plagemann, and V. Goebel, "A methodology to model the execution of communication software for accurate network simulation," *ACM Trans. Model. Comput. Simul.*, vol. 26, no. 1, pp. 3:1–3:31, Jul. 2015. [Online]. Available: http://doi.acm.org/10.1145/2746233

[16] A. Beifuss, D. Raumer, P. Emmerich, T. M. Runge, F. Wohlfart, B. E. Wolfinger, and G. Carle, "A study of networking software induced latency," in *Networked Systems (NetSys), 2015 International Conference and Workshops on*, March 2015, pp. 1–8.

[17] G. Pei and T. R. Henderson, "Validation of OFDM error rate model in ns-3," *Boeing Research & Technology*, 2010. [Online]. Available: https://www.nsnam.org/~pei/80211ofdm.pdf

[18] C. Hepner, A. Witt, and R. Muenzner, "In depth analysis of the ns-3 physical layer abstraction for WLAN systems and evaluation of its influences on network simulation results," *BW-CAR Symposium on Information and Communication Systems (SInCom)*, 2015.

[19] ——, "Extended Abstract, A new ns-3 WLAN error rate model - Definition, validation of the ns-3 implementation and comparison to physical layer measurements with AWGN channel," *Workshop on ns-3 WNS3 2015, Castelldefels (Barcelona), Spain*, 2015. [Online]. Available: https://www.nsnam.org/wp-content/uploads/2015/04/WNS3_2015_submission_34.pdf

[20] N. Baldo, M. Requena-Esteso, J. Núñez Martínez, M. Portolès-Comeras, J. Nin-Guerrero, P. Dini, and J. Mangues-Bafalluy, "Validation of the ieee 802.11 mac model in the ns3 simulator using the extreme testbed," in *Proceedings of the 3rd International ICST Conference on Simulation Tools and Techniques*, ser. SIMUTools '10, 2010, pp. 64:1–64:9.

[21] K. Andreev and P. Boyko, "IEEE 802.11s Mesh Networking NS-3 Model," *Workshop on ns-3 WNS3 2010, Malaga, Spain.*, 2010. [Online]. Available: http://www.nsnam.org/workshops/wns3-2010/dot11s.pdf

[22] C. Hepner, A. Witt, and R. Muenzner, "Extended Abstract, Validation of the ns-3 802.11s model and proposed changes compliant to IEEE 802.11-2012," *Workshop on ns-3 WNS3 2015, Castelldefels (Barcelona), Spain*, 2015. [Online]. Available: https://www.nsnam.org/wp-content/uploads/2015/05/WNS3_2015_submission_33.pdf

[23] ns-3 bug reports, 2016. [Online]. Available: https://www.nsnam.org/bugzilla

[24] WINLAB (Wireless Information Network Laboratory) - Network Simulator 3 (ns-3.16) Patches, 2016. [Online]. Available: http://www.winlab.rutgers.edu/~gruteser/projects/patch/Additional-Backoff-Timer-Trigger.html

[25] OpenWrt, 2016. [Online]. Available: https://wiki.openwrt.org/

Visualization of Urban Traffic for the Management of Smart Cities

Prachi Singhal, Gary Tan
School of Computing
National University of Singapore
Singapore 117417
{prachi.singhal@u.nus.edu, gtan@comp.nus.edu.sg}

Kakali Basak, Balakumar Marimuthu
Singapore-MIT Alliance for Research and Technology, 1 Create Way
Singapore 138602
{kakali@smart.mit.edu, balakumar@smart.mit.edu}

ABSTRACT
Smart cities hold the promise of lowering the cost of traffic congestion, thereby improving productivity and protecting the environment against the excessive emission of toxic gases, thereby promoting sustainability. This paper elaborates on a visualization tool for urban traffic that will be accessible to every user, from students to professionals. The tool is interactive and customizable, to suit the user's preferences. The software is applicable to multiple case studies, with the capability to observe trends in traffic by the naked eye. The visualizer plays another role of verifying the traffic principles implemented for the simulation and reinforces their relevance in the context of future cities. The trends observed for an urban setting are generalized to be applicable to an assortment of urban areas and aid in the policy planning for sustainable growth. Visualization is the gate through which any user can step into the world of simulation and apply it to conceptualize solutions for smart cities.

Keywords
Traffic Simulation Software; Simulation Verification; Visualization; Urban Scenarios

1. INTRODUCTION
An urban area is an ecosystem with a large impact zone, given the high population density. Mobility is essential for urban viability as it grows in tandem with the economy (Abhijit Banerjee, 2012). Data, together with logical implementation of traffic modelling will produce simulations that will provide a means for strategic management of traffic and ultimately benefit individuals, businesses and society. Accurate simulations with customized parameters are the ideal tools to use to forecast and fashion policies for efficient management of traffic. Visualization of the simulations boosts the usability and reach of the tool. Simulations are the result of comprehensive conflagration of traffic engineering, environmental sustainability and computational power.

The aim of this work is to develop a user friendly visualization tool for the simulation output that is generated using the computing tools merged with the theory of traffic engineering.

SIMUTOOLS 2016, August 22-23, Prague, Czech Republic

One such simulator tool is SimMobility, an integrated multi-agent activity based software that models the movement of traffic based on transportation principles (SMART, 2012). It is under development. The potential of the visualizer tool will be realized when it is used by the common user to propose policies. The idea is to make the tool accessible, empowering every individual to take responsibility for and ownership of their environment. The tool allows users to propose policies, simulate the conditions and subsequently observe the simulated results on the visualization. The visualizer is a valuable tool that is perched at the intersection of information technology and strategy management. While professionals who have access to vast amounts of data and work in a team of experts will derive maximum benefit of the simulation, the common user can also design his or her own city and tune the parameters as desired. Advanced computing knowledge or traffic engineering knowledge is not essential to run the simulations. This makes the software distinct and constitutes a conducive platform for the development of innovative ideas.

The visualizer is multi-functional as in addition to painting the simulations on the screen for understanding, it is also used to debug and verify the traffic engineering principles. It therefore serves as a tool that validates the principles that are the foundation for strategies employed for urbanization on a global scale. Traffic engineering algorithms that are applied in the context of future cities that will have automated cars and intelligent systems can be tested comprehensively. The simulations will highlight how applicable the current theories are in the context of future cities. Thus, only tested theories will be used to design the cities of the future and risk level of mismanagement is minimized. The system is agile to accept real time data or user generated data. This will be constructive to accommodate future cities design as there is an absence of data with regards to prospective cities. Unprecedented transition towards unplanned urbanization could stand between sustainability and healthy economies. The visualizer will be constructive to calibrate the traffic engineering principles to match the automated future cities. In addition to verifying the traffic engineering principles, it also plays a role as a debugger for the software developers. Debugging the simulations by following a specific agent in the output file is not only tedious, but also prone to errors. Hence, the simulation verification function of the visualizer is universal and can be applied to other software that output simulations as well.

Smart mobility is growing as is evident by LeEco introducing the driverless car (DAILYMAIL.COM, 2016). It heralds in a new era of safer and smarter mobility. It will become imperative for other traffic elements to work in tandem and make intelligent decisions while on the road so as to derive the maximum benefit from these innovations.

This paper describes the visualizer tool that is accessible to the common man and that doubles up as a verification tool for the extrapolation of traffic engineering principles to prospective scenarios. This will empower more people to contribute to the design and management of resilient future cities. Emerging economies will largely benefit from these tools and spur the development of other software that will serve as an integrated approach to management of future cities.

The layout of this paper is as follows. It introduces four observations in policy implementation for traffic management that could benefit from the use of the visualization tool (Section 2). The tools present in the market currently are described in Section 3. Inspired by the observations, this paper proposes a visualizer tool to achieve the enhanced policy implementations. It describes the structure of the visualizer and how the user will interact with the tool in Section 4. This tool is distinct as it has a larger reach in the context of the users. The features that make the tool versatile are elaborated in Section 5. Section 6 describes the testing of the visualizer and the conclusion and future works to expand the visualizer tool in terms of performance are discussed in Section 7.

2. Observations and Motivations

This section introduces four observations that led to the motivations for developing an accessible visualizer for traffic management for smart cities. The practical applications of the tool in policy formulations and promotion of public participatory planning are highlighted.

2.1 Implementation of odd-even license plate policy for vehicles during peak hours in urban areas

Rome, Paris, Mexico, New Delhi and Beijing. These cities have experimented with policies restricting a percentage of the vehicle fleet from entering high density urban areas in a bid to reign in congestion and toxic emissions (Banerji, 2015). One policy does not fit all, as the policy was extremely successful in Paris but only faced limited success in New Delhi. Given that the population of New Delhi is five times the population of Paris, this was not a surprise (World Population Review, 2016). However, variations of this policy, such as designs to direct traffic to less crowded sections in the city has the potential to produce desirable results. Certain algorithms that guide drivers to escape pockets of congestion would greatly contribute towards the bigger goal of reducing road congestion along popular roads. Hence, empowering the general public with tools to devise and verify simple algorithms for customization to local neighborhoods, given the specialized knowledge of their neighborhoods would result in an effective implementation of a general policy.

2.2 Multi-tier pricing

This policy charges drivers a fee during peak hours with the aim of distributing traffic more evenly during the duration of a day. It has been implemented in major metropolitan areas, such as London. It's success is limited in that the policy does not manage the given traffic, it merely aims to reduce it. The policy has been unpopular with the public as it is regressive and unpopular with businesses as their revenues dwindle (Pettinger, 2011). However, variations of this policy, such as applying multi-tier pricing based on congestion levels, instead of peak hours could be used as a tool in reliably constraining congestion. This could mean relatively lower charges for shopping districts and relatively higher charges for more wealthy neighborhoods. SimMobility, which is a software that forecasts the expected behavior of vehicles can simulate the results and the visualizer will enable quick analysis of such proposed policies. Given the policy planning tool in the hands of students who can even experiment on virtual cities, created by them, will result in an influx of innovative ideas that will shape the smart cities of tomorrow.

2.3 Car free day

Car free day is a trend that emerging economies are hoping to implement, following the success of the policy in the developed countries (teleSur, 2015). However, with the lack of proper infrastructure in the public sector, the effectiveness is limited (Chin, 2013). Having said that, customizations of this policy can be implemented in emerging economies. Perhaps, a more competent implementation of the car free policy in the emerging economies would be to declare pockets of car free zones. France has 30 car free places, whereas India has 3. This illustrates the vast scope of improvement that can be realized. These pockets have to be selected with due consideration on the impact to the drivers. In the future, with smart cars that auto-drive, the routing algorithms will work in conjunction with the dynamic car free places to deliver a first-class experience to the users. Hence, the visualizer would come in handy to delineate the appropriate car free regions. Also, differential pricing can be applied to test out policies such as car-pool days. The impact of having differential pricing for cars in the car-pool category can also be analyzed and verified with the visualizer. Customizations, such as calibrating fees for cars for odd-even days can be determined after analysis from the visualized results. The level of return on investment in implementing this policy will be evident from observing the trends on the visualizer. Hence, the visualizer is a tool that will allow people to experiment, fine-tune policies and propose targeted policies to achieve exceptional results.

2.4 Expansion and integration of public transport infrastructure in smart cities

Emerging economies are moving towards developing their transport infrastructure, with an emphasis on public transport in a bid to provide alternatives to the private vehicular traffic (Morgan Stanley, 2008). Rapid urbanization results in growth of the road network (Rui, 2013). Figure 1 highlights the expected growth in transport infrastructure for Asia to be approximately five times that of the growth in Europe and in the United States. Given the massive scale of the growth, it is crucial to develop tools that are accessible to one and all, and not just for professionals. How do the authorities ensure that this development is organized, integrated with the present and future smart systems, and sustainable to the environment? Public participatory planning will go a long way to provide solutions for impending challenges. The untapped potential of people will add value only after they're equipped with the resources. High levels of mobility in urban areas is achievable through smart design and technology. Hence, designing the transport infrastructure and predicting its impact on the public will be imperative to its success. The visualizer is the tool for that specific use case.

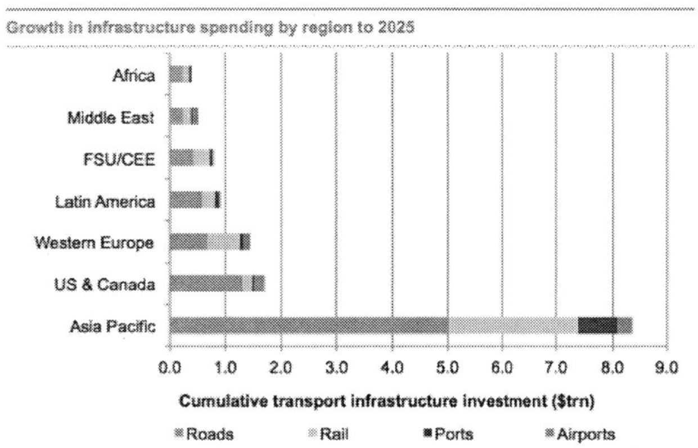

Figure 1 - Infrastructure spending by region, reflecting the immense outreach potential in emerging economies

3. RELATED WORK

Traffic simulation software is gaining momentum as growing urban cities grapple with the issues of congestion and inefficient road networks. The graph illustrates how the rate of increase for car usage (38%) surpasses the rate of increase of population (10%). The trend is expected to continue as there is an expected boom in the surge of the middle class, from 28% to 66%, with consumption too increasing from 23% to 59% (Brookings Institution, 2011).There are a few software that are already in place that run complex simulations on high performance computers. SimMobility and the Visualizer run on both scales, small and big.

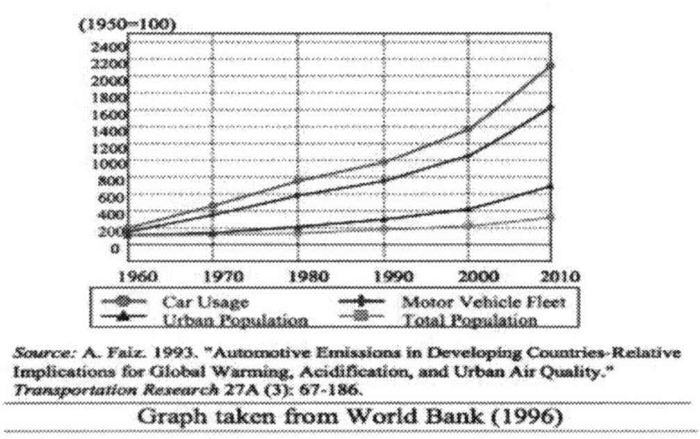

Figure 2 - Growth in Vehicles and Car Usage

The simulators for traffic management are accompanied with their visualizers. These include software such as SUMO, MATSim, Vissim and SimTraffic (Hawick, 2009). MIT Senseable City Labs have developed visualizations for a myriad of applications multi-contextual dimensions which will also be explored. In this section, we focus on the similarities and differences for the visualizer output of the simulations. The relevance to Entry Time based Supply Framework (ETSF) are also discussed.

This paper examines the two most popular open source traffic simulation software, MATSim and SUMO. It also reviews other paid software that also execute traffic simulation, such as Vissim and SimTraffic. These simulators also input information about a city and output the expected movement of traffic, given a certain demand and time in day. The future of urban planning and sustainable development is geared towards responsive cities that are based on big data design. Simulation software also use large amounts of data and often the simulations run on high performance computers over a few days (Daniel Zehe, 2015). Big data is becoming the foundation of high quality decisions. This paper proposes a visualizer tool for individuals and companies who do not have access to the organized big data. These users can build their own network as it is on a small scale.

MATSim is a joint effort by three entities, Technical University of Berlin, Swiss Federal Institute of Technology, and Senozon - a company founded by former research students (MATSim, 2014). MATSim refers to Multi-agent Transport Simulation. It offers agent-based traffic simulation for both private and public transport. Its visualizer is interactive and the user can follow each agent individually. The software is used to model metropolitan cities around the world with high urban density, such as Zurich in Switzerland, Padang in Indonesia and Kyoto in Japan (MATSim, 2014). MATSim has been used to study the traffic scenario in Singapore. It has been used to evaluate critical questions such as forecasting the ridership of new bus services or the effects on traffic of new pricing schemes (Alex Erath, 2013). As Singapore is a growing economy, it is imperative to continuously develop strategies to manage the traffic in order to sustain the substantial growth in standard of living of its citizens. MATSim is also open source and is being further developed by Future Cities Laboratory in Singapore (Singapore-ETH Centre, 2011). The customization done by the laboratory is for Singapore's public transport router and bus route tools.

Moreover, MATSim integrates simulation from medium to long term (ERATH, 2011). Hence, it is used chiefly by large organizations with the resources to engage in policy planning and analysis. The system has a mix of various supply and demand side agents. On the other hand, SimMobility can be used for the above mentioned and also be used by individuals or local groups who wish to improve the mobility in a certain neighborhood. This is because SimMobility provides short- term or microscopic level of modelling that is useful in smaller projects that do not involve supply and demand factors. The simulation results for the mid-term and long-term are also dependent on the types of modelling strategies used to obtain the supply and demand for a given urban area. The scope of the implementation being practical will differ for each urban area as traffic in different cities behaves differently. Hence, one recommendation for improved simulation could include customizing the simulation according to the behavior of the drivers and conditions of roads in urban areas. For example, drivers in cities like Singapore engage in less lane changing, whereas drivers in cities like Delhi engage in more lane changing.

The Institute of Transportation Systems in Germany has developed an open source software for simulation of road and railway traffic (Institute of Transportation Systems, 2015). SUMO is an acronym for Simulation of Urban Mobility. It is used to evaluate policies and algorithms that are used to improve traffic flows in cities. SUMO is a good tool that provides microscopic simulation and online interaction. One feature common to SUMO and SimMobility is that both of the software model private vehicles, public transport and pedestrians (Institute of Transportation Systems, 2015). Another common feature between SUMO and SimMobility is that both the software are implemented in C++. Moreover, they both use portable libraries. SUMO is available since 2001 (SUMO, 2016). Since it is open source, the new versions have additional functionality. For example, it has a feature whereby the roads are color coded according to the speed limit (Sha Tao, 2012). The documentation for SUMO grows constantly as additional plugins are developed to improve the functionalities offered.

PTV Vissim is a microscopic traffic simulation software that is developed by Planung Transport Verkehr in Karlsruhe, Germany

(PTV Group, 1992). The name is derived from Verkehr In Städten – SIMulationsmodell (German for "Traffic in cities – simulation model"). It was first developed in 1992. It has offices around the world and professional training centers that coach people to use the software. A typical introduction course can cost around $1000 (PTV Group, n.d.). Given that formal training is required to work with the software, it will be challenging to increase its reach. Vissim simulates traffic patterns comprehensively as it is applicable to private transport, goods transport, rail, pedestrians and cyclists. It even offers 3D modelling of the city. Hence, it is a large software that will be useful to large corporations looking at urban planning. It has an add on module, EnViVer that gives information about the exhaust emissions from vehicles (PTV Group, n.d.). This is very useful for sustainable planning of urban cities. As Vissim is also based on connectors and roads, it would be plausible to adjust the output from this simulator and feed it into the visualizer tool. The basic model of the nodes and links, which will be elaborated later, makes the visualizer very versatile to be employed with different simulators.

SimTraffic is designed to be used by field traffic engineers (United States Department of Transportation - Federal Highway Administration, 2016). It primarily focuses on traffic signal timing. Hence, it deals less with route planning and policy implementation. A study comparing the output of Vissim and SimTraffic declares that the calibration for both the software are different (Steven L. Jones, 2004). Therefore, while both are microscopic simulators that aim to model the traffic in an urban area, they output different results. The visualizer is a tool that displays the simulated results given that there is a basic road network and some vehicles in movement. The different output from simulators can be adjusted to be input in the visualizer and analyzed from thereon.

MIT Senseable City Labs have developed innovative visualization technologies. The Live Singapore project includes a visualization that shows deformations in the size of the map, thus reflecting the time taken to travel in an area. The Urban Village project displays a multi-dimensional graph that conveys the human interaction levels for different cities. The Art Traffic at the Louvre project demonstrates the visualization of human traffic inside the museum. This is similar to the visualization of the movement of traffic on the roads of a city as depicted by the visualizer proposed in this paper.

4. VISUALIZATION OF TRAFFIC SIMULATIONS FOR OPTIMUM USER EXPERIENCE

Visualization of traffic simulators has been in development for professionals to forecast expected results of certain urban designs and policies. The end user in these cases are institutions with a team of skilled professionals. The traffic forecast for international events such as the Soccer World Cup do call for recommendations from experts. However, small scale implementations that will greatly enhance the quality of life of society in localized urban areas, specially for emerging economies, and be environmentally sustainable, will be possible as this simulator and visualizer tool has greater reach among the youth and budding enterprises.

The process of forecasting the traffic involves two steps. The first step is to process the raw data using a simulator program. The second step is to view the simulation results using a visualizer. There are so many simulation software as each applies the logic for the traffic forecast in a unique manner. The visualizer tool aims to display the simulations that are output from any simulator. As long as the basic structure of the node and the links, as elaborated by the Entry Time based Supply Framework (Yan Xu), are specified, the visualizer tool will work for multiple platforms.

The visualizer is developed using Qt Creator, an open source cross platform integrated development environment. The technical knowledge of C++ is not necessary for the end user to use the tool. The visualizer takes an input file and outputs the desired visualization, i.e. the static road network and the vehicles moving to their destinations. There is a graphical user interface for easy selection of the file and amending the parameters for the display. Installing the visualizer requires three steps. Firstly, the user has to run one command to run a script that installs the visualizer and the related libraries. Then, the user can open the file in Qt Creator and execute it. Lastly, it will prompt the user to select an input file, which contains the static network and the movements of the vehicles, and display the results, as illustrated in Figure 3. The analysis of the results is entirely up to the user. Analytics software may be utilized, but that will be dependent on the inclination of the user to determine the complexity of the visualization.

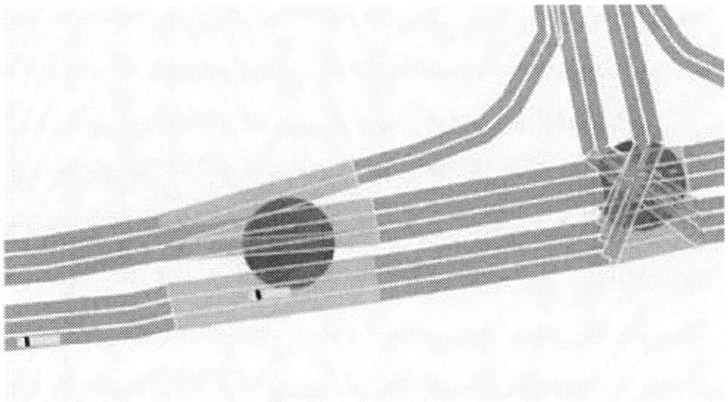

Figure 3 - Sample Visualization

The input file is very critical as it holds the road network and the movement of the vehicles. This file is generated from a simulation software, such as SimMobility. There are other simulation software that predict the expected movement of vehicles. The visualizer can process any file that comes in the similar format. Users can develop their own network of a neighborhood, which can be as small as one roundabout or as big as an entire city. They can then key in the policy implementation logic for the movement of the vehicles and see the results play out on the screen.

The visualizer parses the road network defined in the input file and draws it to the screen. There are options to display only the features desired. The navigation buttons allow to focus on a desired period. There are search options to focus on a particular road. The vehicles move from their origin to destination. Additional information about the vehicles, such as the speed, the acceleration and the identity number can be displayed by enabling the required option.

The visualizer has two main divisions, the geospatial and the temporal. The geospatial deals with any network features. These include the roads, lanes, and turnings. The geospatial handles storing the network data and drawing the network features. The temporal deals with anything that changes with time. This could include the vehicles movement or the traffic signals that change with time. Traffic signals are included in both the geospatial and temporal, as they are both a part of the network and change with time. The format of the data in the input file that is sent to the visualizer is also categorized into two, one major format for the geospatial and the other for the temporal. The consistency makes it easy to add more features, for example more types of vehicles in temporal category, such as auto-rickshaws, mini trucks and motorcycles.

The layout of the network is basic such that there are nodes that represent key points. The nodes are connected with links, which represent the roads. This simplifies the complex road network such that it is accessible to the common man. Creating a new network or creating a network of the neighborhood without the official data is straightforward too. This opens up the platform to a plethora of applications by end users. The level of complexity of the network may be amplified by adding more parameters such as lanes for each road, turnings and conflict points at intersections. The level of complexity is entirely in the hands of the user. The system is robust to the input, from a few hundred vehicles to millions of vehicles. The user has to define the static network, the number of agents and their trips, and the time of the simulation. Three simple steps to obtain the simulation and visualization output. One possibility of making the software even more accessible would be to provide an assortment of the agents information so that the users of the software are fully equipped to run their experiments. One possible plug in could be to obtain real time information from Google maps for the drivers information. This would greatly improve the usability and the accuracy of the tool. A picture speaks a thousand words. This truly becomes relevant in the visualizer as it saves the user from manually tracing the simulation output for each vehicle.

There is scope for more thorough investigations, from the perspective of road safety. Conflict point in transportation engineering is a point where the path of two or more users merge. An illustration is shown in Figure 4. The blue dot is the node that represents an intersection. The light grey paths define the roads that meet at the intersection. Two roads that are connected have a turning path drawn between them. The dark grey paths define the turning paths. The conflict point is placed at the intersection of two turning paths. The red dots are the conflict points.

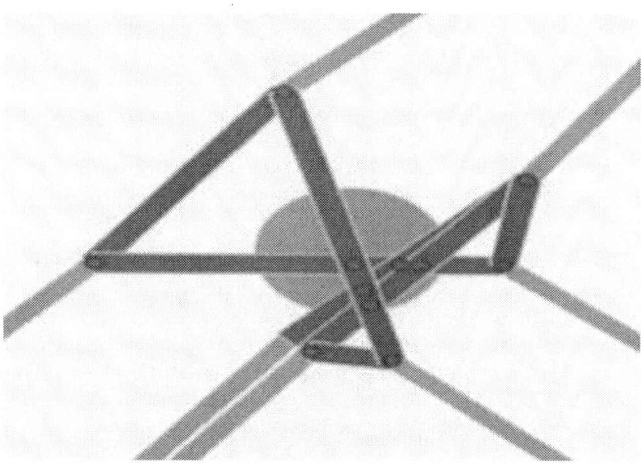

Figure 4 - Conflict Point at an Intersection

Each conflict point is accompanied by two sets of data for turning path – which crossing the point is located at (turning path ID) and the position of the point from the start of the crossing (conflict distance). Visualizing the conflict point is a three step process. First, the data is parsed using the general parser that is universally applied to the network (Figure 5). The property parameters – turning path ID and conflict distance are obtained for each of the two intersecting turning paths. To simplify the drawing, the intersection for the turning paths is taken to obtain the coordinates for the conflict point. Lastly, the coordinates are drawn on the map using the painter device in Qt Creator. Typically, to calculate the coordinates for the conflict point on the map, the vector distance from the starting point of the turning path has to be calculated. This is circumvented by using the data (turning path ID) for the other turning path instead. The conflict distance parameter is hence inessential.

```
1. REGEXP_LINE = QRegExp(QString("\\(") + REGEXP_ID + REGEXP_SEP +
   REGEXP_NUM + REGEXP_SEP + REGEXP_NUM + REGEXP_SEP + "\\{([^[]*)\\}"
   + " *\\)");
2. REGEXP_PROP = QRegExp(QString(" *") + REGEXP_ID + REGEXP_PROP_SEP +
   REGEXP_ID + REGEXP_SEP);
```

Figure 5 - Regex used for parsing data for visualization

An intersection with more conflict points is inherently more prone to accidents. The visualizer gives an option to enable the conflict points to perform risk assessments on the road network. Road safety is a problem everywhere, specially so in emerging economies as oftentimes the drivers do not undergo the required tests for their license. Many accidents are caused due to poor eyesight of the drivers. Technology can be used to alert them when they are arriving at a conflict point. With the drive for the development for smart cities where emergency services have limited time to reach the location, routing for paths with fewer conflict points will be beneficial. For example, four way intersections have 32 potential conflicts whereas roundabouts have 8 conflict points_(U.S. Department of Transportation, 2000). This portrayal of conflict points could perhaps alert the traffic police to manage their manpower accordingly.

The user for the visualization tool can be any person or institution with an idea who is interested to assess its impact. The user experience is unique because the user is in control of the level of complexity the visualization runs in. The simulator can be complex with vast models but the visualizer shows only what the user is targeting at. This will invite more users who have a focus and inhibit them from getting involved with the irrelevant details. The current tools are advanced and require specialized knowledge to operate them. The future of urban management lies in tapping on the potential of the locals so as to implement optimum solutions for each locality. The price of technology has come to a level where it is accessible to the common man. The surge in smartphones applications is a testimony to that. The greatest minds in traffic management will be recruited from the neighborhoods. The traffic of each city reflects its culture. To devise a targeted approach, it will be efficient to engage the local resources. This approach also solves the problem of obtaining accurate data for high density urban areas. Often large corporations are cut-off from the data. When the users create their own network, the probability of error will be reduced. Hence, the energy and passion of the new coders if channeled towards policy implementation will benefit their community manifold.

5. FUNCTIONAL DESIGN – ABSTRACTION AND GENERALISATION

Abstraction is the process of translating a real life scenario to be displayed graphically. It is put into effect in realizing the static network, that is essentially the map of a physical area. Generalization has to be used in caution as beyond a certain limit, it will diminish the required customizations. Generalization, which is extrapolating one idea to fit many contexts, is relatively less erroneous when considering small, localized areas. Therefore, if used on a small scale, its effect can be discounted.

Abstraction is exercised to develop the road network. Every network can be modeled by points and lines connecting those points. The points indicate the intersections between roads or destinations. The level of intricacy in defining points for a self build network is determined by the user. The more points defined, the finer will be the simulation output. For localized simulation, intricate definition of points is very plausible. The same principle is applicable to roads. The roads can be defined more precisely in terms of their orientation by dividing them into sections. This is up to the user's discretion as it hinges on the policy that the user is set out to test.

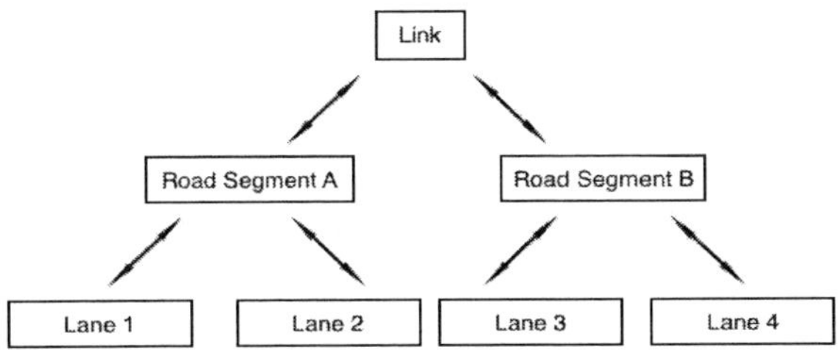

Figure 6 - Network Layout (Link)

Currently there are two abstraction groups, each three levels deep. The first group consists of the link, road segment and lane (Figure 5). A link can have multiple road segments, which can have multiple lanes. The link refers to a road and it is the user is at full liberty to define it. The second group consists of node, turning group and turning path (Figure 6). These are typically at intersections. If the user is working to strategize the movement of vehicles at large roundabouts, such as India Gate in New Delhi, then solely focusing on the second tree will be profoundly advantageous. However, if the user is focusing on policies for highways, the link group will be more relevant to investigate.

The network is essentially defined by points and lines. These lines are referred to as polylines. The lanes and roads are formed by shifting the polylines. This further emphasizes the rudimentary nature of the visualizer tool to model a locality. The use of the same functions to design the links, road segments and lanes makes the calculations efficient. For the calculations to find the intersection points that determine the real life conflict points, the most efficient technique of intersection of two lines was used, as opposed to using complicated vector math that would use more computing resources and adversely affect the performance of the visualizer in terms of time required for the results to be displayed. Every effort has been made to keep the calculations elemental, thereby delivering superlative performance.

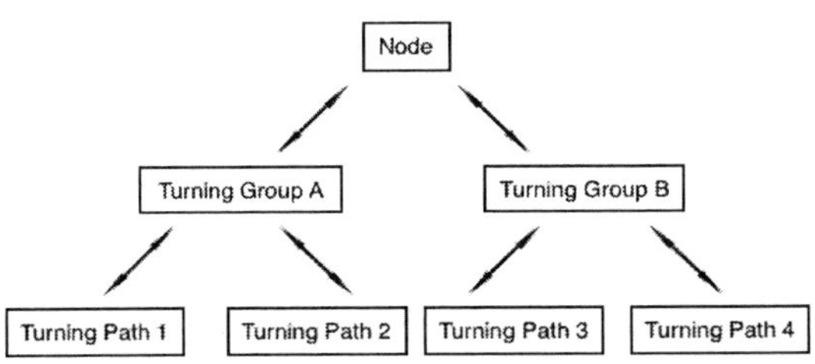

Figure 7 - Network Layout (Node)

The preference manager boasts of multiple options so that the user can display the final visualization according to his or her preference. It includes every network element. This will pave the way for policies that are an amalgamation of command and control and strategic management, and play the indispensable role of forming future cities. The painting of the network features, such as the points and the roads is subject to modification by the user. In addition to the options to display and hide the features, the users can select the colors and also focus on the network features. The agent information for only selected vehicles can be traced. This will be functional if there is an analysis to trace the movements of an ambulance or a fire rescue truck.

The principle of generality is applied to vary the level of complexity for the vehicles. An agent is the top most level that could represent a private car, a taxi, a bus or train. If the policy implementation is focusing on the relationships between public and private vehicles, then the distinction can be made between the agents. However, if a general policy that covers all motorists on a specific road is being evaluated, then the car, taxi and bus drivers will be enabled only. This gives immense flexibility to the user to utilize the program according to his or her needs.

6. TESTING

6.1 Types of testing

The process of testing has two purposes. One is testing to check whether the simulation output is as desired by comparing with the predicted output of the transport engineering principles. This testing involves observing certain behaviors of agents, such as whether the lane changing algorithm is actualized as desired. The second purpose is to run the proposed case studies and observe the impact. There is no comparison to standard results in the second purpose. The visualizer output is the prediction of the impact. This testing will involve understanding the simulated results, and fine-tuning parameters to achieve the most compelling policy customization for a given urban area.

6.2 Observation and Analysis of Visualization

All testing involves defining minimally the area of simulation, the time, number of vehicles, traffic signals and the route choice algorithm. Further analysis such as focusing on a few agents to check whether they complete their trips is useful. Other takeaways such as observing the average speed for an agent or identifying congestion intersections are computed. Observing agent behavior, such as unnecessary lane changing can be highlighted and worked upon in the design stage of the smart city. Future automated cars which can communicate with each other can be simulated as well.

One shortcoming of the simulated results might be the relevance of the assumptions in the context of the testing. One example of such assumption would be the driver reaction time. It can be modeled using various methods based on different scenarios, such as a platoon of vehicles, release of vehicles from the stop line and response to traffic light changing (Basak, 2013). The different modelling scenarios can be tested out to achieve the desirable one for a given case study. Another assumption would be the modelling of buses and bus stops. The SimMobility software assumes that buses will only stop at bus stops. The buses queue at the bus stop. While this might be applicable to developed economies such as Singapore, it is less applicable in emerging economies like India. In India the buses will stop at any lane on the road as long as there are passengers who are alighting. Hence this behavioral modelling can be done using another simulator tool. The visualizer can be used to simulate the output from a personalized simulator, not necessarily SimMobility. Therefore, this limitation can be overcome by careful consideration of the input that is fed to the visualizer.

Testing Parameters for SimMobility Visualiser	
Area	Kallang Paya Lebar Expressway, Singapore
Simulation Time	7.00 am - 7.05 am
Traffic Light	Yes, enabled
Vehicles	More than 10,000
Path	Shortest Path

Figure 8 - Basic testing parameters for policy implementation

The time step of the simulation can be adjusted by the user as well, depending on the level of details required. If the case under investigation is based on traffic management for highways, then a larger time step would be more appropriate Figure 8 shows the simulation for one expressway in Singapore, showing the growth of congestion in 5 minutes, with the test parameters input as shown in Figure 7.

Figure 9 - Sample congestion on one expressway, Singapore

7. CONCLUSION AND FUTURE WORK

This paper described a visualizer tool that can be used to observe the simulated results for traffic simulation of an area. This tool can display the road network and the traffic at different levels of complexity, such as for a local neighborhood and for a large city. It can be used to observe trends in traffic after the implementation of policies. The idea explored in this paper is to engage a bigger community in taking responsibility and being accountable to the environment and future generations by actively participating in the design and management of urban areas. Resilient future cities with automated cars and intelligent systems will require informed and strategic management. The visualizer is a tool that can be exploited to convert risks into rewards.

There are two proposals to enhance the visualizer. The first one focuses on visualization performance, and the second one focuses on delivering an impactful user experience.

The visualization tool can be simplified by breaking down the updating process of the agents into smaller sections. At present, the tool updates the agent information for every agent on the map, regardless of whether the agent is relevant to the user. After the accuracy of the tool in translating the simulation output has been established, the next step would be to update the agent information only in the view shown to the user. This would boost the performance substantially as the time taken for parsing and painting the updates for a certain map view is a fraction of the time taken to update millions of agents. The gains from performance would increase exponentially with the size of the simulation. For the users, they will have a more focused view of the agents and network elements, enabling participative planning for concentrated urban areas. An integrated approach including design, utility, energy and environment can be developed on a focused area.

Moreover, after the performance is augmented, the visualizer can be transferred to the 3D domain. This would contribute to superior user experience, and serve as a marketing tactic to beckon more users to engage in the process of design and development of our future smart neighborhoods.

8. ACKNOWLEDGMENTS

This research was supported by the National Research Foundation Singapore through the Singapore MIT Alliance for Research and Technology's Future Urban Mobility IRG research program. The authors would like to thank Kakali Basak and her entire team of software engineers from Future Urban Mobility Interdisciplinary Research Group in Singapore-MIT Alliance for Research and Technology, for their support in this work.

9. REFERENCES

[1] Abhijit Banerjee, E. D. (2012, February). *On the Road: Access to Transportation Infrastructure and Economic Growth in China.* Retrieved from http://economics.mit.edu/files/7782

[2] Alex Erath, S. O. (2013). *Using public transport smart card data for large- scale, agent-based transport demand simulation using MATSim: the case of Singapore.* Retrieved from http://www.ivt.ethz.ch/vpl/publications/presentations/v470.pdf

[3] Banerji, R. (2015, December). *5 Cities Implemented The #EvenOdd Road Rationing Policy. But Was It Effective?* Retrieved from http://www.indiatimes.com/news/india/5-cities-implemented-the-evenodd-road-rationing-policy-but-was-it-effective-248085.html

[4] Brookings Institution. (2011, June). *The Emerging Middle Class in Developing Countries.* Retrieved from http://siteresources.worldbank.org/EXTABCDE/Resources/7455676-1292528456380/7626791-1303141641402/7878676-1306699356046/Parallel-Sesssion-6-Homi-Kharas.pdf

[5] Chin, H.-C. (2013). Sustainable Urban Mobility in South-Eastern Asia and the Pacific. Nairobi: GRHS 2013: Regional report South-Eastern Asia and the Pacific. Retrieved from http://unhabitat.org/wp-content/uploads/2013/06/GRHS.2013.Regional.South_.Eastern.Asia_.and_.Pacific.pdf

[6] DAILYMAIL.COM, S. L. (2016, April). *Move over Tesla: China's LeEco reveals autonomous electric car concept that could pave the way for driverless taxis Read more: http://www.dailymail.co.uk/sciencetech/article-3550041/Move-Tesla-China-s-LeEco-reveals-autonomous-electric-car-concept-pave-way-fleet-driverless-taxis.html#ixzz46RFIhBEs Follow us: @MailOnline on Twitter | DailyMail on Facebook.* Retrieved from DailyMail: http://www.dailymail.co.uk/sciencetech/article-3550041/Move-Tesla-China-s-LeEco-reveals-autonomous-electric-car-concept-pave-way-fleet-driverless-taxis.html

[7] Daniel Zehe, A. K. (2015, June). SEMSim Cloud Service: Large-scale urban systems simulation in the cloud. *Simulation Modelling Practice and Theory.*

[8] ERATH, K. A. (2011, November). *Urban Sustainability and Transportation: Research Framework for Medium and Long Term Transport Planning.* Retrieved from http://www.lta.gov.sg/ltaacademy/doc/J11Nov-p07Alex_UrbanSustainabilityandTransportation.pdf

[9] Hawick, G. K. (2009). A Review of Traffic Simulation Software. *Institute of Information & Mathematical Sciences*, 35-54. Retrieved from https://www.massey.ac.nz/massey/fms/Colleges/College%20of%20Sciences/IIMS/RLIMS/Volume13/TrafficSimulatorReview_arlims.pdf

[10] Institute of Transportation Systems. (2015). *SUMO – Simulation of Urban MObility*. Retrieved from http://www.dlr.de/ts/en/desktopdefault.aspx/tabid-9883/16931_read-41000/

[11] MATSim. (2014). *MATSim Community*. Retrieved from http://www.matsim.org/about-us

[12] Morgan Stanley. (2008, April). *Emerging Markets Infrastructure: Just Getting Started.* Retrieved from http://www.morganstanley.com/views/perspectives/files/infrastructure_paper4.pdf

[13] Pettinger, T. (2011, November). *Pros and Cons of a Congestion Charge*. Retrieved from http://www.economicshelp.org/blog/143/transport/how-effective-is-a-congestion-charge/

[14] PTV Group. (n.d.). *Emissions Modelling*. Retrieved from http://vision-traffic.ptvgroup.com/en-uk/products/ptv-vissim/use-cases/emissions-modelling/

[15] PTV Group. (n.d.). *PTV Vissim Courses*. Retrieved from http://vision-traffic.ptvgroup.com/en-us/training-support/training/ptv-vissim-courses/

[16] PTV Group. (1992). *PTV. The Mind of Movement*. Retrieved from http://company.ptvgroup.com/en/ptv-group/

[17] Rui, Y. (2013). *Urban Growth Modeling Based on Land-use Changes and Road Network Expansion.* Sweden: Royal Institute of Technology Stockholm.

[18] Sha Tao, V. M. (2012). Real-Time Urban Traffic State Estimation with A-GPS Mobile Phones as Probes. *Journal of Transportation Technologies*, 22-31.

[19] Singapore-ETH Centre. (2011). *MATSim Singapore.* Retrieved from http://www.fcl.ethz.ch/project/matsim-singapore/

[20] SMART. (2012). *Future Urban Mobility.* Retrieved from Singapore SMART-FM: http://ares.lids.mit.edu/fm/

[21] Steven L. Jones, J. P. (2004, June). *TRAFFIC SIMULATION SOFTWARE COMPARISON STUDY.*

[22] SUMO. (2016). *Main Page.* Retrieved from http://sumo.dlr.de/wiki/Main_Page

[23] teleSur. (2015, September). *330 Cities Around the World Celebrate 'Car Free Day'*. Retrieved from http://www.telesurtv.net/english/news/330-Cities-Around-the-World-Celebrate-Car-Free-Day-20150922-0007.html

[24] U.S. Department of Transportation. (2000). *Roundabouts: an informational guide.* U.S.: Federal Highway Administration.

[25] United States Department of Transportation - Federal Highway Administration. (2016). *Surrogate Safety Measures From Traffic Simulation Models.* Office of Research, Development, and Technology, Office of Safety, RDT. Retrieved from https://www.fhwa.dot.gov/publications/research/safety/03050/04.cfm

[26] Basak, K. S.-S.-A. (2013, October). *Modeling Reaction Time Within a Traffic Simulation Model.* Retrieved from 16th International IEEE Conference on Intelligent Transportation Systems (ITSC 2013): dspace.mit.edu/openaccess-disseminate/1721.1/89073

[27] Yan Xu, X. S. (n.d.). An Entry Time-based Supply Framework (ETSF) for mesoscopic traffic simulations. *Simulation Modelling Practice and Theory*, 186.

[28] World Population Review. (2016). *City Populations 2016.* Retrieved from http://worldpopulationreview.com/world-cities/

Implementation of Cognitive Driver Models in Microscopic Traffic Simulations

Roland Cristea, Stefan Rulewitz, Ilja Radusch
Fraunhofer FOKUS
Automotive Services and Communication Technologies
Kaiserin-Augusta-Allee 31, 10589 Berlin, Germany
{roland.cristea, stefan.rulewitz, ilja.radusch}@fokus.fraunhofer.de

Karl Hübner, Björn Schünemann
Technische Universität Berlin
Daimler Center for Automotive Information Technology Innovations
Ernst-Reuter-Platz 7, 10587 Berlin, Germany
{karl.huebner, bjoern.schnuenemann}@tu-berlin.de

ABSTRACT

In order to perform microscopic traffic simulations as realistically as possible, a detailed modelling of each individual driver is essential. Currently established microscopic traffic simulators follow a rather static approach to model the driver's behaviour. Individual emotional influences and temporarily occurring distracting factors are heavy to implement in the established state-of-the-art microscopic traffic simulators. This paper proposes a solution how emotional influences and distracting factors can be integrated in established traffic simulation tools. For this purpose, robot-learning approaches are adapted to model the emotional state of vehicle drivers. In the end of this work, a proof of concept is done to illustrate the strength of the developed approach.

Categories and Subject Descriptors

I.6.7 [**Simulation and Modeling**]: Simulation Support Systems

Keywords

Driver Behaviour Models, Cognitive Models, Distraction, Emotions, Microscopic Traffic Simulations

1. INTRODUCTION

Modelling the movements of individual vehicles as realistically as possible is an essential task of microscopic traffic simulators. The decision making process for each individual vehicle includes various domains, e.g. the present traffic infrastructure, the movements of other vehicles, or traffic cognition is rather rarely modelled in classic car-following models such as Krauß [19] or IDM [33]. There are approaches to model human behaviour via imperfection properties [19], however, this might not be sufficient to model the complex decision making process of human drivers. Especially, with classic car-following models it is not possible to simulate unexpected behaviour of drivers, such as short-time speeding, unexpected lane changes, distracted drivers, or visual impacts.

Moreover, perception is the basis for any further decision making and according to Schaub it is the *"transformation of physical and chemical stimuli to psychological processable information as foundation for action control"* [15]. Additionally, human perception is always related to individual objects on which the driver focuses and, consequently, a driver never has a complete view of the traffic situation and his/her surroundings. Not least because drivers perceive the *"outside-the-car"* world up to 90% by visual sense [6]. However, current microscopic traffic simulators do not consider these important visual senses, but rather apply perfect sight and senses to the driver. For a more detailed view it is important to consider the human factor. As Mesken identified, driving is a highly complex cognitive process which can not be simplified easily [21]. Additionally, drivers are highly influenced by emotions and distraction as a recent study shows [9]. For example, Sullman et al. [32] claim a rate of 40% distraction by inner factors while driving. Also, distraction caused by using the phone is the main risk factor of the 90% driver-related crash causations (emotion, distraction, fatigue, error) [9]. As essence of these studies, external and internal factors are identified which itself can be subdivided. Although drugs (including alcohol) have extremely high risk factor, they occur far less [9] but change perception and coordination dramatically. Table 1 summarises disrupting influences and the affected parameters of the driver.

In this paper, we introduce the consideration of emotional processes and distracting factors in microscopic traffic simulations. That is, each driver perceives his/her environment and assesses the traffic situation differently. Consequently, the resulting emotional state of the driver influences his/her decisions and behaviour. In addition, distracted drivers are modelled which also affects the driver's behaviour. Both

SIMUTOOLS 2016, August 22-23, Prague, Czech Republic

Effected Parameter	Distraction	Age	Drugs	External Factor	Driver Type
	Influence				
Visibility	*	*		*	*
Field of View	*	*	*		*
Estimation Error		*	*	*	*
Safe Distance	*		*	*	*
Acceleration					*
Deceleration					*
Reaction Time	*	*	*		*
Speed	*				*
Lane Behaviour	*				*

Table 1: Influences and Effects according to [9, 7, 26, 11, 35, 23, 17]

concepts and their impacts are implemented and investigated in microscopic traffic simulation environments.

2. STATE OF THE ART

For decades there has been research on the human thinking and decision making. General models specialised on the driving task have been developed and formulated in this period. Most of the models reference explicitly to the classical standards from Michon [22] and Rasmussen [25] who designed multi level models of human information processing. Those were merged by researchers like Edmund Donges [10].

The ITERATE project [16] and the DRIVABILITY model by Bekiaris et al.[3] both studied visual limitations of the perception of drivers. DRIVABILITY additionally considered environmental factors as road and weather conditions. The model of Yuhara and Tajima [36] took the influences of personal characteristics on perception into account. In addition, DRIVABILITY showed that emotions are a big factor that has to be considered. Deml et al. did research in the field of human behaviour characteristics and its representability in driver models. They analysed PELOPS and CosmoDrive as driver behaviour specific models in comparison to general cognitive approaches of QN-MHP and ACT-R [8]. However, neither of those models deal with emotional processes nor does any include temporary distraction (e.g. using the phone or configuring the car's navigation system). In context of representing cognitive processes in microscopic traffic simulations none of the models are suitable.

Analogous to Deml, Treiber implemented driver models in traffic simulators like VISSIM [5] and SUMO [18] which barely consider emotional processes and neglect distracting factors. The mostly used car following model IDM (Intelligent Driver Model) in combination with the lane change model MOBIL can be statically parametrised in terms of sportiness and cooperativeness, but do not yet consider cognitive processes as required [34].

Researchers and developers are beyond dispute about the recreation of human information processing principles in their models to match human behaviour. Therefore, our following concepts have the goal to implement the most important factors of cognitive modelling such as emotional processes and distraction in combination with existing car-following models.

3. CONCEPT

In the following, we present our concepts which introduce the consideration of emotional process and distracting factors in microscopic traffic simulation.

3.1 Distraction

Research has shown internal and external factors that distract and impair drivers [9]. All factors consider a different or for a short time not existing view on the surrounding environment. While people perceive the world at 90% visually [6] [29] the additional 10% can be neglected. Therefore it would be an asset to modify the raw simulation data according to the type of distraction.

Firstly, the *maximum visibility* of a driver is reduced based on daytime, weather conditions, and personal visual performance. For example, glare can reduce visibility by up to 75% [31].

Secondly, the drivers *field of view* is always limited, mainly due to the car's pillars. As Renge et al. researched elderly people lose their head turning ability and have therefore a more narrow field of view [26]. During distraction, the field of view becomes tunnel vision due to the attention which is switched to the distracting task or factor. Figure 1 shows the a 360° field of view. It marks the driver's visible (translucent) and non-visible angles (black). This definition can be easily adapted for any new finding.

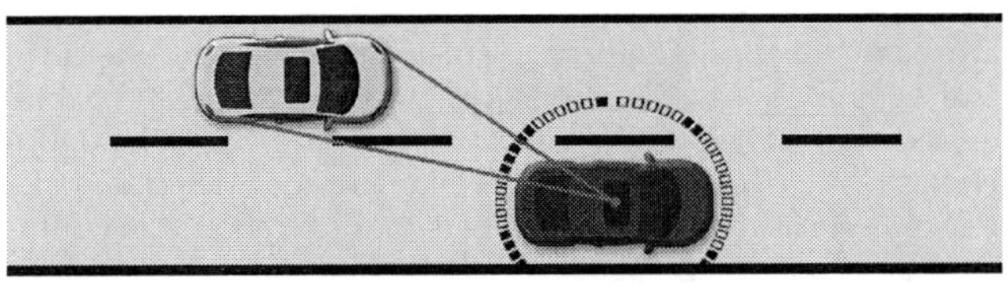

Figure 1: Field of view with non-visible parts (black)

Thirdly, drivers have to constantly estimate speeds, distances and headings of the surrounding vehicles in order to adapt speeds and make decisions. The *estimation error* depends on whether the driver is distracted and what type of driver he or she is. While simulation environments deliver exact values this error has to be included to generate human inaccuracy. This error can be generated randomly inside a previously defined range with the help of a smoothing function.

While both, visibility limitations and the estimation error need to be considered by the car-following model directly, there is also distraction caused by the driver which results in changes in the driving behaviour, according to Cooper et al. [7]. The most important consequences of distraction are massively longer reaction times (up to 100% longer). However, the reaction time is one of the basic factors that defines safety distance and therefore the capability of avoiding accidents. Figure 2 shows the effect of an extended reaction time. Additionally to the extended reaction time, a significantly higher variance in speed (up to 62.5%) can be found, lane changes are reduced, and drivers slip into short gaps while overtaking.

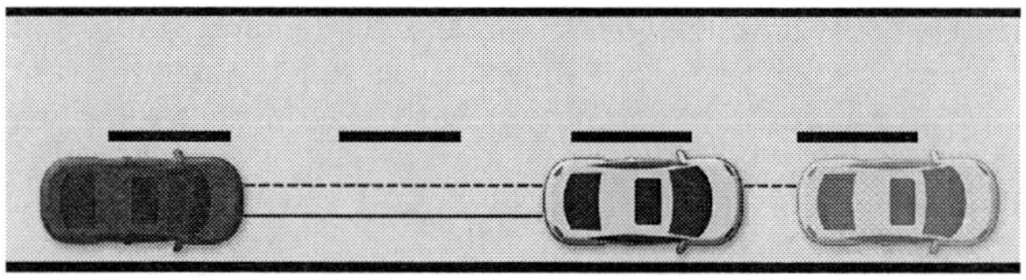

Figure 2: Effects of reaction time on safe distance. The leading vehicle was previously outside the safe distance and is now inside.

Accordingly, we propose to trigger short-time distraction randomly for each driver in the simulation. With a given distraction rate r_d the driver gets distracted for a short period of time more or less often. Given the distraction rate r_d, the current simulation time t_c and the time period t_w in which the distraction should take place, the next point of time t_d at which the driver gets distracted is calculated by equation 1. In order to prevent distraction triggered immediately after the previous distraction period has ended, a minimum pause t_p between two distraction events is used.

$$t_d = t_c + t_p + (1 - r_d) \cdot rand(0, 1) \cdot t_w \quad (1)$$

Finally, each distraction lasts for several seconds in which the vehicle reduces its own speed a bit and is not able to accelerate.

3.2 Emotion

Based on current cognitive research, we propose to consider the emotional state of the driver and its effects on decision making in traffic simulations. Those emotional states are based on basic emotions, such as *anger*, *fear*, *sadness*, and *happiness* [12]. For modelling emotions and their effects, we use the *robot-learning-method* proposed by Gadanho and Hallam [14]. Here, the driver's perception of the traffic situation (*sensations*) as well as personal characteristics influence the *feelings* of the driver. Based on those feelings, the *dominant emotion* can be calculated which then affects the decision making process of the driver. Figure 3 shows the model used for calculating the dominant emotion based on sensations of the driver. This model is basically configured by the emotion coefficients C_{ef} which affect the influence of sensations to emotions, the activation and selection threshold I_{th_a} and I_{th_s} which is required for an emotion to be processed or selected, and the attack gain a_{up} and decay gain a_{down} which are used to increase or decrease the emotion intensities [14].

The following sensations are determined as the most important ones by us and therefore are included in the model. During the simulation for each sensation it is checked whether it is active or not. *Rear distance* determines if the car behind maintains the own preferred safe distance. If this sensation is active, it has increasing influence on the emotions anger and fear. *Duration* is a sensation based on Mesken [21], which tells if the driver's journey takes longer than expected. After a certain amount of time, this sensation gets activated and increases sadness and decreases happiness. The third sensation, *density*, depends on the own velocity and the traffic density. To determine if this sensation is active, the preferred safe distances of the car behind and in front is checked and whether the lane left to the vehicle is occupied or free. In such cases, it increases fear and anger, and decreases happiness. The last important sensation is *speed*, which tells whether the driver's preferred speed is achieved or not. If active, it has increasing influence on happiness, and decreases anger and sadness. As a result of those sensations, the emotion model calculates one dominant emotion which takes effect on the driver's behaviour.

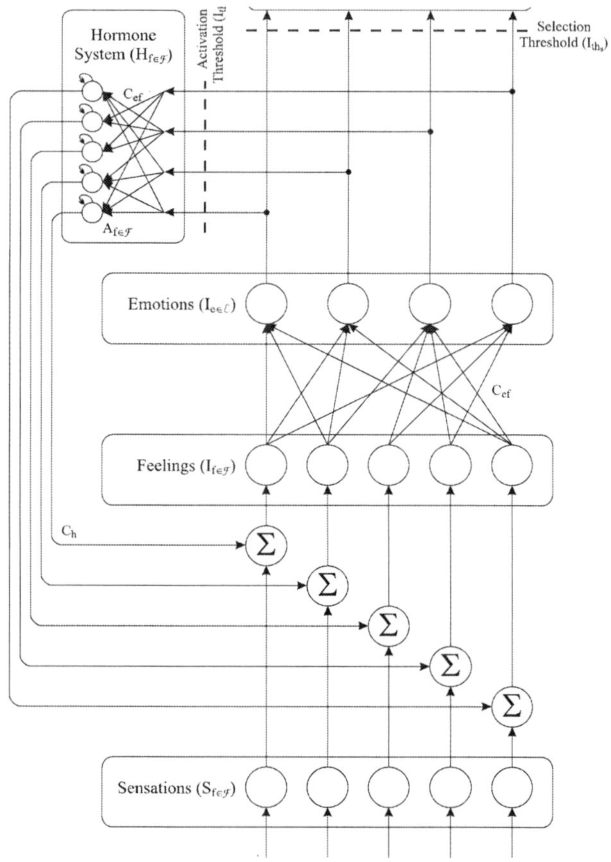

Figure 3: The emotion model (source: [14]) used for calculating the dominant emotion of the driver based on his perceptions.

Anger is considered to be the most frequent emotion and also has the most significant impacts on the driver's behaviour [13], especially on gaining speed and decreasing the safe distance [2]. Furthermore, we propose to adjust the properties of the lane change model in a way, that it is more aggressive, e.g. by deactivating cooperative lane changes and keeping the vehicle on the most left lane.

The emotion *fear* results in the need to increase safety which leads to a reduction of the speed by 20% [20] and the wish to change onto the most right lane. Furthermore, a frightened driver is not willed to adapt his speed to the leading vehicle but maintains his own reduced speed, and keeps more distance between his and the leading vehicle.

Sadness results in strategies to avoid any risks [1, 21], such as decreasing speed and a passive lane change behaviour. The passive behaviour includes cooperative lane changes and an adaptation to the speed of the leading vehicle.

A *happy* driver is ready to gain speed due to this emotion [4]. Accordingly, the preferred speed is increased by 10% which might lead to an exceedance of the allowed speed.

The driver respects other drivers and is willed to adapt his speed in order to act cooperative, which can be realised by adjusting the properties of the lane change model.

3.3 Driver characteristics

Furthermore, next to the consideration of distraction and the emotional state of drivers, we propose to take individual driving characteristics into account. Therefore, three different driver types are defined: *sporty*, *normal* and *cautious*, based on [17]. For each type, different properties can be parametrised according to Schulz et al. who did their research on driver assistance systems [27]: Preferred maximum speed v_{max}, default acceleration a_{acc} and deceleration a_{dec}, the speed factor f_s, and the preferred safety time gaps to the leader and follower t_{gap} describe the basic parameters of the car-following model in the traffic simulation. The politeness factor p is adapted from the lane-change model MOBIL and presents the willingness to collaborate with other vehicles [33] during lane changes. Moreover, each driver type is parametrised with distraction rate r_d.

4. PROOF OF CONCEPT

In order to prove our concept, we choose to simulate a scenario with the proposed modules with the help of the simulation framework *VSimRTI*, which is a flexible framework to simulate and assess complex simulation scenarios on microscopic and mesoscopic level. The main focus of VSimRTI is on coupling different simulators with different emphases [28, 24]. Through the interplay of these different simulators it is possible to conduct investigations in the context of cognitive sciences, such as the viewing of distractions and emotions that may occur during a journey. For our scenario, we coupled VSimRTI with the microscopic traffic simulator *SUMO*, which provides the possibility to use different car-following and lane-change models. By using the socket interface TraCI, it is also possible to interact with the vehicles and their parameters during the simulation. However, this interaction is encapsulated in VSimRTI completely, which allows us to use a high-level API in order to implement the proposed models. This also enables the possibility to replace the traffic simulator in further investigations.

4.1 Parametrisation of drivers

After defining vehicles and their journeys, the drivers need to be parametrised according to the properties in section 3.3, as seen in table 2. Additionally, in order to configure the emotion model, the emotion coefficients C_{ef} found in table 3 are used for our simulations. For example, the emotional value of *anger* is increased by 70% as soon as the sensation *rear distance* is triggered, whereas it is decreased by 10% if the sensation *speed* is active. Further parameters of the emotion model have been configured with the values proposed by [14].

4.2 Traffic Scenario

The scenario to be evaluated represents a familiar commuter route in the urban area of Berlin. Most of the vehicles are emitted along the motorway BAB115 heading north and passing the intersection between BAB115 (AVUS) and BAB100, which is one of Germany's most frequent traffic nodes. Therefore, the focus lies on this bottleneck, as seen in figure 4. Next to this, several vehicles are driving on other motorways in this area, to produce a traffic distribution close to reality. However, we do not have any traffic flow data or realistic origin-destination matrices and therefore we decided to use artificial traffic flow for our simulations. In total, 3,200 vehicles are emitted on four starting points within a simulation period of 3,600 seconds.

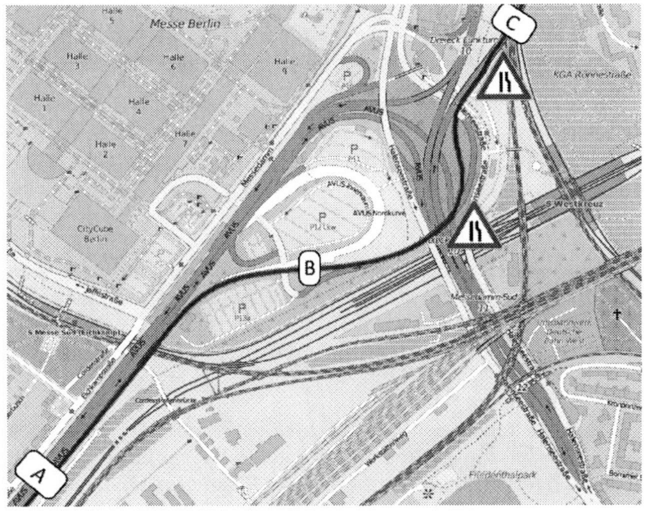

Figure 4: Traffic scenario with route and bottleneck at motorway interception and following on-ramp situation. Also, vehicle flow detectors A, B and C are placed before, along, and after the bottleneck. (Map source: OpenStreetMap)

	Driver type		
	sporty	normal	cautious
v_{max}	160 km/h	140 km/h	120 km/h
f_s	1.1	1.0	0.9
a_{acc}	5.0 m/s^2	3.0 m/s^2	2.0 m/s^2
a_{dec}	10.5 m/s^2	8.5 m/s^2	6.5 m/s^2
t_{gap}	0.8 s	1.7 s	2.8 s
p	AGGRESIVE	COOPERATIVE	CAUTIOUS
r_d	10%	20%	5%

Table 2: Individual parametrisation of vehicles based on driver types.

Emotion	*rear distance*	*duration*	*density*	*speed*
anger	0.7	0.0	0.1	-0.1
fear	0.2	0.0	0.8	-0.1
sadness	0.0	0.3	0.0	-0.2
happiness	0.0	-0.2	-0.1	0.4

Table 3: Emotion coefficients C_{ef} used for our simulations.

4.3 Simulations

In order to examine the various concepts proposed by us, we execute several simulations. The following simulation configurations are used:

0 Plain simulation **without** different driver types, **without** emotions, and **without** distraction triggering. in this simulation run, each driver is parametrised the same, that is with the values of the *normal* driver.

1 This simulation run includes **different driver types** in the simulation, **without** emotions and **without** distraction triggering. 65% of the vehicles are parametrised as *normal*, 15% as *cautious*, and 20% as *sporty* drivers, based on [17].

2A This simulation run includes **different driver types** in the simulation and considers **emotions** for each driver, but still **without** distraction triggering. The drivers are parametrised and distributed the same as in **1**.

2B This simulation run includes **different driver types** in the simulation and triggers **distraction** for each driver. This simulation run is **without** considering emotions. The drivers are parametrised and distributed the same as in **1**.

5. RESULTS

For each simulation run, several measurements are examined. For this purpose, we set up induction loops A, B and C on important points along the main route (see figure 4) in order to observe the traffic flow during the simulation and the distribution of vehicles among lanes. Furthermore, general properties such as the duration of journeys and the average speed of vehicles are measured. Those measures are used to compare the simulation outcomes in order to analyse the impacts of the different domains *driver types*, *emotions*, and *distraction*.

In table 4 general measurements of the different simulation runs can be found. For each vehicle, the travel time and the average speed during the journey is measured. Additionally, the time loss property shows how much time the vehicles lost in average compared to the ideal travel time they would achieve without any traffic. For example, a high value in time loss can indicate dense traffic or even congestion. Furthermore, for the simulation runs which have been mapped with different driver types, the measurements are additionally segmented for each type. Note: 300 vehicles which were inserted at the beginning of the simulation are excluded since they would distort the results.

Figure 5 shows the average speed at all detectors placed along the route. With the help of this, traffic congestion can be identified. For example, it can be seen that the density at detector B is very low as soon as distraction is triggered in the simulation.

Furthermore, figure 6 shows the distribution of vehicles among lanes at detector A. According to [30], a typical lane distribution on a motorway with a total flow of 2,000 veh/h is 33% of the flow on the left lane, 28% on the right lane, and 39% on the middle lane. This distribution can be achieved the best by the simulation which considers different driver types and emotions.

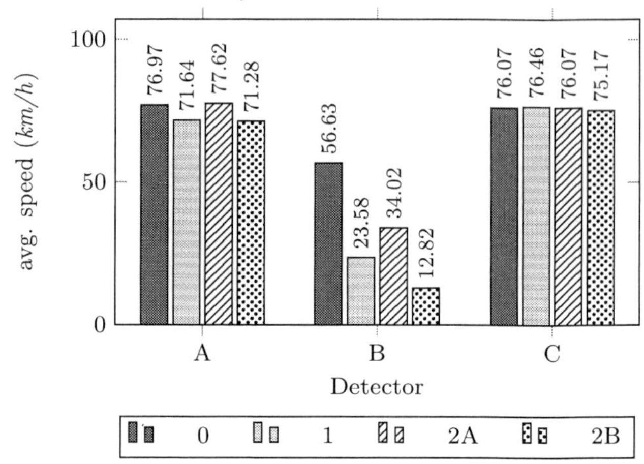

Figure 5: The average speed in km/h of all vehicles passing detectors A, B and C for each simulation run. Amongst other things, congestion can be found at detector B if drivers are parametrised individually.

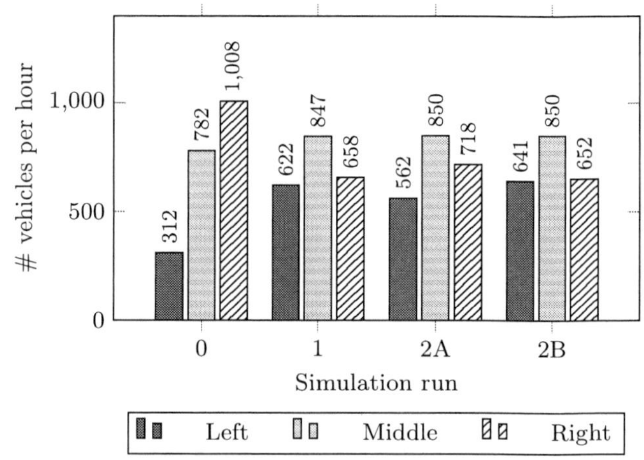

Figure 6: Traffic flow on the different lanes at detector A (AVUS) for each simulation run. It can be seen that a diverse traffic with different driver types leads to a more realistic distribution of traffic on different lanes.

5.1 Configuration 0 - Plain simulation

In this simulation all vehicles are parametrised with equal values and do not differ from each other. There is no traffic congestion throughout the simulation and vehicles can reach their preferred speed during the whole journey. This can be shown by the low average travel time of 650 s and a low value of time loss, which is only 61 s. Due to the constant traffic flow at the bottleneck at detector B, the vehicles can perfectly merge onto the only existing lane without producing any congestion while keeping the maximum allowed speed. Concluding, this simple simulation results in a quite perfect flow of vehicles which is, however, not realistic. Vehicles follow each other perfectly without overtaking, which leads to an unrealistic lane distribution where the left lane is used rarely.

Simulation Run	0 Plain simulation	1 Driver types	2A Driver types + Emotions	2B Driver types + Distractions
All drivers				
Avg. speed in km/h	76.18	71.35	77.72	66.17
Avg. travel time in seconds	650	695	646	780
Avg. time loss in seconds	61	107	95	191
Cautious drivers				
Avg. speed in km/h	-	67.46	73.62	63.00
Avg. travel time in seconds	-	726	676	795
Avg. time loss in seconds	-	72	79	141
Normal drivers				
Avg. speed in km/h	-	71.46	77.62	66.64
Avg. travel time in seconds	-	694	646	770
Avg. time loss in seconds	-	105	94	180
Sporty drivers				
Avg. speed in km/h	-	74.02	81.11	67.03
Avg. travel time in seconds	-	676	622	802
Avg. time loss in seconds	-	141	111	266

Table 4: Results for the different simulation runs

5.2 Configuration 1 - Different driver types

This simulation run introduces different driver types: *normal* (65%), *cautious* (15%), and *sporty* (20%). With this configuration, the traffic flow is much more diverse than in the previous run. A more diverse parametrisation of vehicles results in traffic situations one would expect to find in reality, such as overtaking vehicles, forming of vehicle groups and short-living traffic congestion at bottlenecks (e.g. at detector *B*). This is emphasised by a much better lane distribution at detector *A* (figure 6), which almost meets the typical lane distribution on motorways.

Not surprisingly, the effects of the parametrisation of different driver types can be found in the simulation results as well. Cautious drivers have the lowest speed and longest travel times, while sporty drivers reach their targets fastest. On the other side, cautious drivers have the lowest time loss since their ideal travel time is already high. However, it can also be seen that the average driver is slower than in the previous simulation. This can be explained by the cautious drivers which slow down all other vehicles as well, and by the short-living traffic congestion at the bottleneck (detector *B*).

5.3 Configuration 2A - Driver types and emotions

As previously, vehicles are parametrised in this simulation run. Additionally, the emotional state of each driver is modelled (according to chapter 3.2). The overall flow is very similar to the previous run, where vehicles form groups and traffic congestion occurs. However, it can also be seen that the average driver is much faster and that his journey takes less time. This effect can be explained by the emotional state of the driver.

In order to study the emotional state of the drivers and its influence on the traffic, figure 7 shows the distribution of dominant emotions during the simulation. While *normal* drivers are mainly *happy* since they can reach their preferred speed on the major part of their journey, cautious drivers often show *anger* because of other vehicles which come very close from behind. However, both *anger* and *happiness* result in an increasing speed factor which therefore increases the average speed of all drivers. This also allows sporty drivers to drive faster than usual. Furthermore, the emotion *anger* lets drivers speed up more than allowed. While the speed is limited to 100 km/h on the AVUS, vehicles with sporty drivers occasionally speed up over 120 km/h for a short time, until *happiness* suppresses *anger*. Concluding, modelling the emotional states and its reactions can result in unexpected driver behaviour which is closer to reality.

Furthermore, the general traffic flow is not negatively affected. Actually, the average speed at detector *B* increases due to aggressive lane changes of sporty and *angry* drivers. In addition, the lane distribution at detector *A* matches the usual distribution which can be found at three-lane motorways with a flow of 2,000 vehicles per hour [30].

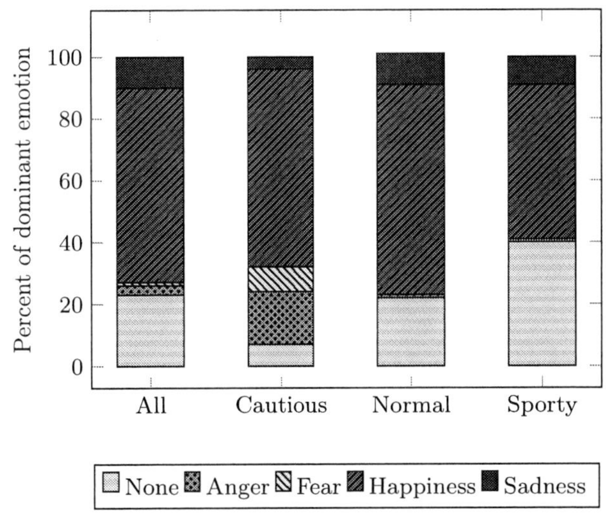

Figure 7: Distribution of dominant emotions in the simulation.

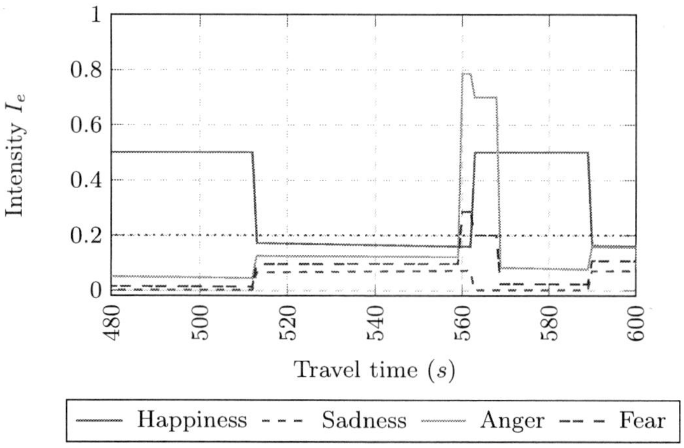

Figure 8: Intensity of emotions of an arbitrary driver during a part of the simulation. An emotion e is dominant at time step t, if its intensity I_e is greater than all other emotions, and exceeds the activation threshold $I_{th} = 0.2$ (dotted line).

5.4 Configuration 2B - Driver types and distraction triggering

In this simulation, different driver types are used again and are configured to experience randomly triggered distraction (according to chapter 3.1). With this configuration, the average speed of all vehicles decreases to 66.17 km/h and the average travel time increases to 780 s. It can also be seen that detector B shows very low speeds due to traffic congestion at the bottleneck. In contrast to simulation **1** and **2A** the congestion does not resolve, which can be explained with the distraction of the drivers.

Whenever a distraction is triggered vehicles keep their current speed and do not accelerate, due to the driver which rather concentrates on other tasks, such as using his phone, configuring his navigation system, or getting distracted by other passengers. This not only has effects on the usual traffic flow (as seen in the decreased speed at detector A), but especially on bottlenecks, where an efficient merging of vehicles onto one lane is required. In such cases, distracted vehicles disturb the merging process from time to time which eventually results in traffic congestion right before the bottleneck. For example, if a vehicle is required to accelerate in order to fill the front gap quickly, distracted drivers delay the following traffic flow by staying at their current position. Concluding, the consideration of distraction in the simulation is able to model complex traffic situations which have influences on the overall traffic flow.

6. CONCLUSION

In this paper, emotional processes and distraction factors of drivers were modelled within a microscopic traffic simulation environment. The emotional state of drivers was modelled with the help of the *robot-learning-method* by Gadanho and Hallam, in which each individual driver perceives the world through sensations which influence their emotions and therefore their decisions and behaviour. Also, each driver experiences temporary distractions in which the driver's reaction capabilities are decreased. Furthermore, drivers are parametrised individually based on current studies and investigations. Those concepts were studied and assessed with the help of simulation scenarios modelling typical urban commuter traffic on a motorway. The results show that all those concepts improve classic traffic simulations in terms of an individual behaviour of drivers. While a sophisticated parametrisation of drivers leads to a more diverse traffic in which vehicles form groups and produce short-term traffic congestion at bottlenecks, emotional processes result in unexpected behaviour of individual drivers, such as speeding or unusual lane changes. Furthermore, temporary distraction especially leads to inefficient merging at bottlenecks and therefore unexpected traffic congestion occurs, whereas classic simulations fail due to perfect and unrealistic models.

Since the results are promising, we plan to make further investigations with other simulation tools. For example, including those models in driving simulators. Also, the emotional model and distraction mechanisms used in our study need to be calibrated with real world data in order to get even more meaningful results.

7. REFERENCES

[1] L. B. Alloy and L. Y. Abramson. Judgment of contingency in depressed and nondepressed students: Sadder but wiser? *Journal of experimental psychology: General*, 108(4):441, 1979.

[2] Andrea Uhr. *Aggression und Emotionen im Strassenverkehr: bfu-Faktenblatt Nr. 12.* 2014.

[3] E. Bekiaris, A. Amditis, and M. Panou. Drivability: a new concept for modelling driving performance. *Cognition, Technology & Work*, Volume 5(Issue 2):152–161, 5 2003.

[4] G. Bliersbach. *Gefühlswelten im Straßenverkehr: Emotionen, Motive, Einstellungen, Verhalten*, volume 10 of *Schriftenreihe Verkehrssicherheit.* Dt. Verkehrssicherheitsrat, Bonn, 2002.

[5] Carsten Werner. Integration von fahrzeugfolge- und fahrstreifenwechselmodellen in nachtfahrtsimulation luciddrive. Master's thesis, Universität der Informationsgesellschaft, Paderborn, 2010.

[6] C. Chaloupka-Risser, R. Risser, et al. *Verkehrspsychologie. Grundlagen und Anwendungen.* Facultas, Wien, 2011.

[7] J. M. Cooper, I. Vladisavljevic, N. Medeiros-Ward, P. T. Martin, and D. L. Strayer. An investigation of driver distraction near the tipping point of traffic flow stability. *Human Factors: The Journal of the Human Factors and Ergonomics Society*, 51(2):261–268, 2009.

[8] B. Deml, H. Neumann, A. Müller, and H. J. Wünsche. Implementierung eines fahrermodells in die simulationsumgebung eines autonomen fahrzeugs. *at-Automatisierungstechnik Methoden und Anwendungen der Steuerungs-, Regelungs-und Informationstechnik*, 56(11):601–608, 2008.

[9] T. A. Dingus, F. Guo, S. Lee, J. F. Antin, M. Perez, M. Buchanan-King, and J. Hankey. Driver crash risk factors and prevalence evaluation using naturalistic driving data. *Proceedings of the National Academy of Sciences*, 2016.

[10] E. Donges. *Handbuch Fahrerassistenzsysteme: Grundlagen, Komponenten und Systeme für aktive Sicherheit und Komfort*, chapter

Fahrerverhaltensmodelle, pages 15–23. Vieweg+Teubner, Wiesbaden, 2009.

[11] T. Dukic, E. Erikkson, and F. Sagberg. Older drivers hazard perception performance. In M. Sullman and L. Dorn, editors, *Advances in Traffic Psychology*, chapter 15, pages 53–61. Ashgate, Farnham England, 2012.

[12] P. Ekman. An argument for basic emotions. *Cognition & emotion*, 6(3-4):169–200, 1992.

[13] B. Frehse and R. Höger. *Kognitive Bewertungsdimensionen von Ärger im Straßenverkehr.* PhD thesis, Lüneburg, 2014.

[14] S. C. Gadanho and J. Hallam. *Emotion triggered learning for autonomous robots*, volume no. 916 of *DAI research paper.* Dept. of Artificial Intelligence, University of Edinburgh, [Edinburgh, Scotland], 1998.

[15] Harald Schaub. Wahrnehmung, aufmerksamkeit und >situation awareness< (sa): 4. In Petra Badke-Schaub, Gesinge Hofinger, and Kristina Lauche, editors, *Human Factors - Psychologie sicheren Handelns in Risikobranchen*, pages 63–81. Springer Berlin Heidelberg, 2012.

[16] M. Hjälmdahl, D. Shinar, O. Carsten, and B. Peters. The iterate project - overview, theoretical framework and validation. In P. C. Cacciabue, M. Hjälmdahl, A. Lüdtke, and C. Riccioli, editors, *Human Modelling in Assisted Transportation - Models, Tools and Risk Methods*, pages 97–106. Springer Milan, 2011.

[17] H. Jöri. Ruhig bis aggressiv - sechs typen am steuer. *punktum. Zeitschrift des Schweizerischen Berufsverbands für Angewandte Psychologie, Zürich, Schweiz*, April 2002.

[18] D. Krajzewicz. Sumo in scientific literature, 2002–2012. In M. Behrisch, D. Krajzewicz, and M. Weber, editors, *Simulation of Urban Mobility: First International Conference, SUMO 2013, Berlin, Germany, May 15-17, 2013. Revised Selected Papers*, volume 8594, pages 160–174. Springer, 2014.

[19] S. Krauß. *Microscopic modeling of traffic flow: Investigation of collision free vehicle dynamics.* PhD thesis, Universitat zu Koln, 1998.

[20] J. Lerner, L. Tiedens, and R. Gonzalez. Toward a model of emotion-specific influences on judgment and decision making: Portrait of the angry decision maker. *Journal of Behavioral Decision Making*, 19:115–137, 2006.

[21] J. Mesken. *Determinants and consequences of drivers' emotions.* s.n.] and University Library Groningen] [Host], [S.l. and [Groningen, 2006.

[22] J. A. Michon. A critical view of driver behavior models: what do we know, what should we do? In *Human behavior and traffic safety*, pages 485–524. Springer, 1985.

[23] M. Praxenthaler. *Experimentelle Untersuchung zur Ablenkungswirkung von Sekundäraufgaben während zeitkritischer Fahrsituationen.* PhD thesis, Universität Regensburg, 2003.

[24] T. Queck, B. Schünemann, I. Radusch, and C. Meinel. Realistic simulation of v2x communication scenarios. In *APSCC '08: Proceedings of the 2008 IEEE Asia-Pacific Services Computing Conference*, pages 1623–1627, Washington, DC, USA, 2008. IEEE Computer Society.

[25] J. Rasmussen. Skills, rules, and knowledge; signals, signs, and symbols, and other distinctions in human performance models. *Systems, Man and Cybernetics, IEEE Transactions on*, (3):257–266, 1983.

[26] N. Renge, M. Tada, K. Renge, and S. Usui. Differences in driving behaviours between elerderly drivers and middle-aged drivers at intersections. In M. Sullman and L. Dorn, editors, *Advances in Traffic Psychology*, chapter IV, pages 207–216. Ashgate, Farnham England, 2012.

[27] A. Schulz and R. Fröming. Analyse des Fahrerverhaltens zur Darstellung adaptiver Eingriffsstrategien von Assistenzsystemen. *ATZ - Automobiltechnische Zeitschrift*, 110(12):1124–1131, 2008.

[28] B. Schünemann. V2x simulation runtime infrastructure vsimrti: An assessment tool to design smart traffic management systems. *Computer Networks*, 55:3189–3198, October 2011.

[29] D. Shinar. *Traffic safety and human behavior*, volume 5620. Elsevier, 2007.

[30] M. Short, M. J. Pont, and Q. Huang. Simulation of motorway traffic flows. *ESL04-02, Embedded Systems Laboratory, University of Leicester*, 2004.

[31] J. H. Sprute. *Entwicklung lichttechnischer Kriterien zur Blendungsminimierung von adaptiven Fernlichtsystemen.* PhD thesis, Technische Universität Darmstadt, 2012.

[32] M. Sullman and L. Dorn. *Advances in traffic psychology.* Ashgate Publishing, Ltd., 2012.

[33] M. Treiber and D. Helbing. Realistische mikrosimulation von strassenverkehr mit einem einfachen modell. In *16th Symposium Simulationstechnik ASIM*, volume 2002, page 80, 2002.

[34] M. Treiber and A. Kesting. *Verkehrsdynamik und -simulation: Daten, Modelle und Anwendungen der Verkehrsflussdynamik.* Springer-Lehrbuch. Springer-Verlag Berlin Heidelberg, Berlin, Heidelberg, 2010.

[35] M. Winninghoff, K. Schmedding, and K.-H. Schimmelpfennig. Die reaktionszeitverlängerung bei dunkelheit unter alkohol- und blendungseinflüssen. *Verkehrsunfall und Fahrzeugtechnik*, Mai 2001.

[36] N. Yuhara and J. Tajima. Multi-driver agent-based traffic simulation systems for evaluating the effects of advanced driver assistance systems on road traffic accidents. *Cognition, Technology & Work*, 8(4):283–300, 2006.

VNE-Sim: A Virtual Network Embedding Simulator

Soroush Haeri and Ljiljana Trajković
Simon Fraser University
Vancouver, British Columbia, Canada
{shaeri, ljilja}@sfu.ca

ABSTRACT

Computer network virtualization and virtual network embedding (VNE) algorithms have gained significant attention in recent years. Performance evaluation of VNE algorithms mainly relies on discrete event simulations. However, modular and scalable VNE simulators are not available. In this paper, we describe newly developed simulator *VNE-Sim* that enables users to define and implement network elements possessing various resources. It also enables researchers to generate various topologies of Internet Service Provider and data center networks for the evaluation of VNE algorithms. Furthermore, *VNE-Sim* provides the infrastructure for implementing both single and batch request processing approaches.

CCS Concepts

•Networks → Network simulations; •Computing methodologies → Simulation environments; Simulation tools; •Software and its engineering → *Abstraction, modeling and modularity;*

Keywords

Computer networks, virtualization, virtual network embedding, simulation tools, discrete event simulations

1. INTRODUCTION

The best-effort service, supported by the current Internet architecture, is not well-suited for all applications. A significant barrier to innovation has been imposed by the inability of the current Internet architecture to support a diverse array of applications. Network virtualization overcomes these shortcomings [1], [2]. The virtualized network model divides the role of Internet Service Providers (ISPs) into two independent entities: Infrastructure Providers (InPs) and Service Providers (SPs). The InPs manage the physical infrastructure while the SPs aggregate resources provide end-to-end services [2]. In the virtualized network architecture, an InP owns and operates a *substrate network* composed of physical nodes and links that are interconnected. Combinations of the substrate network nodes and links may be used to embed virtualized networks.

An InP's revenue depends on the resource utilization within the substrate network that, in turn, depends on the performance of the algorithm that allocates the substrate network resources to virtual networks. This resource allocation is known as the virtual network embedding (VNE) [3], which may be formulated as a mixed-integer program (MIP) [4] or may be reduced to the multiway separator problem [3], [5]. Both problems are $\mathcal{NP}$-hard, making the VNE problem also $\mathcal{NP}$-hard. This is one of the main challenges of virtualization.

VNE algorithms have recently received considerable attention within the research community [3], [4], [6]. Performance of VNE algorithms is only evaluated using discrete event simulations. Therefore, there is a need for a scalable, flexible, reliable, and modular VNE simulator.

Embed [3] and *ViNEYard* [4] are two early developed C-based VNE simulators. They are no longer maintained, lack documentation, and do not provide interfaces for developing new VNE algorithms and performance metrics. MATLAB has also been used for simulating VNE algorithms [6]. However, the MATLAB-based simulator is not publicly available. *Alevin* [7] is a recent VNE simulator written in Java. It has a modular design and provides a graphical user interface (GUI). However, its design does not enable users to define network elements of their choice such as defining CPU, memory, and storage of nodes and bandwidth of links in the substrate network. Furthermore, writing scripts to perform batch simulations is rather cumbersome.

We have developed the *VNE-Sim*, a virtual network embedding simulator that has been used for performance evaluation of a number of VNE algorithms [8], [9]. It is publicly available under the terms of the MIT License. *VNE-Sim* provides extensible interfaces for users to implement algorithms and customizable network elements. Furthermore, being written in C++, *VNE-Sim* offers good memory management and enables performing batch simulations using any scripting language.

The remainder of this paper is organized as follows. The *VNE-Sim* architecture and its components are introduced in Section 2. The core of the simulator is then presented in Section 3. In Section 4, we present a case study and introduce the VNE problem, common approaches for its solutions, and simulation results. We conclude with Section 5.

SIMUTOOLS 2016, August 22-23, Prague, Czech Republic

2. THE VNE-SIM ARCHITECTURE

VNE-Sim is a discrete event simulator written using the 2011 C++ standard (C++11), which introduces smart pointers and lambda functions. These new functionalities of C++11 are employed in *VNE-Sim*. We describe here details of the *VNE-Sim* discrete event simulator and its compilation. The *CMake* build system [10] is employed for compiling the code. *VNE-Sim* relies on several external libraries. While some required libraries are downloaded and installed automatically by *CMake*, the others libraries are expected to be installed prior to initiating the compilation process.

The libraries that are automatically installed by *CMake* are: *Fast Network Simulation Setup* (FNSS) [11] used for generating data center network topologies; the *Hiberlite* library [12] used for writing simulation results to disk; and the *Adevs* library [13] employed for modeling the virtual network embedding process as a discrete event system.

CMake relies on scripts to search for the libraries that should be installed prior to compilation:

- The Boost File System, Log, Thread, and Unit Test Framework libraries [14] are mainly used in the core classes for file handling, logging, testing, and debugging. The test cases and experiments are implemented using the Unit Test Framework library.
- The GNU Scientific Library (GSL) [15] is used for generating random numbers and probability distributions.
- The GNU Linear Programming Kit (GLPK) [16] is used for solving the Multi-Commodity Flow (MCF) [5] problem. It is also employed by the ViNE algorithms [4].
- The SQLite3 library [17] handles simulation results. They are exported automatically as SQLite databases.

VNE-Sim uses modified versions of the *Hiberlite* and FNSS libraries. *CMake* applies the required modifications after downloading these libraries. *VNE-Sim* also contains a modified version of the Boston University Representative Topology Generator (BRITE) [18] that is compiled as a component of the simulator.

Components of *VNE-Sim* and their dependencies are shown in Figure 1.

The simulator includes a number of packages:

- The *Core* package contains classes and interfaces required for implementing various virtual network embedding algorithms. It also contains the discrete event simulation system that models the process of embedding virtual networks as a discrete event system.
- The *network-generator* package is used for generating various network topologies and Virtual Network Requests (VNRs). It employs the FNSS [11] and BRITE [18] libraries for generating network topologies and the GNU Scientific Library [15] for generating probablility distributions of VNR arrival times, lifetimes, and resource requirements.
- The *GRC* package contains the implementation of the Global Resource Capacity (GRC) algorithm [6].
- The *ViNEYard* package contains the implementation of R-ViNE and D-ViNE algorithms [4].

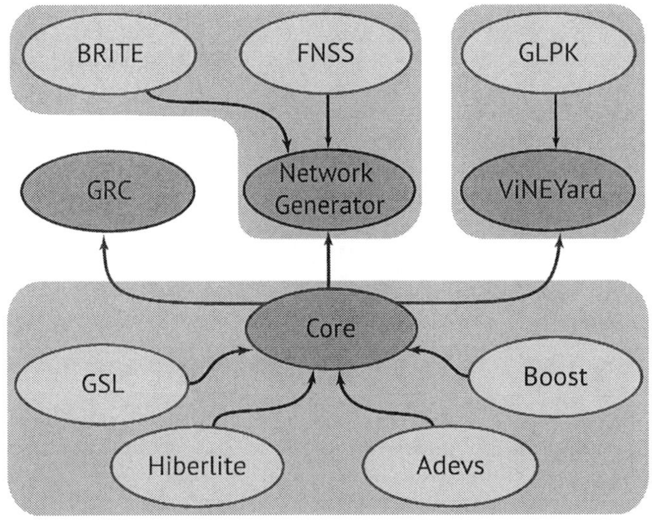

Figure 1: *VNE-Sim* components and their dependencies. Installation of Boost, GSL, and GLPK is required by the user while the other libraries are automatically installed during the compilation process.

3. THE VNE-SIM CORE

Components required to simulate various VNE algorithms are implemented as abstract template classes in the *Core* package. They are divided into five categories:

- *Network Component Classes* provide a framework for defining substrate and virtual nodes and links, substrate and virtual networks, and VNRs.
- *Virtual Network Embedding Algorithm Classes* define an interface for embedding algorithms.
- *Discrete Event Simulation Classes* model the virtual network embedding process as a discrete event system. All these classes are derived from the *Adevs* library [13].
- *Experiment and Result Collection Classes* connect various components to define simulation scenarios. They create SQLite database tables for simulation parameters and for collecting simulation results.
- *Operation Related Classes* provide the basic required functionalities such as managing the configuration file, database access, type definitions, and random number generation.

3.1 Network Component Classes

3.1.1 Substrate and Virtual Nodes and Links

Substrate and virtual network components are implemented as C++ *variadic* templates where their resources are defined by the template arguments. This design enables users to define network components that possess multiple resources. While the VNE algorithms often consider CPU processing capacity as the only node resource, other resources such as Random Access Memory (RAM) and storage capacity may also be provided by SPs. Hence, VNE algorithms should also consider these resources.

3.1.2 Networks and Virtual Network Requests

A network in *VNE-Sim* is defined by the `Network` template class with a node and a link class as its first and second arguments, respectively. This approach enables implementing substrate and virtual networks using one base template class. VNRs are also implemented as template classes where the template argument identifies the type of the virtual network object they possess.

3.2 Virtual Network Embedding Algorithm Classes

These classes define an interface for implementing VNE algorithms. Their backbone is the `EmbeddingAlgorithm` abstract template class with two arguments, which are specializations of the `Network` and the `VirtualNetworkRequest` template classes. Derivatives of the `EmbeddingAlgorithm` base class implement the `embedVNR` function. This design choice accommodates various VNE approaches described in this paper. For example, a two-stage VNE algorithm may be derived from the `EmbeddingAlgorihm` base class by implementing a two-stage `embedVNR` function that sequentially performs the node and link mappings.

3.3 Discrete Event Simulation Classes

The VNE process is modeled as a discrete event system using the discrete event system specification (DEVS) [19] that has been widely employed for modeling social and ecological systems as well as computer networks and architecture. The framework is implemented using the *Adevs* library [13]. This design enables seamless implementation of various VNE approaches including single and batch processing.

The VNRs are first *generated* based on an arrival process. The arrived VNRs are then queued until they are processed by an embedding algorithm. Hence, the VNRs experience both queuing and processing delays. Based on the outcome of the embedding process, a VNR may either be accepted or rejected. When the life-time of a successfully embedded VNR expires, the *release process* begins and an employed algorithm releases the resources.

The directed acyclic graph (DAG) used for modeling the VNE process in *VNE-Sim* is shown in Figure 2. *VNR Generator*, *Embedding Process*, *Release Process*, and *Statistic Collection* are four modules used to model the VNE process. These components are implemented as abstract template classes that require a specialization of the VNR class as their template argument. The *VNR Generator* models the VNR generation process. Upon the arrival of a VNR, the *VNR Generator* sends a signal to the *Embedding Process* and the *Statistic Collection* modules. The *Embedding Process* is used to model the embedding approach. For example, single and batch VNR processing approaches may be implemented as derivatives of the *Embedding Process* template class. If a VNR is embedded successfully, the *Embedding Process* notifies the *Release Process* and the *Statistic Collection* modules. The *Statistic Collection* implements the Observer design pattern [20]. It is used for logging, collecting statistics, and recording the embedding outcomes. The events that occur in the first three modules are transparent to the *Statistic Collection*. A subscription-based approach is employed in this module where various statistical analysis algorithms may subscribe to receive event updates. A logging subsystem is subscribed to the *Statistic Collection* module by default. The logging subsystem employs the *Hiberlite* library to populate event updates into the SQLite database tables.

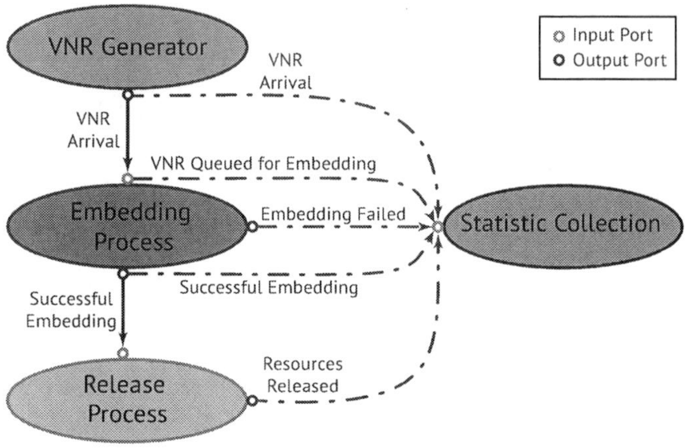

Figure 2: Directed acyclic graph used for modeling the VNE process in *VNE-Sim*. VNRs are first generated and passed to the *Embedding Process*. If a VNR is successfully embedded, it is forwarded to the *Release Process*. The *Statistic Collection* module is an observer that receives information from all input/output ports of other modules.

3.4 Experiment and Result Collection Classes

A *VNE-Sim* simulation scenario is defined using the *Experiment* template class. This class also maintains statistics that are collected during simulations and records them when simulations are completed.

3.5 Operation Related Classes

The `ConfigManager` class reads the simulator configuration file and maintains a *Boost Property Tree* structure of the configurations. This class is a singleton [20] and thus it may be instantiated only once. A pointer to its instance should be acquired first. After obtaining the pointer, a property value may be acquired by calling the `getConfig` function.

The `DBManager` class creates instances of `hiberlite::Database` [12] class and maintains pointers to the created databases in a `map` data structure. This class is also implemented as a singleton. Its interface contains two main functions: `createDB` and `getDB`. The `createDB` function creates a database and returns its pointer. Pointers to the created databases may also be acquired using the `getDB` function.

All network component classes require identification numbers. Classes that have similar types should not possess identical identification numbers. The singleton `IdGenerator` class produces such type-based unique numbers. It generates consecutive identification numbers in an increasing order. The `IdGenerator` interface consists of two template functions: `getId` and `peekId`. The `getId` generates a unique ID for a class type that is given as its template argument while the `peekId` function returns the next ID that will be generated.

The `RNG` class employs the GNU Scientific Library [15]. It is used to generate random numbers and probability distributions. The seed and type of the random number generator are defined in the configuration file. Classes using `RNG` may either use a general purpose random number generator or subscribe to `RNG` class to get a specific generator.

4. SIMULATION OF VNE ALGORITHMS

The VNE problem may be divided into two subproblems: Virtual Node Mapping (VNoM) and Virtual Link Mapping (VLiM). VNoM algorithms map virtual nodes onto substrate nodes while VLiM algorithms map virtual links onto substrate paths. Algorithms that have been proposed for solving VNE are categorized into three categories depending on the approaches taken to solve these two subproblems [21]. The *uncoordinated two-stage algorithms* first solve the VNoM problem and provide a node mapping to the VLiM solver. In this approach, the VNoM and VLiM solvers operate independently without coordination [3]. The *coordinated two-stage algorithms* also first solve the VNoM problem. Unlike the uncoordinated approach, these algorithms consider the virtual link mappings when solving the VNoM problem [4], [6]. The *coordinated one-stage algorithms* solve the VNoM and VLiM problems simultaneously. When two virtual nodes are mapped, also mapped is the virtual link connecting the two nodes.

Most VNE algorithms proposed in the literature address the VNoM while solving the VLiM using the shortest-path algorithms (k-shortest path, Breadth-First Search (BFS), and Dijkstra) or the MCF algorithm [5]. Unlike the MCF algorithm, the shortest-path algorithms do not allow path splitting [3], which enables a virtual link to be mapped onto multiple substrate paths.

4.1 VNE Simulation Performance Metrics

The objective of a VNE algorithm is to maximize an InP's revenue while minimizing the cost of embeddings. The average revenue is directly proportional to the acceptance ratio. Furthermore, increasing the node and link utilizations simultaneously may generate additional revenue. Note that high node utilization is always desirable because it is a result of high acceptance ratio while the link utilization should be maintained as low as possible.

Revenue

Let us denote the available CPU capacity of a node n and available bandwidth of a link e by $\mathcal{C}(n)$ and $\mathcal{B}(e)$, respectively. The revenue $R(G^v)$ is the weighted sum of the VNR's CPU and bandwidth requirements defined as:

$$\mathbf{R}(G^v) = \omega_c \sum_{n^v \in N^v} \mathcal{C}(n^v) + \omega_b \sum_{e^v \in E^v} \mathcal{B}(e^v), \quad (1)$$

where $G^v(N^v, E^v)$ denotes the virtual network graph while the weights ω_c and ω_b are unit prices of the requested CPU and bandwidth, respectively.

Cost

The cost of a VNE $\mathcal{C}(G^v)$ depends on the allocated substrate resources. It is calculated as:

$$\mathbf{C}(G^v) = \sum_{n^v \in N^v} \mathcal{C}(n^v) + \sum_{e^v \in E^v} \sum_{e^s \in E^s} f_{e^s}^{e^v}, \quad (2)$$

where $G^s(N^s, E^s)$ denotes the substrate network graph and $f_{e^s}^{e^v}$ is the bandwidth of the substrate link e^s that is allocated to the virtual link e^v.

Acceptance Ratio

The acceptance ratio is calculated as:

$$p_a^\tau = \frac{|\Psi^a(\tau)|}{|\Psi(\tau)|}, \quad (3)$$

where $|\Psi^a(\tau)|$ and $|\Psi(\tau)|$ denote the number of accepted VNRs and the number of VNRs that arrived in the time interval τ, respectively.

Node and Link Utilizations

Node utilization $\mathcal{U}(N^s)$ is calculated as:

$$\mathcal{U}(N^s) = 1 - \frac{\sum_{n^s \in N^s} \mathcal{C}(n^s)}{\sum_{n^s \in N^s} \mathcal{C}_{max}(n^s)}, \quad (4)$$

where $\mathcal{C}(n^s)$ is the available CPU resource of a substrate node n^s and $\mathcal{C}_{max}(n^s)$ is the maximum CPU resource of the node. Similarly, link utilization $\mathcal{U}(E^s)$ is calculated as:

$$\mathcal{U}(E^s) = 1 - \frac{\sum_{e^s \in E^s} \mathcal{B}(e^s)}{\sum_{e^s \in e^s} \mathcal{B}_{max}(e^s)}, \quad (5)$$

where $\mathcal{B}(e^s)$ is the available bandwidth of a substrate link e^s and $\mathcal{B}_{max}(e^s)$ is the maximum bandwidth of the link.

4.2 ViNE and Global Resource Capacity Algorithms

The Global Resource Capacity (GRC) [6], R-ViNE [4], and D-ViNE [4] are examples of coordinated two-stage algorithms. They are implemented in *VNE-Sim* and we employ them for the case study in this paper. The GRC algorithm relies on a node-ranking approach to solve the VNoM subproblem. The rank of a node is calculated based on the CPU capacity of the node and the bandwidth of the incident links [6]. After calculating the ranks of substrate and virtual nodes, the GRC algorithm employs a *large-to-large and small-to-small* [22] mapping scheme to embed virtual nodes onto substrate nodes. After completing the VNoM assignments, a modified Dijkstra's algorithm is used to calculate the shortest path between mapped nodes in order to complete VLiM. The R-ViNE and D-ViNE algorithms formulate the VNoM problem as an MIP. They employ a rounding-based approach to solve the linear programming (LP) relaxation of the proposed MIP. The MCF algorithm is then employed to solve the VLiM subproblem. MCF treats nodes and links of VNRs as commodities and flows, respectively. When solving VLiM, MCF may use path splitting [3]. It has been shown that utilizing MCF results in better utilization of substrate resources [4].

4.3 Simulation Scenarios

During the development phase of *VNE-Sim*, we have performed various test cases and small scale validation scenarios to ensure the correctness of the implemented algorithms. We present here a simulation scenario that is of comparable scale to the scenarios that are presented in the literature [3], [4], [6].

The BRITE [18] library is used to generate the substrate and VNR graphs. The substrate graph is composed of 50

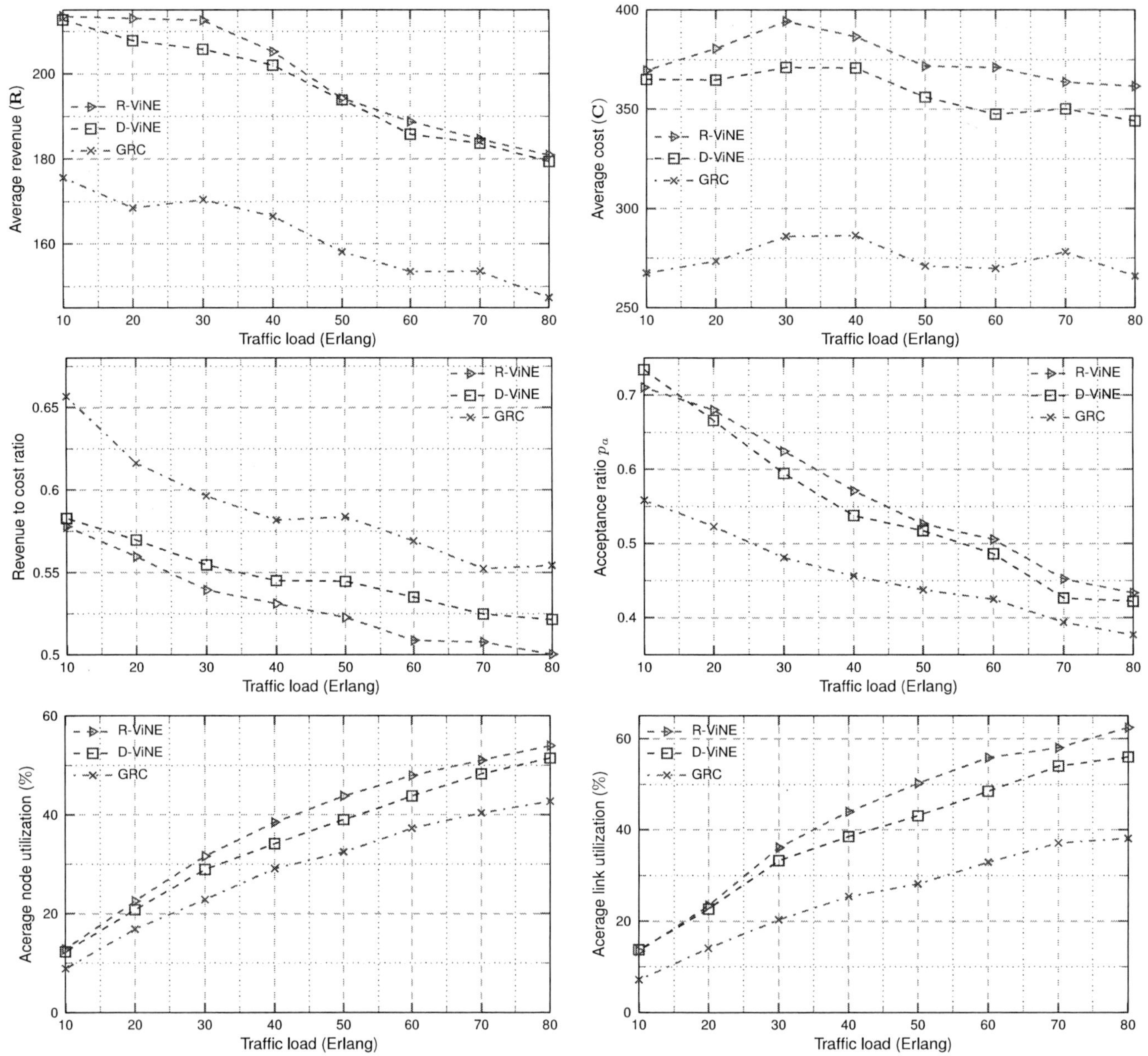

Figure 3: Performance of the ViNE and GRC algorithms. Shown are various performance metrics as functions of the VNR traffic load.

nodes where each node is randomly connected to a maximum of 5 other nodes. The substrate graph that was generated for the simulation scenarios consists of 221 edges. Each node of the substrate network is randomly placed on a 25×25 grid. The VNR graphs are generated using a similar process. The number of nodes in each VNR graph is uniformly distributed between 3 and 10 [4]. The CPU capacity of substrate nodes and the bandwidth of substrate links are uniformly distributed between 50 and 100 units. The CPU requirements of the virtual nodes are uniformly distributed between 2 and 20 units while the bandwidth requirements of the virtual links are uniformly distributed between 0 and 50 units [4]. Performance of the ViNE [4] and the GRC [6] algorithms in terms of revenue, cost, revenue to cost ratio, acceptance ratio, node utilization, and link utilization are shown in Figure 3.

Unprocessed data generated by discrete events that occur during simulations are saved as SQLite databases. These data may be processed using SQL commands or other statistical analysis tools. For example, the output database of the simulation results that are presented here contains a record indicating the outcome of the embedding for every VNR arrival. If a VNR is successfully embedded, the record also includes the revenue, cost, and queuing and processing times of the request. The database entries may then be processed to calculate revenue, cost, and resource utilizations shown in Figure 3.

The R-ViNE and D-ViNE algorithms utilize the substrate link resources more efficiently than the GRC algorithm as a result of employing the MCF algorithm for link mapping. GRC algorithm employs a shortest-path-based algorithm without path splitting to solve VLiM, which is stricter than the MCF algorithm that enables path splitting. For example, consider a virtual node attached to a virtual link that requires 5 units of bandwidth and a substrate node attached to two substrate links with available bandwidths of 2 and 3 units. In this case, while utilizing MCF permits embedding the virtual node onto the substrate node, such embedding is infeasible without path splitting. Superior performance of the R-ViNE and D-ViNE algorithms comes at the cost of higher execution time. In the simulation scenarios, a virtual network embedding required on average 0.596 s, 0.591 s, and 0.017 s using the R-ViNE, D-ViNE, and GRC algorithms, respectively.

VNE-Sim has been used to compare the BCube(2, 4) [23] and Fat-Tree$_6$ [24] data center network topologies for virtual network embedding by employing the R-ViNE, D-ViNE, and GRC algorithms [9]. Simulation results indicate that the Fat-Tree topology is capable of accepting additional number of virtual network requests even though the topology consists of slightly fewer number of nodes and links.

5. CONCLUSION

In this paper, we presented *VNE-Sim* for simulating VNE algorithms. *VNE-Sim* formalizes the VNE process as a discrete event system based on the DEVS framework and uses the *Adevs* library. The modular and scalable design of *VNE-Sim* enables researchers to seamlessly implement new VNE algorithms and evaluate their performance.

The initial development phase of *VNE-Sim* has been completed. Future work includes implementing other VNE algorithms, implementing a source code documentation system, in depth comparison of *VNE-Sim* and *Alevin* in terms of memory usage and capabilities, and implementing a scripting infrastructure for visualization of results.

6. REFERENCES

[1] J. S. Turner and D. E. Taylor, "Diversifying the Internet," in *Proc. IEEE GLOBECOM 2005*, St. Louis, MO, USA, Dec. 2005, pp. 755–760.

[2] N. Feamster, L. Gao, and J. Rexford, "How to lease the Internet in your spare time," *Comput. Commun. Rev.*, vol. 37, no. 1, pp. 61–64, Jan. 2007.

[3] M. Yu, Y. Yi, J. Rexford, and M. Chiang, "Rethinking virtual network embedding: substrate support for path splitting and migration," *Comput. Commun. Rev.*, vol. 38, no. 2, pp. 19–29, Mar. 2008.

[4] M. Chowdhury, M. R. Rahman, and R. Boutaba, "ViNEYard: Virtual network embedding algorithms with coordinated node and link mapping," *IEEE/ACM Trans. Netw.*, vol. 20, no. 1, pp. 206–219, Feb. 2012.

[5] D. G. Andersen, "Theoretical approaches to node assignment," Dec. 2002, Unpublished Manuscript. [Online]. Available: http://repository.cmu.edu/compsci/86/.

[6] L. Gong, Y. Wen, Z. Zhu, and T. Lee, "Toward profit-seeking virtual network embedding algorithm via global resource capacity," in *Proc. IEEE INFOCOM*, Toronto, ON, Canada, Apr. 2014, pp. 1–9.

[7] M. T. Beck, C. Linnhoff-Popien, A. Fischer, F. Kokot, and H. de Meer, "A simulation framework for virtual network embedding algorithms," in *Proc. 16th Int. Telecommunications Netw. Strategy and Planning Symp.*, Funchal, Portugal, Sept. 2014, pp. 1–6.

[8] S. Haeri, Q. Ding, Z. Li, and Lj. Trajković, "Global resource capacity algorithm with path splitting for virtual network embedding," in *Proc. IEEE Int. Symp. Circuits and Systems*, Montreal, QC, Canada, May 2016, pp. 666–669.

[9] S. Haeri and Lj. Trajković, "Virtual network embeddings in data center networks," in *Proc. IEEE Int. Symp. Circuits and Systems*, Montreal, QC, Canada, May 2016, pp. 874–877.

[10] (2015, Dec.) CMake Build System. [Online]. Available: https://cmake.org/.

[11] (2015, Dec.) Fast Network Simulation Setup. [Online]. Available: http://fnss.github.io/.

[12] (2015, Dec.) Hiberlite Library. [Online]. Available: https://github.com/paulftw/hiberlite/.

[13] J. J. Nutaro, *Building Software for Simulation: Theory and Algorithms, with Applications in C++*. Hoboken, NJ, USA: John Wiley & Sons, 2010.

[14] (2015, Dec.) Boost C++ Libraries. [Online]. Available: http://www.boost.org/.

[15] (2016, Jan.) GSL–GNU Scientific Library. [Online]. Available: https://www.gnu.org/software/gsl/.

[16] (2016, Jan.) GLPK–GNU Linear Programming Kit. [Online]. Available: http://www.gnu.org/software/glpk/.

[17] (2015, Dec.) SQLite: Small. Fast. Reliable. Choose any three. [Online]. Available: https://www.sqlite.org/.

[18] (2016, Jan.) Boston University Representative Internet Topology Generator. [Online]. Available: http://www.cs.bu.edu/brite/.

[19] A. M. Uhrmacher, "Dynamic structures in modeling and simulation: a reflective approach," *ACM Trans. Modeling and Computer Simulation*, vol. 11, no. 2, pp. 206–232, Apr. 2001.

[20] E. Gamma, R. Helm, R. Johnson, and J. Vlissides, *Design Patterns: Elements of Reusable Object-Oriented Software*, 1st ed., ser. Addison-Wesley Professional Computing Series. Boston, MA, USA: Addison-Wesley, 1994.

[21] A. Fischer, J. F. Botero, M. T. Beck, H. de Meer, and X. Hesselbach, "Virtual network embedding: a survey," *IEEE Communications Surveys & Tutorials*, vol. 15, no. 4, pp. 1888–1906, 2013.

[22] X. Cheng, S. Su, Z. Zhang, H. Wang, F. Yang, Y. Luo, and J. Wang, "Virtual network embedding through topology-aware node ranking," *Comput. Commun. Rev.*, vol. 41, pp. 38–47, Apr. 2011.

[23] C. Guo, G. Lu, D. Li, H. Wu, X. Zhang, Y. Shi, C. Tian, Y. Zhang, and S. Lu, "BCube: a high performance, server-centric network architecture for modular data centers," *ACM SIGCOMM Comput. Commun. Rev.*, vol. 39, no. 4, pp. 63–74, Oct. 2009.

[24] M. Al-Fares, A. Loukissas, and A. Vahdat, "A scalable, commodity data center network architecture," *ACM SIGCOMM Comput. Commun. Rev.*, vol. 38, no. 4, pp. 63–74, Oct. 2008.

Performance Comparison of Dual Connectivity and Hard Handover for LTE-5G Tight Integration

Michele Polese*, Marco Mezzavilla†, Michele Zorzi*

*Department of Information Engineering, University of Padova, Italy
e-mail: {polesemi, zorzi}@dei.unipd.it
†Tandon School of Engineering, New York University, Brooklyn NY, USA
e-mail: mezzavilla@nyu.edu

ABSTRACT

Communications at frequencies above 10 GHz (the mmWave band) are expected to play a major role for the next generation of cellular networks (5G), because of the potential multi-gigabit, ultra-low latency performance of this technology. mmWave frequencies however suffer from very high isotropic pathloss, which may result in cells with a much smaller coverage area than current LTE macrocells. High directionality techniques will be used to improve signal quality and extend coverage area, along with a high density deployment of mmWave base stations (BS). However, when propagation conditions are hard and it is difficult to provide high quality coverage with mmWave BS, it is necessary to rely on previous generation LTE base stations, which make use of lower frequencies (900 MHz - 3.5 GHz), which are less sensitive to blockage and experience lower pathloss. In order to provide ultra-reliable services to mobile users there is a need for network architectures that tightly and seamlessly integrate the LTE and mmWave Radio Access Technologies. In this paper we will present two possible alternatives for this integration and show how simulation tools can be used to assess and compare their performance.

CCS Concepts

•**Networks** → **Network simulations;** *Mobile networks;*

Keywords

5G LTE tight integration, dual connectivity, simulation

1. INTRODUCTION

The latest Cisco Visual Networking Index forecasts an explosion of mobile network traffic to be expected before 2020, with an eightfold increase of global mobile traffic [5]. The next generation of cellular networks will be required to address connected devices, and to provide improved performance for many different use cases. For example, 5G networks should support [8] (i) a rate of 50 Mbits or more even at cell edges, with peaks of 1 Gbps in particular cases; (ii) ultra-low end-to-end latency below 10 ms, with a stricter requirement of 1 ms for applications such as tactile internet; (iii) ultra-reliable communications, with ultra-high availability and reliability; (iv) massive Machine Type Communications (MTC) with very low power.

MmWave technology may play a major role in allowing 5G networks to meet these requirements. The spectrum above 10 GHz is not as fragmented as the microWave spectrum, therefore large contiguous chunks of bandwidth are available. However, there are several issues that must be studied in order to make mmWave technology well understood and market-ready. MmWave frequencies suffer from high isotropic pathloss, which can be compensated with massive MIMO and beamforming, thanks to the small size of the antennas, but also from blockages from solid materials (i.e., buildings of bricks and mortar) [3, 14].

These extreme propagation conditions offer new design requirements for the PHY and MAC layers [15], however they also have consequences on the higher layers of the protocol stack. In particular, in order to provide an ultra-reliable service, user equipments (UEs) at mmWave frequencies will have to perform handover between neighboring mmWave base stations or to fall back to the legacy LTE network. The LTE base stations may offer a reliable backup in case the link with mmWave BS is disrupted and outage is experienced. However, the current LTE handover procedure may be too slow, and may result in service interruptions and excessive signaling. Therefore, we propose a dual connectivity (DC) solution, in which the UE is connected to both Radio Access Technologies (RATs), and performs fast switching between the two with a single RRC message. The dual connectivity is part of a set of proposals on tight integration between LTE and mmWave RATs, which can be found in [16].

A thorough simulation campaign on dual connectivity or handover between different RATs has however not yet been performed, since current simulation tools for LTE and 5G are not integrated. In this paper we will describe the work done to implement a simulator that offers the capabilities of using PHY and MAC layers of LTE and 5G in the same UE. It is based on the open source simulator *network simulator 3* (ns–3, [11]), and uses the 5G mmWave protocol stack developed by NYU [6] together with the LTE module of ns–3 [4].

The paper is organized as follows. In Sec. 2 we will describe two different ways to integrate LTE and mmWave networks. Then in Sec. 3 we will present the simulation framework and briefly recall some implementation issues. Finally we will show which are the metrics we expect to measure from still ongoing simulation campaigns and present some early results in Sec. 4.

2. LTE-5G TIGHT INTEGRATION

LTE and 5G are expected to integrate at a certain layer and to rely on a common core network infrastructure, following an idea of *harmonization* strongly advocated by several stakeholders [10, 12, 16]. By exploiting existing infrastructure and architectures, the deployment of 5G networks can be faster and requires lower capital expenditure (CAPEX). Mature elements of legacy networks are expected to be used also in 5G networks, and one of the areas that can benefit from this integration is reliability, due to the wide-area coverage of LTE macrocells. The discussion on which is the appropriate layer at which LTE and 5G should integrate is still ongoing. The idea is that from this *integration* layer upwards the two stacks will have common protocols. The integration layer has an interface to lower layer primitives and functions whose implementation differs in the two radio access technologies. A possible integration may be placed at the MAC layer, exploiting the fact that probably PHY layer will be OFDM based, but this would limit the optimization that can be carried out on the design of mmWave MAC layers. The same problem presents for integration at the *Radio Link Control* (RLC) layer, which is tightly coupled with the MAC layer by the scheduling decisions. A more realistic integration can be performed at the *Packet Data Convergence Protocol* (PDCP) layer, which is not strictly dependent on lower layers' functionalities. In this work we assume that the integration is performed at this layer.

Currently, a typical UE supports more than one possible RATs, i.e., it can use GSM, UMTS or LTE networks. However, these three technologies are not integrated and are very different from one another, both in the radio access and in the core network. In order to switch from LTE to one of the two other legacy networks, an involved inter RAT procedure is required. However, for LTE and 5G networks a new inter RAT handover (HO) that requires less signaling may be designed. A good starting point to lower the burden and the complexity of the HO may be to consider mmWave cells as LTE cells, and use the faster intra RAT handover procedure. This may be made possible by the control layer integration between LTE and 5G, which is part of the proposals around tight integration [16].

However, even the intra RAT handover may not be a good solution for a seamless and ultra-fast switch between the two air interfaces. Indeed, it involves signaling both between the two BSs, on the X2 interface, and at the RRC layer, to communicate to the UE the information on the target cell. It also needs a non contention based random access procedure, and a message exchange with the *Mobile Management Entity* (MME) in the core network in order to switch the path from the *Serving Gateway* (SGW) to the BS to which the UE is performing the handover. The processing in the MME may require a one-way latency in the order of 10 ms, and during this interval packets must be forwarded from the BS from which the handover originated to the target BS. Moreover, a handover from a mmWave BS to an LTE cell should be triggered only if the mmWave link is going to be in outage, in order to remain connected to the mmWave cell as long as possible and benefit from its high throughput and low latency. In this case, the control signaling may experience some latency due to packets received with errors and retransmissions, or worse, the UE may not manage to transmit/receive the required messages at all, thereby detecting a Radio Link Failure (RLF). During the random access procedure, moreover, the UE is not capable of transmitting and receiving data, which is buffered at the BS and experiences an increased latency.

A different and more robust solution can be obtained using a dual connectivity (DC) setup, introduced here as an extension of 3GPP's LTE DC proposal [1]. In the proposed scheme, the UE is simultaneously connected to both LTE and mmWave BSs. The LTE cell acts as a backup: since the UE is already connected, when the signal quality of the mmWave link degrades, there is no need to perform a complete handover with a random access procedure, to send path switching messages to the core network: a single RRC control message from the LTE BS to the UE is enough. The LTE cell is also a coordinator of all the neighboring mmWave cells, as proposed in [7], and an access point to the core network for dual connected devices. In this setup the UE transmits pilots that mmWave base stations can use to estimate the link quality (for example by measuring the SNR). These measurements are periodically sent from each mmWave cell to the LTE cell, via the X2 interface. Therefore, the LTE BS knows which is the best mmWave cell for each UE: notice that this reporting is forwarded to the closest LTE eNB, i.e., the one that may offer fallback once all mmWave cells are in outage. Once the UE is within coverage of an LTE cell, it performs a random access to the LTE *evolved Node Base* (eNB) using the standardized LTE procedure. As soon as the LTE BS knows that the UE has successfully completed the access procedure, it instructs the UE to connect also to the mmWave eNB with the best SNR.

In a dual connected setup, in the LTE eNB there is a PDCP and related RLC instance for each bearer, while in the mmWave eNB there is only an RLC instance. Then, data is forwarded from the core network to the LTE eNB, where the PDCP layer decides whether to send it via LTE RAT, or to forward it to the remote RLC layer in the mmWave eNB. The mmWave link is used unless in outage, in this case a switch signal is sent to the UE which starts receiving data on the LTE radio interface. Notice that this scheme allows also to decouple uplink and downlink connections. If the LTE cell detects that another mmWave eNB has a better signal quality than the current one, it may trigger and orchestrate a handover between the two mmWave cells, while the data transmission is switched to LTE.

The PDCP forwards data via the X2 interface, thus, since the mmWave eNB is usually preferred to LTE, and according to the latency of the connection between BSs, the PDCP layer and anchor point to the core network may be moved to the mmWave eNB to decrease the end to end latency of data transmissions.

3. SIMULATION OF LTE-5G TIGHT INTEGRATION IN NS–3

In order to assess the performance of both schemes, we

integrated two already developed tools for LTE and 5G simulations. The first is the LTE module of the ns–3 simulator, whose upper layers are shared by the ns–3 mmWave simulator developed by NYU [6]. This tool has a very detailed characterization of the physical layer, which exploits real measurements in order to model small scale fading, beamforming and channel conditions at 28 and 73 GHz carrier frequencies [9]. This simulator assumes a TDD physical layer, and the physical frame structure can be configured to support different OFDM numerologies.

Even though the mmWave simulator uses the LTE higher layers, prior to this work it was not possible to set up a simulation with devices capable of both LTE and mmWave communications in the same scenario. Therefore, the core of the DC implementation is a new extension of the ns–3 `NetDevice`, called `McUeNetDevice`, which has a double stack: mmWave physical, MAC and *Radio Resource Control* (RRC) layers, LTE physical, MAC, RRC layers, and a single UE *Non Access Stratum* (NAS) layer. The latter has an interface to both RRC entities and is in charge of the exchange of information between them.

An `McUeNetDevice` connects to an LTE eNB and to a mmWave eNB. In a dual connectivity scenario, the UE connects to the closest LTE cell, which in turn selects the mmWave cell with the highest SNR for initial connection of the UE mmWave stack. The mmWave eNB RRC does not interact with the core network when dealing with dual-connected devices, and only the LTE RRC handles the bearer creation and related protocol exchanges. The general scheme of an `McUeNetDevice`, an LTE BS and a mmWave eNB is shown in Fig. 1. In the dual connectivity setup the PDCP layer in the eNB relies on the X2 interface to transmit packets to the remote RLC layers in the mmWave eNB. In the UE, instead, the PDCP is directly connected to both LTE and mmWave RLCs. The `McUeNetDevice` can be used also to simulate the handover between LTE and mmWave cells. Indeed, it can be configured to use a single RRC layer, which can be interfaced with PHY, MAC and RLC layers of both radio access technologies.

Moreover, we extended the mmWave simulator classes in order to support handover and dual connectivity, by (i) providing SNR measurements in each eNB from all the UEs in the scenario; (ii) automatically configuring the UE protocol stack and PHY parameters after the connection to a new mmWave eNB; (iii) allowing disconnection of a UE from an eNB during handover; (iv) adding non contention based random access for initial access during handovers. The methods that allow the LTE macrocell to act as a coordinator in a dual connectivity scenario are implemented in the LTE eNB RRC layer. The LTE BS is thus capable of collecting measures from other mmWave eNBs, triggering handovers between mmWave cells or RAT switching.

The mmWave simulator relies on a helper class (`MmWaveHelper`) which sets all the simulation parameters and objects needed. A `SpectrumChannel` models the mmWave channel. In order to support also communications on the LTE radio access network, the helper is extended with two additional `SpectrumChannel` objects, for LTE uplink and downlink channels, that can be characterized with different models of pathloss and are interfaced with the LTE physical layer. Moreover, we added methods to install in the simulation LTE eNBs, UEs and dual connected devices. The LTE eNBs can be characterized with their own scheduling and handover algorithms.

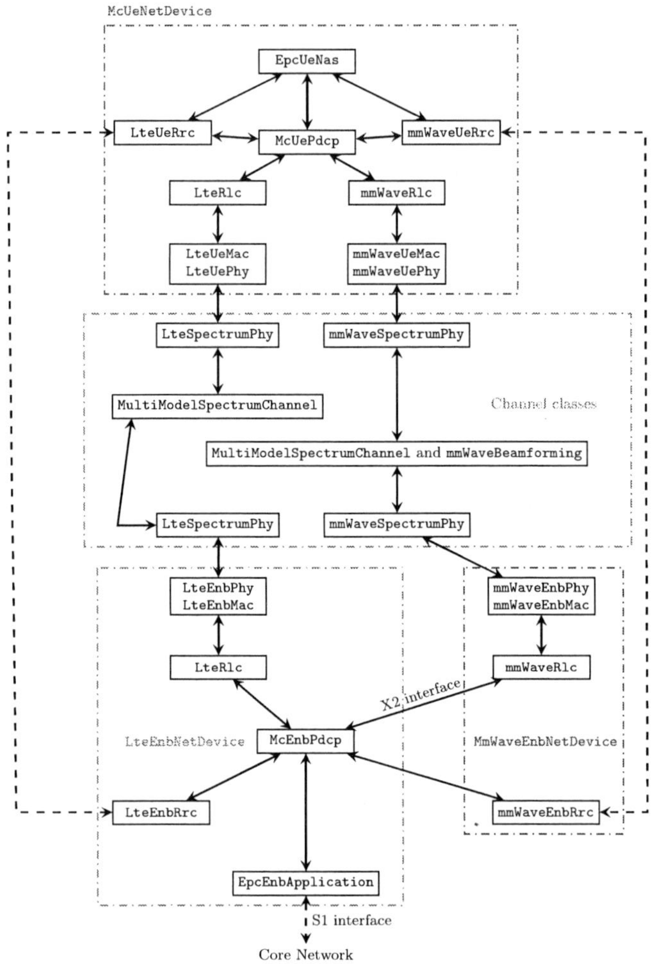

Figure 1: Block diagram of a dual-connected device, an LTE eNB and a mmWave eNB

X2 interfaces are created between all the eNBs, either LTE or mmWave. These links are modeled as ns–3 `PointToPoint` links, therefore it is possible to set the delay, data rate and Maximum Transfer Unit (MTU) of connections between eNBs, and between each eNB, the MME and the SGW.

Actually, in the current implementation of the LTE module for ns–3 the link between eNBs and MME is ideal, whereas in this paper we extended the implementation to allow a more realistic modeling. In particular, the `EpcMme` class of the default LTE module is modified into an application (`EpcMmeApplication`), which is installed on an ns–3 node (`MmeNode`). Then this application is interfaced with the S1-MME endpoint at the MME node. The latter is connected with a `PointToPoint` link to the other endpoint, in the eNB, thus, as for the X2 links, it is possible to introduce a propagation delay, a data rate and an MTU also for S1-MME links. The new `EpcS1Mme` and `EpcS1Enb` classes receive SDUs from the MME and the eNB, respectively, and create PDUs that can be sent over S1-MME by encoding the Information Elements and adding the S1-AP header[1], as specified in [2].

[1]S1-AP is the protocol which runs on top of the S1-MME link.

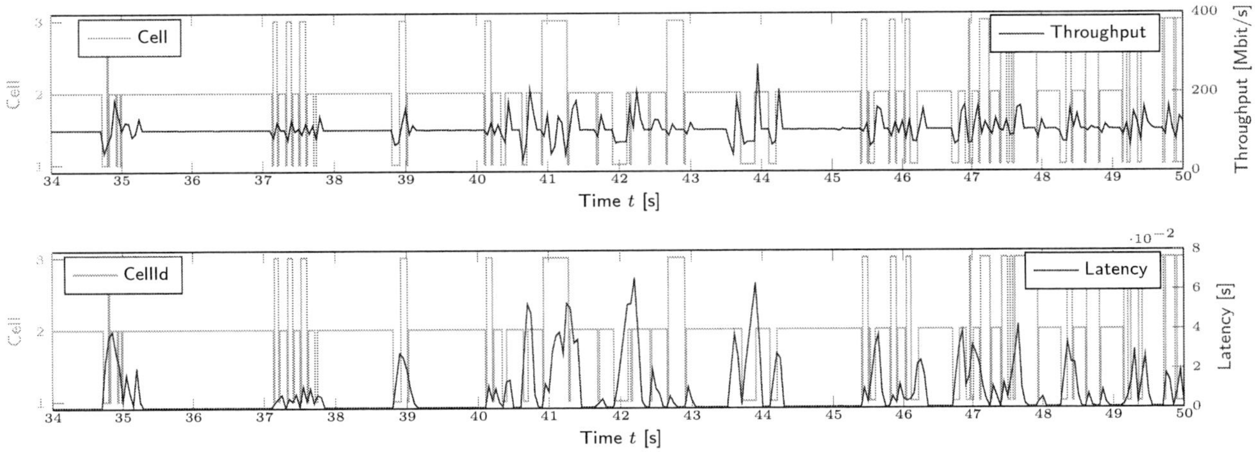

(a) Dual Connectivity setup

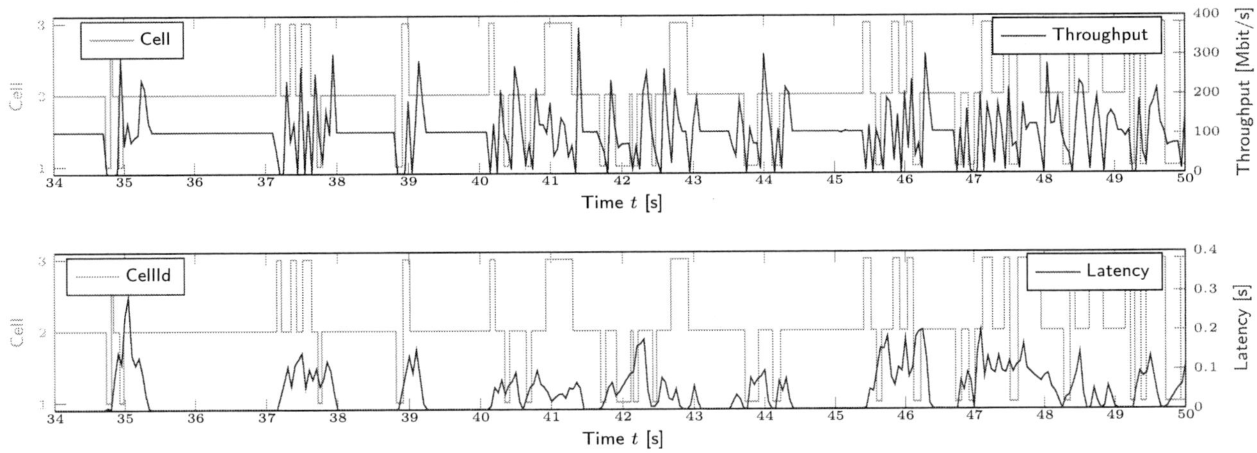

(b) Hard Handover setup

Figure 2: Examples of simulation output: throughput and latency over time, over the cell to which the UE is connected. Cells 2 and 3 are the mmWave eNBs, cell 1 is the LTE eNB

4. METRICS

The main goal of this implementation is to provide a tool that can be used to compare the performance between a system using dual connectivity, with switching, and another where hard handover (HH) is used.

The main benefit of an implementation of the LTE-5G tight integration in ns–3 is the possibility to study the performance of the system by considering a very high level of detail, with realistic interactions among the different parts of the network, from the radio channel modeling to the higher layer protocol message exchanges. Indeed, the comparison between the two systems can be affected by several parameters. The latency of X2 connections may have an impact on how quickly the LTE eNB detects that a UE is in outage with respect to the current mmWave link. The duration of the intervals during which a UE is performing the handover depends on the delay of the connection to the MME, and this affects the latency of data packet transmissions. By using real RRC messages one can account for a different delay and packet error rate in the exchange of control messages between the UE and the eNB. This also makes the parameter space very large, and a thorough simulation campaign to compare the two solutions is ongoing.

There are many metrics that can be computed in a simulation in ns–3 using the developed framework over LTE and mmWave modules. In particular, throughput and latency can be extracted at each layer, from PHY to transport. Packet losses during switching and handover events are also a metric of interest. Another issue that may arise on a high throughput mmWave link is bufferbloat at the RLC layer [17], and latency due to RLC retransmissions. Since ns–3 LTE and mmWave modules offer different RLC implementations, it will be possible to check whether these problems are present or not in the two systems.

The behavior of different transport protocols (UDP, TCP) can be tested, to check which of the two architectures offers higher resiliency in mobility scenarios. In particular it will be interesting to see how TCP reacts to the changes in the link in terms of latency and data rate.

As an example of metrics that can be extracted from the simulator, we present in this paper some early results from a first set of simulations. It is possible to directly compare a simulation with dual connectivity and a simulation with hard handover because by using the same parameters for the

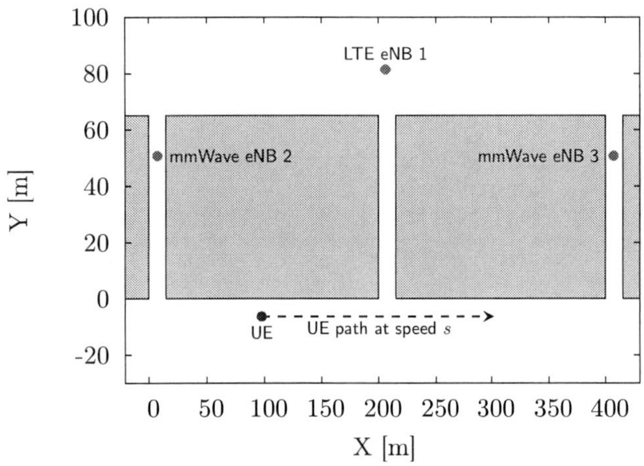

Figure 3: Simulation scenario. The grey rectangles are buildings

Parameter	Value
Outage threshold	-5 dB
mmWave carrier frequency	28 GHz
mmWave bandwidth	1 GHz
LTE carrier frequency (DL)	2.1 GHz
LTE bandwidth	20 MHz
X2 link latency D_{X2}	1 ms
RLC AM buffer size B_{RLC}	10 MB
S1-MME link latency	10 ms
UDP packet size	1024 byte
UDP packet interarrival	80 μs
UE speed s	2 m/s along the x axis (Fig. 3)
Iterations	$N = 10$

Table 1: Simulation parameters

random number generation the channel varies in the same way. Table 1 contains some parameters of the simulations, and the scenario is shown in Fig. 3. The traffic is generated at a rate of 102.4 Mbit/s at the UDP transport layer, and sent from a remote server to the UE. The UE moves along the x axis at $s = 2$ m/s. An example of simulation output is provided in Fig. 2, which shows the throughput and latency at the PDCP layer over time. The UE moves from coordinates (100, -5) to (300, -5), and while moving may experience outage from both mmWave cells (thus the connection changes to LTE RAT either with handover or switching) or perform a handover to the mmWave cell with higher SNR. A hysteresis of 3 dB is accounted for when considering which is the best mmWave cell, and the current cell over time is shown by the green line.

The average values of the throughput and latency, over a set of $N = 10$ simulations for this particular setup, are given in Table 2. It can be seen that the latency of the dual connectivity solution is smaller than that of hard handover. This is due to the fact that the switch is much faster than the handover, therefore packets do not have to be buffered before being transmitted. This behavior is shown also in Fig. 2. For example, at $t = 34$ s there is an outage event, i.e., the connection falls back to LTE cell 1, then the UE returns

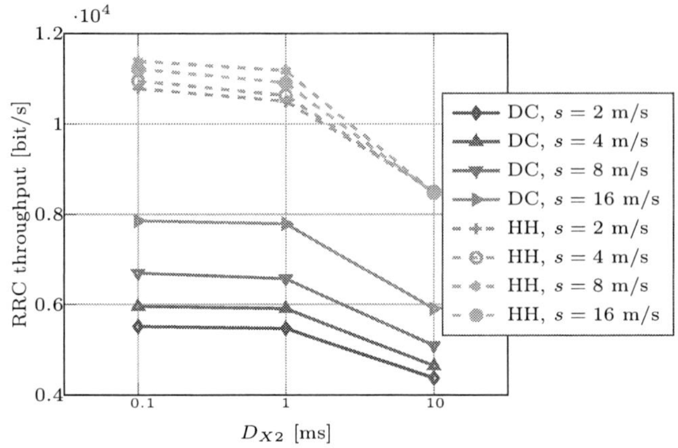

Figure 4: Average RRC traffic per user for DC and HH

	PDCP Throughput	RLC Latency
Dual Connectivity	106.70 Mbit/s	5.1 ms
Hard Handover	104.98 Mbit/s	18.1 ms

Table 2: Throughput and latency for the two setups, for the parameters in Table 1, average over $N = 10$ simulations

to a mmWave connection to mmWave cell 3, and finally it connects to mmWave cell 2. With the DC solution, the latency never exceeds 40 ms, while the HH latency exhibits a spike of 287 ms.

The average PDCP throughput of DC is also higher than that of HH, showing that dual connectivity suffers fewer packet losses.

Another example of metric is shown in Fig. 4, where we present the average traffic per user generated by the RRC layer for different values of the X2 latency $D_{X2} \in \{0.1, 1, 10\}$ ms and for different UE speed $s \in \{2, 4, 8, 16\}$ m/s. It can be seen that the dual connectivity solution, with fast switching, allows to reduce the signaling traffic per user: this reduces the overhead, given a certain number of UEs, or, given the same amount of control overhead, it allows to scale to a larger number of UEs.

5. CONCLUSIONS

In this paper we discussed two possible ways to integrate 5G and LTE networks in order to improve the reliability of next generation mobile networks. We also presented the implementation of a simulation framework that can be used to assess the performance of such systems, integrated in ns–3, and showed that the level of detail of the simulation that can be carried out with such a tool makes it possible to understand and evaluate which is the best solution among dual connectivity with switching and hard handover. We showed some early results, for a particular choice of parameters, as an example of a possible simulation output. A more detailed description of the new software modules and a more comprehensive set of preliminary results can be found in [13]. The application of the proposed framework to extensive simulation campaigns to fully characterize performance trends and to gain key insights for system design is left for future work.

6. REFERENCES

[1] 3GPP. TR 36.842, study on small cell enhancements for E-UTRA and E-UTRAN, v12.0.0, 2013.

[2] 3GPP. TS 36.413, S1 application protocol (S1AP), v13.1.0, 2015.

[3] M. Akdeniz, Y. Liu, M. Samimi, S. Sun, S. Rangan, T. Rappaport, and E. Erkip. Millimeter wave channel modeling and cellular capacity evaluation. *Journal on Sel. Areas in Commun.*, 32(6):1164–1179, June 2014.

[4] N. Baldo, M. Miozzo, M. Requena-Esteso, and J. Nin-Guerrero. An open source product-oriented LTE network simulator based on ns-3. In *Proceedings of the 14th ACM International Conference on Modeling, Analysis and Simulation of Wireless and Mobile Systems*, MSWiM '11, pages 293–298, New York, NY, USA, Nov. 2011. ACM.

[5] Cisco. Visual Networking Index. http://bit.ly/cisco-vni, 2016.

[6] R. Ford, M. Zhang, S. Dutta, M. Mezzavilla, S. Rangan, and M. Zorzi. A Framework for End-to-End Evaluation of 5G mmWave Cellular Networks in Ns-3. In *Proceedings of the Workshop on Ns-3*, WNS3 '16, pages 85–92, New York, NY, USA, June 2016. ACM.

[7] M. Giordani, M. Mezzavilla, S. Rangan, and M. Zorzi. Multi-Connectivity in 5G mmWave Cellular Networks. In *Proceedings of the 15th Annual Mediterranean Ad Hoc networking workshop*, MedHocNet '16, June 2016.

[8] M. Iwamura. NGMN view on 5G architecture. In *2015 IEEE 81st Vehicular Technology Conference (VTC Spring)*, May 2015.

[9] M. Mezzavilla, S. Dutta, M. Zhang, M. R. Akdeniz, and S. Rangan. 5G MmWave Module for the Ns-3 Network Simulator. In *Proceedings of the 18th ACM International Conference on Modeling, Analysis and Simulation of Wireless and Mobile Systems*, MSWiM '15, pages 283–290, New York, NY, USA, Nov 2015. ACM.

[10] Nokia Networks. 5G radio access, *System Design Aspects*. http://bit.ly/nokia-radio-access, 2015.

[11] Nsnam. Network simulator 3. http://www.nsnam.org, 2016.

[12] A. Osseiran, F. Boccardi, V. Braun, K. Kusume, P. Marsch, M. Maternia, O. Queseth, M. Schellmann, H. Schotten, H. Taoka, H. Tullberg, M. A. Uusitalo, B. Timus, and M. Fallgren. Scenarios for 5G mobile and wireless communications: the vision of the METIS project. *IEEE Communications Magazine*, 52(5):26–35, May 2014.

[13] M. Polese. Performance Comparison of Dual Connectivity and Hard Handover for LTE-5G Tight Integration in mmWave Cellular Networks. Master's thesis, Department of Information Engineering, University of Padova, July 2016. Available on arxiv.org.

[14] S. Rangan, T. S. Rappaport, and E. Erkip. Millimeter-wave cellular wireless networks: Potentials and challenges. *Proc. IEEE*, 102(3):366–385, Mar. 2014.

[15] H. Shokri-Ghadikolaei, C. Fischione, G. Fodor, P. Popovski, and M. Zorzi. Millimeter wave cellular networks: A MAC layer perspective. *IEEE Transactions on Communications*, 63(10):3437–3458, Oct 2015.

[16] I. D. Silva, G. Mildh, J. Rune, P. Wallentin, J. Vikberg, P. Schliwa-Bertling, and R. Fan. Tight Integration of New 5G Air Interface and LTE to Fulfill 5G Requirements. In *2015 IEEE 81st Vehicular Technology Conference (VTC Spring)*, May 2015.

[17] M. Zhang, M. Mezzavilla, R. Ford, S. Rangan, S. S. Panwar, E. Mellios, D. Kong, A. R. Nix, and M. Zorzi. Transport Layer Performance in 5G mmWave Cellular. In *2016 IEEE Conference on Computer Communications Workshops (INFOCOM WKSHPS)*, 2016, Presented.

Complex Job Scheduling Simulations with Alea 4

Dalibor Klusáček
CESNET a.l.e.
Prague, Czech Republic
klusacek@cesnet.cz

Šimon Tóth
CESNET a.l.e.
Prague, Czech Republic
simon@cesnet.cz

Gabriela Podolníková
Faculty of Informatics,
Masaryk University
Brno, Czech Republic
xpodoln@fi.muni.cz

ABSTRACT

Simulations have been used for many years in order to either develop, refine or validate new setups of production resource managers, that are used in large computing systems such as HPC clusters, computing grids or clouds. Typically, new job scheduling algorithms or various resource-related policies are first evaluated in a simulator prior to their deployment. To facilitate this, accurate models of both the applied resource manager and the workload being processed are very important to obtain reliable simulation outputs. In this paper we present a new major release of the Alea simulator, that has been developed in order to allow for such detailed and realistic simulations. The simulator allows for detailed emulation of typical scheduling systems that are widely used in nowadays computing centers. Furthermore, it also provides novel approach to properly model dynamic user-to-system interactions. We also present recent real-life based examples where the Alea simulator has been used to improve the performance of an actual computing system, demonstrating its practical capabilities and usefulness.

CCS Concepts

•Computing methodologies → Discrete-event simulation; *Planning and scheduling;* **•Computer systems organization →** *Grid computing; Cloud computing;*

Keywords

Alea, simulation, job scheduling, workload adaptation

1. INTRODUCTION

Large computational systems like HPC clusters, grids or clouds generally involve high complexity and significant operational costs. It is therefore only natural, that their operators expect these systems to operate at peak efficiency. So called *resource managers* are those necessary software components that are responsible for managing access to the *scheduler* which maps waiting jobs submitted by users onto the available system resources. To maintain the efficiency of the system, job schedulers follow one or more *optimization criteria*, such as user-to-user fairness, global or per-user wait times, resource utilization, and so on [7].

The attainable performance of a job scheduler depends on many variables that usually include the type (mix) of users' workloads (e.g., parallel vs. sequential jobs, short vs. long jobs), applied scheduling algorithm (e.g., trivial First Come First Served or more efficient solutions like backfilling [11]) and additional system configuration (e.g., the number of queues and their priorities/limits). Therefore, designing a proper configuration is a truly daunting process due to the complexity of the whole system. Furthermore, even straightforward (conservative) changes in the configuration of a production system can have highly unexpected and often counterintuitive side effects that emerge from the mutual interplay of various components [9].

Simulators that are capable of reliably emulating a particular production system and its configuration therefore play an important role when a new configuration of a resource manager/scheduler is required. In this paper we present a new release of the complex job scheduling simulator — Alea 4. This work represents a major extension of the Alea simulator, which was firstly introduced in 2007 and later thoroughly evaluated in the paper presented at SIMUTools 2010 [8]. Since then, Alea has been further developed to enable truly complex and detailed simulations.

The new version presented in this paper covers several important areas. First, the simulator now allows for detailed emulation of *multi-queue* systems with *queue-related priorities and constraints*, which allows for modeling of complicated systems that are logically/physically partitioned into resource/job pools. A set of priority mechanisms for intra-queue job ordering is also supported, focusing on common *fair-sharing* approaches that are widely used in multi-user computing systems to guarantee fairness.

The second important extension is the new *workload adaptation approach.* For each simulation, a simulator requires a workload trace that provides the simulation data describing the parameters of jobs (job arrival times, the amount of requested resources, runtime, etc.). So far, the common approach was to use historical workload traces [6] capturing previously recorded users' activities. However, recent research has shown that this common practice of relying on a static historical workload trace often leads to totally misleading and skewed results [17, 16]. Instead, a new approach utilizing dynamic workload adaptation has been suggested,

SIMUTOOLS 2016, August 22-23, Prague, Czech Republic

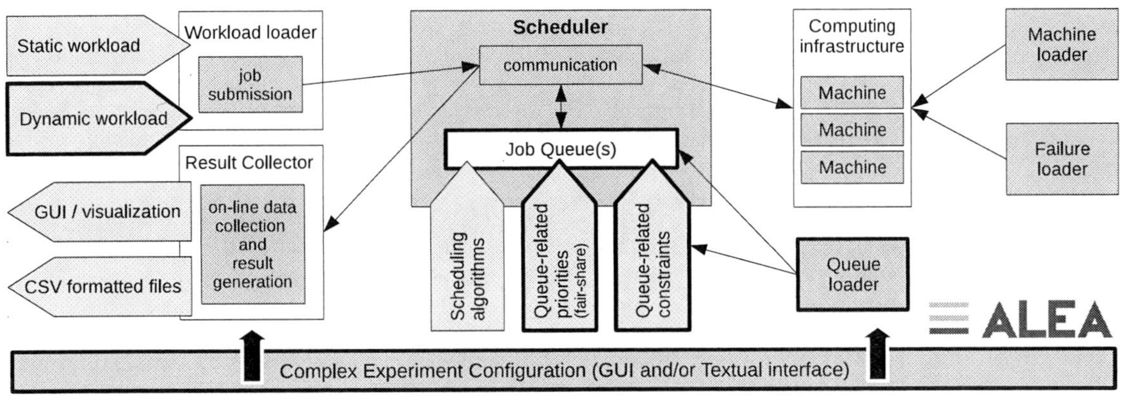

Figure 1: Main parts of the Alea 4 simulator (newly added modules are highlighted with bold lines).

as it provides more accurate representation of common user behavior [16].

As far as we know, Alea [1] is the first publicly available job scheduling simulator, that enables dynamic workload adaptation. Our implementation uses an agent-based model where each user of the system is represented as an independent entity (agent), which brings great flexibility when modeling the overall user behavior. Also, this new approach allows us not only to simulate the interactions of users and the underlying system, but we can also analyze *hypothetical changes* to the workload/system. For example, we can easily model and analyze the admission control process, e.g., add a new user into the system and then explore the effects on the existing users and/or overall system performance.

This paper is organized as follows. Section 2 briefly introduces the architecture of the Alea simulator. Next, Section 3 explains the major extensions of Alea 4 and their importance. Section 4 demonstrates the practical impacts of complex simulations achieved by our simulator. Finally, related work and conclusions are presented in Sections 5-6.

2. ALEA SIMULATOR

The basic architecture of Alea simulator remains the same as was already discussed in our SIMUTools 2010 paper [8]. Therefore, we only briefly present the overall architecture here and put greater emphasis on the recent developments that are described in Section 3.

Alea 4 is an event-based, discrete time simulator built on the top of GridSim simulation toolkit [15] which is used to emulate the underlying computing infrastructure. Alea is composed of independent entities which implement the job scheduling simulation functionality as shown in Figure 1 (newly created modules are highlighted with bold lines).

The main part of the simulator is the centralized job scheduler. The scheduler manages the inter-module communication and maintains the important data structures such as job queue(s). Job scheduling decisions are performed by scheduling algorithms[1] that respect newly added features such as queue-related priorities (fair-sharing) and various queue-related constraints and limits. Additional parts are responsible for simulating the computing infrastructure (including the emulation of machine failures/restarts), workload loading (either static or dynamic), while several additional modules are responsible for the simulation setup[2] and the visualization and generation of simulation outputs. The behavior of the simulator is driven by the event-based message passing protocol. For each simulated event — such as job arrival/completion or machine failure — one message defining this event is created. It contains the identifier of the message recipient, the type of the event, the time when the event will occur and the message data.

The simulator allows for easy extension of its current functionality, thanks to the object oriented paradigm used by both the underlying GridSim and the Alea 4 itself. Alea 4 is platform-independent and freely available at GitHub [1].

3. MAJOR EXTENSIONS

The primary goal of a job scheduling simulator is to allow "safe" and realistic evaluation of new scheduling policies or new setups of an existing physical system. For this purpose, it is necessary to capture all important features of the actual system. Throughout our practical experience in MetaCentrum — a major computing center[3] in Czech Republic — we have repeatedly realized that many promising "theoretical" works based on simulations are not usable in real systems, due to the overly simplified nature of performed simulations. Typically, those works often focus solely on particular scheduling algorithm while none or very simplified model of additional system-related constraints and policies have been used. However, production systems use literally dozens of additional parameters, rules and policies that significantly influence the overall performance of the scheduler [13].

3.1 Queues, Constraints and Fair-Sharing

As we have observed in practice, those "tricky parts" that influence system performance are *queue-related setups and constraints* as well as *fairness-related policies* such as fair-share [9]. Therefore, we have implemented such a functionality in Alea 4 allowing for more reliable system simulations.

First of all, Alea 4 allows to specify the number of job queues, their names, priorities and queue-related constraints.

[1]Alea 4 supports great variety of scheduling algorithms including several advanced meta-heuristics. New algorithms can be easily added using existing simple interfaces.

[2]Recently, a new complex configuration file together with a step-by-step GUI configurator has been added for easier simulation setup management.

[3]http://metacentrum.cz/

For example, we can specify that — beside a "normal" queue — there are other queues, e.g., a high-priority queue for short jobs that can use up to 60% of all system resources and a low-priority queue for very long jobs that can use only up to 20% of system resources. It reflects the rather complicated setups of production systems where system resources are usually partitioned into several (sometimes overlapping) pools, where each pool has a corresponding queue. Users workloads (jobs) are then mapped to these corresponding queues, in order to avoid potentially dangerous saturation of the whole system — either with jobs from a single user, or with a single class of jobs [7]. For example, it would be very unfortunate to saturate the system with long running jobs (i.e., jobs with expected runtime of several weeks) as it would naturally lead to huge wait times for shorter jobs [9]. This functionality is newly implemented in `QueueLoader` and `Scheduler` classes.

Furthermore, the `Scheduler` class now provides several variants of *fair-sharing mechanisms* that are used to prioritize jobs within queue(s) in order to guarantee user-to-user fairness. The goal of a fair-share mechanism is to dynamically adjust job priorities such that the use of system resources is fairly balanced among the users [7, 9].

Still, even simulators that support such advanced capabilities may not fulfill entirely the requirements requested by actual system administrators. As we show in the next section, a major problem relates to a workload being used.

3.2 Dynamic Workload Adaptation

For a proper simulation, a workload trace is required that provides the data describing important job parameters (job arrival times, the amount of requested resources, runtime, etc.). Most commonly, *researchers utilize historical workload traces* that are either extracted from the system itself, or from a public workload trace repository such as the Parallel Workloads Archive [6] or the Grid Workloads Archive [4]. Statistical models can be also employed [5] to generate a synthetic workload, with the model being fitted to match the overall users behavior.

As was repeatedly shown in the past [14, 17], *this methodology is problematic* for several reasons. The biggest problem is that such workloads are static and — unlike real users in real systems — these workloads do not react to the current state of the simulated system, causing the simulated jobs to arrive with unrealistic timing. For example, it is unlikely that a user would submit new jobs if all her previously submitted jobs are still waiting to start/complete. Similarly, if all user's jobs have completed processing quickly, that user is not likely to wait weeks to submit new jobs (even though this timing is present in the historical trace). In other words, static workloads suffer from preordained job arrivals, and thus are not affected by the state and performance of the simulated system. The system throughput is then dictated by the workload being used, which means that the simulation cannot be used to reliably measure differences in achievable throughput/utilization or setups intended to measure various user-aware metrics like fairness [17].

Therefore, Alea has been extended to enable simulations with dynamic workload adaptation, using the novel model of Zakay and Feitelson [16]. Here, each particular user in an existing workload — given a set of rules — now reacts to the changing performance of the simulated system by *adapting arriving times* of their jobs. This is achieved by transforming an existing static workload into a dynamic one by using the dynamic user-aware workload generation approach. It is a two stage process where an existing workload trace is firstly analyzed to identify user-to-system interactions and then job inter-arrival times are dynamically adjusted during simulation based on observed performance.

3.2.1 Workload Analysis

Similarly to the model of Zakay and Feitelson [16], Alea 4 uses an existing historic workload trace as an input. It then processes the workload one user at a time and detects high level structures such as *user sessions*, *job batches* and *batch dependencies*. This information then can be used to replay the workload, while re-introducing at least some of the dynamics that were present during real system operation.

Sessions represent interactive sessions of a given user, that is the time-frame when a user was actively submitting new jobs. A session starts with the submission of a job and ends after a period of inactivity (no new jobs arrived) which is longer than the maximum inter-arrival time[4]. After the analysis is complete, for each user we have a set of linearly ordered sessions, each with a non-overlapping start and end time. Figure 2 presents a simple workload example of a single user, where 3 sessions were detected (s_1, s_2 and s_3).

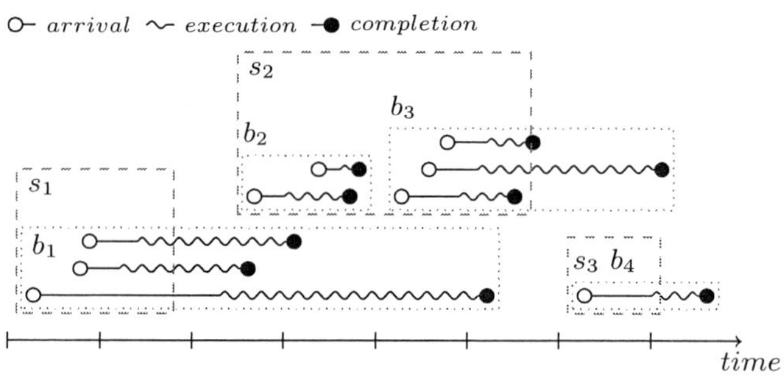

Figure 2: A workload with 3 detected sessions s_1, s_2, s_3 and 4 detected batches b_1, b_2, b_3 and b_4.

Next, in each session we identify so called *job batches*, i.e., independent sets of jobs that do not overlap in their earliest job arrival and latest job completion. In our example in Figure 2, we can see this situation in session s_2 which has two non-overlapping batches b_2 and b_3. All jobs within a single batch must arrive within a single session. While two batches in a single session cannot overlap by definition, two batches in two different sessions can overlap (simply by having long-enough execution time).

After all sessions and batches are detected for each user, logical dependencies between job batches are reestablished in order to define the logical ordering of user "work-flow". Simply put, a batch can only be started if "previous" batches has completed their job submission (so called "follows" relation). Also, within one session a *following* batch can only be started when all jobs from a previous batch are completed (so called "depends" relation). Finally, if the original workload contains two independent sessions where the last batch in the first session completed before the first job of the latter

[4]Maximum inter-arrival times of 30 minutes and 1 hour are commonly used. By default, we use a 30 minute maximum inter-arrival time.

session, then this dependency is also kept. For details please refer to [16] while simple example is shown in Figure 3.

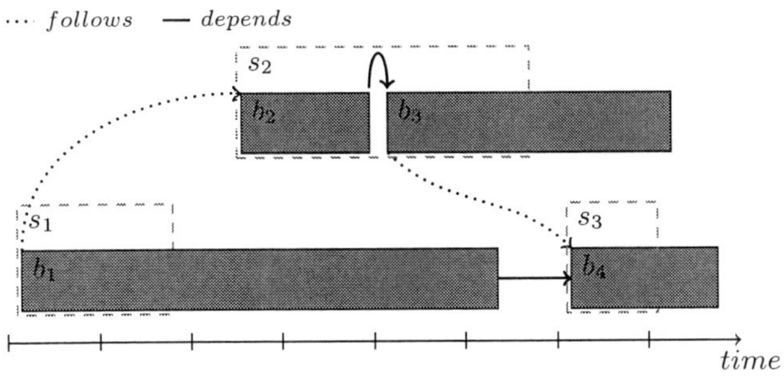

Figure 3: Batches and session from Figure 2 with reconstructed dependencies.

The goal of the dynamic workload adaptation is to adjust the original workload of each user during the simulation to provide a more realistic and representative behavior. This is achieved by *placing the eligible batches into existing sessions* while following the reconstructed dependencies between batches. Each batch of jobs is only allowed to start submitting jobs once all the dependencies for this batch have been satisfied, i.e., all batches with the follow dependency have finished their submission and all batches with the completion dependency (depends relation) have finished their execution. For our experiments, we are reusing existing sessions, i.e., only the batches can be moved forward/backward in time[5]. The inter-arrival times of jobs inside a batch are not adjusted and batches are never interrupted in their submission, so once a batch starts submitting jobs the user will remain active (potentially prolonging the current session) until all jobs have been submitted.

The impact of the new workload adaptation approach is demonstrated in Figure 4, which compares the length of job queue (# of waiting jobs) when either the original (static) workload or the dynamic model is applied. Clearly, the static workload with fixed job arrivals soon produces totally unrealistic system/queue load with extreme queue length.

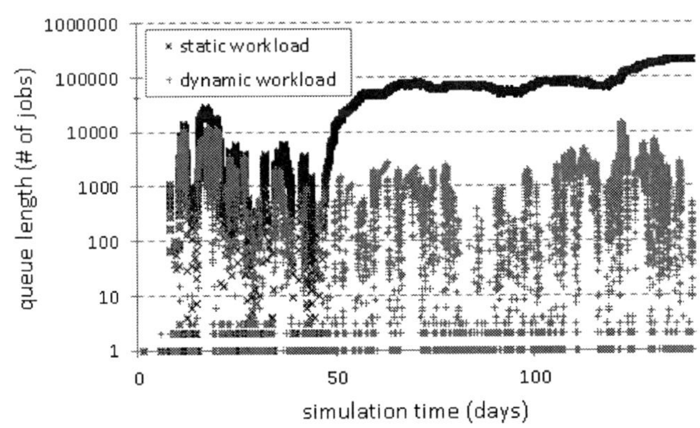

Figure 4: Queue length for static workload replay vs. dynamic workload adaptation.

[5]If we run out of detected sessions, new synthetic sessions can be created. Further details can be found in [16, 12].

3.2.2 *Implementation*

The aforementioned dynamic workload adaptation model is implemented mainly within `AgentDynamic` class, that is responsible for appropriate job submissions of a given user. `AgentDynamic` reacts to the actual performance of the scheduler, using an instance of auxiliary `DynamicBatchManager` class that dynamically maintains a user workload including its inter-batch dependencies. During the simulation, these dependencies are preserved, and a new user's batch is submitted only when all its dependencies are satisfied. This creates the desired feedback effect, as users dynamically react to the actual performance of the system, while major characteristics of the workload including job properties or per-user job ordering are still preserved.

Moreover, since each user has its own independent instance of `AgentDynamic`, it is very easy to either model different types of users (by changing the logic of a particular user agent) or manipulate the workload being used by adding/removing particular user agents to/from the simulation. Beside the increased realism of such a simulation, this newly available user-oriented workload model enables previously unfeasible "what if" simulation approaches, that allow to evaluate effects of newly added users/jobs on the overall performance of the system and/or their impact on existing users in the system.

Furthermore, thanks to the user-oriented workload model, we were able to develop a new experimental model within Alea, that monitors *user (dis)satisfaction* with the system performance. Here we were inspired by the future work discussed in the recent Zakay and Feitelson paper [17], which suggest that (in reality) users may leave the system if the performance is too poor. More details concerning the usefulness of this model are presented in Section 4.2.

4. NOTABLE APPLICATIONS

Alea has been used by many researchers[6], while we have used it for various simulations both for "pure research" as well as for "production" purposes. In the following text, we mention two major successful applications of Alea that helped to improve the performance of the Czech national grid and cloud computing infrastructure *MetaCentrum*.

4.1 Major Queue Reconfiguration

In the late 2013, Alea has been used to verify the suitability of planned major system reconfiguration in MetaCentrum. This reconfiguration was very demanding as it included both total replacement of existing queues as well as deployment of newly developed fair-sharing mechanism. The role of Alea was very important as it was used to mimic the whole reconfiguration, using its aforementioned capabilities to simulate complex queue-related setups as well as fair-sharing policies. These simulations helped to reveal that certain aspects of planned reconfiguration would probably introduce rather unfair behavior. The new setup was finalized using Alea and deployed in practice in January 2014.

A retrospective analysis performed in late 2014 revealed that the new setup has improved significantly the performance of MetaCentrum. For example, the average number of utilized CPU hours has increased by 43.2%, while the system throughput (number of completed jobs) has increased

[6]Alea has over 110 citations in Google Scholar, 13 citations in Scopus and 13 citations in the Web of Science databases.

by 66.3%. Furthermore, even with a significantly larger throughput and utilization, job wait times remained decent. In fact, they were — on average — decreased by 17.9% (4.4 vs. 3.6 hours) which was a good news for system users. More details can be found in Figure 5 that shows the observed difference in system utilization and job wait times. For a detailed analysis we kindly refer to [10].

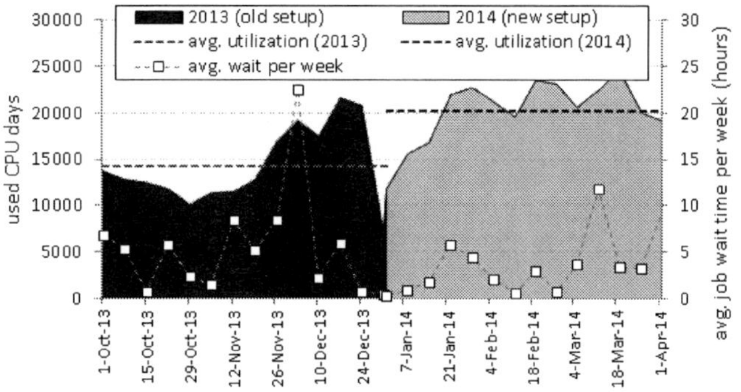

Figure 5: Used CPU days per week before/after reconfiguration (left axis) and the avg. wait time per week (right axis).

4.2 Analysis of New MetaCentrum Scheduler

In the late 2014 MetaCentrum has decided to replace its original job scheduler with a new one, which provided new advanced features such as the use of a *meta-heuristic* to optimize generated job schedule. Alea simulator was extensively used to analyze the suitability of the new solution. Among those "standard" tests one notable experiment was performed — using the new features of Alea — which we present in the following text. While it was quite clear that the new scheduler increases resource utilization and decreases average wait time, a major concern was if the newly applied meta-heuristic algorithm cannot somehow negatively affect selected users in the system. Therefore, a new experimental model to measure *user (dis)satisfaction* was developed and implemented in Alea, using the benefits of *dynamic workload adaptation*.

In this model, each simulated user (an instance of `AgentDynamic`) measures how the system responds to his or her workload. If the agent observes large wait times, it "reports" that it is not satisfied. Also, it measures "how large" this dissatisfaction is by calculating the actual to expected wait time ratio. Here a user agent expects that its jobs shall start in a time which is proportional to job's requirements. In other words, the longer a job is (higher walltime estimate) and the more CPUs it requires the higher is the tolerable wait time and vice versa. This dependency is not linear, since our experience shows that real users usually have some "upper bound" of their patience. For example, if a job requiring 1 CPU starts within one hour, then users are usually satisfied. However, that does not imply that a job requiring 16 CPUs can wait for 16 hours. Similar rule applies to walltime, i.e., user's patience is not linear with respect to job duration, instead it quickly runs out. Therefore, we have developed a simple formula to calculate "acceptable wait time" for a given job which captures this nonlinearity[7].

Figure 6 (left) shows the non-linear distribution of acceptable wait times with respect to job duration and parallelism (# of requested CPUs), as produced by the applied formula. This simple "hand tuned" formula was just a rough approximation being used for our analysis and certainly more realistic models of user's expectations can be developed. During a simulation the model then works as follows. Upon each new job arrival, a *job's acceptable wait time* is calculated. If more jobs of a single user are present in the system we sum up their acceptable wait times. Then, whenever a job is started, a corresponding user agent checks whether the actual wait time was within the calculated overall limit. If not, the user agent "reports dissatisfaction" and calculates the level of such dissatisfaction, which is the actual wait time divided by the acceptable wait time. Otherwise, the job's wait time is within the limit, and the agent just updates its current acceptable wait time limit (i.e., decreases accordingly the value of $acceptable\_wait$).

The results of such experiment are shown in Figure 6 (middle) and (left), showing the number of dissatisfying events per user and all dissatisfying events ordered by their seriousness, respectively. It shows that the newly adopted scheduler has a superior performance, being able to significantly minimize the number of "complaining users", the number of excessively waiting jobs, as well as the "size", i.e., seriousness of such job delays. During the final evaluation of the new scheduler, this particular experiment was very useful as it brought unprecedented flexibility for a per-user evaluation.

5. RELATED WORK

There are several interesting toolkits and simulators that can be used to evaluate scheduling algorithms. To name at least some of them, we must mention the SimGrid[3] — a complex framework for studying Grids, Clouds, HPC or P2P systems. SimGrid provides several extensions that aim at the same "job scheduling" area as Alea, e.g., the SimBatch and the GarSim. Also the GridSim toolkit [15] serves as the basis for specialized job scheduling simulators such as the GSSIM [2]. However, most of these specialized simulators now seem to be inactive or abandoned projects[8].

6. CONCLUSIONS

This paper presents the new major version of the complex job scheduling simulator *Alea*. The core part is dedicated to the explanation of the importance and usefulness of its novel capabilities that include *simulation of complex system setups* and the ability to realistically model *user-to-system interactions* using the dynamic workload adjustment technique. Moreover, we have provided several real-life based showcases that demonstrate how Alea can be utilized for detailed simulation and analysis of an existing computing system.

[7] $acceptable\_wait = (\ln(req\_CPUs)+1)\cdot(walltime/factor)$. Here req_CPUs denotes the number of requested CPUs and job's $walltime$ is divided by an integer ($factor \geq 1$) which increases as the walltime increases, emulating the non-linear user's wait time expectations. Currently, we use five factors $1, 2, .., 5$, which apply for walltimes $< 3h$, $3h..7h$, $7h..24h$, $1d..7d$, $\geq 1w$, respectively.

[8] SimBatch and GarSim are available via SimGrid portal but are not maintained anymore. GSSIM, including its official portal at http://www.gssim.org/, seems to be completely removed (in May 2016).

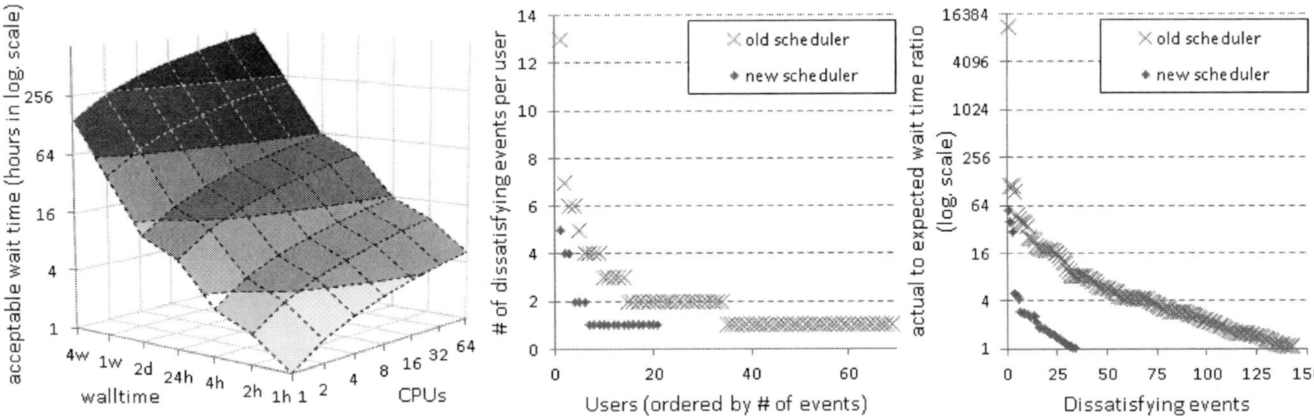

Figure 6: Acceptable wait time with respect to CPU and walltime requirments (left), the number of dissatisfying events per user (middle) and all dissatisfying events ordered by their seriousness (right).

7. ACKNOWLEDGMENTS

We kindly acknowledge the support and computational resources provided by the MetaCentrum under the program LM2015042 and the CERIT Scientific Cloud under the program LM2015085, provided under the programme "Projects of Large Infrastructure for Research, Development, and Innovations". We also highly appreciate the access to MetaCentrum and CERIT Scientific Cloud workload traces. Last but not least, we thank Dror Feitelson for his kind help and explanation concerning the dynamic workload model presented in [16].

8. REFERENCES

[1] Alea 4: Job scheduling simulator, May 2016. https://github.com/aleasimulator.

[2] S. Bak, M. Krystek, K. Kurowski, A. Oleksiak, W. Piatek, and J. Weglarz. GSSIM - A tool for distributed computing experiments. *Scientific Programming*, 19(4):231–251, 2011.

[3] H. Casanova, A. Giersch, A. Legrand, M. Quinson, and F. Suter. Versatile, scalable, and accurate simulation of distributed applications and platforms. *Journal of Parallel and Distributed Computing*, 74(10):2899–2917, 2014.

[4] D. Epema, S. Anoep, C. Dumitrescu, A. Iosup, M. Jan, H. Li, and L. Wolters. Grid workloads archive (GWA), April 2011. http://gwa.ewi.tudelft.nl/pmwiki/.

[5] D. G. Feitelson. Workload modeling for performance evaluation. In M. C. Calzarossa and S. Tucci, editors, *Performance Evaluation of Complex Systems: Techniques and Tools*, volume 2459 of *Lecture Notes in Computer Science*, pages 114–141. Springer Berlin Heidelberg, 2002.

[6] D. G. Feitelson. Parallel workloads archive, July 2014. http://www.cs.huji.ac.il/labs/parallel/workload/.

[7] D. Jackson, Q. Snell, and M. Clement. Core algorithms of the Maui scheduler. In D. G. Feitelson and L. Rudolph, editors, *Job Sched. Strategies for Paral. Proc.*, volume 2221 of *LNCS*, pages 87–102. Springer, 2001.

[8] D. Klusáček and H. Rudová. Alea 2 – job scheduling simulator. In *3rd International ICST Conference on Simulation Tools and Technique*. ICST, 2010.

[9] D. Klusáček and Š. Tóth. On interactions among scheduling policies: Finding efficient queue setup using high-resolution simulations. In F. Silva, I. Dutra, and V. S. Costa, editors, *Euro-Par 2014*, volume 8632 of *LNCS*, pages 138–149. Springer, 2014.

[10] D. Klusáček, Šimon Tóth, and G. Podolníková. Real-life experience with major reconfiguration of job scheduling system. In *Job Scheduling Strategies for Parallel Processing*, 2015.

[11] A. W. Mu'alem and D. G. Feitelson. Utilization, predictability, workloads, and user runtime estimates in scheduling the IBM SP2 with backfilling. *IEEE Transactions on Parallel and Distributed Systems*, 12(6):529–543, 2001.

[12] S. Schlagkamp. Influence of dynamic think times on parallel job scheduler performances in generative simulations. In *Job Scheduling Strategies for Parallel Processing*, 2015.

[13] U. Schwiegelshohn. How to design a job scheduling algorithm. In *Job Scheduling Strategies for Parallel Processing*, 2014.

[14] E. Shmueli and D. G. Feitelson. On simulation and design of parallel-systems schedulers: are we doing the right thing? *Parallel and Distributed Systems, IEEE Transactions on*, 20(7):983–996, 2009.

[15] A. Sulistio, U. Cibej, S. Venugopal, B. Robic, and R. Buyya. A toolkit for modelling and simulating data Grids: an extension to GridSim. *Concurrency and Computation: Practice & Experience*, 20(13):1591–1609, 2008.

[16] N. Zakay and D. G. Feitelson. Preserving user behavior characteristics in trace-based simulation of parallel job scheduling. In *22nd Modeling, Anal. & Simulation of Comput. & Telecomm. Syst. (MASCOTS)*, pages 51–60, 2014.

[17] N. Zakay and D. G. Feitelson. Semi-open trace based simulation for reliable evaluation of job throughput and user productivity. In *7th IEEE Int. Conf. on Cloud Computing Technology and Science (CloudCom 2015)*, pages 413–421. IEEE, 2015.